Even the most psychopathic woman can realize, when staring death in the eyes, that what she valued, in the end, was life all along.
– Tori Telfer

OTHER RELATED TITLES BY TROY TAYLOR

UNTIL DEATH DO US PART (2024)

HELL HATH NO FURY (2021)
HELL HATH NO FURY 2 (2022)
HELL HATH NO FURY 3 (with Amanda Woomer) (2023)

FALLEN ANGEL (2013)
THE TWO LOST GIRLS (2016)
"I WANT TO COME HOME TONIGHT" (2017)
SUFFER THE CHILDREN (2018)

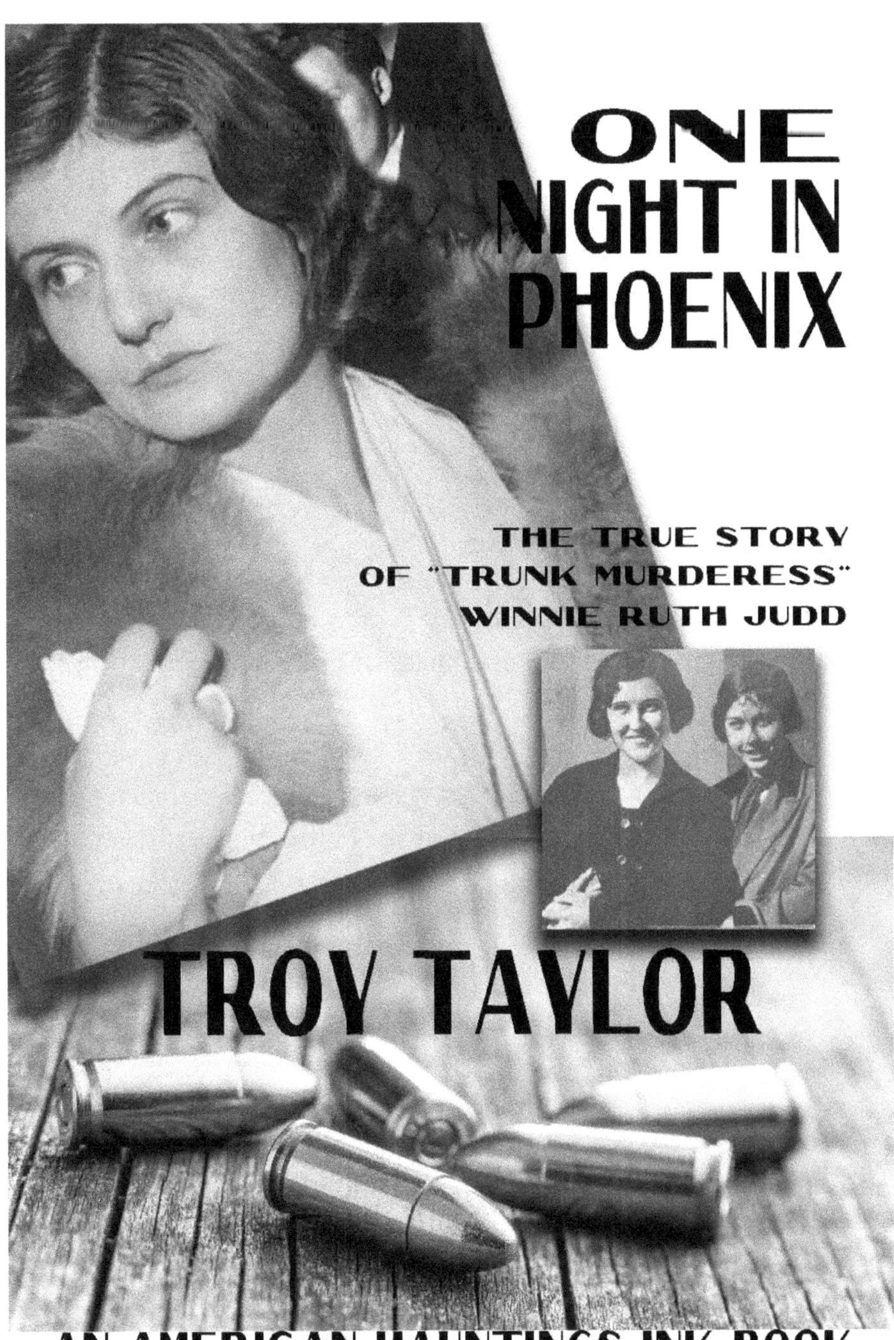

AN AMERICAN HAUNTINGS INK BOOK

ONE NIGHT IN PHOENIX
The True Story of "Trunk Murderess" Winnie Ruth Judd

ISBN: 978-1-958589-21-2
First Edition

Published by American Hauntings Ink
301 East Broadway - Alton IL - 62002
www.americanhauntingsink.com

Cover Design by April Slaughter
Interior Design by Troy Taylor

Printed in the United States of America

TABLE OF CONTENTS

PROLOGUE:
A TRAIN TO LOS ANGELES

OCTOBER 18, 1931, WAS AN ORDINARY AUTUMN NIGHT in Phoenix, Arizona. The thermometer had climbed to 89 degrees that afternoon, the beginning of the "cool" season in the desert community of just 48,000 people. The summer heat had been almost intolerable, and everyone looked forward to the milder days ahead. Most of the country would soon be fending off snow and freezing temperatures, but that kind of winter never came here.

But those warm winters brought many visitors and tourists with money to spend. While the rest of the country struggled with the Great Depression and the record unemployment, Phoenix was hard at work and welcoming more tourists than ever.

Among them were the health seekers, especially those with tuberculosis, seeking out the dry climate just as they'd been doing for a half-century or more. It was generally considered that while it was suitable to come to Phoenix to get well, it wasn't in good taste to talk about it. The city's preferred kind of winter visitors were referred to as "the elderly gentlemen who like to play golf all year around the ladies of all ages who like to applaud them." Many of these "elderly gentlemen" came with a lot of cash, which they used to build sprawling mansions and invest in luxury hotels.

That kind of money was new to Phoenix, even though the town had been around since it was founded as a farming community in 1867. A little over two decades later, it became the capital of the Arizona Territory. However, it was still a frontier town, and Arizona

The Phoenix, Arizona, skyline in the 1930s.

wouldn't become the forty-eighth state in the union until 1912. By the end of World War II, Phoenix had become the largest city in the state, and by 1931, it had started to be considered "civilized." The city finally had more attorneys than blacksmiths and more doctors than saloons. Nearly 50,000 people lived in Phoenix that October and more were always arriving.

And they were spending money and helping the city grow. That fall, it boasted 86 miles of roads and a trolley line that could take you anywhere. Seven buildings in the downtown stood more than four stories tall, including the Westward Ho Hotel, which had 16 floors and would be the tallest in the city until 1959.

However, not all the residents decided how successful the city was based on how much money was in the banks, how tall the buildings were, or how many golf courses had been built. In October 1931, most residents agreed with how the Chamber of Commerce promoted Phoenix - "a city of homes, schools, and churches." Those three things were a top priority, and there were no apologies for the fact that all three were segregated by race.

Life in Phoenix largely revolved around family, home, and a strict moral code that required a husband to be faithful and provide for his family so that his wife could raise the children and take care of the home. Divorce was scandalous, and adultery was out of the question.

Phoenix was an uptight, conservative, god-fearing place - or at least it seemed that way on the surface. For most residents, it was easy and necessary to ignore the seamier side of the community. They pretended there was no prostitution, even though it was thriving. They claimed there was no political corruption, even though it was rampant. And they ignored any hint of extramarital affairs, even when it was an infamous tradition.

It was easy to ignore such things when you had 80 churches in town, all from various denominations - Protestant, Catholic, and even one synagogue. There were also some black churches, but they were relegated to South Phoenix, the poor side of town. Every Sunday, every church was filled with parishioners, most thanking their gods that the Depression hadn't hit Phoenix the way it had hit everywhere else.

The city would recover much faster than most American cities, too. Most people in town hadn't invested in the stock market, and the crash had affected them so little that the local newspapers rarely mentioned it. Those with jobs were careful to hang onto them. They may not have been getting raises - and there may have been a few pay cuts - but at least they were still working.

That may have been what stirred generosity in the hearts of so many in Phoenix. They had learned they couldn't just take care of themselves and ignore the disaster that had caused so much tragedy everywhere else. Churches and civic groups started relief funds and services for the thousands of transients who came to Phoenix hoping for work or at least a break from the winter cold.

Anyone looking at Phoenix in October 1931 - and having no knowledge of what existed under the surface - believed the city lived up to its reputation as a shining city of the American Southwest. They saw it as a place of opportunity - where work, shelter, money, and a climate sheltered them from the chilly winter months ahead.

It was that reputation that would typically bring so many tourists to Phoenix during the winter months. But this winter wouldn't be typical. This winter, the tourists would be coming for more than just nice weather.

They would be coming for reasons stained with blood.

IT WAS AN ORDINARY EVENING FOR MOST PEOPLE IN Phoenix, but not for Winnifred Ruth Judd - whom most people called "Ruthie."

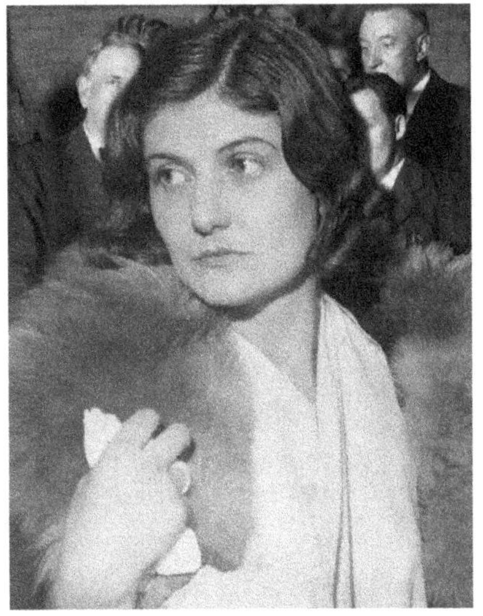

Winnie Ruth Judd, known to most family and friends as "Ruthie."

The 26-year-old daughter of a Methodist minister hadn't spent that day at church as she had on every Sunday of her life while growing up in Darlington, Indiana. In fact, her church attendance had been pretty lax since she'd left home seven years earlier as the bride of a successful doctor who was 22 years older than she was. But she didn't tell her parents that in the long letters she wrote home to them. Her letters were always cheery and betrayed nothing about how her life had turned out.

Dr. William C. Judd hadn't turned out to be as successful as his wife and her family had expected. When your daughter married a doctor in those days, parents expected her to be the wife of a nice family doctor who became beloved in the community where he chose to practice, but that wasn't where Dr. Judd ended up. Instead, he found work as a doctor for American mining interests in Mexico, working for little money and whatever accommodations the company provided. He changed locations often and never stayed anywhere for long. Eventually, he had trouble even getting those jobs, unable to keep any position because he was addicted to narcotics. That fact didn't make it into the letters Winnie sent to her parents either.

Ruthie's husband, Dr. William C. Judd

Ruthie became skilled at taking care of herself. She had come to Phoenix because its dry air offered relief from the tuberculosis she had been diagnosed with. She had arrived in the city from Mexico in 1930 - without her husband - and without the skills to earn a living. She always got by because of her pretty face and "sweet disposition." Under other circumstances, she could have been beautiful, but she never had the money for makeup and fine clothes. Her only good coat had shrunk in a cleaning, so she wore it around her shoulders. The only luxury she allowed herself was to have her long hair cut into a fashionable bob.

Fortunately, she found a six-day-a-week job at Phoenix's first private medical office, the Grunow Clinic. It paid $75 a month, which was quite good for an unskilled woman in those days, and she lied to get it. In her interview for a job as a medical secretary - which meant she would be typing up reports on exams for the clinic's doctors -- she claimed to be proficient at typing. She wasn't, but she quickly enrolled in night classes to develop her skills. So, even though Sunday was usually her one day off, it was not unusual for her to spend part of that day working at home, catching up on reports she'd fallen behind on.

But she didn't mind. Her salary paid her rent and groceries, leaving her a little to send to her husband. She had to keep doing that until he could land a new job, which, she believed, would be any day now. He'd been in California for the last few months pursuing promising prospects. She was sure that luck was going to come his way soon.

The Grunow Clinic in Phoenix, where Ruthie worked in 1931

She usually did the laundry and cleaned her small apartment on Brill Street with the rest of her Sunday. On some Sundays, though, she had dinner with her two best friends, Anne LeRoi and "Sammy" Samuelson, who lived just a trolley ride away. They often pooled their money for something special - fried chicken was a favorite - and Anne would cook. Then, they'd turn up the radio and listen to their favorite shows.

But Ruthie did none of those things on October 18. On that day, she was busy packing. In fact, she had been up all night packing. And now she needed help. She went to see her landlords - Howard and Violet Grimm -- a kind couple who lived just across the alley from her apartment.

Violet knew something was wrong when Ruthie, her tenant, came to the door. She looked tired, and she seemed preoccupied and nervous. Her hand was bandaged with a towel. She told Violet that she had burned it while ironing. She fussed at her and said it should be covered with a salve and appropriately bandaged, but Ruthie insisted it would be fine. She wanted to know if she could use the telephone and if Mr. Grimm could help her with some luggage.

Howard Grimm was reading the newspaper when his wife told him she'd volunteered him and their son for an errand. Ruthie was taking the night train to Los Angeles to see her husband and needed help loading her trunks.

As Howard would later testify, he didn't mind lending a hand to the pretty young woman who had rented one of his apartments. Ruthie was clean, didn't have loud parties, and paid her rent - sometimes a little at a time, but all $45 was always paid by month's end. She had even become friendly with the Grimms' children, especially his 13-year-old daughter, Rita. When the girl had trouble with her Spanish classes, Ruthie had offered to help.

Howard didn't know much about Ruthie, but everything he and his family knew convinced them she could use the help. He hadn't been impressed with Dr. Judd, who had spent some time in Phoenix with his wife before leaving town to look for work again. He couldn't understand what the attractive young woman would see in the plain, older man. He suspected that the doctor liked either his booze or his dope, but that wasn't Howard's concern. Ruthie had no such vices. Her biggest problem seemed to be that she was in a tough spot as a woman alone during tough economic times. Even when his contracting business slowed down, he still made enough money that his Violet didn't have to work. In Howard's way of thinking, Dr. Judd was a failure, unable to provide for his family.

Howard also had a practical reason for helping Ruthie. She was a tiny thing - maybe 110 pounds and not even five-and-a-half feet tall - and she certainly needed help moving anything heavy or bulky.

Like everyone else who encountered Ruthie Judd that weekend, Howard and Violet would never forget the details. Violet later said Ruthie visited her house twice on Sunday to use the telephone. She didn't hear what number Ruthie requested from the operator, but she did overhear her ask someone to loan her $5. She also recalled that Ruthie seemed nervous and preoccupied - not her usual self.

The train to Los Angeles was scheduled to leave at 8:00 P.M., so Howard planned to collect Ruthie's luggage around 6:30. But when he told his son, Kenneth, about the plan, he found it wouldn't work. Kenneth had a youth meeting at church that started at 5:00. The

The train depot in Phoenix

teenager ran across the alley and asked if Ruthie could be ready earlier. She told him she could.

Ruthie was dressed in a plain brown suit when the men arrived. She pointed them toward the bedroom, where they found two trunks. Howard was startled by the weight of the black one and groaned as he tried to lift it. Ruthie apologized for the weight. She said that it contained her husband's medical books, and he'd need them in California if he got the job he was promised. It took Howard and Kenneth both to haul the trunk to their car outside. They tied it to the running board on the passenger side. Kenneth managed the smaller trunk by himself, wedging it between the front and back seats.

Winnie carried out her battered suitcase and a hatbox. She sat in the front seat as Howard drove. Kenneth climbed into the back.

It only took a few minutes to reach the new train depot at Fourth Avenue and Jackson. Howard and Kenneth climbed out to help her. Ruthie had promised to give them $1.50 for their assistance, but she only had a $1 bill. She offered to pay them the rest when she returned, and Howard told her it was fine.

Baggage handler Beverley Stallings was working the evening shift at Union Station when the Grimms' car pulled up in front. Stallings and Kenneth moved the large trunk, and Kenneth fetched the smaller one as Stalling started the paperwork. The trunks were overweight, and Ruthie had to pay an extra $4.48 to get them to Los Angeles.

Fellow baggage handler Avis Boutchee collected the additional charges from Ruthie and asked for her signature. He noticed that her left hand was wrapped in a bandage. He attached one copy of the paperwork to the trunks and gave a yellow copy to Ruthie. Only later did he look to see what name she signed - B.J. McKinnell. He had no way of knowing this was the name of Ruthie's younger brother.

Head Porter John Washington noticed the attractive woman sitting alone in the station when he arrived for work at 5:00 P.M. It was nearly three hours until the L.A. train arrived, and the station was practically empty. He noticed the woman getting up and walking around and later recalled that she seemed very nervous. She always kept her carry-on luggage in sight each time she got up. Washington thought the hatbox looked pretty new, but her brown leather suitcase had seen better days. He eventually asked her if she was going to Tucson, but she replied that she was waiting for the Los Angeles train.

Her voice was trembling when she answered, he remembered later.

When the *Golden State Limited* pulled into the station at 7:55 P.M., Beverley Stallings had already taken his supper break. He helped the baggage boys load Ruthie's trunks onto the train, along with some other luggage dropped off by local passengers. As always, he was in a hurry because the train was only at the station for 15 minutes. But even in his haste, he noticed something leaking from the largest trunk. He thought it smelled like medicine.

Meanwhile, John Washington, the porter, made a point of helping the young woman onto the train with her carry-on bags. She still seemed nervous. Her seat was in the rear of the chair car, third from the right. Washington knew she'd be sitting up for the overnight trip but imagined she couldn't afford a berth. He didn't expect a tip, but she did manage to find him a few pennies, which he thanked her for and tipped his hat as he left her.

The Los Angeles train station where Ruthie arrived in October 1931.

(Below) The station's main waiting room

H.J. Mapes was the baggageman on the train that night, handling the duties between El Paso and Los Angeles. He'd been with the Southern Pacific Railroad for 23 years and had managed thousands of bags, so he immediately knew something was wrong with the large steamer trunk loaded in Phoenix. He noticed a strange smell, and when he looked closer, he was sure it was leaking blood. The scent became stronger as the train traveled across Arizona - and the leaking never stopped.

As soon as he unloaded his car in Los Angeles at 7:45 A.M., he notified district baggage agent Arthur V. Anderson that they had a problem - a contraband deer, he suggested.

Anderson went onto the platform where the trunks had been loaded onto a flatbed truck. Even in the open air, he could smell the horrible odor. As he got closer, he saw blood running down the side of the trunk. He thought Mapes was right. People were always trying to smuggle deer meat on the train to California. Health officials for the railroad had demanded that the practice stop, so Anderson tagged both trunks with a pink hold slip, which meant the luggage couldn't be released without official approval.

NO ONE NOTICED THE YOUNG WOMAN IN THE BROWN suit who disembarked from the train that morning except Stella Conley, a maid in the ladies' room. The woman was carrying a hatbox and was followed by a porter with a banged-up brown suitcase. They passed the storage lockers along the walls and walked directly to the ladies' room. Stella had to step aside to let them pass. The woman asked the porter to place the suitcase behind the restroom door against the wall. She put the hatbox on top of it. She nodded to Stella as she left the restroom and sat on a bench in the large waiting room.

Stella didn't usually let people clutter up her restroom with luggage. That's what the pay lockers were for. But the woman was obviously waiting for someone, so she thought she'd let it pass.

But an hour later, the woman was still sitting there. Stella approached the woman and asked if she was leaving, and the woman simply told her she was not. Stella asked her to check the bags she'd left in the bathroom, but the woman replied that she didn't have the money for a locker. She was waiting for her brother, who was a student at the University of Southern California. She'd sent him a message to meet her, but she wasn't sure if he'd got it before going to his morning classes. If he didn't come soon, she'd have to go and get him, and she only had enough money for a streetcar ride.

Feeling sorry for a woman in her predicament, Stella offered to keep an eye on her bags if she had to go and find her brother. She knew what it was like not to have much money.

A few minutes later, the woman got up to leave. She told Stella that if she missed her brother and he turned up at the station, he would be looking for "Mrs. Judd."

"If your brother comes, shall I let him have your bags?" Stella asked.

"No, don't let anyone have the bags until I come back," the woman instructed. Stella agreed but did ask her to come and tell her when she returned to the station.

After the woman left, Stella tried to move the suitcase farther out of the way so that no one would bother it, but it was so heavy she couldn't lift it. Assuming it would be safe, she left it where it was.

By the time Stella's shift was over at 3:00 P.M., neither Mrs. Judd nor her brother had come to claim the two bags behind the restroom door.

GEORGE BROOKER WAS THE DELIVERY CLERK at the station that day. As he had each day for the past four years, he exchanged claim checks for baggage and filled out the paperwork that went with the job. When he went to record the numbers on the two trunks that were sitting on the flatbed luggage wagon, he got a whiff of a terrible smell. Something dark was leaking out of one of them. Below the cart was a spot about the size of a dinner plate where the liquid had been dripping. He saw that both trunks had been tagged with pink slips. He wasn't surprised they had gotten the attention of his boss.

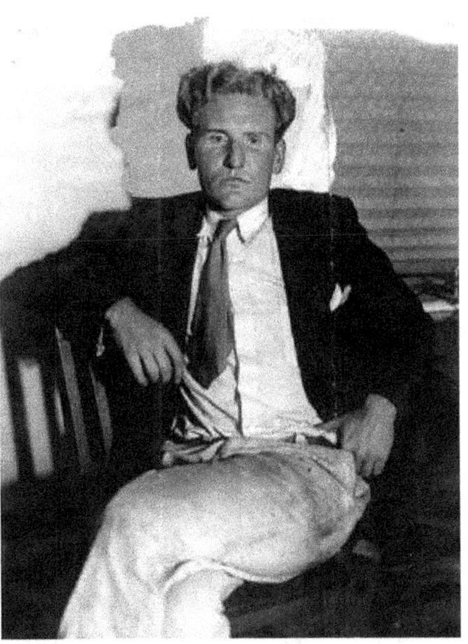

Ruthie's brother, Burton McKinnell, who came to pick her up at the station when she arrived in L.A.

Around noon, a Ford roadster pulled up to the loading dock. Brooker didn't know the attractive woman who got out of the car, but he recognized the young man with her. His name was Burton McKinnell, and he was a college kid who had helped at the station over Christmas, lending an extra hand with the additional holiday mail and luggage.

The young man handed Brooker two claim tickets, and he took them to the front office. Baggage agent Anderson came out personally to handle the situation with the pink tags. "Who does this baggage belong to?" he asked.

Ruthie's trunks, waiting for her at the train station, were found to be leaking a mysterious liquid that seemed to be blood.

The woman said the trunks were hers, and when asked what was inside, she told him that it was personal things and clothing.

"It must be something else," he insisted. "It wouldn't be a broken bottle of booze, I don't suppose?" He laughed, and the woman assured him it wasn't.

Anderson led the woman and the young man toward the flatbed, and they were about four feet away when he asked if they could smell the terrible odor. The woman acted as if nothing was wrong, saying she couldn't smell a thing. Burton, though, looked horrified. He could see the stain on the concrete caused by whatever was leaking off the cart, and he noticed files swarming around his sister's trunks. "Well, I can smell it!" he blurted out.

Anderson led the woman closer to the trunks and asked her to try again. She finally admitted that, yes, she did smell something.

"What could be in those trunks to cause that stink?" Anderson asked her sharply.

"Well, I don't know," she replied calmly. "I can't imagine what it is."

Anderson pointed out the liquid that was still dripping. The woman turned to Burton. "What do you suppose that is?" she asked him, but the young man just stared at her. Anderson said he noticed nothing in the woman's behavior suggesting she was nervous or uncomfortable. In fact, she seemed as confused as he was. The young man with her was totally befuddled by what was going on.

"Please open the trunks, ma'am," Anderson told her. He later said that whatever was leaking would undoubtedly damage the other contents, and he didn't want her to file a claim against the railroad, claiming that she had ruined items. He just wanted to determine the extent of the problem now.

But the woman seemed hesitant, so her brother offered an alternative plan. "It might cause some embarrassment to open the trunks here," he said. "Why not come out to the house and examine the contents there?"

But Anderson refused. The woman opened her purse and fished around inside with one hand - the other was wrapped in a bandage - as though she were looking for keys to the trunks. Then she looked exasperated, "My husband has the keys," she finally said, but Anderson later said he was convinced she was lying.

Quickly, she said she'd have to telephone her husband to bring the keys to the station. Anderson offered the use of his office phone, and she made a show of thumbing through the phone book, claiming that she didn't remember her husband's number and couldn't find it listed.

"I'll have to go and get my husband and bring him down here," the woman eventually said. The man with her still looked like he couldn't figure out what was happening. Anderson and Brooker watched as the pair calmly walked to the Ford and drove away.

They didn't come back.

Anderson waited until 4:30 that afternoon, then called the police and reported two suspicious bags.

Detective Frank Ryan's shift was almost over when the call came in. He hoped to go straight home after a quick stop at the train station. But the 10-year veteran detective was in for a long night.

When Ryan joined Anderson and Brooker on the loading dock, he took one look at the large trunk and knew he was looking at blood. Over his last decade, he'd seen too much of it with the LAPD. Anderson handed him a set of passkeys, and the detective picked open the lock on the larger trunk.

LAPD Detective Frank Ryan opened Winnie's trunks and got the surprise of his career when he discovered the bodies of two women inside.

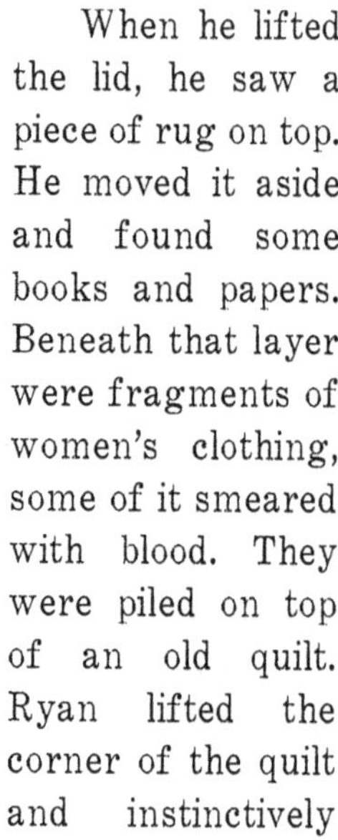

When he lifted the lid, he saw a piece of rug on top. He moved it aside and found some books and papers. Beneath that layer were fragments of women's clothing, some of it smeared with blood. They were piled on top of an old quilt. Ryan lifted the corner of the quilt and instinctively jerked his hand away.

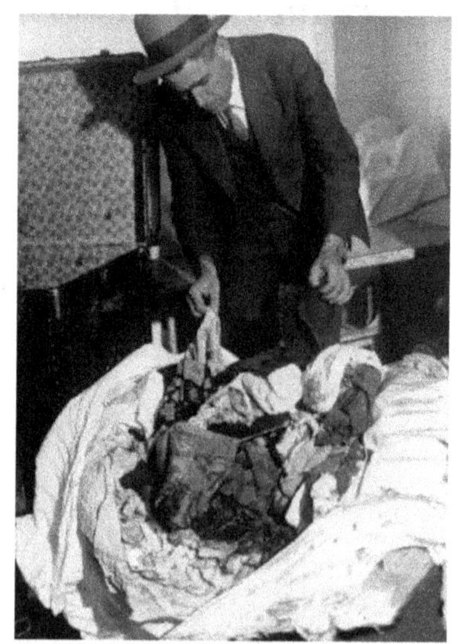

He was looking at a woman's face.

As he pulled his hand back, the quilt was gripped tightly in his fist. It was pulled aside to reveal the body of a woman who was crammed into the trunk. She had dark hair and was wearing pink pajamas. She was on her side, her head in one corner and her knees drawn up to her chest.

Detective Ryan let the lid of the trunk slam shut with a thud, rushed into the depot office, and called precinct headquarters to request fingerprint men and attendants from the morgue.

As he waited for them to arrive, he opened the smaller trunk. Several sheets of paper lay on top, some spattered with blood. A thin cotton blanket was stuffed around the contents. Under it were two bundles wrapped in women's clothing.

He unwrapped the first one - it contained a human leg and foot. It had been severed just below the knee.

The detective tugged at the cloth wrapped around the other bundle - inside was the torso of a woman, from head to navel.

Frank Ryan had seen enough. He'd wait for the boys from the lab and wouldn't touch anything else. But he already knew something that made him feel sick - the pieces in this trunk didn't add up to a whole body.

He didn't know it yet, but two more bags were stashed behind the station's ladies' room door.

Those two bags held surprises of their own.

1. BEST FRIENDS

IN ORDER TO EXPLAIN THE CONTENTS OF THE TWO trunks abandoned at the Los Angeles train station, we have to turn back the clock to a few days earlier - Friday, October 16.

It was around 9:30 that evening, and Anne LeRoi was already in her pink pajamas when Ruthie Judd arrived at the bungalow Anne shared with her roommate, Hedvig "Sammy" Samuelson. Anne had been wearing her pajamas all evening, which she often did when spending an "at home" night with her best friends.

Sammy was already in bed when Ruthie arrived. She spent more time there than she wanted, too weak and sick from tuberculosis to get around much. Her entire wardrobe, it seemed, was composed of various kinds of silk pajamas.

They made quite a pair, and everyone who knew them called them "the girls," which they didn't mind, even though Anne was 32 and Sammy was 24.

Ruthie let herself in through the kitchen back door. She knew the bungalow on North Second Street as well as she knew her own apartment, which was just a few blocks away. She knew the back door was never latched, just as she knew the front door was only used by "company." Ruthie wasn't company. She was a former roommate and still a best friend. She called out a hello as she walked into the kitchen.

It seemed natural that the three women had become friends. All were newcomers to Phoenix and far away from family, familiar surroundings, and hometowns. Anne was from Oregon, Sammy was from North Dakota, and Ruthie came from Indiana.

The two young women who became Ruthie's best friends – Agnes Anne LeRoi (left) and Hedvig "Sammy" Samuelson

The bond between Anne and Sammy was already strong by the time they arrived in town together in 1931. They'd met in Alaska, where Anne had worked as a nurse, and Sammy was a teacher. The wet, cold climate of the region had been terrible for Sammy's tuberculosis, and they came to Phoenix for the same reason that Ruth had come a year earlier - hoping the dry climate would ease Sammy's condition. Ruthie had found that the weather and dry air allowed her to hold down a job and enjoy a normal life. Sammy wasn't as lucky. She was never well enough to work or even do much housework.

Like Anne and Ruthie, she understood the stress of a single woman trying to make it on her own during a time when having a husband who made good money was not just socially acceptable but almost essential. Anne had been divorced twice, Ruth's husband was unreliable, and Sammy had never married at all. Sammy had saved about $400 before she became too sick to work again and lived on that, with help from Anne and some of the other "friends" they'd made in Phoenix.

Anne LeRoi

When the girls arrived in town, Ruthie was already working as a medical secretary at the Grunow Clinic. Anne was hired as an X-ray technician right away, working six days a week and earning $125 a month, which was $50 more than Ruthie. They started visiting during coffee breaks, going to lunch together, and spending time in the evenings. Ruthie invited Anne and Sammy to her apartment for dinner, and they asked her back. Soon, they even became neighbors.

Anne and Sammy lived in a duplex bungalow on the edge of town, just a few blocks off the trolley line. Ruthie moved in when the other half of the house became available in May 1931, and the three women became inseparable.

Ruthie's husband, William, also lived there for a few months off and on. By all accounts, they were a friendly foursome, often having dinner together, playing cards, and listening to the radio. Dr. Judd even had things in common with the girls. He and Anne had both worked at Good Samaritan Hospital in Portland, Oregon, and Anne's parents lived near the Judd family's Oregon farm. Dr. Judd also had two sisters who were teachers, like Sammy, and

The duplex bungalow that the three girls shared, first in two apartments and then in one for a short time.

Sammy had a younger brother who was a doctor.

By October 1931, though, none of the three women had seen Dr. Judd in months. The previous year had been challenging for them, and all their dreams of a "new life" in Phoenix had been dashed.

Sammy Samuelson, whose tuberculosis often made it impossible to work or care for the bungalow she shared with Anne.

Ruth's hopes of settling down with her husband were thwarted by his drug addiction and inability to get a job. Sammy wasn't improving in the desert climate, and worse, Anne had found out that she had also contracted tuberculosis. By June, she was too sick to work and wanted to go home to her family and rest for a few weeks. But she feared she would lose her job if she left, plus she didn't have the money she needed to make the trip. Ruthie lobbied on her behalf, pleading with the doctors at the clinic to hold Anne's job for her and even to give her some traveling money. One of the doctors was so moved by Ruthie's entreaties that he wrote Anne a check for $100.

With Anne gone, Sammy moved into a sanatorium to get the daily care she needed. Ruth moved into the girls' half of the duplex. It was a little larger, and they had nicer furniture than Ruthie's.

By July, things were looking up. Anne's health had improved enough to return to Phoenix and go back to work, so Ruthie moved Sammy back into the duplex, caring for her friend until the three women were reunited in August. While waiting for Anne's return, Ruthie wrote her a friendly letter:

Sammy and I are together every day, waiting for our little Anne to return to the fold. Sure, I think the three of us can get along fine until I go to the doctor ffimeaning Dr. Juddffl. We talk a lot about our Anne and how she is going to behave herself when she gets back.

After Anne returned, the three roommates tried to adjust to living in a one-bedroom house. Not only was it cramped, but they also had very different ideas about housekeeping - Anne was tidy and clean, while Ruth was careless. Their domestic differences led to several "petty arguments," a mutual friend later recalled.

But that was the least of Anne's worries when it looked as though she might not be able to get her job back. One doctor at the clinic wasn't fond of Anne and had trained a young nurse to run the X-ray machine in her absence. He didn't feel Anne's specialized skills were needed anymore. However, Ruthie pleaded again on her friend's behalf, and soon Anne returned to work.

The three women remained living together for only two months. In early October, Ruthie found her one-bedroom apartment on Brill Street. It was only a couple of blocks from the clinic, allowing her to walk to work each day instead of paying the daily fare for the trolley ride from the house.

Ruth would soon come to regret her decision to move.

THE THREE GIRLS HAD MANY FRIENDS - AND MANY admirers. They were always referred to as cheerful, friendly, and pleasant, but more than anything else, all three were beautiful.

Ruthie was the most petite. She had large blue eyes, high cheekbones, and arching brows. When she smiled, she lit up a room. Her light hair was sometimes blond, sometimes hennaed for a reddish tone, and she kept it in the short, bobbed style of the day.

Sammy might not have been quite as pretty as Ruth, but she more than made up for it in personality. Her illness had not caused her to lose any of her striking looks. She was tall and thin with blue eyes and auburn hair that she kept short. Perhaps because she couldn't do much else during the day, she stayed current with the news and was a voracious reader. She wrote frequent letters to her family and maintained a daily journal.

It was common for Sammy to be the center of attention whenever they entertained. Since Sammy didn't go out much, their guests came to them, which meant frequent parties at the bungalow. Ruth was often there, even after she moved to her new apartment, and so were other friends Anne had made in town. There were also plenty of men, including young doctors from the clinic and businesspeople from Phoenix and out of town.

A favorite guest was a tall, handsome, broad-shouldered man named Jack Halloran, whom the other two girls had met through Ruthie. Jack always arrived - not always announced -- with plenty of food and booze, even though Prohibition was still hanging on. He often brought along his friends and other successful businesspeople like him who had families at home but loved spending time with attractive young women. Sometimes, the men brought presents, like a brand new Philco radio, or left cash on the table when they left.

Of the three girls, Anne has been described as the "runner-up in the beauty contest." She was a little larger than the other two girls but gorgeous enough to turn a head. Newspapers would later refer to her as "mannish," but friends called her a "brunette beauty." She was the oldest of the girls and the most capable of caring for herself. She was wickedly smart and realized that while anyone could be a nurse, few had yet mastered the specialized training for the newest diagnostic wonder -- the X-ray machine. She knew this skill would bring job security and better pay than she could make as a nurse.

Anne became the breadwinner in the household and, for that reason, likely made all the decisions. The other girls wouldn't have questioned her authority, and she was never shy about expressing her thoughts. Her biggest worry was Sammy. She constantly talked about her friend's health problems and fretted that the desert climate hadn't done much to give Sammy back her strength. At least a couple of times each week, Anne would pick up something at the drugstore that she thought Sammy would like. This kindness was exclusive to Sammy. To all others, she was the woman in charge. But for Sammy, she would do anything.

It wasn't commonly expressed in those days, but Anne was believed to be deeply in love with the other woman. And the feelings were likely returned. With their good looks, wit, and charm, it was probably expected that Anne and Sammy would find suitable husbands and join the ranks of American housewives. But that wasn't in the cards for them, and they would always be just "roommates."

It was something that Ruthie Judd would never understand. All she had ever wanted was to be a good wife and a mother.

Ruthie grew up as the daughter of a minister in Indiana, where she had an often-troubled childhood.

RUTHIE WAS BORN ON JANUARY 29, 1905, DURING A blizzard in the small town of Oxford, Indiana. She had been born in the parsonage of the Free Baptist church, where her father, Harvey McKinnell, was a minister. She was a late-in-life baby. Her mother, Carrie, was a schoolteacher and was 38 when she married. Ruthie was the first of her two children. Her brother, Burton, was 19 months younger than his sister.

When Ruthie was born, her lungs were underdeveloped. Thanks to the storm, she didn't receive the immediate care she needed and contracted pneumonia. By age four, she'd contracted tuberculosis, which affected her studies when she entered school. Her frequent absences often put her far behind her classmates.

She also had difficulty fitting in socially. While her parents were regarded as a kind, generous couple, beloved by church members and neighbors, they were strict and forbade Ruthie to participate in what they considered frivolous activities - like movies, dancing, carnivals, ball games, and roller skating. She was never allowed to wear jewelry, and her clothing had to be very modest and plain.

Thanks to her repressed childhood, Ruthie had few friends and rarely spent time with men other than her father and brother. She had grown up so sheltered from everyday life that she was often overwhelmed when she finally got her first job.

Newspaper image of Ruthie and her husband, Dr. William Judd.

In 1923, when she was 18, Ruthie was hired as an assistant at an Indiana psychiatric hospital. Almost immediately, she fell in love with a 41-year-old doctor named William Judd. They purposely ran into each other in the cafeteria many times before he finally asked her out in August. She wanted to go to dinner with him but had to deliver a speech about missionary work at her father's church that night. She told him she would go to dinner with him afterward if he accompanied her to church. He agreed, and they began regularly dating until her father married them at his church on April 18, 1924.

Ruthie left home for the first time that same night on a honeymoon trip to Mexico. It was her first train ride, her first night in a hotel, and certainly her first time out of the country.

Dr. Judd took his new bride to Vanegas, Mexico, where he'd landed a job as a doctor for the crew of an American-owned silver mine.

The next three years in Mexico were the only happiness the couple ever shared. Ruthie even realized her greatest dream - telling her husband she was pregnant. However, the weather in that part of

Mexico caused her tuberculosis to flare up, and she believed this caused her to become too weak to carry and deliver the child. Tragically, Ruthie said she lost the baby. A second pregnancy the following year ended the same way.

By the end of 1927, Ruthie was so sick that her husband sent her to a sanatorium in California to get treatment for her illness. In a few months, she was well enough to join him at a new posting in another part of Mexico, but that climate didn't agree with her either. In late 1928, she was back in California for more treatment. She tried joining her husband in Mexico again in 1929 -- at yet another mine, this one northeast of Mazatlán -- but this place turned out to be even worse for her, and she moved to Phoenix alone in 1930. Dr. Judd promised to join her, sure he could find a job in a town that needed doctors, but he never did.

Ruthie often made excuses for her husband's drug addiction, claiming he'd been given an overdose of morphine for a wound during World War I. Whether that was true or not, by the time Ruthie ended up by herself in Phoenix, she knew he had a drug problem from which he likely wouldn't recover.

In Phoenix, she first found work with a wealthy family named Ford, caring for an invalid wife and watching the children. It was room and board and $80 a month. Ruthie was the kind, caring, churchgoing, no-trouble young woman the family wanted. While living with them, she met their friends and neighbors, including Jack Halloran, who lived next door.

Jack was 44 years old and a local success story. He was one of the most prominent men in town, and he and his wife and three children lived in the nicest neighborhood in Phoenix. He was well-liked, admired, and politically connected - you wouldn't find anyone in the city who'd say a bad word about him.

And then along came Ruthie and a relationship that would nearly destroy them both.

Lured away from the Ford family by a political job that paid $125 a week, Ruthie left the family - only to get fired after her new boss lost the election. Luckily, she was soon hired at the Grunow Clinic, established by a Chicago millionaire who wintered in Phoenix. It had been started in honor of his late daughter, who died before an illness she had could be appropriately diagnosed. At the clinic, Ruthie became friends with Anne LeRoi and, by extension, Sammy Samuelson.

Dr. Judd remained in and out of her life for the next year or so, skating into town after losing another job because of his drug problem and then taking off again to look for another. He spent five months in a hospital before landing on Ruthie's doorstep in January 1931. He failed to find a job in Phoenix, tried other towns in Arizona, and then returned to Mexico - but had no luck.

Ruthie loved her husband but had little hope that her marriage would work out. She rarely spoke about her marital problems, confiding only in her brother, Burton. In August 1931, she wrote him a long letter about Dr. Judd's continual failure to find a job. She told Burton she refused to leave Phoenix until her husband had a solid position:

I will stay here until he makes enough to take care of me. I don't want to give up my job and then be broke again. I am all alone. I wish that mama could come out now. I have a little house, and I am all alone. Why don't you come over next weekend? Hike over and visit me. We can talk over how and when we can get mama out here.

Ruthie avoided her problems when she wrote letters home to her parents, always trying to stay upbeat, minimizing her troubles and loneliness, and trying to paint her husband's job search in a positive light. But her folks knew more than she thought they did. Ruthie may have shielded them from the truth, but Burton had been more honest. He'd told them what was really going on, and Harvey and Carrie were worried.

Despite her fears about the failure of her marriage, her letters to Dr. Judd were filled with her undying love, and she often begged him to return to her in Phoenix. "Come home soon," she wrote.

It isn't a pretty home, doctor, but again, we ain't got barrels of money, maybe we are ragged and funny, but we will travel along, singing a song 'side by side,' because we love each other.

But deep down, Ruthie likely knew she was wasting her time and letter-writing efforts. Dr. Judd was lost in his addiction by 1931, and there seemed to be little hope for his recovery.

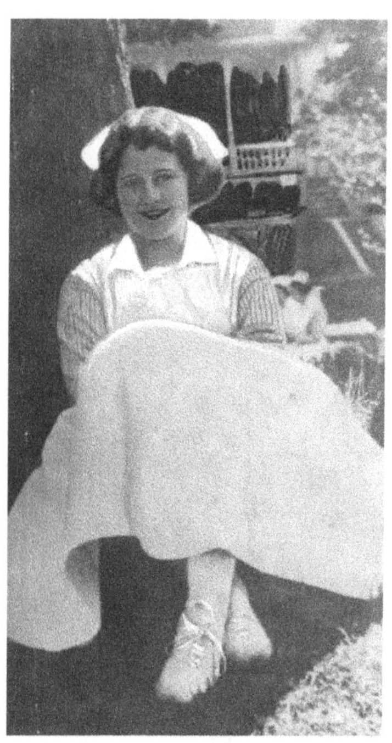

Newspaper image of Anne LeRoi during her nursing training in Oregon.

RUTHIE'S FRIEND, ANNE, HADN'T DONE MUCH BETTER regarding marital bliss. She had married William Mason in 1925 while still in nurse's training in Oregon, keeping the marriage a secret so she wouldn't be kicked out of school. The hospital found out anyway, and she was asked to leave. The marriage fell apart after 18 months, but they parted on good terms. Mason later stated, "We didn't quarrel, but it was a case of incompatibility, and we agreed to a settlement and divorce."

After the divorce became final, Mason said that he insisted Anne return to nursing school. He wished her well and likely knew that Anne would have been much happier in a relationship with a woman - something out of the question at the time.

Little is known about her second marriage to LeRoi Smith, other than that it didn't last, and Anne kept his first name as her new last name when she moved to Alaska. William Mason saw her once after her second divorce when she passed through Seattle. "She had a girl with her that she was taking to Arizona from Alaska," he recalled later.

Mason - as well as friends and employers in Phoenix - would always say that Anne and Sammy were "very, very devoted" to each other.

ANNE WAS SURPRISED ON THE NIGHT OF OCTOBER 16 when Ruthie walked in her back door. Twice that day at work, Anne had asked Ruthie to come to supper. Another friend, Evelyn Nace, was going to stop by, and the four of them could play bridge. Anne had tried everything, even detailing what was on the menu - pork chops supplied by a young doctor planning to rent the other side of the duplex, canned corn, scalloped potatoes, and a salad. But Ruthie had declined both times, saying she was behind with her work and planned to take some of it home.

This was partially true, but the real reason she couldn't come was that she had plans to spend the night with her secret boyfriend, Jack Halloran. The girls, of course, knew Jack, but they didn't know that he and Ruthie had been having an affair for nearly 10 months.

Ruthie was very aware that Jack and his friends spent a lot of time at the bungalow, but he'd told Ruthie that she was the one he wanted regardless of his other flirtations. This didn't do much to cool her jealousy, however. While she'd roomed with the girls, she'd realized that Jack was responsible for more than bringing bootleg liquor to their parties and handing out the occasional gift. He also frequently slipped them considerable sums of money. She'd seen him flirt shamelessly with both Anne and Sammy. She was jealous of them and knew they were envious of her in return - or so she thought. Ruthie was blind to the way the two girls felt about each other.

But Jack hadn't shown up for their date that night, and Ruthie was irritated, deciding she wouldn't be home if he finally decided to come over. She took a short trolley ride to see her best friends instead.

EVELYN NACE HAD TAKEN RUTHIE'S PLACE AT DINNER that night. She also worked at the Grunow Clinic and had a casual friendship with Anne and Ruthie. She didn't meet Sammy until that night.

The living room of the bungalow that Anne and Sammy shared.

Anne put dinner on the table but didn't eat. She said she wasn't feeling well and sipped tea while Evelyn and Sammy ate. Tired of sitting in the kitchen, Sammy said she was too weak to sit up for bridge, so the three women moved into the bedroom. There was just enough room between the two single beds to set up the card table, and they played bridge for about 40 minutes. They talked and laughed, and the party broke up around 9:30. Anne and Sammy walked Evelyn to the door and said goodbye.

Ruthie arrived just a few minutes later, explaining that she'd finished her work earlier than planned. She should stay the night, the girls said. It was already late, and the trolleys would stop running soon. Saturday was a workday, plus they had a big day ahead of them - they were all going to look at a house that Ruthie hoped would be their new home.

Ruthie had been working with a realtor for months to find a large house to buy. Her parents were considering retiring and moving to Phoenix to be near Ruthie. They'd sell their home in Indiana and use the money for their down payment.

Ruth, Anne, and Sammy had come up with an additional part to this plan - if the house had enough space and a separate entrance, the girls would move in, too. Anne and Ruthie's rent would cover the house payments, and Ruthie's mother, Carrie, would be happy to help care for Sammy.

Although I don't think the three young women had really thought about how this living arrangement would work - putting an end to their frequent parties in the home of a Methodist minister - they were all eager for things to work out. Ruthie was especially anxious about it. She missed her parents very much and wanted them close to her. The realtor had told her only yesterday that he'd found a house that might be perfect. Ruthie had arranged to borrow a car so they could all see it.

As she often did, Ruthie decided to spend the night on the pullout couch in the living room. Anne loaned her a pair of pink polka-dotted pajamas, and they all clustered for a talk in the bedroom before they turned the lights out.

It was an unremarkable Friday night for the three women. They had been together like this hundreds of times. There was nothing to suggest that this night would be any different.

But by the time this night was over, Anne and Sammy would be dead, each with a bullet in their head. Anne's body would be stuffed into the bottom of a steamer trunk, and Sammy's body would be cut into four pieces.

And Ruthie Judd would be a murderer.

2. "BODIES OF TWO MURDERED WOMEN HID IN LUGGAGE!"

AFTER THE TWO TRUNKS WERE OPENED AT LOS ANGELES' Union Station, the police traced the license number of the Ford that picked up the mysterious woman to Burton McKinnell. They went to his home in Beverly Glen, but he wasn't there, so they tracked him to Santa Monica. Burton was with his brother-in-law, the perplexed Dr. Judd, who was shocked to learn that the police were looking for his wife. He couldn't imagine that she had committed a crime. Why were the authorities trying to find her?

But Burton already knew. While driving away from the station, Ruthie admitted to him that there were bodies in the trunks.

"What?" he cried out. "Who?"

"The less you know, the better off you are," his sister replied. When the car stopped at the corner of Sixth and Broadway, Ruthie begged for a few dollars from Burton, jumped out of the vehicle, and vanished into the crowd.

The police started a search -- one that the newspapers would call the largest manhunt in the history of the West. Hundreds of officers in California and Arizona were looking for her. Nine blond women who matched her description were detained and questioned. They grilled her husband and her brother for hours. They interviewed her

Baggage handlers and LAPD officers removing Ruthie's trunks from the train station. By now, the search for Ruthie had started.

landlords and neighbors back in Phoenix and everyone she worked with or was even remotely connected to Ruthie and her two unlucky friends. They dug into Ruthie's personal life and the lives of her victims.

And they fed it all to eager reporters who passed the story on to the obsessed public on the front pages of the newspapers. In the early 1930s, the papers were still Americans' number one news source. Radio was just beginning to find its voice with news coverage, and television was still years into the future. The public demanded the printed word - and they couldn't get enough of the story.

Few crimes have ever seen the barrage of coverage devoted to Winnie Ruth Judd, and few criminals have instantly become a household name nationwide. Just as the bandits and bank robbers like John Dillinger, Pretty Boy Floyd, and Bonnie and Clyde would accomplish in a few years, Ruthie's crimes would serve as a distraction and take people's minds off the Depression.

It was just the right kind of crime - and Ruthie was the right kind of criminal - to feed into the excess that defined journalism in the 1930s. Newspapers didn't just report the news. They weren't using words like "allegedly" or looking for multiple sources to confirm their information. Newspapers acted as judge and jury, using a sensational tone designed to attract readers willing to hand over their nickel to read the bloodstained coverage of whatever crime they were covering.

The wall-to-wall coverage about the "trunk murders" began that first day with reporters cranking out stories written to scoop their competition. Of course, mistakes were made, incorrect stories were printed, and wild tales were concocted, but the fear of first-day mistakes couldn't compete with the fear of being beaten to the punch by a rival reporter. Getting the scoop wasn't just a duty but a badge of honor. Reporters had to be on top of every story. They'd be unemployed if they weren't. The battle to break every new turn in Ruthie's story became so heated in Los Angeles that teams of reporters from competing morning papers almost came to blows over the latest revelations.

As the news of the bodies broke that first day, reporters fed the public's fascination with Ruthie. They had a field day with a story that was a morbid mix of disgust and glee. Two-inch headlines screamed about the "Velvet Tigress, "the Blond Butcher," "Wolf Woman," and, of course, the "Trunk Murderess."

Phoenix newspapers were obviously obsessed with the stunning hometown crime, and editors happily shelved other stories to free up more space for their coverage of Ruthie.

But the fascination of Los Angeles papers rivaled even those in Phoenix. They could also claim it was a "hometown crime" since the bodies were discovered there, but Los Angeles had something that Phoenix did not - William Randolph Hearst.

Over the years, Hearst has earned a reputation as the most influential publisher in American history. He remains well-known decades after his death. Books have been written about him, and Orson Welles immortalized him as the inspiration for the film Citizen Kane. He was admired and hated, but mostly, he was feared. If he turned the force of his coast-to-coast newspaper empire in someone's direction, they would be either saved or destroyed.

Hearst also took a personal interest in Ruthie's case. He provided money for her defense, forced a leading California lawyer to lead her team of attorneys, and even offered to pay for an appeal to the U.S. Supreme Court.

But why?

That remains a mystery. One of his biographers suggested that perhaps he just loved a juicy story or had a soft spot for women in trouble. But more likely, he knew her story would sell newspapers.

William Randolph Hearst, whose interest in Ruthie's case was purely a financial one for his newspapers.

In 1931, Hearst planned to turn his Los Angeles Examiner into the city's biggest, loudest, and most profitable newspaper. He fought tooth and nail against the Chandler family, who owned the *Los Angeles Times* and wanted to ensure they were the paper on top. As each side battled for dominance in the market, they went to great lengths to ensure they printed everything they could about Ruthie Judd.

The *Times* - the more conservative of the two papers - likely held its nose as it descended into the muck to cover a sensational murder story, but the *Examiner* had no problem with the idea of "if it bleeds, it leads." Ruthie's story was perfect for Hearst's kind of newspaper. His reporters and editors ran full tilt into a story, never sticking with only "official" sources, never afraid of going too far, and giving readers all they could stomach. Some of the worst reporting in American history was printed in Hearst newspapers - but so was some of the best.

When Ruthie's story first broke, Hearst owned 30 newspapers -- one or more in every major city in the country. He also owned his own wire service, which no other news organization could compete with. His International News Service took stories from his individual papers daily and sold them to other papers nationwide. Even though the Associated Press was bigger, it didn't have the "single voice" that Hearst's empire had - a voice that promised readers all the scandal, intrigue, sensationalism, and blood that the early 1930s could offer.

Immediately, Heart's *Examiner* offered a $1,000 reward for "exclusive information" that led to the capture of Winnie Ruth Judd. Keep in mind, this was as much as most Americans earned in an entire year in 1931. Not to be outdone, the *Times* offered a $1,500 reward.

This would not be the last time either of these papers used cash to obtain information.

Eventually, both papers published their own versions of Ruthie's life story - supposedly written by her for astonishing sums of money. The "battle of the confessions," as the Phoenix press called them, allegedly earned her thousands of dollars from each paper.

Readers in Phoenix were shocked that crime paid so well because the newspapers there weren't paying for anything. The sheriff couldn't even get the County Board of Supervisors to cough up $250 for a reward that led to Ruthie's capture.

But readers in the rest of the country didn't need to wait for Phoenix papers to print lurid stories - they found those everywhere else. Hearst's papers played the story like chapters in a seamy melodrama, making some of the most outlandish and absurd allegations ever written about the case.

They gave readers a bizarre and often deranged story, filled with the smallest details about everyone connected to the tragedy. Newspaper readers were offered personal letters written by the victims and the woman accused of killing them. They were fascinated by theories from so-called experts who tried to explain the "weird" lives they all supposedly lived. But mostly, they were given a lot of really bad information.

By the time Ruthie turned herself in, the public knew all about her childhood, her marriage, her life in Phoenix, her secret boyfriend, the kind of stockings she preferred, that she colored her hair, was skilled at Mexican cooking, and had an open account at Wade's grocery store in Phoenix. Readers knew her family believed she was devoted to her husband, but they also knew she was having an illicit affair.

And they were convinced she was a cold-blooded killer.

ON MONDAY EVENING, OCTOBER 19, EVERYONE WAS searching for Ruthie, but she had disappeared.

The first news about the murders was broadcast on the radio that night, just hours after the discovery at the train station. Radio stations broke into their usual entertainment programs with news flashes that didn't offer much news - bloody trunks were found in Los Angeles, and the woman who had checked them in Phoenix had disappeared.

When the morning papers hit the streets, people were anxious to learn the story's details. The *Times* put the story on page one - above stories about Al Capone facing prison sentencing and the death of Thomas Edison - calling it "one of the most brutal crimes in the criminal history of the Southwest."

The story was printed under a headline that read: BODIES OF TWO MURDERED WOMEN HID IN LUGGAGE. It was followed by a subheading: "Mysterious couple disappear after seeking grewsome death trunks sent here from Phoenix."

The story began:

Ghastly discovery of the bodies of two women, one mutilated and a section missing, crammed into a small steamer trunk and a large wardrobe trunk, was made by authorities last night as they smashed the locks of the luggage after it had been

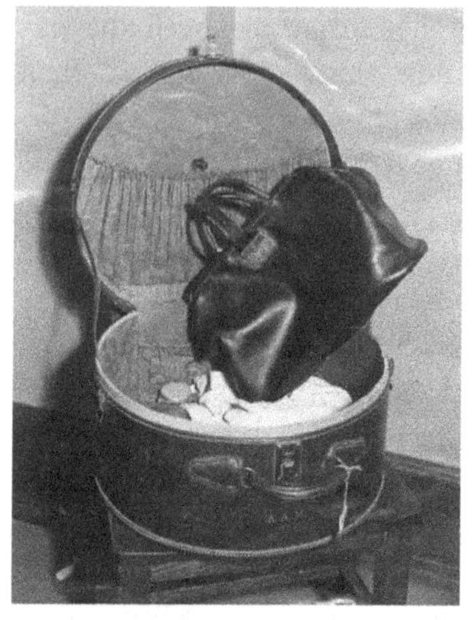

deposited at Central Station earlier in the day by a Southern Pacific passenger train from Phoenix.

Blood issuing from the luggage brought it under suspicion immediately on its arrival at 7:45 A.M. and it was placed under surveillance - but a woman and a man who made an effort to claim the pieces about noon escaped.

It wasn't wholly accurate, but at least it presented the facts, unlike other parts of the same article, which became pretty wild as it continued:

With fiendish irony, the murderer gathered up the exploded shells, one of the leaden slugs and an unexploded cartridge and dropped them into the purse of one of the women. Then he tossed the purse into the trunk with the bodies and clamped down the lids on the remains of his murderous orgy.

Among the grewsome relics of the fiendish act was a green-handled bread knife, about ten inches long, with a cutting and saw-tooth edge. Officer said it may have been the instrument with which the dismembering of the woman was done. Fingerprints etched in blood on the knife's blade may go far toward the identification of the killer.

Wild or not, the picture painted by the article was disturbing and was made even more upsetting when appearing next to the faces of the victims, which were used to illustrate it. No newspaper could have hoped to get photographs like that in the few short hours between the discovery of the trunks and the final press deadline. But the paper noted they were available because the killer had supplied them. The photos, some smeared with blood, had been tossed into the trunks with the bodies.

Sammy Samuelson

Next to an image of Sammy Samuelson, the text read:

Smashed locks revealed the mutilated body of the woman believed to be Miss Samuelson. After being shot through the head near the right ear, in the left arm between the elbow and the shoulder and in the upper abdomen, the body had been separated between the lower abdomen and the knees - the section that is missing. It is believed possibly to be in other luggage not yet discovered. The torso, head, and arms had been wrapped in rags and jammed down into the smaller trunk. Her lower limbs were thrown in the larger trunk with the body believed to be that of Mrs. LeRoi.

There were two photographs of Agnes Anne LeRoi. She was in her nurse's uniform in one of them, and in the other, she was smiling at the camera - a pretty young woman who never should have met such a gruesome fate. Chilling words were printed next to her photographs:

Anne LeRoi

The body believed to be that of Mrs. LeRoi was not mutilated but had been jammed into the larger trunk. She had been shot once through the head.

A bigger scoop was printed in the *Examiner* that morning. Reporters for that paper had managed to get more information from police detectives than the competition had. The

Examiner was about to name the "mysterious couple" who had tried to claim the luggage - Winnie Ruth Judd and her brother, Burton McKinnell.

They also announced the discovery of the missing parts of Sammy's body.

On Monday evening, someone had noticed the old suitcase and hatbox behind the station's ladies' room door, and after the excitement over the bloody trunks, station officials called the police. Inside, they found Sammy's lower torso wrapped in pajamas and a blanket from her waist to her knees. In the hatbox, they found an empty black surgeon's bag, surgical dressings, women's undergarments, makeup, a .25 Colt automatic pistol, and a box of cartridges.

But even this discovery wasn't the biggest bombshell in the *Examiner* that morning. The paper was about to go to press when this new information was announced. Editors quickly inserted a "bulletin" in bold type about the lead story:

BULLETIN: At three o'clock this morning Detective Lieutenant Art Bergeron announced that B.J. McKinnell, brother of Mrs. Ruth Judd, had admitted that Mrs. Judd confessed to him that she murdered the two women shipped from Phoenix in trunks, and that she added she was "perfectly justified."

The story was spread across the country by the International News Service, shocking readers with news of a psychotic butcher who believed their actions could be explained - and worst of all, the killer was a woman.

The *Examiner* offered a slightly different description of the contents of the trunks:

Two murdered women, the body of each crammed into a trunk, arrived in Los Angeles as baggage yesterday! Carefully - one at a time - both trunks were opened. In the larger one was the body of an older and larger woman. She had been shoved into the trunk and

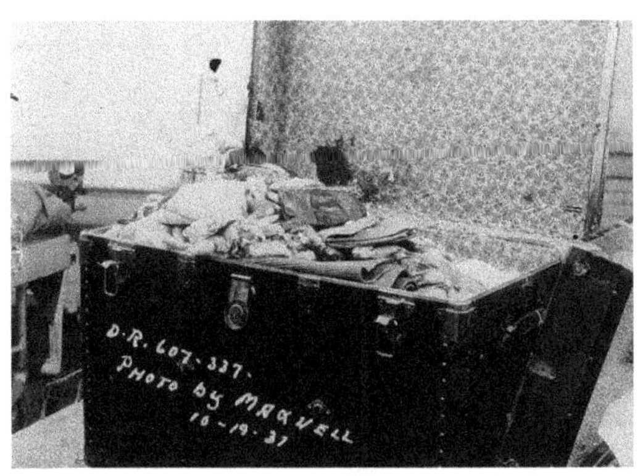

partly hidden by a mass of clothing, blankets, letters, and a jumble of other material, apparently thrown hastily on top of the corpse.

In the body of the younger woman were three bullet wounds. One was in the left temple, one in the left breast, and one in the left shoulder. Too, there was a bullet wound on the third finger of the left hand, suggesting that the girl had died while hopelessly trying to ward off her assailant.

She had been stuffed into the smaller trunk, for the body had been severed by a keen-edged instrument - cut completely into three pieces, but the portion from the waist to the knees was missing. She had been dead not more than two days, the surgeons said...

On the other side of the country, Hearst's *New York Journal* had already speculated on a motive - claiming that the two women had been murdered after an argument over Ruthie's request that they kill a pet cat who was sick.

I have no idea where this idea came from.

Another Hearst newspaper, the *New York Daily Mirror*, even speculated that Ruthie might have "fed bits of her victims to her pet cat."

Blood and gore were great - as far as the New York papers were concerned - but they wanted to make sure the story was sensational enough to hook the readers by printing the first public claims of "queer love" between the victims. Truth or fiction, the papers had no way of knowing. However, they did know that by twisting some ordinary bits of information, they could shock and titillate a country scandalized by homosexuality.

All three women loved "weird thrill parties, purposely subjecting their nerves to shocks and strains," the *Journal* told readers, never explaining that it had reached this conclusion because the girls - like millions of other Americans - were hooked on radio mystery shows. The paper also absurdly suggested that Ruthie had once tried to poison Anne. That was based on a letter in which Anne jokingly complained about what a terrible cook Ruthie was.

Back home in Phoenix, the city's two daily papers - the *Arizona Republic* and *Phoenix Gazette* - also didn't hold anything back. The *Republic* called it "one of the cruelest yet crudest crimes in the Southwest's criminal annals," while the *Gazette* dubbed it "Phoenix's most sensational murder case." Both agreed that Sammy had been "hacked into pieces."

The Republic announced the crime in two-inch-high letters: TWO PHOENIX WOMEN SLAIN. As was the style of the 1930s, the main headline was followed by subheads that highlighted the story:

- BODIES OF VICTIMS, ONE DISMEMBERED, FOUND IN TRUNKS

- MRS. AGNES ANNE LEROI, LOCAL X-RAY TECHNICIAN, AND MISS HEDVIG SAMUELSON, SCHOOL TEACHER, BELIEVED TO BE THOSE BRUTALLY KILLED IN CITY FRIDAY.

- TWO ARE HELD AS WITNESSES ON COAST.

- SOUTHERN PACIFIC BAGGAGEMAN IN LOS ANGELES MAKES GRUESOME DISCOVERY AFTER MAN AND WOMAN CALL FOR CONTAINERS; OFFICERS BELIEVE SOLUTION NEAR.

The story that followed printed the basic facts of the discovery at the train station and noted that Burton McKinnell and Dr. William C. Judd were being held for questioning.

But the highlight of the *Republic's* story was the detective work that its reporters were doing.

Neighbors, the story continued, saw a gray Packard in the driveway of the "death bungalow" for hours on Saturday afternoon, the day before the trunks were shipped to Los Angeles. The "mysterious car" showed up again on Monday night, not long after the trunks were opened in Los Angeles. The police told reporters that the driver quickly drove off when an officer guarding the house turned on a porch light. This same car, reporters would find, was frequently seen at Ruthie's apartment in the weeks before the murders. And yet, somehow, the *Republic* reporters could never discover who owned the car.

But the police knew who owned the Packard, and so did the neighbors. Out-of-state reporters didn't hesitate to print the owner's name, but that information never appeared in Phoenix.

And that wouldn't be the only time in this case that news would appear in out-of-state newspapers that were never found in the papers at home.

By the time the *Phoenix Gazette's* Tuesday afternoon edition was out on the streets, it had the most complete information available on the case. This paper had the advantage of time - morning papers were printed just after midnight, but afternoon editions were printed at noon. It was evident from the coverage that reporters had been working on the story all night. The main headline shouted: MRS. JUDD SOUGHT IN DOUBLE TRUNK SLAYING.

The front page was dominated by nine headlines about the case. Two more pages inside were devoted to related stories. The *Gazette* had managed to piece together an in-depth and astonishingly accurate account of Ruthie's activities around the time of the murders. Readers - especially those who knew her - studied the stories, trying to learn how this ordinary woman could have become involved in such an out-of-the-ordinary series of events.

It was reported that Ruthie, who was "known as a calm person who spent most of her evenings writing on a typewriter," had hosted three parties during the week of the murders. The last party had been on Thursday night and was attended by another woman and some men. Neighbors told reporters it was "a little bit loud."

The victims themselves had also had parties that week, hosting a new doctor from the Grunow Clinic for supper on Thursday and entertaining a nurse from the clinic, Evelyn Nace, for dinner and bridge on the night they died. When Evelyn spoke to reporters about her last evening with the girls, she said both Anne and Sammy seemed happy and were without any sense of apprehension when she left them at 9:30 P.M.

An hour later, a neighbor, Jennie McGrath, was awakened by three gunshots coming from the direction of the bungalow. She said there was one shot, then a pause, followed by two more in quick succession. She looked out the window but saw no lights on in the bungalow. She didn't investigate any further.

Another neighbor, Gene Cunningham, also reported hearing the shots but didn't check them out either. Instead, he went back to bed.

On Saturday morning, the clinic secretary, Mrs. Ernest Smith, took a call from Ruthie, who said she would be arriving at work a little late. Shortly after, a woman who claimed to be Anne LeRoi called to say she wasn't coming to work because she had to make an emergency trip to Tucson. Mrs. Smith angrily told the caller she was already late and Dr. Louis Baldwin would be very unhappy with the situation. She was right. Dr. Baldwin took the call and demanded Anne cancel her travel plans and come in to work. They had a full schedule of X-ray patients that day.

Mrs. Smith was still on the line. "That wasn't Mrs. LeRoi," she told the doctor after he hung up. "I think that was Ruth Judd."

When Ruthie arrived at the clinic later that morning, Mrs. Smith confronted her about the call, but Ruthie denied making it. No one believed her, especially after they got a look at her. Evelyn Nace remembered her looking "white as a ghost and nervous." Others thought she looked "untidy" and as if she "had been up all night."

The most shocking information, though, came from Richard Swartz, a driver for the Lightning Delivery Company. A woman had called his office on Saturday night and asked for a trunk to be picked

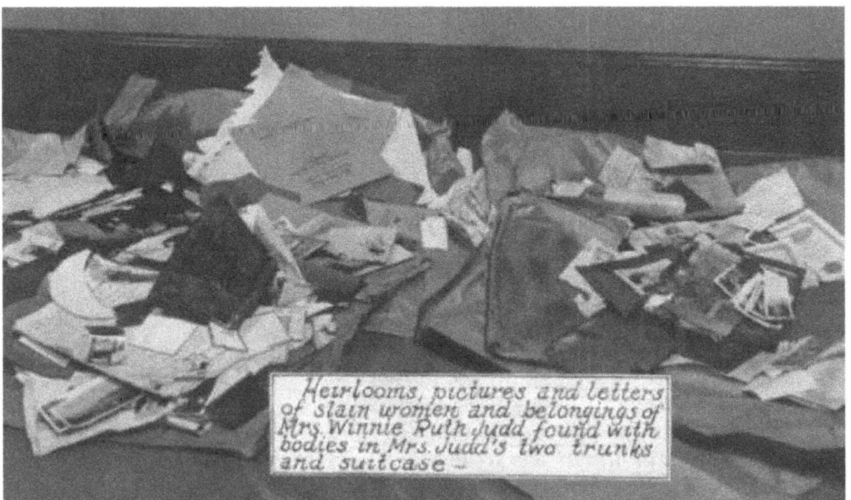

Items that belonged to Ruthie that were found inside the trunks and suitcases that contained the bodies of Anne and Sammy.

up at the bungalow and delivered to the train station. When he arrived, he found the house dark and a single trunk in the living room. It was so heavy that he needed help from two of his assistants to lift it. When he asked what was in it, the woman said it was books. Swartz warned her that a heavy trunk couldn't be shipped as luggage. He said she hesitated for a long time, looking confused, and then asked him to deliver her and the trunk to an apartment on Brill Street instead.

Swartz recalled that the woman acted as if she were in a daze. He had to ask her to move out of his way three times so that he could get past her with the trunk. When he had driven away from the Brill Street apartment, he said she was standing in the doorway, completely still, "like a statue."

He also commented that she'd promised to tip him but never did. This was the behavior that seemed to offend him the most.

Ruthie had apparently moved Sammy - or pieces of Sammy - in the smaller trunk and the suitcase she was later found in. The police found a satchel of surgical instruments in her apartment on Brill Street, and while she could have dismembered Sammy there, it seems

A photo showing the missing section of rug that been had cut from the bedroom at the bungalow. The rug – covered in blood – was found in one of the trunks.

more likely that this was done at the bungalow so Sammy's remains could be moved more easily.

When detectives searched the bungalow, they became convinced Anne and Sammy had been killed in the bedroom. Both mattresses were missing. The corner of a bedroom rug had been "crudely hacked out with a pair of surgical scissors." Blood spatters were under one bed, covering the floor and splashing up as high as the baseboard. There was no blood on the walls.

The police later found one mattress - with no bloodstains - in a vacant lot miles away from the bungalow. The other mattress was never found. The bloody piece cut from the bedroom rug was found inside the bloody trunks.

But why had the murders happened at all?

Ruthie's recent move to her own apartment was cited as proof of "friction" between the three women. Bits and pieces of letters written to family and friends were widely quoted to demonstrate the growing animosity that officials claimed had broken the friendship - but really, they only show that the housekeeping styles of Ruthie and Anne clashed. The girls were much better friends, living separately.

Sammy wrote to her sister on August 10: "Ruth Judd is staying with us, but somehow, it seems she doesn't belong here. I don't know how it will work out, but if the doctor gets a position, she will probably join him. It doesn't bother me, but I don't think Anne likes it."

On September 28, Anne had written in a letter: "Ruth is leaving us in a few days. Dr. Judd is coming home so she will take an apartment. It really hasn't worked out so well having three of us. We are very fond of her, and she is a sweet girl, but three just seems to be a wrong number when one is used to living by oneself and just one other very congenial one."

On October 2, in the last letter her parents would receive from Sammy, she wrote: "Ruth Judd, the girl that was staying with us, moved so we are alone again, and we like it so much better. Three never get along very well."

One of the letters to Ruth from her husband that police found in her apartment contained a slight hint of trouble. Dr. Judd wrote: "I don't want to write a letter to lie around for Sammy and Mrs. LeRoi to read. I had supposed you thought so much of those two girls that you would be perfectly happy with them, but if you are not, it puts a different face on matters. I am not at all surprised at what you tell me. I do not dare write you freely because you are so careless with letters."

When asked later, Dr. Judd refused to elaborate on any problems between his wife and the girls, saying only that Ruthie disapproved of Anne's "lifestyle." Of course, he had no idea that his wife was having an affair with Jack Halloran at the time she was living with the girls, so her "lifestyle" wasn't exactly one that would have met with approval from many people.

The newspapers used the letters they'd obtained from the police to try and show that the three women had become antagonistic with each other - or at least toward Ruthie. They used small quotes from letters that were otherwise benign or even joking. Anne wrote to her brother that she'd been subjected to another of Ruth's Mexican dishes and joked, "It almost did me in." When reporters asked about this, the brother stated clearly that Anne's comment hadn't been serious.

None of the letters - even those that seemed happy about Ruthie finding a place of her own - sounded threatening, and none of them offered any hint of the horrible violence to come.

But there was one letter that the police revealed to substantiate that there had been some violence between them in the past. It was the last letter that Sammy ever wrote. It was a three-page letter to her sister, penned on the day she died. It was found, waiting to be mailed, on the desk in the bungalow. During a press conference, a police officer read a section aloud from the letter to reporters:

We are much happier by ourselves as Ruth and Anne clashed on so many things and their quarrels were sometimes violent.

That sounds bad, but there's a slight problem - this is *not* what the letter says. The handwritten letter is still preserved in the files of the Arizona historical archives, and it actually reads:

We are so much happier here by ourselves. Ruth and Anne clashed in so many things. We get along so well, but it shows there has to be a lot of tolerance which comes from love.

The police were desperate to show the press that Ruthie had some sort of motive for killing her friends, and they even purposely misread from Sammy's letter to try and give her one. Even if Ruthie and Anne did "clash in so many things," that hardly seems to be terrible enough to lead to such a gruesome murder.

There had to be more.

Famed detective William J. Burns

Internationally known detective William J. Burns, who wintered in Phoenix, wrote about the case for the *Gazette*. Based on his experience, he told the reporter, "I feel that the motive is the deepest mystery in the crime. The fact that the murderer or murderers in this case sought to hide their crime by shipping the bodies to Los Angeles indicates that the mind of the criminal was inflamed. It was not at all a calm individual who killed the two women. The trunk murder case was handled very clumsily, and it is quite possible that the crime was committed without much deliberation."

Was Ruthie insane? Or was she a killer who carefully premeditated and orchestrated the death of her best friends, as the prosecution in her case would later tell the jury?

Or more intriguing was the theory suggested by a few detectives and newspapermen that Ruthie hadn't committed the murders at all. She had just badly tried to cover them up.

Did Ruthie Judd have an accomplice?

3. ANOTHER KILLER?

RUTHIE'S BROTHER, BURTON - THE SECOND HALF OF the "mysterious couple" at the train station - was immediately suspected of being his sister's accomplice. Detectives initially figured that he had either helped her plan the murders or, at the very least, knew in advance that she was bringing her victims to L.A.

William Judd was also an immediate suspect. It was suggested that he might've taken a secret trip to Phoenix and assisted his wife with her crime.

But it quickly became apparent that neither man was involved. Neither of them had been to Phoenix in months, and both had solid alibis for the night of the murders. Both were as confused and alarmed about Ruthie's involvement as her friends back in Phoenix were.

However, if these two men weren't involved, then who was? Because the police in both Los Angeles and Phoenix were convinced that Ruthie had help.

A headline in the *Gazette* read: "Phoenix officers hunt accomplice in brutal killings." The authorities assured reporters that loading the trunks was "a feat believed beyond the unaided strength of Mrs. Judd."

County Attorney Lloyd Andrews told reporters: "From the evidence gathered by the police, Mrs. Judd's complicity is evident - we know she attempted to dispose of the bodies. It would be foolish, considering everything that we've learned, to go on the theory Mrs. Judd alone was responsible for the slayings. She is a woman of slight build, and it would have been impossible for her alone to have handled the bodies. There is little doubt a man was involved in the packing of the bodies into the trunks."

As a result, he filed a warrant charging Ruthie Judd and an unknown man with first-degree murder in the death of Sammy. A second warrant was filed against Ruthie alone for Anne's murder.

The paper's readers, though, were just as confused as the police about the whole situation. They were expected to believe that Ruthie and her accomplice, for some unknown reason, killed the two girls and then tried to conceal the crime in the most ridiculous way imaginable. Why hadn't the bodies been dumped in the thousands of square miles of empty desert around Phoenix, where coyotes and buzzards would have eaten the evidence and scattered the bones? Why would anyone take the bleeding bodies by train to Los Angeles?

Famous detective William J. Burns was right - nothing about this crime had been thought out very carefully. From the very first day, it seemed there was more about this case than just two horrible murders. It seemed possible - even likely - that someone else was involved in this crime.

And for many people, that possibility has never gone away, even all these years later. Some believe the truth of the story has never been revealed - and some even believe that Ruthie never killed anyone at all.

AS THE SEARCH FOR RUTHIE CONTINUED, THE newspapers continued to point out what seemed obvious - that Ruthie Judd was a killer. Whoever else was involved, they would be found out later. They were confident the police would discover the accomplice, but for now, it was clear that Ruthie needed to be caught and punished.

For the next three days, the search went on without success, and then suddenly, the *Gazette* announced that the police had found "startling" evidence at the bungalow that proved there was an accomplice, but they never spelled out what that evidence was. Either detectives never told reporters what they'd found, or the reporters decided to keep it a secret. Investigators were quoted about making progress in the case and were confident they would soon identify the accomplice.

But then, officials abruptly changed their minds. Los Angeles detectives - who were 500 miles away and never set foot in Phoenix - told reporters they had "wholly abandoned the theory that Mrs. Judd had a male accomplice."

The Phoenix police quickly backtracked, too, telling the press that, regardless of their earlier theories, it was clear that Ruthie had acted alone. County Attorney Andrews also weighed in. He told reporters that he suddenly found it reasonable that Ruthie was solely responsible for the crime. He would later take this theory - no matter how ridiculous he once believed it to be -- to the jury at her trial.

There was no explanation in the newspapers for this change of mind. No one even tried to explain the evidence that detectives supposedly had. The police simply said they'd been wrong - it was Ruthie, by herself, all along. She had killed Anne and Sammy and then had tried to ship their bodies to Los Angeles. They announced they'd been horribly wrong at the start, but now they were on the right track.

This abrupt change of theory caused whiplash in those closely following the case. To make matters worse, the police had been so sure that Ruthie had an accomplice that their sudden denial that she'd had help seemed absurd. Many people weren't initially convinced-and some never were. They would always believe that the prosecutors and the police had railroaded Ruthie, and no follow-up articles or "corrections" by the press would change their minds.

They were convinced by the earliest reporting on the case - the stories that were the observations of what experienced detectives had observed and deciphered. Those first stories had no political considerations or concerns about whose toes were being stepped on. They were the "who, what, when, and where" stories - the "why" would come later.

Of course, all the worries about politics and city insiders would begin very quickly. However, in the first hours after the discovery of a horrific murder, no one was thinking about those things.

For newspaper readers, those early stories always colored their first impression of what happened. Journalists know nothing sticks in the reader's mind like that first story. A shocking story like this one guaranteed that many papers would be sold, and while hundreds of articles would eventually be written about Ruthie, most people would remember the first ones as the best. And wrong information, even if corrected later, would still be stuck in the reader's mind because that was what they heard first.

From the very start, substantial misinformation was presented as fact in Ruthie's case.

Burton McKinnell

One of the greatest errors was Burton McKinnell's report that his sister had confessed to him. Burton always insisted that he was misquoted and never told the police that. He soon became a champion for his sister, even publishing a 12-page booklet at his own expense that proclaimed her innocence. He also moved to Arizona to be closer to her - as did his elderly mother and father - and became an amateur detective working on her behalf. At the beginning of the case, however, the public believed he had betrayed his sister.

A few newspapers, including the *Los Angeles Times*, later ran lengthy stories that allowed Burton to set the record straight, but most papers paid little attention to his protests. Some stated that he had "recanted and changed his story," while others said Burton "claimed he was misquoted." He was old news by then, and reporters wanted to move on to the fresh developments in the story.

But Burton continued to protest - and based on his interview with the police, he had good reason to keep complaining.

While being questioned, Burton told a roomful of detectives that his sister had shown up on campus around 11:00 A.M. on Monday and ordered him to get his car because she wanted him to take some trunks out in the ocean and "sink them."

Burton told the police: "I asked her why such drastic measures and she told me she didn't want me to ask any questions - that the less I knew, the better off I would be and a sentence like that has a certain amount of significance, whereupon I saw if I assisted her in getting the desired trunks that there would be no dispute."

A detective questioned: "Did you guess what was in the trunks?"

Burton: I didn't. I asked her what was in the trunks, and she refused to answer me."

Question: "Did you keep asking her?"

Burton: "I didn't because I saw the logic of it... I anticipated there was something wrong, of course, or she wouldn't want the trunks sunk at sea and to press that question in the face of that supposition, I felt that she was right - that I should not know."

Burton was then asked what he thought when station agents refused to give them the trunks at the baggage depot.

Burton: "We left, and I said, 'Ruth, what's in that trunk, a man or a woman?' And she said, 'Burton, I am not going to answer any questions,' and she said, 'I can justify everything.' When she said she was justified, I said, 'I'm not interested in your justification and think the thing to concentrate on now is what the next step is to take' and then we were silent, the both of us for some time and then she asked me for money because she said she had to leave and I said, 'I think that is the best thing you can do' and I said, 'I wish you all the luck in the world, kid,' and she left."

Burton gave her a $5 bill - the only cash he had - and she stepped from the car at a stoplight and vanished into the downtown crowds.

The interview went on from there, and Burton was asked the same questions repeatedly and always gave the same answers. Never, at any time, did he claim that his sister had confessed to murder.

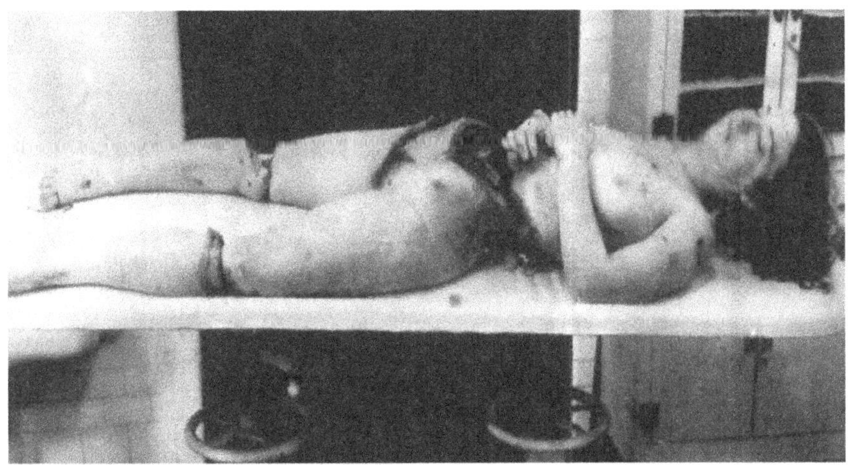

Sammy's body after it had been re-assembled by the coroner.

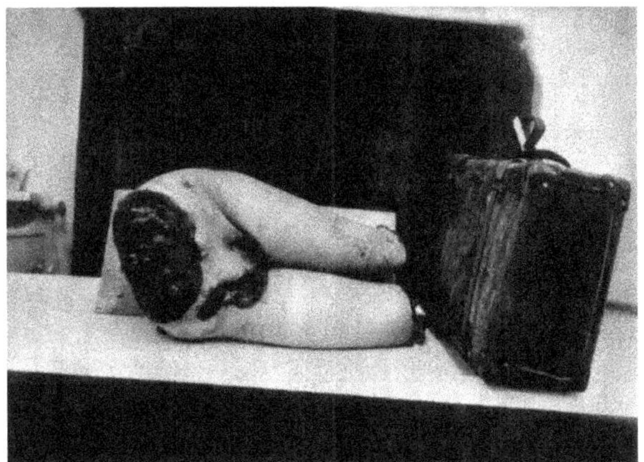

The condition of Sammy's body shows that it was not "hacked" as the reports claimed. This shows her waist and upper legs, which were found in the suitcase next to the corpse.

As it turned out, though, misquoting Burton McKinnell was not the biggest mistake in those early reports. There was another piece of misinformation that became accepted as fact and which still haunts this case today.

In the initial stories, the International News Service described the condition of Sammy's body as "grisly butchery." The Associated Press used the phrase "hacked into pieces." Those descriptions conjure up an image of horror - a body brutally hacked apart with some sharp instrument - and were the ingredient that made the case

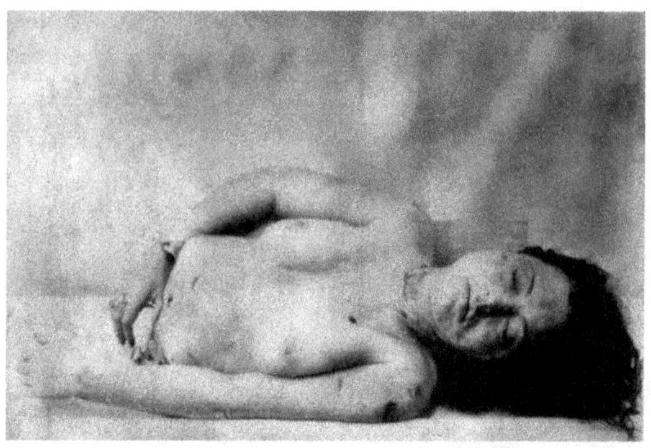

Sammy's "butchered" body was always the most memorable part of the Ruthie Judd story, despite misleading information being offered about photos the public didn't see.

so sensational. If Sammy's body hadn't been "butchered," the case might have been just another unusual homicide, and we wouldn't still be talking about it nearly a century later.

The multiple traveling trunks that contained sections of Sammy have always been the most memorable pieces of this story - so to speak. Several books have described how Ruthie cut her friend up to fit her into a trunk, a suitcase, and a hat box. Author Marvin J. Wolf in the book *Fallen Angels*: "Winnie got a surgical saw and a butcher knife. She hacked Samuelson's body into pieces..."

It's easy to assume this was the case, especially since so few people saw the autopsy photos. The county attorney who prosecuted Ruthie and her defense lawyers saw them, but the judge who presided over her case did not. Neither did the jurors who decided her fate. They were never printed in newspapers, of course. They were considered too terrible even for the sensational press of the 1930s. This meant that the public had to rely on the written word, and even the newspaper reports that said Sammy's body had been "dismembered" didn't steer clear of descriptions like "hacked" and "savaged." Anyone reading those words in the newspaper instantly imagined a woman's body that had been chopped up into pieces.

I have seen the photos - I've even reprinted them here for those who have the stomach to look closely - and while they are horrific, it's clear that Sammy was not "hacked apart." Her body was undoubtedly severed, cut apart so that she would fit into separate cases, but despite the newspaper wording, it didn't look like a chainsaw or an axe had done it.

The legs, lower torso, and upper torso were severed so cleanly that the coroner was able to stitch the body back together again.

Does that make this any less horrific? Not really.

But seeing the photographs does make it clear how inaccurate the printed stories of the murders were. I believe the descriptions in the news articles influenced everything about this case, from start to finish.

They were likely one reason why the police stopped looking for Ruthie's accomplice - but they weren't the only reason, as will soon be apparent.

4. SEX AND SUNSHINE

CLAY GEORGE'S HANDS WERE SHAKING AS HE DROVE home from work on the evening of October 19. He was just a plumber, he thought; he wasn't supposed to be mixed up in anything like this. Pulling into the driveway, he turned off the car ignition and sat behind the wheel for a few minutes, working up the nerve to go into the house where his family was waiting for him to sit down for dinner. He knew his wife, Ruby, would be able to tell he was upset, and then she'd ask questions he wasn't supposed to answer.

Clay worked for a local plumbing company, Hudlow and Fleetner, and, except for today, he'd always loved his job. His bosses were genuinely good men. They had kept the shop open during the Depression, knowing that Clay and their other employees had families to support. Because of that, they had Clay's loyalty, and when he was asked to go to a bungalow on North Second Street that day, he didn't hesitate.

But he'd never forget what he'd been asked to do there.

He looked up and saw the curtain in the kitchen window open, and he saw his wife look out at him. He knew he had to go inside. He grabbed his lunch pail by the handle, got out of the car, and went to the back door as he always did.

When he entered the cheery, brightly lit kitchen, he saw Ruby putting the finishing touches on supper. He could hear the radio playing in the other room and the rambunctious noises of all six of his children throughout the house.

The bungalow on Second Street that Clay George visited after news of the murders broke. His visit there was never recorded by the police.

As soon as he stepped inside, his daughter, Edna, appeared from nowhere and wrapped her arms around his waist in a hug.

She had no idea how much he needed that.

Ruby looked over at her husband and daughter and smiled, but the smile quickly faded from her face. "Edna," she said quickly, "go tell your brothers and sisters to wash up for supper. I need to talk to your Daddy."

When Edna ran off, Ruby's became serious. She could see that Clay's face was ashen and pale. Before she could ask what was wrong, another news flash - like the ones she'd heard all afternoon - came on the radio. It was the same as all the others, announcing that two young women had been killed in Phoenix, and their bodies had been taken to Los Angeles on the train.

When Clay heard the news, his knees seemed to grow weak, and the little color left on his face drained away. "That's strange!" he gasped. "The police told me not to talk about it."

Ruby gasped. "What do you mean?"

Clay told her that he'd been sent to a bungalow on Second Street that day, and when he got there, he learned that it was a murder scene - the very place that was being talked about on the radio. Detectives had asked him to clean out the drains in the bathroom, but he'd found bits and pieces of skin, flesh, bones, and hair in the pipes. The police, he explained, wrapped it all up and took it away. He was told not to talk about what he'd done, where he'd been, and what he had seen there.

But as he was leaving, he overheard two of the detectives talking, and they said they thought the killer's boyfriend had something to do with the murders. Clay even thought he'd overheard the man's name.

If Clay George ever spoke about that day again, no one ever remembered. Many years later, his daughter, Edna, who was by then a grandmother, did remember being with her father when he drove past the bungalow in the days and weeks that followed. She also remembered that their mother always hushed them whenever she or her siblings asked about the incident. The children were always bothered by how disturbed their father was about the case.

In an interview, Edna recalled, "My brother said Daddy was afraid, that's why he didn't talk about the story. I never thought Daddy was afraid of anything, but I think he was afraid of this. He expected to testify at Ruth Judd's murder trial. Much to his relief, he was never called."

This seems like a strange mistake for the county attorney to have made - not calling a witness who could testify to the chain of custody for the evidence found in the bathroom drain at the bungalow - but it gets even stranger.

There is no police record of Clay George cleaning out any drain. Whatever flesh, bone, and hair was found was never submitted as evidence in the trial. Instead, the police stated they had found no evidence in any drain - either at the girls' bungalow or Ruth's apartment. As proof, they released a report from a different plumber they sent to check out both drains on October 26, a week after Clay had already recovered all the evidence.

But why? Why conceal that evidence? Why lie about what was in that drain? And why would the authorities tell Clay - a family man who desperately needed to keep his job - to stay quiet about it?

Perhaps it had something to do with what the police already suspected - and what Clay overheard as he left the bungalow that day. Perhaps they feared that Ruthie's secret boyfriend, one of the most prominent men in Phoenix, was somehow involved in the mess.

To those who knew Ruthie, it had come as a shock when they heard she was responsible for two murders. They assumed there had to be some sort of mistake.

Ruthie's first employer in Phoenix, Leigh Ford, even told police, "If a thousand people were standing in a row and I was called upon to pick the person who might commit a crime of his kind, Ruth Judd would be the last one that I would pick."

But could the same be said for her secret boyfriend?

ALMOST FROM THE START, PHOENIX PLAYERS AND politicians suspected that Ruthie Judd wasn't involved in the murders alone. And with that realization came speculation about who else might be involved. Many local men left town for a while to let things cool off, fearing they'd be drawn into the case, exposed as men who had partied with Ruthie and her two friends.

In the 1930s, Phoenix presented itself as a God-fearing, morally strict city where "everybody knew everybody." Not surprisingly, though, under the surface, it was just like any other town, and it wasn't hard to find prostitution, gambling, bootleg liquor, drugs, political corruption, payoffs, and worse.

There was a "political machine" that ran Phoenix in those days. It handed out jobs during a time when jobs were hard to find, got a cut from the illicit businesses it allowed to operate, and made sure that none of its friends got into serious trouble. There was a subculture of cops, attorneys, playboys, and party girls, and the authority figures were among the most powerful in the community. If they wanted to protect a friend, they could easily do so. They could also make sure that Phoenix's image stayed untarnished. The town needed to keep growing and prospering, and the only way to do that was to keep the dirty side of things swept under the rug.

Jack Williams -- who not only reported the news on the radio in Phoenix at the time of Ruthie's trial but also became Arizona's governor - told a story about how things worked in the city at that time:

Like every other decent-sized city in the 1920s, Phoenix had its share of crime and political corruption during this volatile era.

A political candidate known for his excessive drinking ended up in jail on a Friday night just before the election. The police chief called the party chairman and asked what should be done with the guy. The chairman said it would be convenient if he stayed in jail until after the polls closed on Tuesday. No problem, the chief said.

If the police were doing that kind of political favor to keep a drunk politician off the street, just imagine what they were capable of doing when faced with a serious problem. As a reporter for the Republic named James E. Cook once said, "If they wanted to lose evidence, they could. If they wanted to protect their friends, they could."

But it was more than just protecting a friend. Many insiders feared the Judd case would expose one of the city's long-standing traditions - the "summer bachelor."

It had been going on for years. As soon as Arizona temperatures hit the triple digits, every businessman in town sent his wife and children away to someplace cooler. That meant the men left behind were free to do whatever they wanted during the summer months.

Legend says that as one train left the station with the wife and kids, another brought in the "summer wives." Those not imported were local girls - like Ruthie, Anne, and Sammy.

Most families spent the summer in the mountain town of Prescott, about 100 miles north of Phoenix and conveniently linked by rail line. The businessmen could take the train on Friday nights to spend the weekend with their families, then return early Monday morning in time for another work week and the ladies waiting for them in the desert heat.

The freedom afforded to the summer bachelors allowed affairs to happen, but they were never supposed to be long-term. There were only two rules - that the summer girlfriends disappeared in the winter, and nobody was supposed to get caught.

But now it looked like Ruthie's boyfriend was about to get caught - and all thanks to the murders. There was a genuine fear in the community that the publicity from the whole mess might destroy the careers, reputations, and entire families of some of the most important men in town.

Of course, when they got wind of this scandalous behavior, the Hearst newspapers ate it up. This was just the kind of juicy information their readers loved, and the first stories ran within a few days of the discovery of the bodies.

The International News Service announced:

Astonishing new secrets of the intimate diary of Agnes Anne LeRoi, "trunk murder" victim, leaked out from two sources today and rocked Phoenix official and social circles with threatened exposure of "playboys" who helped Miss LeRoi and her chum, Hedvig Samuelson "enjoy life."

The diary was said to have been divided into two parts, one containing the intimate details of the "party lives" of the slain girls. This section of the diary is said to be in the hands of an attorney who is guarding the contents in the interest of wealthy men clients whose names may be drawn into the baffling "all-woman triangle." The weird contents of the diary were discussed everywhere on the streets

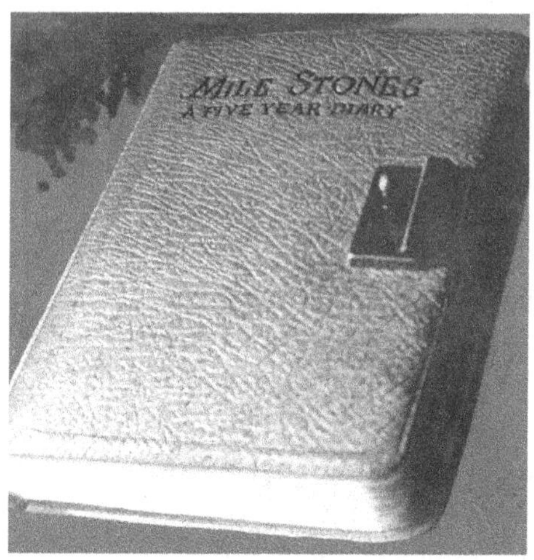

The infamous diary that detailed the parties hosted by Anne and Sammy at the bungalow. The names it contained were kept secret and the diary was never used at Ruthie's trial.

today and names were mentioned that adorn the social register of the capital city.

Deputy County Attorney Harry Johnson confirmed the existence of the diary. He was asked if he had the diary or had seen it. "I have not been able to obtain the diary," Johnson said. Questioned as to why the diary could not be produced through an official demand, Johnson replied, "I have been instructed by County Attorney Lloyd Andrews by telephone not to give out anything to the press.

A prominent resident of Phoenix said he had seen the diary shortly after it was found in Miss LeRoi's rooms. A representative of a local organization, this resident said, had taken the diary to an office and it was locked up in a safe. Revelations of the contents of the diary, it was admitted, would wreck several prominent homes and efforts were being made to keep names in the diary from being drawn into court records.

Again, not surprisingly, those efforts worked. The names stayed hidden. There is no record of the authorities ever trying to get that diary away from the private attorney or any record of him even being questioned about it. The diary was never discussed at trial. Officials just pretended that it didn't exist, even though it was mentioned repeatedly in newspapers in other cities.

It was not, however, even mentioned within the pages of the *Arizona Republic* or the *Phoenix Gazette.* The local papers selectively edited the stories that hometown folks were allowed to read. They didn't print anything about the diaries, and they didn't name names. Maybe they just figured that in a town where "everybody knew everybody," the locals already knew that Ruthie's secret boyfriend was none other than the big-shot businessman who was known to his pals as "Happy Jack."

But Jack Halloran wasn't going to stay happy for long.

AS USUAL, JACK HAD BEEN BUSY DURING THE WEEK WHEN the girls died.

Jack Halloran

He was a lumberyard to run. He had meetings at the Phoenix Country Club, where he was on the board of directors alongside the city's top attorneys, politicians, and businessmen. The Community Chest campaign was preparing for a charity drive, and Jack was head of its industrial division.

His family was back from their summer cabin in Prescott's Hassayampa Mountain Club, and the children were busy at school. A pal named Ed Ryan was in town from El Paso for a few days, and that always meant a party.

And, of course, any spare time he had was always filled with Ruthie Judd.

Jack Halloran - successful businessman, community leader, family man, on the board of the Chamber of Commerce, member of the Knights of Columbus, president of the Southwest Golf Association, and Elks Club member - was also a serial philanderer. And while he'd always been merely a "summer bachelor" like most of his friends, he'd made the mistake of keeping his fling going after the summer temperatures had gone away.

The bungalow where Jack Halloran lived in 1931.

It was a mistake that had the potential to be very costly.

Jack was a charming man; there's no doubt about it. He had an easy, carefree way about him that served him well in business and his personal life. He first came to Phoenix in 1915 when he was the Arizona sales manager for a California wholesale lumber company. He loved the city and, four years later, purchased a controlling interest in the Bennett Lumber Company, which traced its roots in Phoenix back to 1892. He renamed it the Halloran-Bennett Lumber Company and began an ambitious expansion plan that earned him great respect from the other businessmen in town.

LUMBER
THE YARD OF SERVICE
Halloran-Bennett Lumber Co.
PHOENIX, ARIZONA
Phones 24505 32800
2nd Ave. and Madison

By October 1931, his lumber yard occupied two city blocks in the heart of Phoenix, and he and his family lived just a dozen blocks away in a Craftsman-style bungalow built in 1920. It was, of course, in the best part of town.

Jack's activities during the week of the murders can be pieced together from police reports and detective work done by Ruthie's brother and other supporters.

A large part of his week was spent organizing a big hunting party for the weekend. He planned to go to northern Arizona with some doctors from the Grunow Clinic and a few friends. Ruthie dreamed about going along, too, but knew their affair would be exposed. She did know a nurse at the clinic from northern Arizona, though, who supposedly knew the best hunting spots.

Jack was happy to hear this and asked Ruthie to set up a dinner with the nurse on Wednesday night. But he got drunk with friends instead and didn't show up at Ruthie's apartment until after 9:00 P.M. She was angry that he'd blown off their dinner date and kicked him out. But first, Jack sweet-talked her into rescheduling the date for the next night.

As he was leaving, Jack made a flirtatious remark to Maude Marshall, a pretty schoolteacher who lived in the apartment next door to Ruthie's. She was coming home just as Jack was leaving Ruthie's place. She was offended and ignored him, but when she got inside, she scribbled down his car's license number in case she ever needed information about a pest that was bothering her.

Things were better on Thursday. Jack picked up Ruthie at her apartment, and then they picked up Lucille Moore at her home. Lucille was a young woman who had moved to the "big city" from a small farm community in the White Mountains and didn't have many friends in town. She'd occasionally had lunch with Ruthie at the clinic and knew Anne, but only by sight.

The plan for the evening was simple. They were supposed to return to Ruthie's apartment with a bottle of tequila, and Ruthie was going to make huevos rancheros, a Mexican dish she'd learned to prepare while south of the border with her husband.

But on the way back, Jack announced that he needed to stop at Anne and Sammy's place. Ruthie begged him not to stop. She had

Ruthie's acquaintance, Lucille Moore, who was with Ruthie and Jack when they stopped by the girls' bungalow before the murders.

turned down an offer to join Anne and Sammy for supper with the new doctor from the clinic, claiming she had work to do. How would it look if they found out she lied to them?

But Jack insisted they stop. Ed Ryan and another friend were visiting the girls at the bungalow, and he needed to pick them up. Ruthie and Lucille could wait in the car. He wouldn't be long. Ruthie made him promise he'd hurry and promise he wouldn't tell her friends she was in the car.

Jack parked in the driveway next to the bungalow, leaving Ruthie and Lucille in the car. They were chatting while he was in the house, and it would turn out that some of what was said during those few minutes would become crucial to the prosecution's case against Ruthie.

Lucille later told the police that Ruthie asked, "What do you think of Jack?"

"I think he's nice."

"He's better than that," Ruthie replied. "He's perfectly grand. Anne and Sammy think so, too. You know, I used to live here with Anne and Sammy, but we had a little difference, and I moved away - in fact, that's what I moved, over our difference about Jack."

Then, to Ruthie's dismay, both Anne and Sammy came out of the house. She rushed from the car and embraced them both, not bothering to introduce them to Lucille. The girls insisted that everyone stay at their home for supper. The new doctor from the clinic, H.J. Brinkerhoff, was already inside, and they'd make a party of it. But Ruth declined. Supper was already planned at her apartment, and they had to leave.

Jack and his friends piled into the car, and they drove off. Ruthie scolded Jack for breaking his promise, but he laughed it off.

Lucille later remembered that she was uncomfortable when they got to Ruthie's apartment, and her husband wasn't there. It seemed improper for Ruthie to be entertaining men when she lived alone. Lucille asked for someone to drive her home, but Ruthie insisted it was all innocent fun and they were just friends. She convinced Lucille to stay.

Lucille never got over her uneasy feelings that night. She had assumed that Ruthie, being married, was faithful to her husband. She'd never met Jack before but knew who he was and that he had a family. She was disturbed by the "considerable affection" between him and Ruthie.

Around midnight, Jack and Ruthie drove Lucille home - but her life would never be the same again.

EARLY ON SATURDAY MORNING, SCHOOLTEACHER MAUDE Marshall was awakened when someone dropped Ruthie off at her Brill Street apartment. Maude had gotten home only an hour or so before, just after midnight, and Ruthie's apartment had been dark. There was no sign that anyone was home.

It was around 1:30 A.M. when Maude heard a heavy car pulling into the driveway, pausing only briefly. Someone got out and entered Ruth's apartment as the car pulled away. Maude assumed the awful man who had tried to flirt with her two nights earlier had dropped Ruthie off at home.

By the time Maude became mixed up in the case, Anne and Sammy were already dead. The police established they had been killed about 10:30 P.M. Medical experts would eventually conclude that Anne's body was placed in the trunk within six hours of her death before rigor mortis set in. They also discovered that the dismemberment of Sammy's body occurred within a few hours of death. Her blood hadn't yet started to coagulate. Any longer, they

A photograph of Ruthie's apartment complex at 1130 Brill Street. She occupied the apartment shown by the arrow, located on the left side of the complex. Maude Marshall lived next door.

stated, and her blood would have stayed in her body. But the autopsy showed she'd been completely drained of all blood and bodily fluids.

The police came to Maude's door after the trunks were discovered. She told them what she knew and added that she *assumed* the car she heard on Friday night was the same one she'd seen on Wednesday night. She didn't see it on Friday; she'd only heard it, so she couldn't say for sure. But she did hand over the paper on which she had written the car's license number. The police had no trouble tracing it - the vehicle belonged to Jack Halloran.

Even though Maude couldn't say for sure it had been the same car, her story did alert them to a significant element of the case - that Ruth Judd had no car, so someone was driving her around in the hours after the murders.

But Maude was not the only one who told the police about Jack Halloran's possible whereabouts that night. Dr. R.B. Raney, who lived across the street from the girls' bungalow, was out late on Friday night, celebrating his birthday. When he came home around 11:00 P.M., he saw two cars parked at the bungalow. One was a large gray car, but he couldn't recall the color or make of the other. Dr. Raney said he was called almost immediately after getting home for an emergency operation at St. Joseph's Hospital and returned home again around 1:00 A.M. He noted the large car was just then turning around in front of the bungalow and driving away without its headlights on.

The police now had cars at both the bungalow and Ruth's apartment in the early morning hours of Saturday, but this never became part of any official record.

However, what was revealed by neighbors was that Jack's gray Packard was parked at the bungalow "for hours" on Saturday afternoon. They gave the information to the police and the Phoenix press, but no one ever publicly identified the owner of the "mysterious car." Out-of-state papers, though, noted that the car belonged to Jack Halloran.

The witness statements given by Maude Marshall and Dr. Raney were never used at Ruthie's trial. No one seemed interested in tracking Jack Halloran's activities that night.

But what about Ruthie's activities?

According to her own statement, Ruthie fled from the bungalow earlier that night and ran to her apartment on Brill Street. However, a trolley driver later testified that he took her most of the way, dropping her off a few blocks from her apartment because the line was closing for the night, and she wouldn't be able to make her usual connection.

Ruthie said that Jack showed up soon after she got home, drunk and boisterous and then unbelieving of the story she told him about the girls being shot. She said he drove her back to the bungalow and then took over. He dropped her back off at her apartment about 1:30 A.M. - something Maude Marshall could have verified if her witness statement hadn't vanished.

Ruthie also believed Dr. Raney knew whose car he saw parked outside the bungalow that night. She said they were leaving just as the doctor came home from the hospital. Jack had turned off his headlights, so he didn't draw attention. He feared Dr. Raney would recognize his car because Raney had recently treated Jack's son.

By concealing the statements from Maude and Dr. Raney, the police showed from the start that they had only a narrow interest in what happened that Friday night. Ruthie had not been alone, and doubt would have been raised about who dismembered Sammy's body.

But that didn't happen because, in the 1930s, the police were under no legal obligation to reveal what they had uncovered in an investigation. They told the press what they wanted to tell them and told defense attorneys nothing.

Many times in this case, the police told one thing to the press, even though the witness statements said something else altogether. In many instances, the cops simply "forgot" to document the information they found.

This was also an era when evidence discovery was not yet mandatory in Arizona courts. Today, it's required that both prosecutors and defense counsel get copies of all police reports and witness statements in a case. If information is hidden now, it's grounds for a reversal or new trial. But in the early 1930s, defense attorneys were kept in the dark. They had no legal right to see police reports or evidence and usually had to hire their own detectives to investigate a case. Their best hope was to trick a police officer on the witness stand into admitting there was an official report. If they managed this, the officer would be forced to produce it so it could be submitted into evidence. There was no way to trip up a witness and get them to admit they'd changed or embellished a story between their original police interview and their testimony in court.

Police officers at the time - just like today - saw their role as proving guilt, not helping the accused. They were taught how to avoid getting tricked by a slick defense lawyer. During Ruthie's case, none of the officers who testified said they'd refreshed their memories from a police report - they always said they consulted their notes. Frank Ryan, the detective who had opened the trunks in Los Angeles, told the court that he had burned his notes so he couldn't produce them. That was the way it was played for decades - cops were careful never to admit there was a police report. When rules on discovery finally became standard in the 1960s, most officers thought it was the end of law enforcement as they knew it.

BASED ON WHAT PHOENIX OFFICIALS SUSPECTED about Jack Halloran and his part in the murders, it seems baffling that they allowed him to reveal Ruthie's "motive" for the murders, but that's precisely what happened.

Hearst's notoriously unreliable *New York American* said it was all because of a kiss.

According to the paper, the sensational theory was advanced by authorities in Phoenix after Halloran presented them with the motive of jealousy. He admitted that while he was at a drinking party on the Thursday night before the murders, he had kissed Sammy. Ruthie was also at the party and saw the kiss. She wasn't the only one. Jack said Lucille Moore and the new clinic doctor, H.J. Brinkerhoff, saw it too. The police told the *American* they intended to question both witnesses.

And they did - but the cops then neglected to tell anyone that Jack's story didn't check out.

Lucille told the police that she never attended any party at the bungalow. She'd never even been inside, only in the driveway. And the only kiss she'd seen that night had been Ruthie kissing Jack at her apartment - and Jack hadn't done anything to stop her.

Jack's story further fell apart when Dr. Brinkerhoff was questioned. Being new in town, he was happy to have dinner with Anne and Sammy. He said that at about 6:00 P.M., three men who were obviously old friends of the girls had arrived. One was named Jack, another was Mr. Ryan from El Paso, and Brinkerhoff never got the third man's name. Ryan set up a radio, and then Jack left, returning later to pick up the other men. After they left, the young doctor said he had a pleasant dinner with the two women. Both girls casually mentioned Ruthie, and he thought Anne and Sammy seemed "very friendly toward her." He left the bungalow between 10:30 and 11:00 P.M., and he never saw Jack kiss anyone.

When the "deadly kiss" angle - the newspapers called it that - didn't work out, investigators switched to general jealousy as the motive. Ruthie was insanely jealous, believing that Jack loved the other girls more than he loved her. She killed them to eliminate any competition for Jack's affection.

According to their theory, Ruthie had been at home on Friday night, fuming over her friends' imaginary affairs with Jack. She snapped, grabbed a gun and her husband's surgical tools, and went to Sammy and Anne's bungalow. She killed them both, and not knowing what to do with the bodies, she cut them up, stuffed them into her traveling bags, and took the corpses to Los Angeles for reasons unknown.

Prosecutors told the press they would show all this when Lucille Moore - their "star witness" - took the stand at trial.

Lucille did testify about the dinner party on Thursday night but was not asked a single question about any kiss. Nor was she asked about the affection she had witnessed between Ruthie and Jack. The most damaging thing she recalled was Ruthie's offhanded comment about the three women having a "difference" over Jack, which led to Ruthie's change of address. Ruthie's defense attorneys never asked her any questions at all.

Both Lucille and Dr. Brinkerhoff played very innocent parts in the events. Under normal circumstances, there was nothing wrong with trying to make new friends and accepting dinner invitations. That was all either of them had done, and yet, both would suffer because their names were part of the case.

Lucille would never work as a nurse in the city again, which she'd intended to. Instead, she returned to rural Arizona for the rest of her life.

Dr. Brinkerhoff's out-of-state fiancé quickly called off their pending wedding. Years later, after his connection with the story had faded, he finally married a local woman and lived the rest of his life in Phoenix.

But what about Jack Halloran?

Naturally, he denied having anything to do with the murder. His only sin had been in associating with the girls. "I am guilty of no greater fault than being indiscreet," he said. He later issued a lengthy statement to the Phoenix papers blasting the "sensational" coverage of the Los Angeles papers that called him a "millionaire playboy."

They might have had it out for him in L.A., but Phoenix's newspapers were much kinder. Most of the information that the police learned about him was never revealed, and it was made clear by editors that they didn't want anything negative reported on Jack Halloran. Even the county attorney, Lloyd Andrews, balked when asked by a Los Angeles reporter for a comment about Jack's involvement in the murders: "That's nonsense. Jack Halloran is a friend of mine. He's a fine fellow."

Everyone liked Jack. He was an esteemed member of the community - he wasn't a single woman like Ruthie, living on her own, barely making enough money to make ends meet, whose best friends were a couple of party girls known for entertaining a variety of men.

Jack was a great guy. Just ask anyone.

Former U.S. Senator Paul Fannin later stated, "I knew him well and never believed he was involved. He was very highly respected. He and his family were very embarrassed by it. He made the mistake of being associated with them - going to parties and things of that nature, but he in no way was involved in any sense. He was a good friend of mine, and I always respected him."

Another esteemed businessman, Tom Chauncey, agreed. "Jack was a handsome man about town," he later said. "He was very generous and very kind. He was terribly well-liked. He had a fantastic business then. He was one of the most prosperous men in the valley. He was very prominent in social circles, as prominent as any man in Phoenix. This destroyed him. It was a terrible thing. He was ostracized. His business went to hell. I always thought he was unfairly accused. I don't think he had a damn thing to do with it."

The list of Jack Halloran's admirers included Harold Spotts, the business manager for O'Malley Lumber Company, which dominated Arizona's building and supply business for decades. "Sure, he knew a lot of politicians," Spotts later said in an interview. "He had business dealings with attorneys and lots of businessmen in town." But he noted that the same could be said for anyone of importance in Phoenix in those days.

Spotts always admired Jack because he was "a great salesman," but admitted he had a reputation as a playboy. "He had a lot of friends of the same type," Spotts said, "they had more money than good sense."

While everyone seemed to love Jack Halloran and were determined to keep him out of trouble, what was happening behind the scenes was another story.

According to Harold Spotts, the brothers who owned the O'Malley Lumber Company were concerned about Jack and invited him to their office for a private chat. The O'Malleys were one of Arizona's more respected and powerful families. They had a very profitable lumber business with dozens of subsidiaries - including the Halloran-Bennett Lumber Company.

Unknown to the public - or anyone aside from the principals involved - Jack's company was really owned by the O'Malleys. It was just one of the many lumberyards they owned around the state but listed under someone else's name. They believed it was better for business if people didn't think they owned every lumberyard in the state. It was sketchy - although not illegal. It simply made it appear that various independent companies were available for lumber needs.

The O'Malleys had no interest in jeopardizing their name or having their business associated with the biggest mess that Phoenix had ever seen. They were not just concerned that Jack was being connected to Ruthie - they were also concerned about the rumors hinting that he had been involved in the girls' deaths.

Spotts stated that after the meeting, the O'Malleys were convinced that Jack wasn't a killer. It was too bad that he'd been involved with the three women but was simply in the wrong place at the wrong time. "Obviously, he wouldn't have anything to do with a murder," Spotts added.

Although the O'Malleys allegedly believed in Jack, they decided to cut ties with him soon after the meeting. They sold the lumber company that everyone thought Jack owned. He started again and bought another lumberyard, but it was never very successful.

Ironically, when the O'Malleys sold the lumberyard out from under Jack Halloran, they also took over all the property the business had accumulated in repayment for bad debts.

One of those properties was a duplex located at 2929 North Second Street - the bungalow where Anne and Sammy were killed.

5. SURRENDER

RUTHIE FINALLY GAVE HERSELF UP ON OCTOBER 23, 1931.

Across Los Angeles, officials breathed a sigh of relief and were finally able to call off the fruitless searches for the missing murder suspect. But they soon learned, much to their dismay, that she had been hiding under their noses at places she'd known well while living in L.A.

When she'd left Burton's car on October 19, she vanished by walking nearly 20 miles to the La Vina Sanatorium, the tuberculosis hospital where she'd once been a patient. She hid in the building for three days, sneaking into the kitchen at night for food.

La Vina Sanatorium in Altadena, where Ruthie hid out for three days after vanishing from her brother's car in traffic.

From there, she returned to Los Angeles and the Broadway department store where she'd once worked. She stayed out of sight and was locked in the store overnight. She slept there, covered by a rug. By now, the wound on her hand had become badly infected and throbbed unmercifully.

Ruthie stayed in the store most of the day until she

overheard a woman reading from a newspaper and mentioned Ruthie's name. There was an advertisement, the woman said, placed by Dr. Judd, begging her to give herself up.

The Alvarez and Moore Funeral Home, where Ruthie surrendered to the police.

Ruthie called Dr. Judd's attorney, Richard Cantillon, who told her to phone another attorney, Patrick Cooney, later that day. When she did, Cantillon and Dr. Judd were also there. Judd pleaded with her and finally convinced Ruthie to surrender.

She met her husband in the lobby of the Biltmore Theater, and they walked to Alvarez and Moore, an undertaker's establishment at Court and Olive Streets. Dr. Judd treated her infected hand there as they waited for the police to arrive.

When they did, Ruthie's condition shocked the officers and reporters who accompanied them.

She looked small, frail, and confused in the newspaper photographs on front pages across the country. Her hair needed to be washed, her dress was dirty, and her face was gaunt with hunger. She seemed to be near to collapsing. Dr. Judd kept a protective arm around her shoulder, which appeared to be the only thing holding her upright.

Reporters took one look at Ruthie, and when they heard the first words out of her mouth, they knew the case had taken a significant turn.

As she was taken into custody, she sobbed, "I had to shoot her, I had to shoot her!" This didn't make sense to the cops or the reporters at the time, but it soon would.

An attorney hired by Dr. Judd read a statement from Ruthie aloud:

I had gone to the girls' home to remonstrate with Miss Samuelson for some nasty things she said about Mrs. LeRoi. Miss Samuelson got hold of a gun and shot me in the left hand. I struggled with her and the gun fell. Mrs. LeRoi grabbed an ironing board and started to strike me over the head with it. In the struggle, I got hold of the gun and Sammy got shot. Mrs. LeRoi was still coming at me with the ironing board, and I had to shoot her. Then I ran from the place.

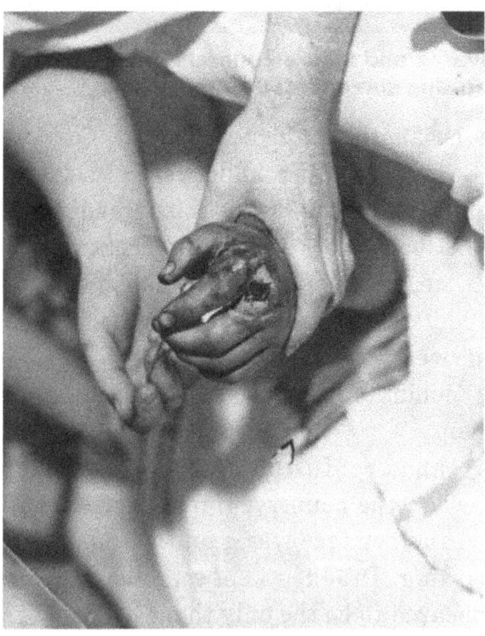

Ruthie's hand was badly infected by the time she was arrested. The bullet was still embedded in her when she reached the county hospital under guard.

Ruthie managed to show off and cling painfully to the proof of her "dramatic plea of self-defense" at the same time. Her left hand was purple, swollen, and horribly infected. A bullet was still embedded in it, which wasn't much of an endorsement of Dr. Judd's physician skills.

Officials quickly realized that they had a problem on their hands. The case no longer seemed so cut and dried. They had a woman who admitted to being a killer but who had a justification that would allow her to walk free. Killing in self-defense was not a crime.

But what about the dismembered bodies, the bloody trunks, the bizarre train journey, and Ruthie's disappearance? People who kill in self-defense don't usually cut up their victims and hide them in trunks. They also don't travel hundreds of miles to get rid of the bodies or do anything else that the police believed Ruthie had done. Her claim of self-defense made the whole case even more baffling - or if you were the cops, it just made it "absurd."

The bullet that was removed from Ruthie's hand while in LAPD custody.

But to prove her story was preposterous, the authorities had to prove she couldn't have been wounded on Friday night during an argument and that she'd shot herself later to cover up what she'd done. And that was what they proceeded to do - or what they told the public they were doing anyway.

The following day, the *Phoenix Gazette* reported on the efforts of the police:

The self-defense plea is characterized as "inconceivable" by officers and investigators here and in Los Angeles. Deductions from a cursory survey of circumstantial evidence and facts led to the belief that the bullet wound in Mrs. Judd's hand was self-inflicted and probably occurred while she was unloading the death gun in her apartment at 1130 East Brill Street after the double tragedy.

Detectives revealed to reporters that they found a .25-caliber cartridge shell in her apartment, the same kind of bullet that had killed the girls.

The newspaper went on to add that some people who saw Ruthie on Saturday claimed that her hand was not bandaged, as it should have been if she'd been wounded Friday night. However, some witnesses claimed that it had been bandaged. The article made it clear: "This factor, it is believed, will be an important cog in the prosecution of Mrs. Judd."

It would be crucial to the case. Obviously, Ruthie couldn't have been wounded in a fight on Friday with no sign of a wound the following day - a day when she encountered at least a dozen people at the Grunow Clinic. Just as obviously, a woman with such a severe wound to her hand could not have packed the trunks with the heavy bodies of the victims.

Even more importantly, how could a wounded woman have performed the dismemberment of Sammy's body? Even prosecutors grudgingly admitted they didn't have an answer to that. Deputy County Attorney G.A. Rodgers told the *Arizona Republic*, "If her story of being wounded in the hand on the night of the slayings should be true, it would absolutely preclude her having disposed of the bodies without the aid of an accomplice."

But then Rodgers quickly added, "It is, however, inconceivable. Evidence tends to show that if she has a wound in her hand, it was self-inflicted. We have witnesses who saw her sometimes with one hand bandaged, sometimes the other, and some witnesses who saw her the morning after the slayings with neither hand bandaged."

If any of this were true, I would say that the prosecutor had a serious problem with his witnesses. It wasn't. Rodgers was lying.

Later, detective work by outside agencies would reveal that police officials knew that Ruth had turned up at the Grunow Clinic on Saturday with a wounded hand. They even had a witness who swore she had the bandage on her hand Friday night, immediately after the murders. It was all in the police records - records they chose to hide.

Fay Ayres had seen Ruthie's bandaged hand - and so did Grace Mitchell. It was also seen by Stella Kerkes and her father, Mike, Emil Clemens, and B.W. Jurgemeyer.

Faye Ayres was a secretary at the Grunow Clinic. "I saw her go out the front door with a bandage on her left hand. I know it was her left hand," she told detectives.

Grace Mitchell had a doctor's appointment at the clinic on Saturday morning. She told the police, "When I walked in the door, I noticed Mrs. Judd looked fearfully bad. I noticed her eyes looked so bad. She looked in pain to me. She looked distressed, but she also looked like she was suffering."

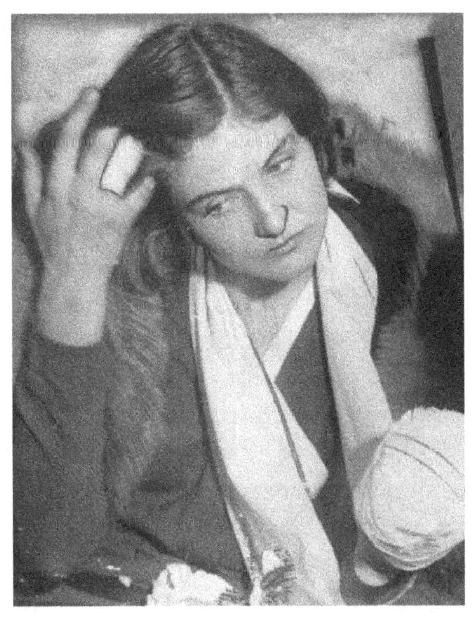

Ruthie with a bandaged hand after her surrender.

Ruthie got up from her desk in the reception area and took Grace into an exam room to be weighed. Grace hadn't noticed her bandaged hand until they were in the room. She asked what had happened, and Ruthie replied, "I burned it."

Grace recounted, "It was the left hand. I said, when the murder came out, that she was in physical misery. I told my husband I wagered she had been shot."

Mike Kerkes and his daughter, Stella, had driven to Phoenix from their home in rural Wickenberg that morning so Stella could see a doctor. They were already in the waiting room when Ruthie arrived. Mike told an investigator for the county attorney's office, "She come in the door with her left hand bandaged and she sat down. I looked up and talked to her. I knew her for some time, and I asked what is the matter and she said, 'Burned it up on the stove last night.'"

Stella remembered that Ruthie was pale, and "she seemed like she was restless or something." She recalled a large bandage on Ruth's hand. She told the investigator, "I noticed it, but I didn't say anything and Daddy noticed it and he asked what is the matter with it, and she said, "Oh, just burned it.'"

Emil Clemens, a handyman at the clinic, also distinctly remembered seeing Ruthie that Saturday morning. He said he knew she had a bandage on her hand but couldn't recall which hand it was.

Despite all the bragging they'd done to the press, investigators could only find one person who remembered that both of her hands were fine on Saturday morning - Dr. Brinkerhoff, who had shared a Thursday night meal with the girls. Considering how much trouble he must've felt that Ruthie had caused him, I doubt he put much effort into remembering anything that would help her.

The investigators also found one person who thought he'd seen her right hand bandaged - Dr. Henry L. Franklin. His statement to officials wasn't exactly solid, however. He told them, "As well as I can remember, it was her right hand."

Considering how things seemed to confirm Ruthie's version of events, it's not surprising that officials decided to bury the statement they received from B.W. Jurgemeyer.

Jurgemeyer was driving the Indian School trolley line the week the girls were killed. His Tuesday to Saturday shift began each day at 4:00 P.M. and ended when the line closed at midnight. During two separate interviews with county investigators, he swore that he remembered Ruthie getting on his trolley that weekend - but couldn't remember if it was Friday or Saturday night. He knew it was one of those evenings, though, because he recognized her as a frequent passenger.

On whichever night it had been, he'd picked Ruthie up around 9:30 P.M. at the same spot where he always did - on Third Street, about eight blocks from her apartment. She had a trolley transfer voucher connecting her to his route.

Then, about two hours later, she boarded his trolley again, going in the opposite direction. He noted the time at 11:30 because he clearly remembered her asking for her usual transfer. He was about to give her one but realized the other line was no longer running because it was so late.

Prosecutors had Jurgemeyer testify about this round trip at Ruthie's murder trial, making sure the jury knew he was the trolley

Trolley on the Indian School Line in the 1930s

conductor who had unknowingly taken her back and forth to the scene of her terrible crime.

After that, he was dismissed from the stand. That was all they wanted him to say - that Ruthie had traveled by trolley to commit murder.

They never asked Jurgemeyer if he noticed anything unusual about Ruthie on her return trip, which had occurred just minutes after she'd allegedly killed her two best friends. They didn't ask because they didn't want him to repeat what he already told the authorities two times: "Her left hand was completely wrapped. I noticed it before she got onto the car." He also remembered that she had to use her right hand to put her token in the farebox.

Of course, Ruthie's attorneys never asked Jurgemeyer a single question because they had no idea that he'd given the police information that could back up Ruthie's claim of self-defense.

The prosecution team must have breathed a sigh of relief when the defense attorneys didn't ask their own questions and again when Jurgemeyer left the stand. If, somehow, his account of seeing Ruthie with an injured left hand after the murders had been heard in court, it could have badly damaged their case.

Ironically, though, Jurgemeyer couldn't have seen Ruthie on Friday night, going to and from the murders. The encounter he described could only have happened on Saturday. As Ruthie later admitted, she did take the trolley to the bungalow on Friday night, but in her terror, she ran home to her apartment. She didn't take the trolley until the following night, she said.

When the deliverymen removed the trunk from the bungalow, she noticed blood dripping onto the porch. She could do nothing about it without drawing attention, so after the trunks were dropped off at her apartment, she took the trolley back to the bungalow to wash the blood from the porch. On her return trip, she asked the driver - B.W. Jurgemeyer - for a transfer, but he told her it was too late to catch the other trolley.

The prosecutors never realized their mistake. They believed they had an eyewitness who had seen Ruthie with an injured left hand immediately after the murders, and they didn't want anyone to know that.

Just how far the prosecution went to keep this from the defense wouldn't be known for years. Unbelievably, by the time Ruthie went on trial, the authorities knew she was being truthful about when the hand wound occurred and also knew that a doctor at the clinic where she worked had even offered to dress the wound on Saturday morning. Publicly, though, they still insisted her hand was never injured during the murders at all.

But could Ruthie have shot herself in her apartment after the murders? Absolutely. She took the gun home with her, so the opportunity was there.

But if she did, it would have been at some point in the early morning hours, before she went to work at the clinic at 9:00 A.M. That makes it likely that someone - especially nosy neighbor Maude Mitchell - would have heard the shot. If the sound of a car pulling into the driveway could awaken her, surely the sound of a handgun being fired would have done the same. But she didn't hear anything. Nor did anyone else who lived in nearby apartments. If the police had found someone who heard a shot, they certainly would have used that information to bolster their case - and they'd have had no reason to hide the statements from witnesses who saw the wound to Ruthie's left hand on Saturday morning.

But what if Ruthie shot herself at the bungalow, perhaps at the same time those who lived nearby heard gunshots? Was this possible? Definitely - and would've just as effectively damaged her claim of self-defense.

However, even if it's possible that the prosecution was right and Ruthie shot herself, the effort they put into hiding evidence that disagreed with their theories was ridiculous - and should have been criminal. I know - the laws were different back then, but everything we have ever been taught about right and wrong and someone deserving a fair trial seems to have gone out the window in this case.

Hoping to strengthen their public statements that Ruthie was lying about her wounded hand, prosecutors used the testimony of Howard Grimm and his son, Kenneth, who had taken the trunks to the train station on Sunday afternoon. The *Republic* announced their testimony was "particularly strong" and destroyed Ruthie's credibility.

Howard and Kenneth insisted that Ruthie's right hand was bandaged when they took her to the train station. Howard even offered this belief as testimony on the stand at Ruthie's trial.

No one seems to have considered that either the Grimms were mistaken, or the prosecutors were lying to the jury - because they couldn't have it both ways. They couldn't tell the jury the cartridge found in her apartment proved she'd shot herself in the left hand before leaving for Los Angeles, and also claim that the Grimms were correct, and she'd left her apartment for the last time with her right hand wounded.

Ruthie had the .25-caliber handgun in her bag when she boarded the train. The only way the Grimms could have been correct was if she had been faking a wound when she left Phoenix and shot herself on the train. But the prosecution never argued that. They already had plenty of eyewitnesses who had convinced them that couldn't be true.

It didn't help the prosecution's case that Sheriff John McFadden wasn't playing along with them. While the rest of law enforcement pretended that Ruthie couldn't have suffered the gunshot on Friday night, Sheriff McFadden told the Associated Press he was sure she had. He surmised from his reading of the evidence that the wound occurred when a bullet passed through Sammy and stuck Ruthie's left hand. He initially told the press that he wasn't convinced Sammy had shot her; however, months later, he changed his mind, but no one bothered to report that in the papers.

By the time the case went to trial, Ruthie's lawyers had managed to find some people at the clinic who testified to her left-hand wound, but their attempts to drive that home with the jury were half-hearted, at best. The prosecution countered their efforts with contradicting witnesses, turning the argument into a confusing mess of "he said, she said," and causing the jury to lose interest.

In addition, by then, it didn't matter anyway. Ruthie's attorneys had stopped arguing that she'd killed in self-defense. By the trial, they were claiming she was insane.

How different would things have been if the defense team had known about the trolley driver or had access to the list of people who swore she'd been wounded in the left hand?

There's no way we'll ever know.

BY THE TIME REPUTABLE DOCTORS IN LOS ANGELES - and not just Dr. Judd - were able to treat Ruthie's wounded left hand, gangrene had set in. She had been taken from the jail to the George Street Receiving Hospital, where she was put under sedation so the bullet could be removed.

Doctors insisted on checking her for other injuries, and a nurse brought a paper for her to sign to authorize the exam, but Ruthie refused to sign it. She was upset, confused, exhausted, and had barely eaten for a week. The nurse left and then returned a few minutes later. Several men followed her, and she pointed to one of them and told Ruthie he was her lawyer. She'd find out later that his name was Judge Russill, and he instructed her to sign the paper.

Ruthie had never been in trouble before and had never needed an attorney. Her husband had always handled their business matters, so Ruthie shrugged and signed the paper.

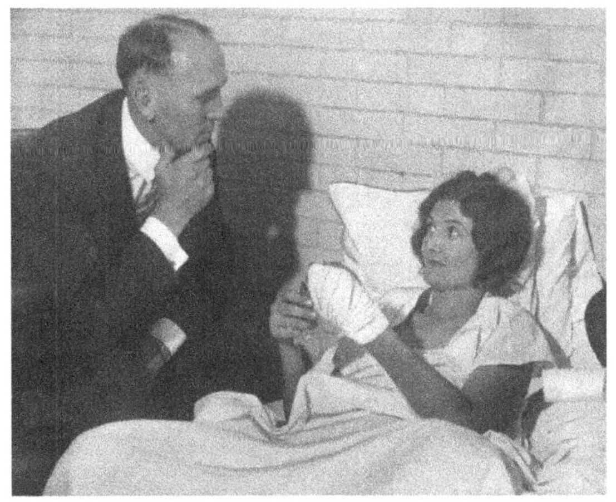

Ruthie being examined at the county hospital on George Street after her arrest.

The nurse returned with two doctors, and Ruthie was checked for other injuries. There "were innumerable bruises all over her body," the *New York Times* reported. In fact, doctors counted 147 of them on her body. Ruthie said that she had gotten the bruises and abrasions during the fight as she rolled around the kitchen floor, tussling with Sammy and trying to dodge the "braining" that Anne was trying to deliver with the ironing board.

But how did the *New York Times* find out about the exam? Judge Russill told them about it, which wouldn't sit well with Dr. Judd.

At some point later that day, a staff reporter for William Randolph Hearst came to Ruthie's room with an envelope that contained several thousand dollars. He told her, "When you are asked who your attorney is," the reporter told her, "Say Schenck." Ruthie later claimed that she had no idea what happened to the envelope he'd brought her, but if I had to guess, I'd wager it found its way to Dr. Judd.

A little later, more men arrived in her room, and with them was the man she'd met last night, Judge Russill. When one of them asked who her attorney was, Ruthie replied, "Schenck."

Russill's face turned red, and he sputtered, "Little lady, this is the sorriest thing you have ever done!" He stomped off, leaving Ruthie more confused than ever. She had no idea what was happening and only did what she was told.

That same day, Dr. Grace Homman examined Ruthie at the request of her defense attorney, who I assume was "Schneck." She also took dozens of photographs with Ruthie wrapped in a bedsheet. Large bruises - some as small as pinches and others as large as heavy blows - could be seen on both arms, both legs, and her back.

In a letter Dr. Homman later wrote to Arizona officials, she stressed that she had volunteered to conduct the exam but had not been paid for it. In other words, her observations came from a trained physician, not from a paid expert witness.

She wrote:

I have a complete record of my examination with a detailed report of the many bruises. Because of them, it has always been my impression that Mrs. Judd put up a tremendous fight for her life.

But a fight with whom? Anne and Sammy? Anne was the largest of the pair, but Ruthie claimed she'd been rolling around wrestling on the floor with Sammy - the tuberculosis patient who was too weak to even hold a job, do housework, or spend much time out of bed.

Could the girls have done this kind of damage to Ruthie? Maybe. By the time she was examined, Ruthie weighed only 103 pounds and was very ill.

But she hadn't been sick on that Friday night. Even in good health, could she have picked up the dead weight of Anne and Sammy and put them into the trunks, dismembered them, and then moved the trunks alone?

Or had there been someone else involved? And was it that person with whom Ruthie had been in a "tremendous fight for her life?"

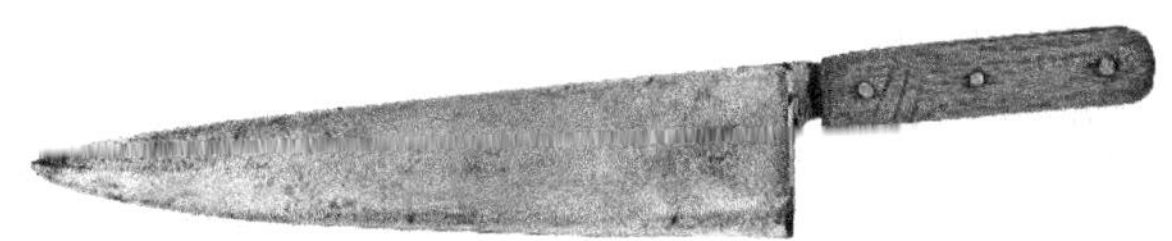

6. ONE CONFESSION AFTER ANOTHER

RUTHIE WAS IN CUSTODY FOR LESS THAN 24 HOURS before she confessed - twice. Or so it seemed. Two Los Angeles newspapers had already printed "exclusive confessions" they claimed she had written for them. The papers reportedly paid her between $5,000 and $15,000, but whatever it was, it was a fortune.

By the time she had been in custody for 36 hours, the story that she was telling was starting to fall apart.

After 48 hours behind bars, a plumber at the Broadway department store found a torn, water-soaked letter to Dr. Judd that Ruthie had written while she was hiding there. The so-called "Drainpipe Letter" would be what finally sealed her fate.

"MY STORY" - THAT'S WHAT THE *LOS ANGELES TIMES* called its exclusive and claimed it was written in Ruthie's own hand. A by-line appeared under the headline that was supposedly her signature.

"My Own Story in My Own Words" was what the *Los Angeles Examiner* called its confession. Ruthie had dictated it, they said, but didn't handwrite it.

Both versions included the story of Ruthie's life, but neither sounded as though it was anything she'd written. The wording was different than what appeared in her letters before and after the murders. The stories also don't sound like a woman frightened or

The Record

HOME EDITION 2c

WINNIE RUTH JUDD'S OWN STORY

WHEN "TIGRESS" SURRENDERED

EARLY LIFE TOLD BY TIGRESS SUSPECT

WRIT ISSUED TO HALT EXTRADITION TO ARIZ.

CRACKS IN THE RECORD

LIONS IN CLASH WITH GRAY FOG

S.C.-BEARS MEET ON SOGGY FIELD

RADIO BOARD MAY STOP BOB SHULER

shocked by the crime she was accused of. They sound very chatty - as though Ruthie was having tea with a couple of reporters and decided to pass on some gossip. For a woman who would eventually label the press "a bunch of morbids," these stories are a strange start to what became an antagonistic relationship.

But that's assuming Ruthie actually wrote or dictated these stories. There's a better-than-average chance that she didn't. But if she did, she admitted some astonishing things. In the *Times* story, Ruthie stated:

It has been charged that I had an accomplice either before, during, or after the actual tragedy. This is not true. I alone shot and killed both these women, who were once my friends. I did it in self-defense to save my life, and for no other reason. I alone disposed of the bodies. I had no help of any kind from anyone.

Sunday morning, I dragged Sammy to the bathroom and in the bathroom, I severed her body, placing parts in the trunks and the suitcase.

Law enforcement members -in L.A. and Phoenix - were skeptical about the authenticity of the "confessions," but no one bothered to try and determine their validity until 1933. The Arizona Attorney General found out from editors at both papers that the stories had been dictated to reporters by none other than Dr. Judd, who claimed he'd run both past his wife before they were printed. Needless to say, he didn't. However, he did cash the checks that were given in exchange for them.

The so-called "confessions" - and the money they supposedly earned for Ruthie - would haunt her case. Crime wasn't supposed to pay, but for the people back home in Phoenix, it looked like their hometown killer was cashing in. Local reporters and readers made no attempt to hide their disgust over the "battle of confessions" going on in Los Angeles. The *Gazette* reported that agents from the *Times* had been sent to the county jail hospital to offer Ruthie "the biggest price ever paid to a criminal in Los Angeles for his or her own story."

No one cared whether Ruthie had written the stories or not. In fact, as far as the prosecution at her trial was concerned, they wanted the jury to believe she had written them - that in a moment of conscience or greed, she sat down and told the world that she alone was responsible for every part of the horrible crime.

Folks in Phoenix, though, after getting past the idea that someone might have paid an astronomical sum for a killer's story, didn't believe either confession. Most still believed that Ruthie was covering up for someone. There had been too many hints, even in the local press, and too many rumors going around for them to believe otherwise.

For many women in Phoenix, Ruthie was starting to look less like a murderess and more like a romantic heroine protecting her man. That, they said, is why she wouldn't name her accomplice. Later, many of these women would be jammed into the courtroom, whispering words of encouragement to Ruthie as she stood trial.

Many law enforcement officials in Phoenix already knew what the public suspected. Their investigation, which they failed to share with her defense, showed that Ruthie couldn't have acted alone.

They knew she couldn't handle those trunks alone.

And they knew the story of her wounded left hand was true.

And they knew Jack Halloran's car had been seen at both Ruthie's apartment and the bungalow on the night of the murders.

And they knew physical evidence at the bungalow indicated an accomplice had been present.

And they knew Sammy had been precisely dismembered with a skill Ruthie didn't possess.

And they were also aware that Ruthie was lying when she got the time and place of that dismemberment wrong. The official autopsy report would show that Sammy was cut apart "within hours" of her death on Friday night - not on Sunday morning, which is what the newspaper "confessions" claimed. That meant it had happened at the bungalow long before the trunk was moved to Ruthie's apartment.

But those officials didn't talk. Publicly, they simply stated that the "confessions" were proof that Ruthie was guilty and that she alone should be punished for the murders.

IF POLICE AND PROSECUTION OFFICIALS REALLY WERE covering up the role of someone else in the murders of Anne and Sammy - who was it? It appears it was the two men she loved equally: her husband, Dr. Judd, and Jack Halloran.

Ruthie would come to consider the death of her friends "a tragedy" but would consider her affair with Jack "a sin." As a minister's daughter who had been taught that being faithful was the cornerstone of a marriage, she saw her affair as the worst of the two. She claimed the tragedy had been unavoidable because she'd been attacked, but her affair was unacceptable and wrong in the eyes of God and society.

She also knew that the affair would devastate her husband. Even though their marriage had been far from perfect, the one thing each had always believed about the other was that they were faithful. Ruthie had never been with another man - until she met Jack and then slept with him on Christmas Eve, 1930. A family man should have been at home with his wife and children on the holiday, Ruthie later said, but Jack had shown up at her door to provide "comfort" for a lonely young woman.

Dr. Judd had been in the hospital again on that Christmas Eve, strung out once more on narcotics. He hadn't even sent Ruthie a Christmas card. She hadn't been in Phoenix long and had few friends, but after meeting the handsome, charming, and loving neighbor of the family she worked for, Ruthie fell hopelessly in love with him.

As their affair continued, Ruthie became aware that she wasn't the only woman in Jack's life. She justified her acceptance of this by believing she saw more of him than anyone else. She never stopped loving her husband, even as she spent every possible moment with Jack. She truly believed that she could love two people at one time.

With these two men, Ruthie hoped to realize the one thing she'd been dreaming about her entire life - becoming a mother. Since her teens, she had been obsessed with having a baby. She once even claimed that a neighbor boy had gotten her pregnant, even though he'd only kissed her. She had been pregnant twice in Mexico with her husband but had lost both babies because of her poor health.

Dr. Judd later admitted that sometimes Ruthie wrote him letters in which she pretended one of the babies survived. She told him stories about the baby's activities throughout the day and about the cute things he did. She sometimes worried for days about what to name this phantom baby. Dr. Judd said at first that he thought she was joking, but then he realized that in her mind, Ruthie thought the baby was real.

It was later discovered that in the month before the murders, Ruthie thought she was pregnant again. This time, the father was Jack Halloran. Doctors at the Grunow Clinic admitted to the police - who buried the report - that she had been given a pregnancy test, but it was negative. Ruthie believed she had miscarried again and bled for 12 days, ending only a week before the murders.

In the dazed and terrified state that she was in during the weekend after killing her friends, Ruthie had to contend with not only the deaths of Anne and Sammy but with her need to protect the two men in her life - one from his role in the tragic events and the other from the knowledge that she was unfaithful.

It's believed that she had a plan in her head before she ever boarded that train in Phoenix. She decided she would protect Jack by taking all the blame. With his role hidden, her husband wouldn't need to learn about the affair. In return, Jack would use his influence to ensure law enforcement treated Ruthie well.

When she finally gave herself up, Ruthie had convinced herself her plan would work, but within hours, it had already started to fall apart.

Reporters were waiting wherever she went - at the funeral parlor where she surrendered, at the hospital where she received medical treatment, at the jail where she was kept for two weeks before she was extradited to Arizona - and they questioned her constantly. She quickly learned to say nothing.

But she did break her silence one afternoon when a reporter from a Phoenix paper told her he was bringing her a message from "a wealthy man" back home. According to an account of the incident that was printed in the *Phoenix Gazette*, the reporter said: "He asked me to tell you he wanted you to clear him in connection with that visit you made with him to the home of the girls the night before they were killed."

Ruthie snapped at the man: "He couldn't have sent that message. He knows all about it."

The story in the newspaper added:

Remembering that her attorneys had warned her not to talk at all, Mrs. Judd refused to comment further. She was asked if she meant the man knew all about the visit to the girls or if she meant that he knew about the circumstance of the slayings.

'I won't answer any more questions,' she said to all queries.

By the way, the *Gazette* ran 10 stories about Ruthie's case in the newspaper that day and the "wealthy man's" name wasn't mentioned in any of them.

For Ruthie, though, the message from Phoenix was terrifying. Although it's more likely that the reporter was trying to get information from her and didn't have a message from anyone, Ruthie was convinced it had come directly from her beloved Jack. She began to think that maybe he was trying to "clear" himself because something had gone wrong.

Her mind filled with doubt, and she tearfully confessed the affair to her husband. She tried to make it seem meaningless, but Dr. Judd understood what had happened. He didn't blame her for being lonely; he told her he forgave her and would stand by her. Dr. Judd had often failed his wife, but he kept his word this time.

To the rest of her family, Ruthie always denied that Jack was anything other than a friend. Her brother, Burton, never believed that but decided that her image as a "good wife" would gain more sympathy for her than the truth. In the fund-raising booklet he published, he presented Ruthie as a faithful wife who was preyed on by her friend Jack.

Burton later said that after the reporter's visit, Ruthie started to fear that Jack was trying to hide his part in things, but she continued to cling to the story she was supposed to tell. He said she instructed him to go to Phoenix, go and see Jack, and tell him that Ruthie hadn't talked. She wanted to know what Jack planned to do. Burton tried to do what his sister asked, but Jack refused to see him.

No matter what Jack did or said, Ruthie remained in a state of panic for the next several months. She believed he'd stand by her, then feared he'd abandon her, then became convinced that he'd never let her hang.

Her fear was painfully illustrated in a psychiatric report that was filed by Dr. Joseph Catton, who examined her for the prosecution on November 27, 1931. He wrote:

She showed scorn for Jack Halloran, stating that he was acting as do the rest of men. He had forsaken her. He would not raise a finger to help her, even though she may be hanged.

During the examination, Dr. Catton recorded an exchange between himself and Ruthie:

CATTON: Would there have been any Ruth Judd case without Halloran?

RUTHIE: No.

CATTON: Could Halloran help you if he wanted to?

RUTHIE: He certainly could.

CATTON: Why don't you tell the complete story?

RUTHIE: Because I can't see where it would do me any good and it would make trouble for others.

CATTON: Possibly it would do you some good.

RUTHIE: My husband is telling me that every time he sees me and urging me to tell everything, and so is my attorney, but what shall I do? I don't know what I shall do, it won't do me any good anyway.

It was a strange line of questioning by the psychiatrist, considering that Jack supposedly had nothing to do with the murders. The prosecution had never linked him to the case, so it seems odd that this would have been allowed.

Regardless, when Dr. Catton interviewed Ruthie two months later, her attitude toward Jack had inexplicably changed. This interview took place on January 7, 1932. It was less than two weeks before the start of her trial, and at this point, Ruthie seemed to believe that Jack was going to save her.

RUTHIE: Jack Halloran still loves me and always has.

CATTON: But you told me before that he had forsaken you, that he was like the rest of the men and that he would not raise a finger to help you, now which is so?

RUTHIE: No, he still loves me. He has sent word to me in jail here that he still loves me and that makes things different. He would come up to see me if he could, but you know as well as I do that he couldn't do that because there is a warrant out for his arrest and he would be picked up if he dared to come here.

Apparently, Jack had told Ruthie that he was in trouble, which was why he couldn't come to see her, but this wasn't true. Dr. Catton knew there was no warrant for his arrest, but he was not particularly surprised that Ruthie had fallen for the lie.

Later in the interview, Dr. Catton continued a line of questioning he'd asked her about many times before - what story would she tell on the witness stand?

CATTON: Won't you tell or aren't you going to tell the complete facts of the case?

RUTHIE: If things do not go the way they tell me, if things do not go the way they are planned, believe me, I will get up there and tell them everything.

But she never did.

AND THEN CAME THE "DRAINPIPE LETTER" - THE PIECES of paper on which the prosecution stated Ruthie had written her own death sentence.

It was found because something was clogging up one of the drains at the Broadway department store, where Ruthie had been hiding before her surrender. A plumber was called, and he found a thick wad of paper while cleaning out the trap. Someone had written a rambling letter in pencil to "Darling." The pages were coming apart, but the last sentence sent the plumber immediately to the police. That final line read:

I killed in defense. Love me yet, doctor.

Ruthie had written the letter while at the store. She was apparently contemplating suicide and wanted to explain everything to her husband. But then she changed her mind, tore up the letter, and flushed it down the toilet - or so she thought.

A few days later, she turned herself in to the police, and after 48 hours in custody, the plumber made his discovery. Detectives carefully pieced the "Drainpipe Letter" back together again, and later, Arizona prosecutors could gleefully show it to a jury.

When the news of the letter's discovery broke, the *Phoenix Gazette* rushed an EXTRA edition on the streets to announce it. Telling readers that it was quoting directly from the letter, the paper claimed that Ruthie wrote: "I knew that Mrs. LeRoi would give me up to the authorities, so I had to killer her, too. Sammy shot me through the hand. I grappled with her and finally gained possession of the gun. Then I shot her twice. I had to kill Mrs. LeRoi to keep her from giving me up."

This made for sensational reading, but it's not what the letter said. This is closer to what the prosecution at the trial would interpret the letter to have meant, but it wasn't what Ruthie actually wrote.

The press also offered their own version of Ruthie admitting to dismembering Sammy's body. They reached that conclusion from these words: "It was horrible to pack things as I did. I kept saying, 'I've got to, I've got to, or I'll be hung.'"

This time, these were Ruthie's words, but what she was saying was not what the papers decided it meant. They decided to pick and choose phrases that were different from what happened. The lines weren't about cutting up Sammy but about packing the parts of her into the baggage. Faced with a trunk too heavy to be shipped on the train, she had to lighten the large trunk by placing Sammy's remains in a second trunk and a suitcase.

This misinterpretation was never corrected - it wouldn't have been as lurid if it had been.

THE "DRAINPIPE LETTER" IS STILL PRESERVED TODAY. It's been archived by the state of Arizona and accessible to the public, although few have reason to seek it out anymore.

I debated whether to include the entire letter here since the first part of it really has nothing directly to do with the murders, but in the end, I decided that I would. I did so simply because it gives the reader a glimpse inside Ruthie's mind when she wrote it.

The best word I'd use to describe her at that moment was "unhinged."

I'm not using that word to be comical. Ruthie had just murdered two people, transported their bodies in trunks a few hundred miles, went on the run, hid out in a sanatorium, and was now lurking in the drapery department at the Broadway store. The letter was meant to be her last words to her husband before she committed suicide.

Even so, she chose to lie to him. She was still trying to conceal her affair with Jack Halloran. She claimed the murders happened on Saturday morning and continued to say she had no accomplice. Obviously, even dead, she wanted Dr. Judd to think well of her.

The letter had been written on 10 blank sheets for telegrams, and one page of it was a note written to a Los Angeles physician asking him to deliver the letter to Dr. Judd. That note was partially obliterated by water, but it read:

Dear Dr. Moore:

I am being sought by the police and can't get any message to my darling precious husband, Dr. Judd. I've got to tell him...

So will you deliver this let...
To it and deliver the messa...
Be kind to my poor hus...
I do love him...
I'm crazy...
When I get tired in...
Worried mentally and sick mind and...
Then finding me for my crime...
Tell Dr. Judd forgive him...
Tell him...
To please not die of grief...
I love him and hope he won't hate me for being wicked.

Thank you and Mrs. Moore for having been so good and sweet to me in the past. One of my hands is about shot off so I can scarcely write. Do me this favor to let Dr. Judd know what happened. I can't...

I love him but through...
Nobody but my dear husband...
And parents believing me...
I'm... away from the police...
Best regards and hoping you do this...

Before we get to the letter to Dr. Judd, it should be mentioned that when the police confronted her with what they considered her confession to double murder, Ruthie denied writing the letter and denied attempting to destroy it. However, police experts stated that the writing on the pages was an exact match to Ruthie's handwriting. They also believed that it contained information that only she would know.

The full letter follows. I'll warn you that it's rather long but worth reading, if for no other reason than you'll hear the story that Ruthie chose to tell - whether truth or fiction - and it just might give you a better idea of what she was really like than I've been able to present so far in these pages.

Aside from some editing to fix spelling errors and a few grammatical additions, nothing in the letter has been changed so that the wording makes more sense. Even with these additions, though, it didn't always work.

Darling:

A confession I've kept from you for life because I was so happy with you and loved you so why tell you. I am crazy only when I am angry or too tired physically my brain goes wrong. One obsession I've always had is wanted or saying I had a baby. First when I was seven years old, I wanted a baby at our house so bad I told at school that mother had one and for days told the neighbors we had one and such cute antics it did far beyond an infant's ability.

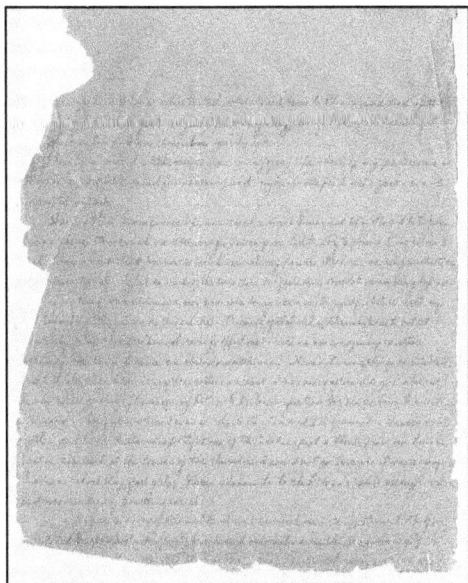

Then when I was 16, on my birthday, a fellow I was going with and I had a split up. I was furious, my girlfriend was the cause. Curiously, I liked her just as well. We chummed together, but this boy's cousin antagonized me by crowing that someone could take him from me. I had taken her boyfriend months before from her. The man's name was Fred Jensen. He wished to be friends but like my chum Laura Walters. I was OK until j-y Burns. I hate her, always will. (I had taken a fellow Ronald Carpenter from her, later they married). I told Fred Jensen about it and asked him not to go with Laura. I loved Laura, but I hated Joy and her crowing. Fred thought I was doing it for meanness, etc. and so finally, as so many unmarried girls in that part of the woods were having babies, I conceived of stating that I was and would make Fred marry me if necessary. I was 16. He was 26. Fred Jensen never touched me. I had never had intercourse with him or with any man until I met you. Fred, I believe, is honest. He cried and cried and told daddy he'd never touch me. He used to tell me I was crazy. I said, well quit going with Laura or I'll send you to the Pen. I won't be tormented by Joy Burns.

I was going pretty good at school then. My teachers loved me. I was good in English class. My stories were published in the school paper and in the city paper. The teachers all like me and I did splendid in Modern History. My classmates like me and I them but I got so worked up I quit school and said I was pregnant and swore out warrants against Fred, made darling dresses, all kinds of dainty things I later gave for little girl's dolls. Fred would walk home from church with me and tell me I was crazy. I said I knew it, but if I started this thing I would finish it. I wanted him to go away until I went back to college then go with Lauras, but please not then. I had an insane temper.

So, finally after about ten months, I decided I'd have to confess a lie or do something drastic, so I proceeded to hope out of my window one night in cold October in my gown and I grabbed a few gunny sacks and overshoes and run away and say I'd been kidnapped. First, I wrote a letter that I had a baby girl (why I don't know) then I ran away. Was going to get some clothes at my home sixteen miles from there and be gone awhile and my Fred had had me kidnapped and I got away. I brought suits against him and assumed as soon as Joy moved, I dropped charges and that was the end.

This is the first time I have ever told this. My parents believed Fred wicked. I did it all myself and never have told it to anyone until now. I've always wanted to tell Fred I was sorry. He was a good boy. He thought it was funny until I had him arrested for rape and kidnapping, etc.

I'm sorry to tell you this, doctor. Here is a confession I should have carried to my death. If I had been intimate with any man I would have told you but I didn't tell you anything to hurt you. I've wanted your respect, confidence, and love. There in Mazatlán or rather Tyolita, I was sick a couple days so as Mrs. Heinz had been so thrilled over being pregnant, I decided I'd say I was. I had hoped for three weeks I might be until I came unwell so when you moved, I wrote I had a miscarriage. Then again, I told Mrs. Heinz and Mrs. Aster I was where you saw I was menstruating the very week we left there. I don't know what possessed me to tell that I had a little boy. I even showed pictures of you with a baby and showed Dyers baby pictures as my baby who was with Mama, so I'm crazy on that line.

Aside from that and occasionally a rage I get into, I seem quite bright. I was working so hard at Phoenix when you went to Bisbee, then something went wrong in my head and I registered under an assumed name and called you up and gave a fictitious address just to hear your voice and see you, then cried all night for doing it. Got a car next morning to sooth my nerves at the garage below the hotel and drove to Warren. Then finally wanted you to soothe me and told you I was there. You know how I cried and cried. I was crazy. You said I was at the time. I came back and Mr. H came out the next evening. He had been on the coast and he said what's the matter, you look terrible, you look crazy. My two doctors said I looked terrible. I've written you for a month how my nerves were doing.

Then Thursday, Mr. H bought the girls a new radio. Mr. Adams had let them have his but they didn't like him so they hated to use his radio. Mr. H wanted me to get some other girl and go with him out to the house. I knew a pretty little nurse who is taking Salvarsan ﬁdrug for the treatment of syphilisﬂ but she has nothing contagious now. I certainly am not expecting them to do wrong, anyhow, so saw no harm. She's pretty and can be interesting so we went to the girls' house.

Dr. Brinckerhoff and a couple Mr. H friends were there. The girls didn't like it, so Mr. H asked us to have dinner with them. I refused so he got dinner and came over to the house. The first time he had ever done it, but it was a nice clean evening. I truly didn't even take a drink. You can ask. The remains of their drinks are in the ice box.

Next day, Anne came over and we had lunch together - the remains of dinner the night before. She wanted me to go home with her that night. Denise Reynolds was going. I had some histories to do and I couldn't. I said if I get time I'll come over and play bridge, but I stayed all night. The next morning all three of us were yet in our pajamas when the quarrel began.

I was going hunting. They said if I did, they would tell Mr. H I had introduced him to a nurse who had syphilis. I said, Anne, you've no right to tell things from the office. You know that only because you saw me get distilled water and syringes ready and she hasn't been contagious, so the doctor lets her work nursing. Well, Anne said, I asked Denise, and she thinks I should tell Mr. H, too. And he certainly won't think much of you for doing such a thing. You've been trying to make him like you and Mr. D, too. When I tell him you associate with and introduce them to girls who have syphilis, they won't have a thing to do with you. And when we tell Mr. P about it, he won't take you hunting either.

I said, Sammy, I'll shoot you if you tell that. We were in the kitchen, just starting breakfast. She came in with my gun and said she would shoot me if I went hunting with this friend. I threw my hand over the mouth of the gun and grabbed the bread knife. She shot. I jumped on her with all my weight and knocked her down in the dining room. Anne yelled at us. I fired twice, I think, and since Anne was going to blackmail me too, if I went hunting by telling them this patient of Dr. Curtis' was syphilitic and would hand me over to the police. I fired at her.

There was no harm introducing this nurse, who is very pretty, to men. One doesn't get it from contact, but they were going to kill me for introducing this -- her initials are D. E. - to their men friends. Anne said before Sammy got the gun, Ruth, I could kill you for introducing that girl to... and if you go hunting, I will tell them and they won't think you're so darn nice anymore.

I don't want to bring Mr. H into this. He has been kind to me when I was lonesome at the first place I worked and has trusted me with many secrets of all he did for the girls, such as caring for Anne, giving her extra money and the radio, and he's a decent fellow. It would separate he and his wife and he'd been too decent.

Mr. D kept Anne in an apartment here in L.A. for several days, then got her state room to Ph and she was mad enough to kill me when he helped move me over. Part of my things are still in the girls' - 3 hats, thermos bottle, black dress, cookbook, green scarf you got me in Mexico, and a number of things.

Doctor, dear, I'm so sorry Sammy shot me, whether it was the pain or what, I got the gun and killed her. It was horrible to pack things as I did. I kept saying, I've got to, I've got to, or I'll be hung. I've got to, or I'll be hung. I'm wild with cold hunger pain and fear now. Doctor, darling, if I hadn't got the gun from Sammy, she would have shot me again.

Forgive me, not forget me. Live to take care of... sick. Doctor, but I'm true to you.... The thoughts of being away from... it me crazy. Shall I give up to... don't think so, the police will hang me. It was as much a battle as Germany and the U.S.

I killed in defense.

Love me yet, doctor.

I think that after reading the letter, you understand what I was trying to say when I prefaced it with some explanation. The letter really is "unhinged." Do I believe that Ruthie fit the legal definition of insane - that she couldn't tell right from wrong when she committed the murders and was unable to aid in her defense? No, I don't. But do I think that Ruthie was mentally ill? Yes, I do.

Simply read the first section of this letter - before getting to the alleged reason for the murder - and it's hard to argue that she was a woman with a disturbing history. She accused one man of raping her and getting her pregnant when she clearly wasn't and then faked at least two more pregnancies when she was in Mexico with her husband. She wanted a baby so badly that she not only convinced herself that she was having one but became so caught up in her imaginary pregnancies that she even suffered the symptoms of miscarriages.

I hate to admit it, but I'm not surprised that her mental issues led to murder. But, of course, that's not all there is to her story.

The prosecution read the "Drainpipe Letter" as an admission of cold-blooded murder despite the errors and the outright lies that it also contained. While it's a confession, I don't think we can accept it at face value. I read it as Ruthie trying to explain things to Dr. Judd before she killed herself. She wanted to convince him not to think less of her or himself. It was all her fault - none of it was his.

But the letter is so disjointed and rambling that it shows that Ruthie was unbalanced when she wrote it. It makes her look insane, so much so that it seems difficult for it to have been faked. The prosecution could argue that the letter was self-serving and that she was trying to establish a story, but I don't find that to be the case.

The letter is not helpful to her case. It's full of incriminating things that Ruthie writes about herself.

But it also raises more questions than it answers. The letter shows a flaw in the prosecution case against Ruthie because there is no anger or hatred toward the girls in the letter. There is not even a hint of animosity. If anything, Ruthie seems shocked that her friends have turned against her. She makes a good case for self-defense - if we accept the letter as the truth.

And that's a big "if." I have some serious concerns about that, primarily because of the other things missing from the letter - like a motive.

What was the motive behind the murder? Did she kill Anne and Sammy because she was jealous? It doesn't seem like it. If we believe that, why was she jealous? There is no "why." The only "why" seems to be that she acted in self-defense because of a fight. But why was there a fight? If we believe Ruthie's version of events, her friends suddenly decided to murder her. But why? Because of a nurse she'd introduced to Jack Halloran? That seems ludicrous and doesn't explain the violence that occurred in the bungalow that night.

Prosecutors will always say that they don't need a motive to prove someone committed murder. Technically, that's true, but a case is much easier to prove to a jury if they have one. A jury - especially one that's hearing a death penalty case - wants justification when they convict someone. They want to know if they did the right thing. So far, the prosecution in Ruthie's case couldn't offer them one. The letter they said was so damning to Ruthie didn't provide one.

And there was one other thing the letter didn't provide - the name of an accomplice, or at least the admission that someone else was involved. Even the police believed Ruthie hadn't acted alone. Of course, they wouldn't tell her defense attorneys that, but they knew Ruthie had someone helping her that night. Even if she committed the murders alone, she had an accomplice for the gruesome acts that followed.

And keeping the secret of that person's identity was slowly driving her mad.

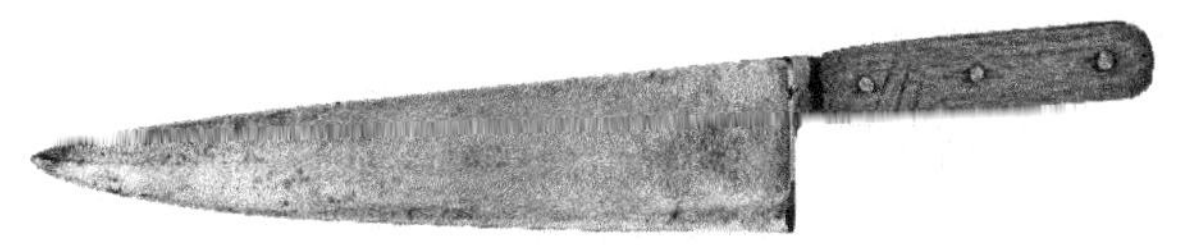

7. EXTRADITION

ON SATURDAY, OCTOBER 24, EXTRADITION PAPERS were sent by special plane to Arizona Governor George W. P. Hunt for his signature. When they arrived, Sheriff McFadden returned on the same plane to present the papers to California Governor James Rolph, Jr. in Sacramento. The sheriff was accompanied by a jail matron who would be in charge of his female prisoner.

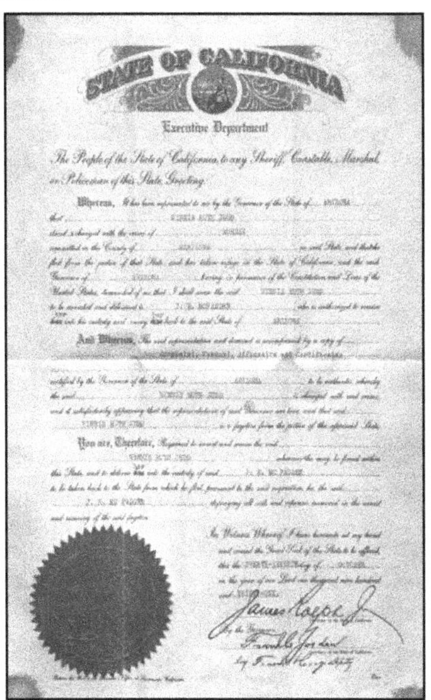

STATE OF CALIFORNIA

Executive Department

The People of the State of California, to any Sheriff, Constable, Marshal or Policeman of this State, Greeting:

[illegible]

During Ruthie's questioning by detectives that day, she indicated her willingness to return to Arizona. But Dr. Judd quickly told her, "You know we're going to fight extradition to Arizona."

"We are?" she asked. "Why?"

"We think you'll be better off here," he replied.

"Why I like Arizona," Ruthie told him. "It's the only place for me."

Nevertheless, one of her attorneys obtained a writ of habeas corpus from Judge Charles Burnell, which prevented her extradition until after a hearing scheduled for November 3.

Sheriff J. J. McFadden of Phoenix serves Undersheriff Eugene Biscailuz of Los Angeles with extradition papers to take Ruthie to Arizona for trial. Also pictured are Chief Deputy Sheriff Frank Dewar of Los Angeles (Left), and County Attorney Lloyd Andrews of Phoenix (right).

Three days later, on October 27, the California deputy attorney in Sacramento approved the extradition papers, and Sheriff McFadden left for San Franciso in a state automobile with the governor's driver. Governor Rolph was sick and was being cared for there at St. Francis Hospital. He signed the papers while in his sickbed, and McFadden headed south to Los Angeles.

Ruthie, who had finally been convinced by her husband that she needed to stay in California, wept hysterically when she learned that the papers had been signed. "They can't do that!" she cried. "I have tuberculosis! My hand is hurting terribly. I can't be moved."

Her attorneys announced they would fight extradition by forcing an examination of the papers. One of them, Louis P. Russell, announced: "The reason we seek to delay her return is not because we have a desire to hinder justice. We are reliably informed, however, that in Phoenix the feeling against our client is high, and we believe this hysteria should subside before Mrs. Judd can be assured a fair and impartial trial."

Sheriff McFadden was unfazed by the attorney's statement. "She'll go back in a few days. She knows me. We became acquainted when she helped nurse my wife once. I told her I'd see that she was cared for properly on the trip back. I don't think she wants to kill time."

At the jail hospital on Wednesday, Ruthie told reporters, "I'm not afraid of returning to Arizona for trial. I think that the jury will believe that I had to fire in self-defense. In addition, I have received word from a man who will be the star witness in the case that he will back me up."

By Thursday, Ruthie not only changed attorneys but also dropped any effort to fight extradition. Her new attorney, Paul Schneck, conferred with her and Dr. Judd as she prepared to leave for Phoenix.

They departed in a caravan of cars later that night, October 29. Ruthie was in the custody of Sheriff McFadden, County Attorney Andrews, and the jail matron, Mrs. Jewel Jordan. In the 1940s, Jewel became the first woman elected Maricopa County Sheriff and eventually pleaded for clemency for Ruthie.

On that day, her prisoner was in good spirits, especially after she discovered that Dr. Judd was riding in one of the other cars. She didn't know he could leave Los Angeles, where he was under a bond for practicing medicine without a license.

When she spotted him at a rest stop that night, Ruthie called out to him and asked him for a kiss. Dr. Judd had been warned to stay away from his wife, but Sheriff McFadden allowed this brief encounter.

At Yuma, the group stopped for breakfast. Cameras flashed, and reporters pushed toward the windows outside. As locals struggled to glimpse Ruthie, they found a section of the diner had been closed to the public. Ruthie sat at her table, eating alone, while Dr. Judd ate with Andrews and a few of the newspapermen who had been allowed access to the caravan.

When the cars reached Gila Bend, Ruthie learned that about 1,000 people were waiting for her arrival at the courthouse in Phoenix. She begged the sheriff to do something, but all McFadden could promise she'd be well-protected.

About 20 miles outside of Phoenix, the caravan was met by a police escort arranged by the police chief and a deputy sheriff to clear

The crowd of onlookers and reporters gathered outside of the Phoenix jail, waiting for Ruthie to arrive from Los Angeles.

traffic. Ruthie became increasingly upset as the cars approached their destination, where the onlookers had gathered since early morning.

The caravan arrived in the early afternoon. As she stepped out of the car, Ruthie was ringed by photographers, and she was given a bouquet of flowers by three women who had fought their way through the crowd. Inmates in the women's section of the jail had decorated the window bars with paper flowers. Under close guard, Ruthie was taken to the county jailer's office.

"Please, Sheriff," she said to McFadden, referring to the reporters, "don't let them come in here now. I can't face any more of those flashlights and cameras."

But McFadden allowed newsmen and photographers a half-hour with Ruthie anyway. She had nothing sensational to tell the reporters, but she posed for the photographers, who were, at that moment, making her the most photographed woman in America.

One of the photographers tried to get a closeup of Ruthie and the bench she was sitting on. "Hey! You can't do that!" Sheriff McFadden shouted at him. He stepped in front of the bench, where a former inmate had carved an inscription that read: "This is a Hell of a place, and how!"

"We haven't painted over that yet," the sheriff explained.

When Ruthie was taken into the cell, she was given a cell by herself. Acting on behalf of Paul Schenck in Los Angeles, Phoenix attorney Herman Lewkowitz conferred with Ruthie over the weekend. No other visitors were allowed.

While in L.A., Ruthie had started receiving "fan mail" - good and bad - and it continued in Phoenix. And, just over that first weekend, more than 300 strangers tried unsuccessfully to visit her in jail.

Ruthie and her attorney had nothing to say, but this didn't stop people from speculating. Rumors spread that she might see a change of venue, which could be granted by the judge presiding over her arraignment. It was also rumored that she might plead insanity rather than self-defense, which she'd been claiming since her surrender.

County Attorney Andrews commented about that rumor: "I don't believe Mrs. Judd will succeed with an insanity defense. I am convinced she was perfectly sane when she killed Agnes LeRoi and Hedvig Samuelson, and I am sure I can convince an Arizona jury of it."

If he did convince a jury, it was possible Ruthie would be convicted of first-degree murder. Previously, Arizona had convicted only two women of first-degree murder. Only one, Eva Dugan, was hanged in February 1930. The rope decapitated her.

There were other kinds of speculation, too. Superstitious people began to believe that Friday - the customary day for hangings at the state penitentiary - was an unlucky day for Ruthie. The murders had occurred on a Friday, Ruthie had surrendered on a Friday, and it was on a Friday that she returned to Phoenix.

Count Louis Hamon, known by the stage name of "Cheiro"

Count Louis Hamon, an internationally famous palm reader, astrologer, and author who visited Phoenix to observe Ruthie and cast her horoscope, enhanced these spooky suggestions about Ruthie's fate. In his opinion, she was fully capable of committing the murders - or at least of accepting someone else's guilt, "even to the limit of fanatical glory of martyrdom in going to her own doom."

Known professionally as "Cheiro," Hamon had analyzed Britian's Lord Kitchener at the request of the British Admiralty and had predicted in 1900 that Mata Hari would be shot as a spy 17 years later. Hamon said that adverse influences in Ruthie's life climaxed on October 16 or 17. He later wrote:

She would be likely to commit crime, under suggestion, hypnotism or narcotic of any kind, or easily be deluded into the idea that she had committed crime.

Without going into technicalities, it is an unfortunate horoscope from the start, indicating financial uncertainty with great difficulties, trials, adversity, mental imbalance, and a brain that was never normal after the age of puberty had passed. Further, the intensity of her love nature is so apparent that she would shield anyone she loved at this period of her life.

This woman is an actress in every sense of the word. Had conditions been more fortunate, there are indications she would have succeeded in a dramatic career.

Ruthie had a way of creating drama all around her, so we have to give "Cheiro" a little credit for that observation. However, I'm not sure she was always aware she was doing it.

Trouble, it seems, had a way of finding Ruthie Judd.

Ruthie appeared in court after her return to Phoenix so that a date for her preliminary hearing could be set.

ON NOVEMBER 3, RUTHIE APPEARED BEFORE JUDGE Clarence E. Ice and was charged with murdering Anne and Sammy. A large crowd had already packed into the county building before she'd arrived. Wearing a black dress and no makeup, she appeared pale and nervous. When the judge took the bench, attorney Lewkowitz commented that she wasn't feeling well and was allowed to sit instead of standing. The charges were read, and Lewkowitz then asked for a hearing. The date was set and agreed upon by Lewkowitz and County Attorney Andrews.

But the interaction between Andrews and Ruthie's L.A.-based attorney, Paul Schenck, wasn't so agreeable.

In an interview with Los Angeles reporters, he took Andrews and Sheriff McFadden to task, claiming they had broken promises made to Schneck and his client. He stated they'd both said Ruthie would not be subjected to lengthy questioning or unnecessary harassment while in Phoenix. However, Schenck claimed that, according to reports, she had been repeatedly questioned for 60 hours with no attorney present. He angrily told the press:

I want to know, and I shall find out, just why the Arizona authorities are rushing headlong into a most drastic investigation and attempting to drag my client along with them.

The days of the Inquisition and such methods are gone, and I intend to see justice meted out in this case. She will not be harried and worried with continual visits from newspapermen and forced to tell and retell again the story of the slayings and her attempt to do away with the bodies. This harrowing experience has been related by this woman twice already to my knowledge.

When the County Attorney read the defense lawyer's allegations, he reacted sharply, particularly about the alleged harassment by reporters:

Mrs. Judd has been advised both by myself, and by all others in Phoenix who have questioned her, as to her constitutional rights. This is always done by ethical prosecutors.

I made no trade with Schenck or anyone else. I did agree, however, that her preliminary hearing would be delayed by a reasonable length of time. This has been done and will be done. Mrs. Judd has not been made the target of lengthy questioning by my officers or others since her arrival. In fact, she has been allowed the first rest she has received since her arrest. Neither has she been subjected to unnecessary harassment. The statement that she had been or will be questioned for 60 hours is so ridiculous as to be merely noise by any person in his right mind.

Andrews also argued that Ruthie had not been "molested" in any way, even by the "usual routine in questioning." The prosecutor stated that she had been so exhausted by her 14-hour trip from Los Angeles that they had allowed her two days to rest. The longest questioning session since arriving in Phoenix had been four hours - and she had been conferring with her own attorney.

He added that since her arrival, newspapermen had been barred from her cell, but then he got nasty:

The "harrowing experience" of telling and retelling her story of the killing referred to by Mr. Schenck was an experience through which, according to the press, Mrs. Judd received thousands of dollars. It was her own story - one for which she was paid real money. And the only story she has told has been voluntarily made to newspapermen. I have yet to see one of her purported "confessions" made to the constituted authorities.

Any questioning that Mrs. Judd may be subjected to in Phoenix will not be for the purpose of lining her pocketbook, but to determine how women were killed in violation of the law of Arizona. It seems to me that the real purpose of the general charges of harassment and molestation and breaking of promises can be for no other reason but to work up public sympathy for this confessed killer.

On Thursday, the sparring between the prosecution and defense shifted from verbal to legal grounds. Herman Lewkowitz was forced to obtain a court order permitting him to visit the house where the murders took place.

Deputy County Attorney Robert McMurchie argued against the order. He remarked to the judge, "Your Honor, you might just as well order the county attorney to divulge all the evidence against the defendant to her attorney."

Remember - it was a different time.

The judge snapped at him: "That is not a proper comparison! Thousands of people have inspected the house and now the county attorney refuses defense counsel to visit it for the purpose of preparing his case in justice court."

After McMurchie had concluded his remarks, Lewkowitz began his argument, but Judge Phelps interrupted him and told him not to bother - the order would stand. He could visit the crime scene. The prosecutor continued to argue, but the judge cut him off.

Soon after the hearing, County Attorney Andrews retaliated, although he would have claimed that was not true if questioned. However, almost immediately after, Ruthie was transferred from her private cell to the women's general population. Sheriff McFadden told the press, "There is no reason to pamper her at the expense of the

Police matron Jewel Jordan, Ruthie, and Sheriff McFadden on their way into the courtroom.

county." The authorities also refused to allow her to have visitors, except for her attorney and occasionally her husband.

On November 9, Ruthie was back in front of Judge Ice, escorted by sheriff's deputies and the matron, Mrs. Jordan. Still without makeup, Ruthie wore a black ankle-length dress as she entered the crowded courtroom once again. The audience, packed into the seats, were primarily women. When one woman fainted at the sight of the prisoner, she was carried, with great difficulty, to the sidewalk outside, where an even larger crowd was gathered.

The courtroom held only two dozen reporters and photographers and about 60 spectators. The coming and going of newsmen looking for a telephone became a problem, with some reporters forced to remain outside while court was in session. Occasionally, fights broke out between the sheriff's deputies and those who wanted inside.

During the hearing, Ruthie sat at a corner of the counsel table between the matron and Joseph B. Zaversack, an associate of Lewkowitz.

The state called 11 witnesses to the stand, two of whom cast considerable doubt upon Ruthie's version of the murders. In her previous statements, she had asserted that she was shot in the hand during the struggle in which Sammy was killed and that she had fired from a position on the floor when Anne attacked her with the ironing board. But Dr. J.D. Mauldin, a Maricopa County physician, testified that both women were killed by bullets fired downward through the brain. Powder burns were noticeable on both bodies, which meant whoever fired the gun had to be close to them.

John W. Pritchett, an employee of the Lightning Delivery Company, testified that Ruthie's hand was not injured or bandaged when he picked up the trunk at the bungalow. "I saw Mrs. Judd's hand clearly," he testified. "It was not bandaged and had no wrapping of any kind. Her right hand had none either. She paid me with that one."

Ruthie in her cell at the county jail

At Ruthie's suggestion, Lewkowitz asked, "Did she tip you for your work?"

"She promised to twice, but she never did," Pritchett replied.

Ruthie laughed at this and turned to her husband, who was seated behind her. But Dr. Judd had missed the exchange. He slept through most of the five-hour session.

The hearing ended just after 4:00 P.M., and Ruthie continued to be held without bond. She returned to her cell and spent the following day visiting with her husband and conferring with her attorney.

Meanwhile, Ruthie's parents were traveling from Darlington, Indiana, to be with their daughter during her trial or, as they called it, "her ordeal to come." Church members and neighbors donated money that allowed the elderly couple to make the trip to Phoenix.

The McKinnells arrived by train on Friday, November 13. They were met at the station by Herman Lewkowitz and Rev. J.G. Fritz, a local Free Methodist minister. Anxious to see their daughter, the couple rose early the next day and waited for word from the sheriff.

Ruthie's parents, Reverend and Mrs. McKinnell

When it came, they rushed to the jail and privately met with McFadden in his office. Then, he took them to a cell on the fifth floor.

He didn't allow any reporters or photographers to accompany them. The sheriff said, "I don't want these old people to go through more than they may have to. Let's leave them alone as much as possible until they get used to the conditions."

Nevertheless, Rev. McKinnell was overheard reassuring his wife as they waited in the cell for Ruthie. "Be brave, mother, be brave. Don't worry - al this is going to come out all right. I don't believe anyone knows all in this matter. Have faith in our girl. Be glad to see her and be brave."

Finally, Ruthie appeared with the matron, and Sheriff McFadden left them alone to talk. After an hour, though, her father left the cell. He told reporters: "It is more important that her mother should be with Ruth. I will have a lot of running around to do. Dr. Fritz wants Mrs. McKinnell and me to stay with them, but I can't do that. We must look for a boarding place - a moderately priced one, too, for you know we ministers are notorious for being poor."

The reporters laughed, already warming up to the kindly older man. When they asked him how he found his daughter, the minister replied:

I can't say. We were so glad to see her, and she was glad to see us. She looks like she is well cared for, and Mr. McFadden surely is a splendid man. I would not have been surprised had he searched me to find saws and other things, but he didn't. He treated us like we were his friends, and he is going to let Mother see her every day. She may stay with her for two hours if she wants to, so he said, and he said that I would be given ample time with her, too.

Everybody wants to do something for us. I don't know how I am going to return all these kindnesses. We are in deep trouble, indeed, but how much lighter has our burden been made by kindness. I feel certain that Ruth will be treated fairly. You can't imagine how grateful we are to find friends instead of enemies. The horror of it all has disappeared much since last night. You know, I have never been so far away from home, and today we are in a strange land. But everything appears so bright here - the sun is brighter and the people are so kind."

Rev. McKinnell acknowledged that Ruthie was "not herself" but added, "Maybe we are not ourselves." But there was one point that he made very strongly that day: "I want my daughter to tell the truth. No matter what happens, she must tell everything truthfully."

If everyone involved in Ruthie's case had followed the direction of Rev. McKinnell, I have no doubt that the story of these murders would have turned out very differently.

But so many lies had already been told - why stop now?

WHILE RUTHIE AND HER LAWYERS WERE PREPARING FOR trial, the Phoenix Police Department and the county attorney's office were putting the finishing touches on the case they had against her - one that even former Phoenix officers would later agree was botched from the beginning. Captain Hugh Ennis, who retired in 1981 after 22 years on the job, never believed it was an accident.

"So much of what happened in this investigation smacks of exactly what it probably was - political interference," he said in a 1992 interview. "Remember, this was a small town and part of the policeman's job was to know who was doing what to whom - they knew out of self-defense because that's how you kept your job in those days."

Court records would show that the first officers to arrive at the bungalow were M.S. Frazier, a 12-year veteran of the department, and George F. Larison, who'd been a cop for three years. It was just after 8:00 P.M. on Monday night, October 19, a short time after the LAPD had telegraphed the Phoenix police about the discovery at the train station. Both officers would testify that reporters showed up almost immediately and were allowed into the house.

Officer Larison testified: "I told the reporters not to touch anything and any time I saw anyone molesting anything at all, I told them to leave it alone. I told them to leave that stuff alone until the fingerprint man got there."

The fingerprint man didn't arrive until nearly two hours later, and according to Frazier, "there must have been a half dozen people" in the house that evening, including reporters and neighbors. He said that they all walked through the three rooms of the bungalow - kitchen, living room, and bedroom - and said he "didn't think" anyone picked anything up because he told them not to.

Looking back now, we assume that perhaps the integrity of a crime scene wasn't as serious in 1931 since there were no DNA or forensic evidence tests, but that's not the case. It was standard operating procedure at the time to be sure that any evidence that existed - especially in a murder case - was not destroyed, damaged, or stolen. There was no excuse for the way things were handled that night. Phoenix was, admittedly, a small town, but it certainly wasn't the first homicide investigation the department had investigated.

And things went from bad to worse.

The landlord of the bungalow went to police headquarters the following day and pleaded with officers to protect his property because "curiosity seekers were destroying valuable furniture and furnishings." The department did assign an officer to stay at the house, but apparently, that was only for show, because he did nothing to keep away the sightseers and trespassers.

Apparently believing that if he couldn't beat them, he'd join them, the landlord quickly ran ads in the two local papers to let the public know that he was offered tours of the bungalow for 10 cents a head. Newspapers reported that "thousands" of people paid to gawk at the city's most gruesome attraction for the next three weeks.

Crowds flocked to the bungalow after the murders and the police and the owner of the house allowed hundreds of people to visit the crime scene.

It wasn't until November 13 - 28 days after the murders - that the county's chief investigator was sent to collect blood samples from the house.

By then, there's no question that the entire scene had been contaminated many times over. That was why defense attorneys didn't expect an argument when they objected to all the blood evidence by reminding the judge: "By the advertisements in the newspapers, the entire population of Maricopa County visited the place."

But their objection was overruled. In fact, the presiding judge turned out to be very forgiving of all the mistakes made by police officers and investigators. Every objection that defense attorneys raised about the "tainted physical evidence" - and they objected to all of it - was overruled. Eventually, they gave up trying to discredit the case because of shoddy police work. It was useless.

To many, the neglect shown to the crime scene was the first clue that the police weren't really interested in the truth of the case. It's standard with a homicide case to look at the evidence and develop a theory about what happened. This is especially true when it's a case of circumstantial evidence, like this one, with no witnesses to say they

Ruthie in trial with her attorneys and her husband, Dr. Judd, who stands directly behind her.

saw the murders occur. In that kind of case, everything must fit the theory. If one piece of physical evidence doesn't fit, it must be explained. In this case, there were pieces all over the place that didn't fit their theory, but they never tried to explain any of them.

In fact, it's difficult to find any evidence that *did* fit the state's theory of the murders. Not even the contaminated blood samples held up under scrutiny.

The scene that the state described for the jury was that the girls were lying in their beds asleep when Ruthie put a gun to their heads and, one at a time, shot them dead. The state suggested that Anne was shot first, dying from a single .25-caliber bullet wound to the skull. It was then suggested that Sammy was awakened by the gunshot, partially raised up in bed, and threw out her hand in a "defensive gesture" toward her attacker, being struck by the first bullet in her hand. The fatal shot was fired into her head. Prosecutors tried to convince the jury that Ruthie's statements about the girls being killed during a fight in the kitchen were absurd.

The bedroom where prosecutors said the girls were killed was really a small sleeping porch with just enough space for two single beds and a dresser. Anne's bed was on the north wall, and Sammy's was on the south wall. There was a walkway - only slightly wider than the dresser - between them.

According to testimony, the only blood in the bedroom was found under Anne's bed. A corner of a rug under the bed was covered with blood - it had been cut out and thrown into the trunk with the body. Besides that, there were a few spatters on the floor around Anne's bed that went up the wall no higher than the baseboards. There was no blood on the bed's springs - the underside of the mattress - and no blood on the wall by the bed.

And there was no blood at all on Sammy's bed. None on the walls above the bed or on the springs under the bed. There was no blood on the floor near or under the bed and no spatter anywhere near the bed.

It seems impossible - based on the blood evidence - that the girls were killed in the bedroom. If they had been shot there, there would have been blood on the walls - especially around Sammy's bed since she allegedly raised a hand to ward off the bullets. There should have been blood all over the bedroom, around both beds. Head wounds are known for how much they bleed, so where was all the blood? It seems possible that one of the bodies eventually ended up on Anne's bed - based on the blood that dripped onto the rug - but the evidence shows no one was killed there.

The blood in the bedroom showed that the state's theory about the girls being murdered there was wrong, so where and how were Anne and Sammy killed? Was Ruthie making up her version of events? If so, what did she have to gain? If she was in the house, she had to know what the physical evidence would show. Why didn't she say the fight was in the bedroom - like the police did - if that was the only place she knew that blood would be found? It doesn't make sense that she'd insist the girls died in the kitchen unless that's what she remembered. These were questions the police should've asked, but they didn't.

Ruthie's defense attorneys poorly handled the blood evidence. Not once did they point out the lack of blood on the bedroom walls, which would make it evident to the jury that no one was killed in the room. They did try to make the jury suspicious about the state not being straightforward about the blood it found, but the point was never driven home. The right questions were raised, but the jury was never given the answers they needed.

The state's blood expert was Dr. H.L. Goss, who testified that he was taken to the bungalow by the county's chief investigator, John Brinkerhoff - no relation to Dr. Brinkerhoff from the clinic. Goss stated that the only human blood he found was inside the bedroom. He said he did not make an independent inspection of the house but took samples *only* where the investigator indicated.

When cross-examined, Goss was asked questions that suggested there was actually blood all over the house. He was asked if he was told to check for blood in the hallway, under the kitchen linoleum, in the hallway, and in the bathroom. Each time, he answered that he wasn't.

The questions raised a lot of suspicion because they seemed so specific - was the defense just fishing, or did they know there had been blood in those places?

But there is a legitimate question that comes from this - why was no blood found in the bathroom? The state's own witness claimed Sammy's body was dismembered shortly after her murder, so it would've had to have happened in the bungalow. It seemed very unlikely that an adult woman could have been cut apart anywhere in the house without leaving a speck of blood behind. Even if the body had been dismembered in the bathtub, there should have been blood around the drain at the very least.

But what we know - and the police knew - is that there had been evidence found in the tub's drain. The plumber, Clay George, had been called to the scene on the night of October 19 when a detective had directed him to clean out the drains in the bathroom. He'd found bits and pieces of skin, flesh, bones, and hair in the pipes, but none of that had ever been entered into evidence.

Ruthie's attorneys suspected blood was found that hadn't been reported, which is why they questioned Dr. Goss the way they did. So why didn't they hire their own experts to take blood samples? This seems like a terrible mistake, but it's more likely they'd been blindsided by the reports the state had. They had never seen the police reports or any of the evidence in advance. They found out about the state's evidence when it was revealed during the trial. They had no chance to prepare for anything.

But they should've had that chance. Even then, the government was supposed to reveal all the physical evidence. In theory, law enforcement is not supposed to be on anyone's side. They're not supposed to be trying to get a conviction or an acquittal. They're just looking for justice. But this time, it appears this wasn't the case. Many believe the prosecution had a predetermined outcome and only revealed the evidence that fit their theory.

The most blatant example of this was a large bloody thumbprint that was found when the police first entered the bungalow on October 19. It was visible on the window shade in the bedroom, left behind when someone likely pulled it all the way down. Defense attorneys couldn't have seen the print - it was long gone by the time they toured the house in late November - but the defense had explicitly asked Dr. Goss about it on the stand. Since it had not been entered into evidence, Goss probably never saw it either.

But Ruthie's attorney had asked about it probably because she had told him who had left the thumbprint on the shade. However, no one ever admitted to seeing it, including the fingerprint man at the house on the night the trunks were discovered in L.A.

Years later, a document was found in which Sheriff John McFadden admitted to personally cutting out the section of the window shade that had the print on it. But that evidence was never produced at trial - like the evidence found in the bathtub drain - and Ruthie's lawyers certainly never saw it.

And then there were the mattresses. Neither of the beds had a mattress on them when the police first entered the bungalow. They should've immediately questioned why they were gone, where they were, and who took them. Instead, the mattresses were ignored. The press eventually reported that a mattress was found miles away from the bungalow but that the police didn't think it was connected to the Judd case because there was no blood on it.

Obviously, the mattresses were important. There was either something on the mattresses the killer didn't want to be seen - or the mattresses didn't fit the state's case. How can you explain that there's no blood on a mattress when you've got a theory that claims the girls were shot in their beds?

The very fact that the mattresses were removed from the house is revealing on its own. Whoever took them had to have some kind of transportation to haul them away. Ruthie didn't have a car, so who removed the mattresses?

The 25-caliber Colt automatic (with cartridge and bullets) that Ruthie used to kill Sammy and Anne. They were discovered in a hat box found in the bathroom of the railroad station, along with a suitcase containing part of Sammy's body.

There were also issues with the state's plan to prove Ruthie committed premeditated murder. To show premeditation, you must show where the gun was that night. If Ruthie came to the bungalow that night to kill Anne and Sammy, the state had to show she had brought the gun with her. They didn't do that because no one knew where the gun was. There were never any tests done to see if she had fired a gun, even though a dermal nitrate test can show gunshot residue for up to two weeks after a gun has been fired.

They could have shown premeditation with the bullets, too. The police not only had the bullets from the bodies but had found both fired and unfired .25-caliber bullets tossed into the trunks. Premeditation could've been shown by producing evidence that the suspect had bought a box of shells, that six were missing from the box, and that six were fired during the commission of the crime. But no one ever testified to anything like that. No one knows where the bullets came from.

Besides physical evidence, the suspect's actions are also important when showing premeditation. It's imperative to show that a plan was made and carried out. The police investigation into Ruthie's activities in the days before the murders revealed no evidence of premeditation.

She met with a realtor on Thursday evening - 24 hours before the killings - to secure a house that was large enough for herself, her parents, and her friends, Anne and Sammy. She told the realtor that she and the girls would look at the house together on Saturday.

On Friday, she had lunch with Anne, and the pair were seen by Dr. Brinkerhoff walking back to the clinic "arm in arm." That same day, she spent all but $2 of her paycheck paying rent and grocery bills.

Then, Saturday night, without any cash of her own, she was prepared to leave town on the late train, obviously knowing that someone was paying for her ticket. On Sunday, she spent the day trying to borrow money for food on her trip.

Saturday and Sunday were, of course, after the murders, but none of the things that she did leading up to Friday night seem indicative of a person carrying out a murder plot. She wasn't saving her money to flee Phoenix or arranging to see the girls so she could kill them - only to wait two days before she left town. Instead, Ruthie appeared to have been a person in a predicament who had to improvise.

Today, the evidence that the police gathered likely wouldn't have made it to a preliminary hearing or a grand jury. There just wouldn't be enough to prosecute her now, but there apparently was in 1931 - in Phoenix, anyway.

As Ruthie Judd, her friends, family, attorneys, and the people of Arizona were just about to find out.

8. THE WHOLE TRUTH AND NOTHING BUT THE TRUTH

CROWDS FILLED THE HALLWAYS AND COURTROOM ON November 16 when Ruthie was escorted to her arraignment before Judge Howard C. Speakman, who would be the presiding judge at her trial.

Like all Arizona judges, Speakman was an elected official. He had won his seat as a Democrat in the fall of 1930. Originally from Oklahoma, he moved to Arizona in 1920. He was a World War I veteran and had seen every side of legal work. Six times during his six years as a prosecutor, he'd convicted murderers who went on to face the death penalty. As a defense attorney, he'd never lost a capital case. In the few years that he'd spent on the bench, he'd already heard nine murder trials, but none of those convicted had been sentenced to die.

When Ruthie arrived in his courtroom for her arraignment, she was accompanied by Dr. Judd, Sheriff McFadden, and the jail matron. On her way to the counsel table, her father gave her a kiss.

When her case was announced, Ruthie stood as the court clerk read the charge against her for the murder of Agnes Anne LeRoi. Herman Lewkowitz entered a plea of not guilty on Ruthie's behalf.

FINAL SPORTS MARKETS

Ruth's Trysts Mock Many 'Playboys'

Evening Express

MRS. JUDD SWOONS IN GRIP OF TERROR

MOHLER, SMITH BADLY HURT IN GAME WITH CAL

Late News Bulletins

LA TIGRESSE

12

As Ruthie's trial heated up, writers and reporters from all over the country rushed to Phoenix to cover every minute of it.

The judge asked how long it would take to try the case, and County Attorney Andrews stated that the prosecution estimated it would take a few days.

"Probably a week," Lewkowitz spoke up, "but we won't be ready for more than a month. We have to obtain depositions from the east."

Andrews objected, and Judge Speakman asked if the defense could be ready by December 15. When Lewkowitz said no, the judge ignored him. "We will set it for December 15," he said, "and if the defense is not ready, it may make a showing for a postponement."

Lewkowitz shook his head. "You'll never bring her to trial on that date," he replied.

A second complaint was then read, charging Ruthie with the murder of Hedvig Samuelson, and again, a not-guilty plea was entered. The trial date was again set for December 15.

"May the record show that we object to the trial date?" Lewkowitz asked. His objection was noted, and the hearing was concluded.

After the arraignment, Paul Schenck, still in Los Angeles, announced that he and Dr. Edward Williams would soon be in Phoenix so that the doctor could examine Ruthie. A local doctor would also be called in to consult.

On Saturday, November 28, Ruthie received physical and mental examinations. Williams spent nearly three hours with Ruthie, and later in the afternoon, she sat down with the state's psychiatrist, Dr. Joseph Catton, whose interview was mentioned in an earlier chapter.

A week later, Catton revealed that Ruthie had concealed many details of the crime. He announced to reporters, "Mrs. Judd told me she could reveal a great deal more about what happened than was generally known, but she claimed she had not decided whether she would tell it. I also asked her about the confession found in the Los Angeles drainpipe and she replied she 'didn't know whether she was going to say she wrote it or not.'"

The statement made by Herman Lewkowitz that Ruthie wouldn't be brought to trial by December 15 turned out to be true. Judge Speakman granted a continuance until January 19. The defense asked for the delay to permit them to obtain depositions from relatives and friends of Ruthie's who lived in the East. He also added that some of the depositions would be coming from mental hospitals in Ohio, Indiana, and Illinois, where some of Ruthie's relatives had been patients.

This was the first indication that the defense would include a plea of insanity - but I doubt anyone was surprised.

While all this was happening, Ruthie waited. Her hand had healed, so she had finally been fingerprinted. The State Bureau of Criminal Identification also identified her with this description:

26 years old.
Blue eyes.
Golden brown hair.
65 inches tall.

109 pounds in weight.
Fair complexion.

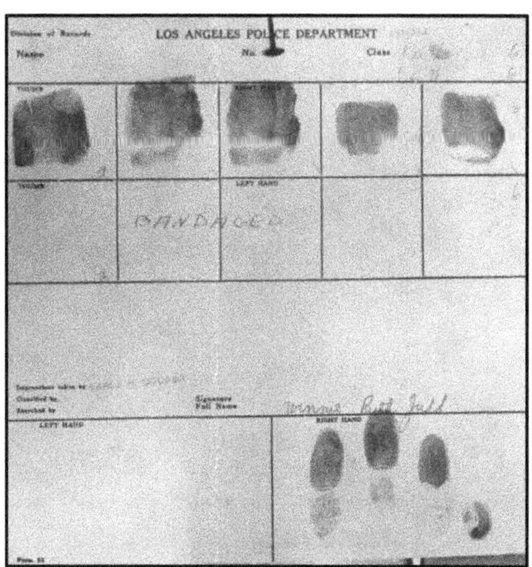

Ruthie's fingerprint record with the State Bureau of Criminal Identification.

Ruthie spent one monotonous day after another in her cell, conferring with her lawyer and spending time with her husband and parents. But Sheriff McFadden told the press she'd been a model prisoner. "She's been under a terrific strain, and she's bearing up well," he said. "She's been a good prisoner, and she hasn't asked for any special consideration. She hasn't said a thing about the slayings. I tried a number of times to get her to tell me certain details, but she has been tight-lipped. I told her if she would talk, we might be able to help her, but she refused, so I've abandoned the idea of encouraging her to tell all."

More than a week before the trial, Judge Speakman announced that there would be no passes or reserved seats that assured admission to the trial. He had received letters from people and the press throughout the country trying to guarantee seats, but he was not allowing that. The courtroom would hold only about 200 people, and, according to the judge, it would be strictly "first come, first served."

Newspaper stories were also ramping up in anticipation of the start of the trial. Reporters had been fighting for news about Ruthie for over a month, and now the story was active again. The nicknames were flying again - "The Blond Butcher," "Tiger Woman," and, of course, "The Trunk Murderess." They described her as a vicious predator and wrote sensational stories that promised new

Ruthie's official mugshot

developments that were coming soon. A story in the *Phoenix Gazette* - under the sub-headline "Sensations Promised" - included this:

Startling developments of a case that already has stirred the nation and gained world-wide attention are freely predicted for the trial. Almost unparalleled in gruesomeness and remarkable features ass was the double killing - the trial is expected to rival the event itself in its new disclosures.

A blood-hued web of facts, speculation, and mystery is woven around Mrs. Judd. Lines of this amazing tangle apparently are entwined around the lives of individuals here and in other cities.

County Attorney Andrews' task will be to unravel these threads of evidence and analyze them so that a jury may determine whether or not the state is correct in its contention that Agnes Anne LeRoi and Hedvig Samuelson were victims of premeditated murder.

Mrs. Judd must give a jury her answer to these accusations. Upon this answer rests her chance of escaping a penalty - possibly the hangman's noose.

More wild speculations followed, including the discovery that Ruthie had once claimed she was kidnapped and seduced in Calhoun, Illinois when she was young. But, just like the story she'd spun about the boy who supposedly raped her and got her pregnant, she later retracted the story and admitted it wasn't true.

Reporters were also excited on January 17 when Dr. Catton revealed more details about Ruthie's earlier examination. He hinted that a second person might've been involved in the crime. He said, "From all aspects of the case as I know them, almost anything may develop." He illustrated this statement by quoting something Ruthie had said to him during his exam - "If things don't go the way they tell me, and don't go the way they are planned, believe me, I'll get up and tell everything."

In response to a question about the crime, he added that Ruthie told him, "I have never even cut up a chicken in my life, doctor."

Catton went on to say, "Mrs. Judd told me there had been no man in her life until Dr. Judd, her husband, came into it, and no other man until about one year ago. She has admitted association with this other man up until the time of the murders. She refused to discuss whether she had seen him after the killing and was tight-lipped about the events of the murder day. She also told me that statements she made about quarreling with Mrs. LeRoi and Samuelson were true."

He also had something else to add that hadn't been mentioned before. According to Catton, Ruthie claimed to be the mother of a boy who was living in Mexico. Even so, Catton said that he believed she was sane and that her intelligence was normal for her age.

And he wasn't the only one who thought so. Word leaked that Dr. Paul Bowers of Los Angeles, another expert for the state, had previously examined Ruthie and announced she was sane. Two of the five physicians who'd been retained by the defense - who weren't identified - judged that Ruthie was insane.

By the eve of the trial, the state had more than 60 people on its witness list. The defense had around a dozen. The attorneys on both sides were reluctant to discuss what they planned to present, and the defense refused to say whether Ruthie would take the stand on her own behalf.

County Attorney Andrews would be assisted in the prosecution by Deputy Attorneys G.A. Rodgers, Harry Johnson, and Robert McMurchie. They planned to try Ruthie first for Anne's murder, and if they failed to obtain a guilty verdict, they'd try again with the murder of her friend, Sammy.

They were determined to convict Ruthie, one way or another.

The jury for Ruthie's murder trial. In those days, women didn't yet serve on juries in Arizona. So, not exactly a "jury of his peers."

THE TRIAL BEGAN ON JANUARY 19, ALTHOUGH THE FIRST TWO days were spent selecting a jury. The prospective jurors were asked questions about their religion, occupation, family matters, and matters more relevant to the case. With the very first candidates, Lewkowitz began probing for possible reactions to pleas of self-defense and insanity.

He asked each possible juror if they were willing to find a not guilty verdict if it was proven that Ruthie only killed to save her own life. He then prodded them for an answer if they could find Ruthie not guilty if they knew she committed murder but was not of sound mind and couldn't distinguish between right and wrong.

The question of where the burden of proof rested in a plea of insanity quickly became a subject of contention between the defense and the prosecution. During the questioning of one potential juror, Judge Speakman resolved the question by asking, "Aren't we trying to cross a bridge before we get to it? In other words, the question of burden of proof is not included in the question and doesn't pertain to the question propounded to the juror."

The judge then turned to the man whom the attorneys were questioning. He addressed the man: "The court instructs you that after the close of this case, if after and when this case is submitted to you, if you entertain a reasonable doubt as to the sanity of the this defendant as defined by the court, then I instruct you that it is the duty of the jury to return a verdict of not guilty. In view of that instruction, what is your answer to the question?"

The man cleared his throat. "If it is your instructions, I would abide by your instructions."

Lewkowitz further pressed the juror about any preconceived notions he might have about the case: "You wouldn't rely on newspaper stories that you've read or discussion that you have heard to tie her to other facts to find a verdict of guilty, would you?"

"Absolutely not," the man replied.

Most jury candidates admitted to having read about the case and discussing it. However, few of them claimed to have any firm opinions because of the publicity given to the case over the last several months. One was an exception, though. He was asked: "But did you form an opinion as to the guilt or innocence of the defendant from reading these articles and discussing them?"

The juror shrugged. "Yes, sir."

Lewkowitz challenged him, and despite objections from G.A. Rodgers, he was excused from jury service.

Another potential juror had firm opinions of his own, which apparently didn't come from news coverage of any kind. Neither did they, he testified, come from his personal acquaintance with Jack Halloran, a friend of Ruthie and the two murdered women.

The potential juror knew Halloran was a regular at the parties thrown at the bungalow, and Ruthie had introduced him to Doris Easton - which wasn't her real name, but we'll come back to that. She was the nurse who worked at the Grunow Clinic that had become the subject of debate - according to the "Drainpipe Letter" - because she was being treated for syphilis. He had been at a party with Ruthie and the others on October 15. The party was a long one that "got a little loud." One participant later told the police that Ruthie was "drinking and having a great time kissing one of the men at the party."

When questioned, the potential juror was asked if, in his business, he interacted with Jack's lumber business.

"No, I never have," he replied.

"Or with Jack Halloran?" Lewkowitz questioned him.

"Yes, I do."

"You know him personally?"

"Yes."

"Known him a long time?"

"Oh, six or seven years."

"It is a fact that you saw his name mentioned in the newspapers you read concerning this case?"

"Yes, I have."

"And is it because of that you do not feel that you can sit as a fair and impartial juror in this case with the idea that he might or might not be mentioned, is that it?"

"It is not at all."

The prospective juror finally explained, uncomfortably, that there were some "unconscious things" that might influence his verdict.

Lewkowitz sighed and asked, "Are these unconscious things - probably I have asked you before, but I want to ask you again - things that you know about the matter, things that you believe because of the persons who have told them to you or friendships with people who is it alleged were connected with it, are them any of those three?"

"The things I believe, yes."

"From someone who has told you?" Lewkowitz prodded him.

"No."

"From reading the newspapers?"

"No."

"Couldn't evidence eradicate that belief?"

"It might," the man shrugged again.

"Whoever has that belief to eradicate from your mind starts, in a way, with a handicap so far as you are concerned?"

"Yes."

Lewkowitz threw up his hands a little in frustration and turned away from the juror. "We challenge for cause," he said to the judge.

But Judge Speakman turned to the juror. "Do I understand you to say you did or did not have an opinion as to the guilt or innocence of the defendant?"

"No opinion as to the guilt or innocence," the man replied.

"Is there any reason," the judge then asked, "that may be known to you alone why you could not sit as a fair and impartial juror if you were selected?"

"Yes."

"There is a reason that is known to you alone?"

'Yes."

The judge shook his head and turned to the county attorney. "Do you resist the challenge?"

"We do not," Rodgers replied.

"Stand aside," said the judge. "Call the next juror."

What the prospective juror and friend of Jack Halloran knew about the case that would have influenced the verdict remains a mystery.

JURY SELECTION CONTINUED FOR TWO DAYS. MORE potential jurors were excused for many reasons. Several of them were opposed to capital punishment. A father with 16 children was excused due to back problems.

One candidate who was accepted became mired in controversy surrounding the jury's decision. Defense attorneys would allege he had been initially biased and had swayed other jurors to vote for the death penalty to get Ruthie to talk. However, nothing out of the ordinary appeared in his responses to the questions asked of other jury members by both the prosecution and defense.

On January 21, 1932, 12 jurors and one alternate were selected and sworn in - all men. Their jobs included clerk, dairy farmer, machinist, watchmaker, and salesman.

After they were sworn in, Judge Speakman was careful to stress to the jury that they should avoid all publicity about the case. He warned them not to read newspaper accounts about the case, listen to radio reports, or even discuss the case with anyone except for other jury members.

From the day they were impaneled, the men were sequestered in a makeshift dormitory on the top floor of the courthouse. No visitors were allowed. When they left their dorm for dinner at a downtown restaurant each evening, they would march in double file, with one bailiff in front and another in back. They sat in a reserved section of the restaurant. Once, they were taken to see a film, and the authorities purchased all the seats in one row in front of them and one behind them so that no one could sit near them. They were paid $4.50 per day.

Even with attempts to keep them entertained, the men were used to reading a daily newspaper or switching on the radio for the news, but that wasn't allowed. Besides, they would have more than enough drama to keep their attention inside the courtroom. They wouldn't need to look for it in the newspaper.

DURING THE TWO DAYS OF JURY SELECTION, RUTHIE expressed an air of indifference about what was going on around her. But that suddenly changed to a display of anger on Thursday morning when Dr. Joseph Catton, the state's psychiatrist, walked into the courtroom and greeted her.

Ruthie jumped up and shouted at him, "Get away from me! Get out of here!" She twisted toward her attorneys and demanded, "Make him get out!" She snapped at Catton, "I don't want you near me. You said you wouldn't talk about me, and you've been talking about me in all the poolrooms!"

Dr. Catton didn't react. He merely continued walking past her.

When the court was called to order, the clerk read aloud, charging that Winnie Ruth Judd did "willfully, unlawfully, feloniously, and of her deliberate and premeditated malice aforethought, kill and murder one Agnes Anne LeRoi, a human being. To which information, gentlemen of the jury, the defendant has entered a plea of not guilty."

County Attorney Lloyd Andrews brought in the state's witnesses to have them sworn in. Judge Speakman explained that they had to leave the courtroom and wait to be called to testify, clearing the way for Andrews to make his opening statement.

Lloyd Andrews was a handsome, well-liked man who'd lived in Arizona most of his life. Most people called him "Dogie," a nickname he'd picked up playing varsity baseball at the University of Arizona in Tucson. When the trial began, he was 36 years old, the youngest man ever elected to the office of Maricopa County Attorney. He had won his seat in the same election - and on the same Democratic ticket - as Judge Speakman.

Andrews' success in Ruthie's case should have been his ticket to even greater success. Instead, he saw his political career evaporate. Just nine months after the trial, he was beaten in his own party's primary by a young Democratic lawyer named Renz Jennings. In 1934, Andrews tried for a political comeback, running in a four-person contest for the Democratic nomination for Arizona attorney general. The winner walked away with 34,000 votes - Andrews came in dead last with just 3,122. He continued to work as an attorney but never achieved fame. He died in 1964.

On the other side of the courtroom was Ruthie's defense team - three warring attorneys who would turn on each other after the trial and whom Ruthie would fire for "mishandling" the case.

The top lawyer was, of course, one of California's top criminal attorneys, Paul Schneck. He was a large man with a snow-white head of white hair and was 58 years old when the trial began. He'd spent 30 of those years making a name for himself in Los Angeles and was famous for introducing the insanity plea in the California courts system. Time after time, he had saved defendants from the noose by convincing juries that his clients were insane at the time of the crime.

Ruthie's L.A. celebrity attorney, Paul Schneck, who was allegedly paid by William Randolph Hearst

He soon discovered that in Arizona, that kind of defense was still considered something of a dubious idea.

By the time he took on Ruthie's case, Schneck had cut back on his legal work and was in semi-retirement. He was coaxed into taking the case - and secretly paid for his services - by William Randolph Hearst.

Ruthie's case would be the tragic end to his illustrious career after he was fired after the trial and publicly blamed for botching her defense. He died just 10 months later.

Herman Lewkowitz and his law partner, Joesph Zaversack, were at the top of a very short list of criminal attorneys in Phoenix at the time. Both men had busy schedules, but they commonly juggled several cases at once. None of the cases they'd handled in the past came even close to the importance of Ruthie's murder case.

Zaversack was a behind-the-scenes lawyer who gathered evidence and organized strategy. He passed away shortly after the trial ended.

Lewkowitz went on to handle 114 murder cases during his career. Ironically, he represented two defendants in two different murder cases that occurred on the same night in October 1931. The same day he lost Ruthie's case in one courtroom, he saved a young pharmacist named Jack West, who'd killed his girlfriend in another. Lewkowitz arranged a plea bargain with County Attorney Andrews that saw West's charges reduced from murder to manslaughter. Lewkowitz had argued for a suspended sentence, but the judge considered some jail time was necessary. West was given three to five years in prison but only served 23 months before going free.

Courtroom scene shot at the beginning of the Ruthie's murder trial. At the counsel table, left to right: Herman Lewkowitz, Paul Schenck, and Joe Zaversack, and Ruthie at far right end of the table.

Lewkowitz was a thin man who wore wire-framed glasses. He was known for his easy-going manner, which quickly became ferocious when questioning witnesses in a courtroom. He died in 1951.

Zaversack and Lewkowitz were also paid by Hearst.

LLOYD ANDREWS DELIVERED THE OPENING STATEMENT for the prosecution. He told the jury that Ruthie was on trial only for the death of Anne LeRoi and that a second trial would be held later for the death of Hedvig Samuelson. But prosecutors would introduce plenty of evidence into the trial about Sammy's death and dismemberment, which made it hard for the jury to distinguish between the two murders. This was, of course, precisely what the county attorney had planned.

Andrews promised that his evidence would prove that Ruthie had planned to kill her friends for a long time. He claimed the relationship between the three women had been "deteriorating for five weeks," becoming so bad that Ruthie had moved out of the bungalow in early October. He told the jury he would prove that her plan had developed in the weeks that followed and that she had killed them in cold blood - an offense that deserved the death penalty.

Ruthie's nemesis – County Attorney Lloyd Andrews

A parade of witnesses made their way to the stand, starting with an assistant county engineer named E.A. Woodworth, who was asked to identify a map he'd drawn of the bungalow. He was followed by Denise Reynolds, an employee of the Grunow Clinic, who'd spent a quiet evening with the victims. She identified a grocery boy as the only other visitor to the house before she left at 10:00 P.M. Next was Beverly Fox, another employee at the clinic, who spoke with Ruthie on October 17 about coming to work.

After a break for lunch, Dr. Laurence Dunn of the Grunow Clinic took the stand and stated that he was Anne's employer. He stated that she had not made any arrangements with him to be absent on October 17.

Most of the rest of the afternoon was filled with testimony from men who had moved baggage from the bungalow and Ruthie's apartment. There were also witnesses like Jennie McGrath and Gene Cunningham, neighbors who'd both reported hearing three gunshots on the night of the murders.

There was some wrangling between the attorneys over the admissibility of evidence when Phoenix and Los Angeles railroad employees testified. Schenck argued that the suitcase shouldn't be admitted because it contained some of Sammy's body parts and, as such, was evidence that should be separated from the case then on trial. Judge Speakman overruled the objection.

The following Saturday, Andrews called Detective Lieutenant Frank Ryan of the Los Angeles Police Department to the stand. He was asked about his examination of the larger trunk and replied that he'd found two women's purses in it.

"What did they contain, if anything?" Andrews asked.

"One purse contained a temperature thermometer, and, in addition, there were two empty shells of.25-caliber and one lead bullet. In the other purse, there was one empty shell."

"And what did you do with these shells and this bullet, if anything?"

"I turned them over to Mr. Moxley, our ballistics man."

After a few other questions, Ryan was asked, "Can you describe the position of the body which was in the large trunk?"

"It was laying sort of on the side, it would be laying on the left side, the head up in the corner of the trunk. The body then, the knees were drawn up and the seat down in the opposite corner, in the lower - in the bottom of the trunk."

"Was the body intact?"

"It was."

"Now, with reference to the smaller trunk, you were present when it was unpacked?" Andrews asked the detective.

"I was."

"And what was found in that trunk?"

Ryan paused for a moment before he replied, "There was several - quite a number of sheets of blank paper. A light cotton blanket was tucked around over the articles underneath. When that was pulled back, there was found to be two bundles wrapped in some articles of women's clothing. And when these were unwrapped, they proved to be the feet and legs up to the knees of a human being. There were - right under them was the head and shoulders and body down as far as the navel of a woman. This was lying in the small trunk on its back with the hands folded across. Each one of the feet then were laid up alongside the head."

Andrews asked him, "And those were the only portions of that body which were in that trunk?"

Detective Ryan examining Ruthie's trunks for a newspaper photographer.

"They were."

When he was asked whether he knew if arrangements had been made with his department for the surrender of the defendant, Ryan replied, "No, I do not."

The detective was followed on the stand by Ray Pinker, a forensic chemist for the LAPD. He had been called to the county morgue on October 19 to examine the baggage. He explained, "I opened the hatbox, and in the hatbox, I found some surgical dressings, miscellaneous cosmetics, a blue dress, I believe, and a small kit of surgeon's tools, scalpels, and a .25 Colt automatic pistol."

The deputy coroner from Los Angeles, R.R. Creasey, testified next, describing his examination of the trunks.

Andrews asked him, "Which one of the trunks did you open first?"

"We opened the larger trunk."

"And what was disclosed when the trunk was opened?"

"Well, without delving into the contents, the head of Mrs. LeRoi was disclosed first." He confirmed Detective Ryan's testimony that the body was intact and folded into the trunk.

Andrews then asked him what else was in the trunk.

Creasey replied, "Soiled bedding, several articles of clothing, a piece of rug that looked as though it had been cut from a larger rug, a pair of ice skates attached to boots."

"And what did the smaller trunk contain?"

"It contained parts of the body of Miss Samuelson."

"Will you state just what portions of the body it contained?"

"The head, arms, upper part of the trunk, and just the lower limbs from the knees down."

"Were you present when the missing portion of the body was brought in?"

"Yes, sir."

"Do you recall who brought it in?"

"I recall one of the officers. I think it was Mr. Pinker."

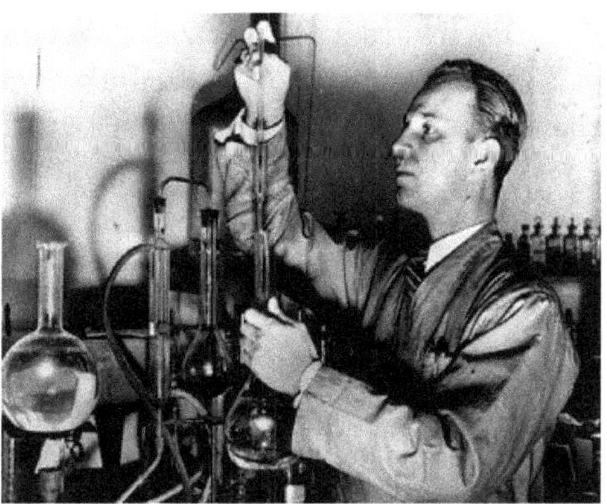

Ray Pinker, the forensic chemist for the LAPD, who testified at Ruthie's trial.

"And what was the missing portion of the body brought in?"

"It was the pelvis and the thighs and upper legs."

"Now, what was this portion of the body contained in?"

"A brown leather suitcase."

When the Los Angeles County autopsy surgeon, Dr. A.F. Wagner, took the stand to talk about the bullet wounds, the jury had already heard from two witnesses - Jennie McGrath and Gene Cunningham - who'd heard three shots ring out from the bungalow around 10:30 P.M. that Friday night. The prosecution now just needed to show there were three bullet wounds in the victims, and everything would fit.

The prosecutor asked him about the nature of the bullet wound in the head of the body removed from the larger trunk.

Wagner stated, "It was my opinion that the gun was up against the head."

"And was there any evidence of powder burns on the temple at the point of entrance of the bullet?"

"There was a dark smudge which appeared to me to be powder - I mean the carbon on unconsumed powder, gunpowder."

Andrews then asked about the direction the bullet had likely traveled. "The direction was downward?"

"Downward and backward," Wagner replied.

The surgeon also testified about the wounds and lacerations on the body taken from the smaller trunk. He said the two women might have been killed at the same time and that the dismembered body had been severed relatively soon after death.

From Dr. Wagner's testimony, it is easy to conclude that there were three wounds - two in Sammy and one in Anne. That was what the jury heard, but it was not exactly what the doctor said.

According to an examination of the records, the autopsy revealed Anne was shot once -- a single "contact wound" to Anne's head that was so close it left a powder burn behind.

But the autopsy also revealed that Sammy had *three* bullet wounds - not two. She was struck by one bullet that entered her left chest and traveled through her body, lodging in the left arm. Another bullet struck the ring finger of her right hand. Neither of those wounds were fatal. She died from a bullet wound to her head, shot, like Anne, at close range.

The autopsy found one other wound in Sammy's body - a superficial puncture wound on the left side of her neck. Dr. Wagner testified that he was not certain what had caused this stab wound but suggested it was from an instrument so flimsy that it couldn't do much damage.

Ruthie's attorneys dropped the ball on the bullet wounds. They never asked the jury to consider that if the neighbors heard three shots, when was the fourth shot fired?

They also never raised any doubt in the jury's mind about the strange puncture wound in Sammy's neck. Was this a stab wound inflicted by Ruthie during the right? Why was she wounded that way when the prosecution stated she was shot in bed, execution-style?

No one asked.

ANDREWS THEN BROUGHT SPENCER B. MOXLEY, a ballistics expert for the LAPD, to the stand. Moxley testified that the three shells and the bullet turned over to him had been fired from the .25-caliber gun in evidence.

For some unknown reason, Schneck attacked Moxley's qualifications as an expert and moved that his testimony be stricken from the record. The motion was denied.

Testimony continued as Dan Lucey, a Phoenix Police Department detective, was called to the stand. He was asked about his examination of Ruthie's apartment because the state was trying to prove that a shell found there on October 20 had come from the gun found in her baggage.

The defense objected. Lucey had examined the apartment four days after the murders, and it was not in the same condition when the detective arrived as it had been when Ruthie left.

The objection was left hanging. Judge Speakman adjourned court until Monday morning. He was, apparently, suffering from a head cold and wanted a fresh start after the weekend.

THE SECOND WEEK OF THE TRIAL OPENED with the courtroom so packed that one woman fainted and had to be carried out through the crowded hallways. Ruthie arrived in the ankle-length, black crepe dress she'd worn at her preliminary hearing. Her face was drawn and pale. As she took her seat at the defense table, she appeared unconcerned with the proceedings, even as the prosecution was introducing the critical empty pistol shell that might damage her story of self-defense.

Ruthie arriving in the courtroom at the start of the second week of her trial.

Detective Dan Lucey was back on the stand. He testified that the shell had been found in Ruthie's apartment, picking up where he'd left off on Saturday. When Andrews asked him precisely where the shell had been found, he replied, "In the southwest corner of the bedroom, under a chair."

This shell - as well as the first three in evidence - was said by ballistics expert Moxley to have been fired from the same automatic pistol.

Over renewed objections from the defense, Judge Speakman allowed the shell to be put into evidence. The jury was left to decide whether this might have been the shell that held the bullet that wounded Ruthie's hand, which the state claimed had been fired after the murders.

At this point, Andrews called Ruthie's landlord, Howard Grimm, to the stand to testify about the state of Ruthie's apartment, which had been a point of contention for the defense. He stated that the apartment had been empty from when Ruthie left on Sunday, October 18, until the detectives began their investigation.

Andrews called his investigator, John Brinkerhoff, to the stand to establish the identification of the bodies and their return to Phoenix.

He also called Phoenix detective McCord Harrison to testify about his investigations on the evening the bodies were discovered in L.A.

As soon as Andrews asked about his examination of the murder scene, the defense objected, "We object to it until the proper foundation is laid that the matters and things investigated were in the same condition as at the time of the alleged offense."

The objection was overruled but was soon renewed. Herman Lewkowitz spoke up. "If this is going in," he said, referring to Harrison's testimony, "I want to show the court some newspaper items and things in those items."

"Newspaper items?" Andrews asked.

"Yes, advertisements at 10 cents a head," Lewkowitz replied.

The jury was excused from the courtroom, and it was at this point that the defense presented the newspaper stories that showed that the owner of the house had been offering tours of the property between the time of the murders and some of the investigations conducted by the police.

"Can the state show whether or not this house was locked?" the judge asked.

"No, we can't show that," Andrews told him, but then said he could show that an examination of the murder scene had been made before the crowds began touring the bungalow. And he would - but, as mentioned earlier, we do know that more investigation was conducted later and that evidence was destroyed or "misplaced" during the interval.

Even though I already mentioned neglect by the police and the behavior of reporters and the public, I wanted to include some of the testimony here. If it wasn't so embarrassing to the police department and the prosecution - and to the court, which didn't see it as problematic - it would be comical.

Phoenix police officers George P. Larison and M.S. Frazier testified about being at the bungalow, about the back door being unlocked, and "about the half-dozen people that stopped by." Lewkowitz asked Larison about people touching things and picking them up.

"I don't recall seeing anyone pick up anything to carry it away," Larison said.

"Not to carry away, but to look at it. Did you see them with anything in their hands and tell them to put it back, and they followed your order?"

"I saw one of them over in the fireplace messing around where some stuff appeared to have been burned, and I told him to leave it alone," Larison sniffed as if he'd done his duty.

"Whatever was in the fireplace, this man disturbed it?"

Larison shrugged. "He probably messed around with his hand and stirred it up. There were just some ashes there, as far as I could see."

"And nothing else they touched?"

"I didn't see nothing else. There were papers on a table, and I told them to leave that alone. I recall in the kitchen there was someone looking around - and I told them to leave that stuff alone until the fingerprint man got there."

Of course, even in 1931, it was too late. The crime scene was contaminated beyond all hope.

The two officers were also asked about the blood they found in the house, and, once again, the defense dropped the ball - never questioning why, if Anne and Sammy had been shot in the head, there wasn't more blood in the bedroom.

After the police officers left the stand, Dr. H.L. Goss was called to testify about the tests that he performed on the blood samples from the bungalow.

Assistant County Attorney Rodgers asked, "Calling your attention to such examination as you made at that time, where did you find the blood spots that you examined?"

Goss replied, "We found certain spots throughout the entire house, with perhaps the exception of the front or living room, the reception room. We made... we took samples or purported blood from the bedroom and from the bathroom, from the dining room and the kitchen... I think a little breakfast room. Some of these were blood, and some were not."

Rodgers then directed him to explain to the jury what he did to determine which were blood spots and which were not and where he had found them.

"The spots in the bedroom on the floor and the floorboard we found to be blood," Goss continued. "At one spot in the dining room the kitchen, rather, the linoleum, those were the only spots which gave a positive test for blood. The others were all negative."

"Referring to the spot again that you said was out in the kitchen," Rodgers quickly spoke up, "were you able to determine from your analysis and investigation whether that was human blood or otherwise?"

The prosecution couldn't take the chance that blood in the kitchen meant that Ruthie's story was true - that she and the girls had fought there. It was a kitchen, though, so prosecutors wanted to imply it might be from some meat cooked there.

Ruthie, looking very concerned, speaking with Dr. Judd during the trial.

"No, I was not," Goss answered. "It was given a simple test for blood, but there was not enough to do a qualitative test to differentiate from other forms of blood."

Sticking with the theme of blood - and noticing there was no testimony about the mattresses, which prosecutors implied must have been "covered in blood," which is why they vanished - Mrs. Roger Thorpe was called to the stand. She and her husband owned the duplex. She identified the piece of blood-stained carpet found in the trunk as having come from the bedroom.

No one asked why, if the girls were shot in that room, there wasn't more blood on the rug than just enough to soak one of its corners.

THE AFTERNOON SESSION ON MONDAY BEGAN WITH Anne's dentists in Phoenix. By examining her dental work, he'd been able to identify her body. A second doctor had identified Sammy's body.

The realtor that Ruthie had been speaking with about renting the house for herself, the girls, and her parents testified that he'd last seen her on Friday, October 16, at his home between 5:30 and 6:00

P.M. She asked to use his car on Saturday so that she and her friends could visit the house.

The next witnesses were a former housekeeper for Anne and Sammy and Earle Riley, the Broadway department store plumber who'd removed the telegraph blanks that had become known as the "Drainpipe Letter" from the store's clogged sink.

Ruthie's jail fingerprint card was offered as evidence, and the defense immediately objected. Lewkowitz asked B.O. Smith, the county's fingerprint man, "At the time you obtained the data on this card for identification, was this party under arrest?

"Yes, sir."

"Did she have a lawyer present?"

"No, sir."

"Was she told of her constitutional rights?"

"No, sir."

"You just took her hand, put ink on it, and rolled them on the card?"

"Yes, sir."

Following a ridiculous discussion about whether Ruthie's constitutional rights had been violated by taking her fingerprints, even though she'd already been arrested and advised of her rights, Judge Speakman patiently asked, "At the time you say Mrs. Judd signed the card, was there any force used by you or anyone present?"

'No, sir," Smith replied. "In fact, she volunteered to do that several times before it was done."

The objection was overruled.

It's not clear why the defense attorneys were bickering over silly things like this while more important stuff - like the destruction of the crime scene and a lot of missing blood - was going right over their heads.

ON TUESDAY, THE PROSECUTION CALLED THEIR LAST witnesses, and they intended to save the strongest for last. They had been trying to create a scenario where Ruthie had killed her friends because of jealousy and rage - premeditated murder.

Andrews wanted to hammer that point home with the jury by presenting "proof" of that motive. To do so, you might expect that he brought in a line of witnesses who could show the growing state of her anger, but he didn't. He presented just two last witnesses, but they were enough.

The first witness was Mrs. Arthur Lepker. Her husband was a professional boxer who had recently been prosecuted for murder by Lloyd Andrews and had been sentenced to prison by Judge Speakman. There are no police reports that show detectives ever questioned Mrs. Lepker about the case. Her name appeared in this case for the first time when she took the stand that day.

She told the court that she had seen Ruthie only twice in her life - meeting her at some point during the summer and then seeing her in August when she came to the Grunow Clinic for a checkup. During that second meeting, she testified that Ruthie confided in her about her boyfriend. "The last name I do not know," she said, "whether it was Jack Halloran or Jack anybody."

Her remarks about "anybody" were stricken from the record before she was allowed to continue.

Mrs. Lepker continued: "And she made a remark that Jack was going to Los Angeles and that he was coming back for a day and then was going on to the eat to stay for two weeks. And she was indeed glad he was gone because she thought Sammy was trying to take Jack away from her. Who Sammy was, I do not know."

The prosecutor asked her what else was said during the conversation, and Mrs. Lepker added, "Mrs. Judd said that Sammy's boyfriend was here and that perhaps he would stay here, be here when Jack came back. And she said she got so angry at times about Jack and Sammy that she could - the remark she made was 'either go crazy or die,' or something like that, something to that effect."

During the cross-examination, Lewkowitz basically called the woman a liar. He questioned her almost angrily, suggesting it was very odd that Ruthie would share such intimate information with a clinic patient that she barely knew. "Why would she tell you such a thing?" the defense attorney repeatedly demanded.

"I don't know!" Mrs. Lepker snapped.

His efforts did nothing to discredit her with the jury.

But the prosecution's "star witness" was Lucille Moore - the woman referred to in records as "Doris Easton" to protect her anonymity because she was being treated for syphilis. That was something people didn't talk about in those days, and it could have even been damaging to the reputation of the Grunow Clinic if her condition became public.

Assistant County Attorney Rodgers asked Lucille about her activities the day before the murders: "And calling your attention to Thursday evening, that being the 15th day of last October, did you see the defendant, Mrs. Judd, on that evening?"

"Yes, I saw her that evening."

"Where did you meet her that evening?"

"She came to my home after me about 7:00 in the evening."

"Jack Halloran."

Rodgers asked her to recall the conversation that took place in the car on the way to the bungalow on North Second Street.

"When we started out to the apartment of Miss Samuelson and Mrs. LeRoi, Mrs. Judd asked Mr. Halloran to remember that he promised her if we went out there that they were not to know she was in the car, that she was there at all, and he said he would remember."

Rodgers then asked, "Now, when you arrived out there at the apartment of Miss Samuelson and Mrs. LeRoi, what is the fact as to whether or not you or Mrs. Judd went into the house?"

"Neither one of us went into the house. We both stayed in the car."

"Calling your attention to Jack Halloran, did he go into the house when you arrived there?"

"Yes, sir."

"And where did you and Mrs. Judd stay during the time he was in the house?"

"We remained in the car that was parked in the driveway."

"Now, as you were sitting there in the car at that time, did you have any conversation with Mrs. Judd?"

Lucille Moore – who had appeared in records as "Doris Easton" – while testifying at Ruthie's trial.

"Yes. When we drove up to the house, Mrs. Judd asked me if I knew who lived there. I said, 'No.' She answered, 'Well, I won't tell you then.' I said, all right, that if she didn't want me to know, that was her affair. Just after that, Anne came to the window and stooped down in front of the window and picked up something, I believe. Mrs. Judd looked at me and said, 'Now, you know who lives here.' I said, 'Yes.' A little bit later, she said, 'What do you think of Jack?' I said, 'He seems very nice.' Mrs. Judd then said, 'He is nicer than that; he is perfectly grand.'"

And then came the part of Lucille's testimony that the prosecutors had been waiting for. When he opened the trial, Lloyd Andrews promised to show that the relationship between Ruthie, Sammy, and Anne had been deteriorating for a long time. However, none of the witnesses had managed to do that up to this point, so Andrews saved a statement from Lucille Moore for the end of the prosecution's case. His entire theory was based on a single sentence Ruthie had supposedly uttered to Lucille the night before the murders:

Anne and Sammy think so, too. You know I used to live here with Anne and Sammy, but we had a little difference, and I moved away - in fact, that is what I moved over, our difference was about Jack.

When she was finished, the crowd in the courtroom waited eagerly to discover what questions Ruthie's attorneys would ask to lessen the blow caused by Lucille Moore's testimony.

But the defense counsel didn't ask her a single question.

They didn't try to counter the impression that Jack Halloran was the only reason Ruthie moved into her own apartment three weeks before the murders.

They could have reminded the jury that Ruthie was in the middle of negotiating the rent on a house large enough for herself, Anne, Sammy, and her parents.

They also could have used Anne's own words in the letter she wrote to show there was another motivation: "Ruth is leaving us in a few days. Dr. Judd is coming home so she will take an apartment. It really hasn't worked out so well, having three of us. We are very fond of her, and she is a sweet girl, but there just seems to be a wrong number when one is used to living with oneself and just one other very congenial one."

Or they could have used Ruthie's version of why she moved: "I found an apartment $5 a month cheaper and closer to the clinic, so I can walk to work and save the trolley fare." That had been in a letter to her husband.

But the jury never heard any of that.

They also never heard about how - just two days after she testified - Lucille Moore disappeared. She was found a week later in her hometown of Williams. She'd fled Phoenix, she said, because of ominous threats. Months later, a reporter for the *Los Angeles Examiner* wrote a story headlined, "Girl Nurse Reticent about Threats That Forced Her to Flee Trunk Killings Inquiry."

According to the story, Lucille got two death threats before she left town. The first time, a man called her on the telephone and said, "You've talked too much. You'd better quit." Soon after, an unsigned message was delivered to her home, warning her to leave Phoenix.

Who those unnamed callers and letter writers might have been remains a mystery. What else did they think Lucille knew? And why did they think she'd talk? No one knows.

HERMAN LEWKOWITZ BEGAN THE DEFENSE CASE with several minor witnesses. Among them were Mike Kerkes and his daughter, Stella, who testified to noticing Ruthie's bandaged left hand at the clinic on October 17. He also called the realtor, George E. Reese, who had been looking for a house large enough for Ruthie, the girls, and her parents. He'd last seen her on the night of October 15.

Ruthie's mother, Carrie McKinnell, who was always a difficult witness for attorneys – especially the prosecutors.

The first major witness called for the defense was Ruthie's 66-year-old mother, Carrie McKinnell. Lewkowitz asked her about an incident concerning a baby that had occurred when Ruthie was seven years old.

Carrie replied: "Well, she told some of her schoolmates and some of our neighbors that we had a baby at our house."

"Who had the baby?"

Carrie answered that she did. "The neighbors came to see it and told us they came to see the baby, and I could not imagine what they meant. They said, 'Why, Ruth said you had a baby,' and there was none."

"There was no truth to the matter then?"

"Not a bit."

Lewkowitz changed the subject. "About that time what were her habits insofar as being able to control herself in bedwetting?"

"Well, she had that habit for about 12 years."

"From infancy up to 12 years of age?"

"Yes, sir."

The attorney then asked about other unusual incidents in Ruthie's childhood.

Carrie sighed. "When she was 10 years of age, she took a notion she would make her own living and started to run away to Chicago. She went to one of the members of the church to tell her goodbye, and she told her where she was going to go - to Chicago. Well, she started, and they let us know about it. Mr. McKinnell went to get her, and he traced her through the cornfields. She would go back and forth like it was in her mind like she didn't know whether to go or come back. She would start one way and then start back. He looked around and followed her tracks as near as he could. He went back to the house where this girlfriend of hers lived, and she was there. Of course, he brought her home with him."

"How long was she gone that time?" Lewkowitz asked.

"Oh, it wasn't very many hours. They let us know immediately."

"Did anything occur when she was 16?"

"Well, yes."

"What was it?"

"She went with a young man, and we think that he was indiscreet."

"What was his name?"

"Fred Jensen."

"Fred Jensen," the lawyer repeated. "How old was Ruth then?"

"Sixteen."

"And how old was this young man?"

"He was 20... about 24."

"Where were you living?"

"We were at Olney, Illinois."

"Tell us about the incident."

"She was going to school in Greenville, Illinois. School was out in June, and she came home. This young man, when he saw her at church, wanted to bring her home. She says, 'No,' she says, 'I have company, and I have got to go home with the one I came with.' She said he asked her the third time right while she was with the other young man for her company, and she wouldn't go with him. He says,

'Well, maybe some other time.' Then he made a point to try and go with her. He would come and go with her to church sometimes, and sometimes he would take her to shows and sometimes go out car riding. Mr. McKinnell followed him out to the car one night and said, 'Fred, be good to my little girl. She is all the little girl I have.' He took her car riding and went way off quite a distance and came to a turn-off place that led into the woods. He stopped and asked her to get out. Well, she wouldn't do it. He took ahold of her and tried to pull her out. She held to the car, and she said she just asked God to let some car come along that would start them on so that he would let her alone."

Ruthie, deep in thought, during her mother's lengthy testimony.

Mrs. McKinnell paused in her account of the story that Ruthie had told her, obviously embarrassed by recalling such a story in front of a crowded courtroom. She went on: "I don't think she said that he had what he desired. I don't think that took place then. I don't remember what she said about that. I don't think it did, but when he got in, he said, 'Ruth, you are an angel, and I am a devil,' and he cried or pretended to cry, and so he brought her home. I don't know when this took place, but anyway, she thought he ought to marry her."

Then she told the court, "And the reason why I thought there must be something wrong, I found her making clothes for a baby."

A short time later, Carrie said that she took Ruthie to see Dr. Weber in Olney, and he examined her. He said she wasn't pregnant. When Lewkowitz asked her what happened next, she replied that she had woken up one morning and found that her daughter was gone.

"How old was she then?" the attorney asked.

"She was about 17."

"And what month was it?"

"I think it was October."

"When did you next locate her - er, how long after that did you locate her?"

"She was gone all that day and the following night and the next day. We were looking for her all the time, had people out looking for her. She came home that evening, the second evening."

"By herself, or did someone bring her?"

"She came by herself to our house, but she was brought from Calhoun by the Methodist preacher there."

"When she came home, where did she tell you she had been, or what, if anything, had happened to her?"

"She said she had been kidnapped, and these people had taken her to a house in Brown Station and put her in there. She said she stayed there all that day."

Lewkowitz told her to continue with the story.

"At night, she heard some voices," Carrie continued. "There were men's voices, talking to a woman where they put her - put her in a house where there was two women. She heard some voices of some men there. She went to a window and opened it and tore off the mosquito bar. That wasn't wire screen - it was just a screen - tore it off and slipped out. She said she just asked the Lord to direct her the way home, and she started the right way. She said she came down the railroad until she got to Calhoun. That was just about morning then, just about light. She said she went and got up into the loft of a garage so that she would not be seen in her nightclothes and a gunny sack that she had cut holes out to put her head and arms through."

"How long did she stay there?"

"She stayed there all day, or nearly all day. This preacher had occasion to be down there to the garage, and he climbed up in there. She had been asleep. When she saw him, she said, 'You get away from here!' and he said, 'I'm not going to hurt you.' He said, 'Why are you here?' She said she tried to find out why she was there, and he saw that she had a gunny sack on and he got clothes for her and brought her home."

Lewkowitz then asked her, "What, if anything, did your daughter do concerning Fred Jensen?"

"I hardly know how to answer that... She swore out a warrant to have him arrested."

"Your daughter did that?"

"Yes."

"Do you know if he was arrested?"

"Well, he wasn't there. I think I caught on to it that he was going to be arrested, and he skipped."

Mrs. McKinnell said that Ruthie was examined for pregnancy once more, and the doctor told her, "I don't think she has ever - that she has even been pregnant."

"Mrs. McKinnell, to your knowledge, has your daughter ever had a child?"

"No, sir, not to my knowledge."

When Lewkowitz was finished with his questions, Judge Speakman asked whether the cross-examination of the witness would be long. When Rodgers replied that it would, the judge - still suffering from his cold - adjourned court early that day, they would return at 9:00 A.M. the following morning.

Before Wednesday's session, Ruthie appeared more relaxed than she had been during previous days. She even embraced her parents for a cameraman making a newsreel about the trial.

But she became increasingly nervous when Mrs. McKinnell's cross-examination by the prosecution began with County Attorney Andrews reading to the jury from the now infamous "Drainpipe Letter," which debunked - in Ruthie's own words - many of the stories that she'd told her mother about Fred Jensen and her phony rape and kidnapping incidents.

Rev. McKinnell, dressed in his clerical collar and coat, followed his wife to the stand. He confirmed much of his wife's testimony for Lewkowitz and then went on to cite several instances of alleged insanity in their family history. They included his father's mother, his

Rev. McKinnell paused to kiss Ruthie on the cheek after he left the witness stand, where he described his family's long history of insanity.

father's brother, and his sister's son, who committed suicide at 27. He also mentioned two cousins of Ruthie, one who had died in an insane asylum in Peoria, Illinois, and another the family described as "mentally deficient."

During Rev. McKinnell's testimony, Andrews objected to testimony about hereditary insanity. However, Schneck argued that it was relevant and introduced a series of depositions from witnesses that corroborated the claims of mental illness in Ruthie's family.

When Rodgers began his cross-examination, he went straight to the question of Ruthie's own mental health and whether she met the criteria for being legally insane.

"When your daughter was a child, and during her young womanhood, Rev. McKinnell, she had good manners and behaved herself well, did she not?" Rodgers asked.

"Yes, sir, generally," Rev. McKinnell replied. "She manifested a hot temper, angry, and then she would be over it quickly."

"In other words, she became angry about in the way that people ordinarily do about things, didn't she?"

"I think so."

"She was usually, outside of the little incident to which you have referred in your testimony, obedient to her parents, wasn't she?"

"Fairly so, yes, sir."

"She seemed to have affair sense of right and wrong, did she not?"

"Well, except when she would get mad - then she did not have."

At the conclusion of the cross-examination, the judge called a recess so that a doctor could examine one of the jurors, who had become sick with a cold. Court was then recessed until 1:00 P.M. on Thursday since the doctor had ordered the juror to stay in bed until that time.

When the crowd of spectators - which had started gathering at 10:00 A.M. - returned on Thursday, though, they were disappointed to learn there would be no trial that day - or for the next few days. Because of the illnesses, Judge Speakman postponed the proceedings until the following Monday.

Friday was Ruthie's 27th birthday, and while Sheriff McFadden told the press, "Birthdays are the same as other days in jail," he allowed Ruthie's parents to stay with her for most of the day.

SHE WAS TOO SICK, SHE SAID. SHE COULDN'T POSSIBLY SIT in that cold courtroom all day.

On Monday morning, with the trial ready to continue, Ruthie claimed to be sick. She said she had pains in her side. An examination by the county physician, though, could find nothing wrong with her, and she wasn't running a fever. When Ruthie was still not ready by 8:30 A.M., she was told that she would be handcuffed and taken to court in a wheelchair. She miraculously improved, and she and the jail matron walked into the courtroom just after 9:00 A.M.

The defense began with more depositions to establish insanity in the McKinnell family and the reading of them droned on for an hour. Both the jury and the audience were becoming bored when Lewkowitz shocked everyone to attention by announcing that his next witness was Dr. William Judd.

In the testimony that followed, Judd explained that during his 22 years of medical practice, he had supervised or been on the staff of mental institutions in Oregon, Minnesota, and Indiana. He spoke of Ruthie's strange behavior in Mexico and several peculiar incidents after returning to the United States.

Dr. Judd testified, "I took her to Mexico, to an ideal location for her - a high, dry altitude. She had a perfectly open dwelling upon a mountain and the finest water and trees surrounding there. I tried to give her, as well as I could, just the treatment I would give a patient in an institution. I had two girls take care of her."

"For tuberculosis?" Lewkowitz asked.

"Yes, for tuberculosis."

The attorney then asked about the state of Ruthie's health when she and Dr. Judd had gotten married.

"She was tubercular at the time," Dr. Judd said. "She was coughing continually. She was having night sweats and had been for some time losing weight, having lost, I believe, in the last year, about 20 pounds."

He went on to say that her health had improved briefly after they were married, but it didn't last. Then, in 1925, Ruthie became pregnant, he said, but her health began to fail again.

"And the pregnancy, did it continue to the time of the birth of the child? What happened, if anything?" Lewkowitz asked.

Dr. Judd replied, "After about three months of pregnancy, her condition, mental and physical, had become so serious that I called another American physician from the Smelter Hospital, a few miles away, in consultation. After studying her case for some time, we thought we were justified in performing an abortion, which was done."

Dr. Judd looked uncomfortable as he continued, "She suffered very severely from the nausea of pregnancy so that she could retain almost no food whatever and was growing very weak. She was able to see that herself. She consented to having the abortion performed because she could see that she was failing too fast that she could not stand it the coming months."

"As to her mental condition?" the attorney questioned.

"Yes," the doctor sighed a little. "She was in a hysterical state a great deal of the time. She would have periods of weeping, sobbing, with no reason that one could know. She would have periods of laughing and dancing around, waving her hands, snapping her fingers as though in a state of exhilaration with nothing to cause any such outburst of pleasure or celebration. She showed some delusions.

For instance, she spoke a number of times of the baby as though it had been already born, spoke of it as though it was now in existence."

By now, most eyes in the courtroom had turned toward Ruthie. Most weren't outwardly staring but were staring at her sideways, wondering how she might behave as her husband began to discuss her mental deterioration. But Ruthie showed little emotion, she was sitting, staring at the table in front of her. She wasn't looking at Dr. Judd, who remained stiff and upright on the witness stand.

After his testimony on the witness stand, Dr. Judd was seen weeping while sitting on a bench in the hallway outside the courtroom.

Lewkowitz gestured for him to go on with his testimony. "She had several spells," Dr. Judd admitted. "I suppose I might say, to put it plainly, when she would be frightened by something which would be in her mind. In the night, she would spring out of bed, run clear out of the bedroom, hide in a closet. I could usually bring her out of this by taking her out and walking up and down the room. Several times, she remarked to me, 'I know I am dreaming.' She would go on with her sobbing, 'I know I am dreaming.' It would be several minutes before she could escape from this fear."

He glanced over toward his wife and then continued, "Altogether with her rapidly diminishing weight, her growing weakness, her recurrence of temperature, this mental condition was so serious so early in the pregnancy, we thought we were warranted in terminating the pregnancy when we did."

"And then, Doctor, during the rest of your married life, did pregnancy occur at any other time?" Lewkowitz asked him.

"Yes."

"When, Doctor?"

"1929."

"And where were you living then?"

"At Tayalto, Durango, Mexico."

"Was there anything about her getting in that condition that was unusual, Doctor, because of the circumstance of your married life?"

"Yes."

"Will you tell the jury what it was?"

Dr. Judd shifted again on the hard wooden chair and looked uncomfortable again. Then he spoke, "Because of her physical condition and because I was in no position, being uncertain as to my future as to where I would live or what I would do, to have a child, I had refused to permit her to become pregnant from the first day of our marriage. She had continually beseeched me, begged me to permit her to have a child. I told her that as soon as we could possibly do so, she could have one, but the time was not yet."

Dr. Judd shifted his gaze over to Ruthie, looking stunned in her chair at the defense table, before he looked back at Lewkowitz and continued, "I could reason with her. She'd admit what I said was true, was right, but at the end of our conversation, she would come again to 'Oh, I want a baby.' She would dwell upon what she would do with a baby, that she must have a baby. At the time she became pregnant, I had prepared for her to use an antiseptic douche, and the way it was used was a fairly sure prophylactic. After she had become pregnant, I found that she had deceived me in that she had not used the douche. She would go to the bathroom, running the douche water down through the toilet bowl, never using it at all. Of course, she only told me this afterward. I knew nothing about it at the time she was doing it."

"And you say she did become pregnant again. In what month was it, do you remember - 1929?"

"I would say it was in early May."

"And did she have a child with that condition - was a child born, or did something happen to it?"

"I did not know. I never knew she was pregnant," Dr. Judd confessed. "As soon as I found out she was pregnant, she said nothing whatever about it but asked me to let her go out to California and visit my sister and aunt there and revisit the La Vinia Sanitarium, where she had been some six months as a patient, a tubercular. I did not know this until long afterward. She went to California. I let her go, and there, in Santa Monica, while visiting my aunt and sister, she had an uninduced abortion. Of this, she told me nothing until long afterward."

"Do you know how far along she was at the time?"

"No, I don't."

"Now, will you explain to the jury what the term 'uninduced abortion' means?"

"One that was not caused by any operation?"

"Commonly called a miscarriage?"

"Yes."

"That happened about what month in 1929 if you recall?"

"July or early August, I would say."

"Doctor, during your married life, was there ever a child born to the marriage?"

"No."

"Did you ever, during the married life have a child living with you, a small child?"

"No."

"Nor your wife, to your knowledge?"

"No."

"You have not gone through any adoption proceedings for a child?"

"No."

"Nor had the care of one for such a length of time or in such a way as to have it in your home with you for any length of time?"

"No."

"And your wife has not done that to your knowledge?"

"No."

"Now, you lived in Mexico, and you and your wife were there. Under what circumstances did your wife come to Phoenix, Arizona?"

"We were at Agua Aita, Coahuila, Mexico. We came out together to the Port, a border town, Eagle Pass. I bought her a ticket to Indianapolis, Indiana, with her Pullman ticket. I boarded the train with her, and we went to Spoffard, Texas, a junction point for the railroad. She went on the train to Indianapolis. I took the next train going west to El Paso, where I had the promise of another position. About two weeks afterward, I was staying at the Del Norte Hotel, and she appeared there to see me. I had been wondering why I had not heard from her from Indianapolis, or rather from her home rather, in Indiana, Darlington. She told me she had taken the train to San Antonio and left the train, come to a hotel, stayed all night, the next morning gone to the station, the ticket office, cashed in her ticket to Indianapolis, and bought a ticket to Mexico City."

Dr. Judd paused for a moment. He looked almost as confused as the spectators, trying to keep up with this strange travelogue and understand how it would get Ruthie to Phoenix.

The doctor took up the narrative again: "When she reached Eagle Pass on her return, she found that she did not have money enough to allow her to continue her trip to Mexico City. So she had left the train then at Eagle Pass, just before reentering Mexico, and had sold her ticket to Mexico City, and now had come from Eagle Pass to El Paso in an automobile with a woman who wanted to drive from Eagle Pass to Los Angeles. I tried to get her to explain why she was going to Mexico City why she had bought a ticket to Mexico City, and for the first time, she showed a species of confusion and could give no explanation, saying she did not know herself. She had no friends in Mexico City, had a cousin living out of Mexico City in a mining town, but I don't believe Mrs. Judd ever knew where she was. Apparently, the reason she didn't go - she had only $16 and some cents in her pocket. It wouldn't even buy her a Pullman ticket to Mexico City. Well, the two women left the next day, starting on for Los Angeles. The next thing I heard of Mrs. Judd, she wrote me from Phoenix. They

Dr. Judd and Ruthie during a break in the trial.

had reached Phoenix and started for Los Angeles. Something about the car broke down. She came back to town, and she said she had got herself a job here. She was going to work here in Phoenix for a while. That is the story of her coming to Phoenix."

"At the time she left you and boarded the train going to Indiana, you may state whether or not the relationship between yourself and your wife was congenial?" Lewkowitz asked him.

"Absolutely," Dr. Judd exclaimed. "We never had a serious quarrel in all the time we were together - a statement I hate to make because so few women believe it, but it is true."

Lewkowitz then asked about Dr. And Mrs. Judd's residence at the duplex bungalow on North Second Street. "And how long were you neighbors, you and your wife, with Miss Samuelson and Mrs. LeRoi?"

"Six weeks, I should say."

"During that six weeks' time, state whether or not you were visiting back and forth, your wife and yourself?"

"Very frequently."

"And the two women?"

"We spent many evenings there, and the girls were back and forth, Sammy not so much - she spent most of her time in bed, Miss Samuelson did. Mrs. LeRoi was back and forth, and Mrs. Judd and I were in and out of their place frequently. We frequently went over there for dinner, and the girls came over and had dinner with us."

"For how long a period of time, to your knowledge, did the relationship of Mrs. Judd and these two ladies continue?"

"From January up until August 8, 1931."

"And then you left Phoenix, did you?"

"Then I left Phoenix."

"Now, when you left, where did you go?"

"Bisbee, Arizona."

"And from Bisbee, do you come back to Phoenix?"

"No, I did not."

"Where did you go from Bisbee?"

"To Los Angeles."

"And at the time of going from Bisbee to Los Angeles, did you notify Mrs. Judd of your leaving?"

"Yes."

"And was the relationship between you and your wife still continuing as friendly?"

"Perfectly so."

"And you remained, as I understand, in California and were there during the time this is alleged to have occurred in October?"

"Yes."

Lewkowitz asked Dr. Judd to describe an incident that occurred while he was living temporarily at the Copper Queen Hotel in Bisbee, trying to obtain a position at the local hospital. Ruthie had called him there just before lunch on Sunday, August 16, 1931.

He explained, "I thought at first that she was calling me in Bisbee from Phoenix. I asked her what was the matter. She said, 'No, I am not in Phoenix. I am in Bisbee.'" He asked her where she was staying, and she was also at the Copper Queen Hotel in room 27. At that moment, he assumed she had come down from Phoenix with a group

The Copper Queen Hotel in Bisbee, where Ruthie turned up unexpectedly while her husband was there seeking a job.

of friends, so he went to the desk to see who was in room 27 and discovered it was a single room booked to a woman named Lucy Rider. The register had been signed, and he recognized Ruthie's handwriting with the signature.

"And did you or did you not have any conversation with her about the registration at the hotel?" Lewkowitz asked.

"Well, as soon as she opened the door and I stepped in, she threw herself into my arms," Dr. Judd explained. "She threw her arms around my neck and went into a paroxysm of sobbing and crying as though she was in the deepest distress one could possibly be. She was almost hysterical. She was sobbing so loudly that I knew the other guests of the hotel would hear her. I drew her over to the bed and laid her down on the bed while I closed the transom, and went over and sat down beside her. I tried to get her to explain to me what was the matter. She was entirely incoherent. About the only words I could understand was, 'I don't know what is the matter. I don't know what is the matter. I don't know what is the matter with me.'"

Dr. Judd continued: "I think it was half an hour before I attempted to hold any conversation with her at all, and then I thought I might shift her mind from her trouble, whatever it was, for a few moments by changing her environment, getting her out of that room. So, I persuaded her to leave that room and come up to my room. Then I tried to talk with her and tried to get her to explain how she came to be in Bisbee, and why she came down. Her only answer was, 'I don't know. I don't know what is the matter. I guess there is something the matter with me.'"

"Did you learn anything else?" Lewkowitz asked him.

"Finally, she told me she had come down the night before. When she told me she had come there a little after 10:00 the previous evening, had spent the night in that hotel there with me, not 100 feet away from me, and had never called or communicated with me until noon the following day, I told her, 'Well, Ruth, I guess you are right. I guess you are crazy.' I thought that might irritate her enough that she would give me some explanation, but it didn't."

Dr. Judd kept talking, explaining further what had occurred in Bisbee in August: "She spent the afternoon there with me. Several times, I reverted to the subject, 'Now, Ruth, come on and tell me what it is, what is the matter, why did you come down here and stay the night, and all this forenoon, and never communicate with me?' She didn't know why. The only explanation she could give was that on the way down, in some way, there was a fire started in the bus. She went down on one of these Greyhound buses. There was a fire started in the bus, and she was asleep. Somebody shouted in her ear and awakened her. She sprang up and jumped out of the bus, fell down, and soiled her dress. She ran down the road a ways in fright, and she said she went into the hotel, the lights of the hotel showed her how soiled her dress was."

Lewkowitz asked him why Ruthie had registered under a false name, but he wasn't sure. Dr. Judd stated, "She just hated to register there as my wife, so she thought she'd register under another name, I suppose, then call me up. Then, she didn't know what was the matter. She could never force herself to go to see me or to notify me that she was there in the hotel, but she did call me twice by phone. She disguised her voice so that I didn't know who it was until afterward. Once she called me and said nothing except, 'Who is this, who is speaking?' until I lost my temper and hung the receiver up. The second time, she called up and gave me a fictitious call to answer. She said she just wanted to see me go out of the hotel."

The defense attorney then asked about Ruthie's arrest. Now, I will ask you if you were not called at the time of the arresting of Mrs. Judd?"

"Yes, I was."

"You were in court when Officer Ryan testified that he arrested Mrs. Judd, mentioning the street. I forgot just where he said it was, did you hear that testimony?"

"Yes."

"I will ask you if you were familiar with the circumstances leading to her arrest on that day at that time?"

"Yes, I am."

"And will you state whether or not, to your knowledge, any arrangements were made for her being delivered into the custody of the officers, arrangements in advance, prior to her arrest?

"I cannot say definitely what arrangements were made, "Dr. Judd admitted." I had my arrangements with Mrs. Judd, and she met me when I went up to the Alvarez Undertaking parlors. Several hours afterward, the county officials, police, and deputies were there. Just what time Mr. Cantillon and Judge Russell notified them to come, I do not know."

The prosecution had only a few questions for Dr. Judd. Rodgers delved into their married life and some of the strange behavior Dr. Judd had testified to, which Ruthie had mentioned in the "Drainpipe Letter," but he didn't want to spend much time with those stories. He was convinced that Dr. Judd had been well-coached to make his wife's behavior look as peculiar as possible, hoping to score points with the jury with the insanity defense.

Rodgers had no interest in helping them with that.

THE BATTLE OF THE PSYCHIATRISTS BEGAN ON MONDAY afternoon. The defense first called Dr. George W. Stephens, superintendent of the Arizona State Hospital. Schneck began by asking about his qualifications, clarifying that he had an extensive background in neuropsychiatry and that he'd visited Ruthie at the county jail between 20 and 25 times.

When asked whether Ruthie knew right from wrong on October 16 - if she had committed the act she'd been charged with - Stephens replied: "She did not know the nature of the act and was irresponsible." He admitted that, at the beginning of the trial, he felt he could not make a positive diagnosis, but he had seen enough during the trial to convince him that he "need not have hesitated a moment."

Dr. Stephens recounted some of the incidents that occurred while examining Ruthie, including once when she had asked him if he'd seen her baby.

He replied: "No, have you a child?"

Ruthie told him, "Yes, I want you to help me get that child." She claimed that her child had been taken from her by an unnamed woman who lived on East Thomas Road.

Ruthie asked him if he wanted to see a photograph of her baby, and when Dr. Stephens said that he did, she showed him a picture pinned to the underside of the mattress above her lower bunk. He also noticed that photos of Anne and Sammy were similarly pinned up in the same spot.

He also cited instances of what he considered Ruthie's delusions, including her alleged mistreatment by county officials.

Schneck asked him, "And what particular classification did you give to the form of insanity you deem here present?"

"Dementia praecox," Dr. Stephens stated confidently. "I first came to that conclusion that it was psychosis with a psychopathic personality." When asked, he added that he believed there was a paranoid trend to her insanity. "Yet there are other trends that go to make up dementia praecox - we call it schizophrenia."

"What does dementia praecox mean?" Schneck asked.

"Dementia praecox is a definite disease or insanity which is an insidious one coming along about the time of adolescence - usually between the ages of 15 and 25, had definite characteristics which fix it as that type of disease. There are a number of types of insanity or psychosis."

"May I ask you, Doctor - the two terms, dementia praecox, what particular significance has the word 'dementia' there?"

"The word 'dementia' is deterioration of the mind."

"Actual physical deterioration of the mind, is it not?

"Yes, sir."

"And 'praecox' means youth?"

"Yes, sir."

"Now, then, you said schizophrenia was but another name of dementia praecox. Will you split that word up if you can and tell us what it means?"

"Well, that means - as far as I can define it - it means rather an ego eccentric existence, living within one's self, or rather, I don't know exactly how I could express it to the jury."

"May I ask you, does not the word 'schizo' mean to split?"

"Yes, split personality."

"I don't want to lead the witness," Schneck said, "but maybe we can get it reduced to language we may understand."

County Attorney Andrews objected to Schneck's attempts to simplify what he called "these great long jaw-breaking names." This got a chuckle out of some jury members, which Schneck undoubtedly hoped for. He was trying to make things easier for the salesmen, farmers, and clerks in the jury box to understand that his client was insane and how medical science could reveal this. He was fighting, he knew, an uphill battle, but if he could dumb things down, so to speak, he might have a chance.

Andrews added, "We are willing for the counsel and witness to do that, but let the witness boil it down, not the counsel."

The judge agreed, and Schneck asked Dr. Stephens to continue. "You say you made a definite diagnosis of dementia praecox?"

"Yes, sir, and I didn't definitely say paranoia dementia praecox. I think it is a mixed type, and I haven't definitely decided."

Schneck asked him to explain what he'd based his findings on, and Dr. Stephens answered, "I based this on the deterioration of this young woman almost from infancy to the present time and particular deterioration that has come about in the last two years."

He gestured over toward Ruthie, sitting at the defense table. "I counted one minute, and she folded that handkerchief four times, which would make about, I think, 1,640 folds to the day's work." He also recalled her emotions during one recess when he said, "The emotions jumping from blazing anger, you might say, to mirth - and that is not normal."

He concluded, "She has no connected train of thought."

Schenck asked whether Ruthie's delusions were hereditary.

"They certainly are," said Dr. Stephens. "They certainly come from hereditary traits that are handed down." He said that he also found that many cases of dementia praecox were associated with tuberculosis.

Prosecutor Rodgers began his cross-examination of Dr. Stephens by attacking his qualifications. Questioned about the political nature of his position. Dr. Stephens confirmed that he had been replaced by one of his assistants for two years.

"And so then, you came back at the beginning of 1931, when the political complexion changed again in the state?" Rodgers asked him.

"That is correct," Dr. Stephens sniffed.

Rodgers hammered Stephens repeatedly about his diagnosis, forcing him to repeat himself several times. Exasperated, the doctor finally retorted, "I have talked pretty thoroughly on it, but, of course, the council doesn't get it."

"Don't worry about me," Rodgers snapped, "you just take care of yourself."

"Oh, I'm going to," Dr. Stephens assured him.

On Tuesday, a second medical expert, Dr. Edward Williams from Los Angeles, was called for the defense. His specialty, Schneck obtained from him, was "nervous and mental diseases." Williams had examined Ruthie once in jail and testified that she wouldn't have known the difference between right and wrong if she had committed the act charged. His diagnosis was similar to that of Stephens, but he added a reference to the endocrine glands as a causative factor for Ruthie's insanity.

Ruthie listened to the parade of doctors who testified about her mental health with seemingly little interest.

Dr. Williams focused particularly on the thyroid glands, the reproductive glands, and others. He said the use of the thyroid for curing insanity "happened to be a most important event in psychiatry." Citing the number of cases cured in mental institutions, he said, "They have cleaned out all the back halls because they have been given this treatment." He added that the reproductive glands "play a very important part in most cases, at least a high percentage of cases of dementia praecox."

Schneck gave him the space to continue, and Dr. Williams went on: "In this defendant, she is an undeveloped - she is not a fully developed woman in this sense, that there has not been a sufficient action of her - of the ovarian secretion so as to produce a person who is entirely normal in physical makeup. That is, she is what we call a 'eunuchoid,' a eunuch being a person with no organs of reproduction, and eunuchoid being one with those not acting enough - the arms being too long, legs too long, and pelvis too narrow. She is underdeveloped."

Dr. Williams maintained that dementia praecox usually began in puberty and said, "She has a history of beginning menstruation at 13, and then she skipped for almost a year, and then another period, and then skipped again for a year. That shows faulty development during the time she was in this episode about the young man and the supposed pregnancy when I believe she did not menstruate."

"What particular sphere of mental activity is first affected by this disease - volitional, emotional, or intellectual? Schneck asked him.

"Well, it is emotional. It is the judgment and so forth, not the intellect. That is, many of these people can remember, many of them continue to be very smart, continue to be very intelligent, but it is the emotions, their feelings, the emotional sphere, as we call it, in distinction from the intellect."

He added that people suffering from dementia praecox showed, as a rule, a lack of emotion or feeling. At other times, "they will laugh, silly laughter about nothing, or have crying spells about something."

When the witness was passed to the prosecution for questioning, Rodgers cited a book called *Insanity Plea* that Williams had written. Williams acknowledged that, as he had written in his book, he did not feel expert witnesses should be questioned by a person who doesn't know as much about insanity as a doctor. He explained, "My theory being, which I believe is held by every intelligent and honest physician, that these cases should not be brought before a jury of laymen because it is unjust, and that the doctors should make their reports, come to their conclusions as they please, be appointed not by either side but by the magistrate himself and make their reports to him."

When Rodgers asked him if malingerers or frauds have ever fooled experts in insanity, Dr. Williams answered, "I suppose they have, but when we find them malingering, we know the majority of malingerers are insane."

Rodgers then asked him if he thought Mrs. Judd knew right from wrong. Dr. Williams stated, "She did not know right from wrong, not anything like in a normal sense. If she had, she would have certainly, in this case. If she did this, she would have certainly taken a more intelligent means of getting rid of the bodies. She had every opportunity in the world to have it made out that it was a case of suicide and murder. She took, if she did it, the most absolute asinine way to get rid of the bodies imaginable."

As Rodgers was completing his cross-examination, he referred again to Dr. Williams' book and the view expressed in it that because under the present law, physicians had to testify before a jury of laymen, they would be justified in tailoring their testimony to fit the legal definition of insanity if, in their opinion, the accused was medically insane. "In other words," Rodgers clarified, "you believe that in certain contingencies - what you term in your book as a slight bending of the truth - is warranted?"

"I have said so in the book, so I must believe it," Dr. Williams replied.

Rodgers completed his cross-examination, but Schneck had more questions before his witness left the stand. He asked Dr. Williams if he had read a book called *Manual of Psychiatry* by Dr. Paul Bowers.

Before Williams could answer, the jury was excused from the courtroom, and Judge Speakman cautioned the defense attorneys. "Don't go adrift into the realms of mysteries so far as we laymen are concerned, except upon the questions involved in this case."

Schenck turned back to Williams and asked, "You would consider Freudian theories of repressed desires as an exploded theory, would you not?" By that, Schneck meant that the theory had been disproved or discredited.

"I think so," said Dr. Williams. "He had a lot of words that were good, but I consider the general theory as exploded."

The defense called one more expert witness to the stand. Dr. Clifford A. Wright had started the Psychoendocrine Clinic with Dr. Williams. It was then a department at the Los Angeles General Hospital. Dr. Wright said he had specialized in endocrinology for about 15 years and, on the stand, confirmed much of the testimony already offered by Stephens and Williams.

But he did have some additions: "This girl was born in a religious family, was repressed. She says the earliest recollections are being taken to protracted religious meetings, revival meetings, kept up until 10:00 or 11:00. It made quite a feature in her family. Very early, she worried about the meaning of the religious songs as pertaining to herself."

He continued, "Now she has delusions surrounding recent events. She feels that the District Attorney, Mr. Andrews and Mr. Harris, are in a league against her. She says they play golf together and put up a job to have her hanged. She says that Mr. Harris would kill her on the streets if he could. She also has a delusion of men on the roof of the jail. They come over there nearly every night, call her by name, and a few nights ago, they had a flashlight there. At first, she thought these people were friends. Now, she feels they are there to kill her."

THE STATE BEGAN ITS REBUTTAL TESTIMONY WITH several witnesses that were called to confirm the state's contention that Ruthie was sane during the months leading to the murders.

Dr. Paul Bowers followed them to the stand, and his testimony so angered Ruthie that she attacked him after court had adjourned for the day. Walking in the hallway, she grabbed a jail matron's arm and shoved her at Dr. Bowers, who was knocked against the wall. When Sheriff McFadden grabbed hold of her, Ruthie kicked him, but her fury was still directed at Bowers. "My husband will get you!" she shrieked.

After he had been qualified as an expert in psychiatry, Dr. Bowers told the jury that Ruthie was sane on October 16 and was capable of knowing right from wrong. He had given her a neurological and mental examination.

"I asked her if she was happy or sad, or indifferent or elated," Bowers explained. "Her answer was, in substance, 'Why talk about that? Nobody likes to be in jail. I am here on a serious charge. I wish my husband was here. I don't like to talk when he is not around.'"

Bowers continued, "When she wanted to answer questions directly, her answers were always to the point and correct. At no time was her conversation incoherent, irreverent, or absurd. She said that she had sexual relations with her husband when he was well and experienced orgasms and that she wished to become pregnant. She was wild about children and said she was anxious to have a baby with Mr. Halloran, that she had sexual relations with him for a number of months, that sex relations with him were satisfactory. She says she felt that she loved her husband, but she loved him in a maternalistic way, that he had been sick. She said she felt differently toward Mr. Halloran, a romantic feeling toward him. Said she worried about the fact that she told Dr. Judd about the sexual relations. She grieved because this information hurt him, and she was sorry for that."

The prosecutor steered him toward whether Ruthie was aware of right and wrong. Bowers replied: "I inquired of her if it was right to steal, to lie, to commit burglary, to commit adultery, to kill. She said it was wrong to lie, to steal, but in self-defense one might be excused for killing. Said she didn't care to talk about adultery and if one were really in love with a person, that adultery was not so wrong as it might seem."

"And what did she say about her defense?"

Bowers replied, "She was asked what her defense was going to be, in other words, 'What story are you going to tell?' She said, 'That depends on the kind of a break I get. I may tell everything that I know. I will just have to wait and see. Mrs. Halloran will help me, but he is not in a position to do so. They would have him arrested if he came around here.'"

"I asked her," Fried continued, "if she ever had any homosexual relations, and she vehemently answered, 'No, I never had. I am not that kind of girl. Sammy and Anne may have had those kind of relations. They seemed to have loved one another more than usual, but I won't say they did have. I won't talk about them like that.'"

On Wednesday, Paul Schneck had his go at Dr. Fried, and things quickly became hostile. They waged a verbal battle for almost six hours, each attacking the others' opinions about Ruthie's mental health. Discussing various definitions of insanity, Bowers said, "I'm not a Freudian, and neither do I agree with White. I don't agree with any author, particularly in all his entirety."

"Let's go back," Schneck quipped. "We will be over in Germany in a minute."

"Stay in Arizona," Judge Speakman warned.

Throughout most of the cross-examination, Bowers was hostile and sarcastic. At one point, Schneck asked about Ruthie's skeletal structure. "I don't think she was ever very fat," he said.

"The bones are always slim," Bowers dismissed him. "I never saw any fat bones."

"If you meant to be facetious, we will try that," Schneck replied.

Asked if he agreed with the author of a book called *Dementia Praecox*, Bowers said, "Inasmuch as it agrees with my own personal experience. I accept no authority as absolute other than God Almighty."

Bowers stated that he thought Ruthie was malingering or faking insanity. Schneck asked, "She punched you in the back yesterday?"

"Yes, I think she did. She punched me quite vigorously, with a little purpose."

"You think that was malingering also?"

"Her foot slipped accidentally on purpose, kind of gave me a real good bump, so I knew she was around."

During Bowers's testimony, Schenck had a blackboard brought into the courtroom, and he used it to illustrate Ruthie's family tree and Mendel's theory of heredity to establish that she suffered from inherited insanity. Mendel's theory, by the way, states that traits are passed from parents to their offspring through genes, with each individual inheriting two copies of a gene - one from each parent - and leads to predictable patterns of what the child inherits.

So, if enough people in Ruthie's family were crazy, according to Schneck, then it makes sense that she was crazy, too.

But Bowers wasn't buying that - and neither was the prosecution. They continually objected to Schneck's questions, diagrams, and family trees, while Bowers kept saying that he couldn't comment on Schneck's diagrams because they didn't conform to Mendel's law. Judge Speakman just kept trying to arbitrate the confusion as Schneck drew one diagram after another.

Psychiatrists for the state at Ruthie's trial – Dr. Joseph Catton (Left) and Dr. Paul Bowers

During his redirect examination, Rodgers asked Bowers if the Mendelian theory had anything to do with the case and the doctor replied that there was no way to say. Even if there was some defect in the defendant's family history, it was just as likely that Ruthie didn't inherit it as if she did.

Dr. J.D. Maudlin, the county physician, expressed his belief that Ruthie was sane and was pretending to be mentally ill.

The last of the state's rebuttal witnesses was Dr. Joseph Catton, the assistant professor at Stanford Medical School who had already made waves in the case by revealing portions of his interviews with Ruthie to the press. He continued to create a sensation in the courtroom during his testimony.

He referred back to his interview with Ruthie. He recalled asking her, "Did you drink anything at the girls' house that night?"

"No," she had answered.

"Did anybody drink there, or was anybody drinking there that night?" he asked, and Ruthie had replied that only Jack Halloran had been drinking, and then, Dr. Catton said, "She quickly put her hand over her mouth and said nothing further."

Dr. Catton spent most of the day on the witness stand, taking four hours to answer a 17-word question that had been put to him in the morning session. This was a man who loved to hear himself talk.

"It is my opinion that she was sane," he said, "so that she was able to comprehend the rightness and wrongness of the act if she committed it." He added that she responded to his examination in the same way that any normal average person would have done.

Catton testified that he had given Ruthie a physical as well as a mental exam. "As a matter of fact," he said, "I believe if Mrs. Judd had about 15 pounds more weight, that she would make a very good model for a woman of her particular height and size in some dress establishment. In addition to looking over her body for various defects and about those endocrine glands, let me tell you this under oath --- I would be the most ridiculous ass if I said this girl was a eunuch or eunuchoid.

He shook his head as if responding to the ridiculousness of this claim. "Mrs. Judd gave me absolutely a clean bill of health regarding hallucinations," he said. "Never had them in her whole life."

Catton added, "I found this girl to be a little tiny more than average modest. She kept covering her shoulder if this thing would drop down when I was examining her. She had that little refined business of putting her skirt down a little further when I examined her, and I found her emotions showed her related to modesty."

He said Ruthie's emotions were characterized by modesty, sympathy, and pity. "She showed revulsion," Catton told the attorney, "to the fact that the girl was cut up. She showed average normal feelings of bitterness over the reactions toward her of the two girls who had been killed, telling me that these girls didn't treat her squarely. That in spite of the fact that she used to wait on these girls when they were sick - she used to shampoo their hair, rub their scalps, do this and that for them - there was no reciprocation. As a matter of fact, they treated her meanly rather than by reward. She showed bitterness in that connection. She showed scorn, scorn for Jack Halloran, telling me that this Jack Halloran had come into her life and, just like the rest of men, wouldn't raise a finger to help her even though she may be hanged."

Dr. Catton said that he tried to discover the depth of Ruthie's jealousy toward the girls but said that the moment he mentioned her jealousy, Ruthie hesitated and seemed deep in thought. She spoke rapidly to him, "I am not a jealous woman. I have never been jealous in my life. Why, Dr. Judd used to have mistresses before he was married. I insisted - I not only allowed it, but I insisted - that he write to those people now. I want to tell you that Jack Halloran, while I love him with my whole heart and soul and more passionately than I ever loved my husband, I have not been jealous of him."

Catton stated, "She said she never violated her marriage vows until December 24, 1930. Ruth Judd says that night she slept with Jack Halloran and sex relations took place. She says from that time on, until the time that these crimes were committed, that even including 10 of the 14 days preceding October 16, this love life continued."

Catton said that he asked: "Mrs. Judd, is it ever right to take a human life?"

"Yes, in self-defense," she had answered.

"Is it ever right under any other conditions?"

"No," she said.

Catton had asked her about the "Drainpipe Letter," and Ruthie became upset: "Now, just a minute, Doctor, I have never admitted that I wrote that letter. I don't know whether I am going to say I wrote it or not. Some of the lawyers in Los Angeles told me I wrote it, and Mr. Cantillon told me I didn't. Mr. Lewkowitz says I didn't. And I don't know whether I am going to say I wrote it or I didn't."

Ruthie had reportedly received as much as $5,000 for writing an article for one of the Los Angeles newspapers, and Catton asked her about the article. He said, "I asked her if she had written this article for the paper, and she informed me that she had not written it. I told her that she had previously told me that she had written the article, but that in some places she had been misquoted, and she said, 'I did not write that article.' I asked her if it was true that she had received $5,000 for writing that article, and she said, 'Yes.' I asked her if she had any other sources of finances to help her in her trial and she closed her lips tightly and turned away. She said, 'I will not answer that.' I asked her specifically if Jack Halloran or any other person was putting up the money, and she said she would not answer that."

When he asked her about comments she'd allegedly made about Anne and Sammy, Catton claimed that she told him that doctors she worked for at the clinic had warned her to stay away from the girls. She was told they were "homosexual perverts," Catton said. "She had seen them sleeping together and making rather excessive love, one with the other."

Catton recalled an examination of Ruthie when he discovered that she had not lost a sense of humor. When informed that the doctor had arrived, she said, "I know doctors. They always keep us waiting, so now they can wait for me."

"She didn't cry at all on the second examination," Catton told the court, "not a tear, unless she cried when I was out of the room. She did smile, and at one time when we were talking about revival meetings, she quoted some little song. I don't remember all of it, but she included something about wanting to go to heaven on roller skates. Then she volunteered, 'Do you know, I used to imagine out and act out all of those songs?' When she thought back to when she was forced to attend revival meetings with her parents, Ruthie told him, "I used to picture myself doing things and being in the places they were talking about."

During that second examination, Catton had asked her again about her defense: "Mrs. Judd, as a matter of fact, you have never cut a human being in your life."

She answered, "I am going to say that I did."

"Please answer the question," he urged her. "Have you ever in your whole life cut a human being under any condition?"

She replied, "Dr. Catton, I have never even cut a chicken."

"Won't you tell, or aren't you going to tell, the complete facts of this case?"

"If things do not go the way they are planned," she had replied, "believe me, I will get up there and tell them everything."

When the state was finished with Dr. Catton, court was adjourned until Saturday morning. Friday was Arbor Day, which was then a legal holiday.

When both sides returned to the courtroom on Saturday, sharp remarks were exchanged between Paul Schneck and Dr. Catton, with Schneck even going as far as to belittle him over the fact that he'd never been given a full professorship at Stanford.

After a lengthy back and forth, Catton acknowledged "that it is entirely possible that any symptom of insanity may be more or less apparent at one time and not so apparent at another time." But that was as much as Schneck could get from him. Catton managed to withstand the attorney's other attacks on his testimony.

Schneck finished with Catton on the stand at 4:32 P.M. A night session had seemed possible, especially after Judge Speakman had announced that they would stay "until midnight if necessary" to allow Schneck to finish his cross-examination of Catton. Thankfully, they didn't have to stay.

Court was recessed until 9:00 A.M. on February 8 when - the jury and spectators in the court believed - Winnie Ruth Judd would tell her story. She was fighting for her life, and it seemed impossible to everyone watching the case unfold that she wouldn't get on the witness stand.

BUT SHE DIDN'T.

Ruthie's original version of events was that the murders were committed in self-defense. Her lawyers claimed she was insane. The prosecution maintained that it had all been premeditated - the work

Ruthie with her attorney, Paul Schneck. She would always claim that she had wanted to testify at her murder trial, but her attorneys wouldn't allow it.

of a jealous woman. But what Ruthie was thinking during the trial remains unknown.

Even though a defendant is never required to testify in the American justice system, it would turn out later that many of the jury members thought it strange that Ruthie wasn't asked to tell her story. Her silence seemed to cement the idea that she had something to hide. The jurors surmised that the defense didn't have her testify because they were using an insanity plea, and they didn't want her to get on the stand and act sane.

Many of the courtroom observers were just as disappointed. They didn't understand why she didn't get up there and set the record straight. They thought she claimed it was self-defense, so why doesn't she tell us what happened?

But they weren't the only ones who were disappointed. Herman Lewkowitz was also very unhappy with the decision. He constantly found his hands tied by Paul Schenck. The defense team had fought about Ruthie taking the stand throughout the trial. Lewkowitz continually advocated for her testimony and always felt he would have won the case if she had testified. Schneck was firmly against the idea, though.

When the trial was over, Lewkowitz was so frustrated that he even petitioned Judge Speakman for a new trial on the grounds that

Ruthie had "not received adequate defense counsel." He claimed that Schneck "called the shots" during the trial and ignored his advice and efforts in mounting a vigorous defense. The judge rejected the petition.

Many years later, in an interview, Ruthie Judd claimed to be angry that she could never testify. Lewkowitz had insisted that she could, and she wanted to take the stand, even claiming that she still thought she would get to testify on the day the judge pronounced her sentence. "I didn't know it was over," she claimed. "I didn't know what was happening. I didn't know anything about the law. The judge said it was too late."

But others don't believe she ever planned to testify. In her own interview, Francie Andrews, widow of the county attorney, later said that her husband repeatedly begged Ruthie to tell her story. "He gave her lots of opportunities," she stated, "but she never said anything."

Jury members turned out not to be impressed with the testimony given about Ruthie's mental state. They dismissed the stories from her parents because she hadn't lived with them for a long time and were bogged down by all the technical jargon about dementia praecox and insanity caused by tuberculosis, which caused her to have delusional fantasies, behave erratically, and be unable to carry out a complicated plan.

But as a juror named Stewart Thompson said during an interview more than 60 years after the trial, "But she never opened her mouth once, so how are you going to tell? Her actions seemed like she knew what she was doing."

He also recalled, "They had all these high-priced psychiatrists on both sides talking about schizophrenia. We didn't know what schizophrenia was. And one of them said she was suffering from that, and the other side said she wasn't."

The jury's confusion over the insanity testimony was cleared up by Judge Speakman in their final instructions. Thompson added, "We knew it was a very serious matter we were in, and we wanted to do the right thing, and we wanted to follow the judge's instructions. The judge told us all we had to determine was if she knew right from wrong. If she didn't, she was crazy. If she did, she wasn't. The evidence showed that she tried to hide it. Someone who knows the difference between right and wrong - that's what they'd do, try to hide everything."

That's not entirely accurate -the judge actually gave the jury six possible verdicts to choose from, but only the right-from-wrong one stuck in their minds.

But the bodies in the trunks, the plan to dump them in the ocean, getting her brother to help - all those things said to the jury that Ruthie knew right from wrong.

Francie Andrews never had doubts. "She wasn't legally insane," she later said. "For that, you don't know the difference between right and wrong - but she was nuttier than a fruitcake. She was a mean, bad woman. She killed those girls all by herself. She shot herself in the hand. And she cut up that body by herself, too."

But it wasn't that cut and dried for many other people. There seemed to be little doubt that Ruthie had shot Anne and Sammy, but many were still convinced she'd had help along the way. And they couldn't understand why her accomplices were not exposed during the trial.

Jack Halloran's name was mentioned repeatedly during the trial, and although he had been sworn in like other witnesses, he was never called to testify.

It had created a stir in the courtroom on the day that Jack was spotted with the other potential prosecution witnesses being sworn in. He looked at Ruthie, some claimed, but she turned away. A short time later, Halloran's name was conspicuously absent when Lloyd Andrews read off his witness list. The press reported that Jack whispered something to Andrews as he left the courtroom, and he was never called back. Andrews was quoted as saying that he only intended to use Jack as a rebuttal witness if he needed him.

As for Halloran, he issued a formal statement at the start of the trial that said, in effect, he was "innocent but perhaps indiscreet."

Francie Andrews was convinced that her husband was voted out of office in retaliation for never calling Halloran as a witness.

But would it have made any difference?

ON THE MORNING OF FEBRUARY 8, ASSISTANT County Attorney Rodgers began the state's closing arguments, followed by the defense. They continued until 4:40 P.M., only interrupted once when a woman in the audience fainted and had to be carried out of the courtroom.

County Attorney Lloyd Andrews (front left) conferring with other prosecutors about the Judd case, including Los Angeles D.A., Buron Fitts (front right)

He attacked the defense plea of insanity as an "excuse for the crime. I don't criticize the attorneys for their attempt. It was to be expected. There is nothing else they can do. But that doesn't mean you gentlemen must swallow it, that you should free this defendant on opinions here expressed on her insanity. When all other defenses fail, look over and anon for the claim of insanity. Subterfuges, however, are neither here nor there when measured by the standard of human justice which says, 'Thou shalt not kill.' I shall not presume to tell you men what you should or should not do, but it occurs to me if you desire to protect and secure the lives of your own loved ones, you must not let this crime pass."

Attorneys Lewkowitz and Schneck followed with their own lengthy arguments for the defense. When Schneck concluded, he said, "I believe the court will instruct you and that the state then will take this defendant in hand, not as a felon, but as an ill person and will keep her in custody along as she remains insane."

He compared Ruthie's condition with that of someone with a physical ailment. "Smallpox patients are not hanged, they are isolated. This woman is suffering from a mental illness. Why hang her if the smallpox patient is spared?"

I'm not sure that was as great of an argument as he must have thought when he presented it, but that's just my opinion.

County Attorney Andrews closed the arguments, calling the insanity defense "just bunk." Leaning over the jury rail, he concluded, "Arizona statutes provide for the infliction of the death penalty in a proper case. If this case does not deserve it, I have never seen one that did. It is in your hands."

Judge Speakman then began his instructions to the jury. As mentioned, he offered them a choice of six verdicts:

- Guilty of murder in the first degree with the death penalty.
- Guilty of murder in the first degree with life in prison.
- Guilty of murder in the second degree.
- Guilty of manslaughter.
- Not guilty by reason of insanity.
- Not guilty.

The jury began deliberations at 5:12 P.M. Stewart Thompson, a 26-year-old salesman and the youngest man on the jury, was elected foreman. He later admitted that everyone agreed that Ruthie was guilty during the first ballot. Then, they took a supper break. It took them five more ballots to agree on the penalty.

The deliberations took just two hours and 40 minutes, not counting that supper break. Court was reconvened at 9:15 for the reading of the verdict.

Judge Speakman addressed the jurors: "Gentlemen of the jury, have you arrived at a verdict?" Thompson silently handed the folded verdict slip to the bailiff, who passed it to the bench. The judge glanced at the paper and admonished the spectators and press, "Before this verdict is read, I want you to know there will be no demonstration in this courtroom, regardless of what this verdict may be."

But the uproar that followed wasn't caused by the crowd–it was the clatter of the reporters as they rushed for telephones to call in their stories.

First, though, complete silence gripped the jammed courtroom as the slip was given to the clerk of the court for the reading. He turned to the jurors and asked, "So say you all?" The jury nodded, and he began reading. Dr. Judd, sitting next to his wife, became noticeably tense.

"We, the jury," the clerk read," find the defendant guilty of the crime of murder in the first degree and fix the punishment at death."

Dr. Judd had slipped his arm around Ruthie's shoulder as the clerk's words rang out in the courtroom. His hand tightened convulsively on her shoulder, his fingers shaking.

The defense counsel looked stunned. The blood seemed to have drained from their faces, leaving them looking pale and haunted.

But Ruthie stared straight ahead, twisting and untwisting the handkerchief in her hands.

A dispatch in the *Phoenix Gazette* read:

Even the nerve-hardened newspapermen cringed. But not Ruth Judd.

Nerves, a rage, a frenzy, a scene? Nothing like that. Ruth Judd was easily the most indifferent person in the courtroom.

Why? Has she something hidden away in the secret recesses of her mind that she knows will save her life if she only says the word?

If not, Ruth Judd is made of things as hard as steel. She may outdo the iron men who have faced death on the gallows without a flinch.

But maybe she does not realize the appalling significance of her act. Regardless of what she was when she killed Agnes Anne LeRoi in the trunk double murder, Ruth Judd is an enigma now.

Ruth looked stunned when the verdict was read but showed little other emotion.

She appears more like a little girl who is watching wide-eyed, and she doesn't know what it is all about. She may be acting. But if she is, what acting in the face of death? Only an omniscient God can tell.

Within minutes after the verdict was read, Judge Speakman set February 23 as the day he would pronounce the death penalty and fix the date for the execution.

Ruthie's trial lasted three weeks and was the longest trial to date in Maricopa County. It ended without testimony from Jack Halloran and, of course, Ruthie herself.

During the next few days, several letters were received by Governor George W.P. Hunt, requesting that he intervene and prevent Ruthie's hanging. One mysterious telegram even arrived from Prague in Czechoslovakia that read: "Stay your hand. Winnie's sacrifice not necessary. Await information. Innocent."

When the defense and prosecution returned to Judge Speakman's courtroom on February 23, Ruthie's attorneys had a stack of affidavits in hand charging that one of the jurors had been biased and prejudiced against Ruthie before and during the trial.

Three of the jurors had sworn the affidavits, and all pointed an accusing finger at fellow juror Dan Kleinman, a 56-year-old rancher and former mayor of Mesa, Arizona. He was an affable man who seemed to know everyone the jurors met on the street during their evening walks for meals. He was known as an upstanding man with a strong belief in morality. When he was mayor of Mesa, he passed blue laws that closed businesses on Sundays and started a 9:00 P.M. curfew for children under 18.

But, according to one affidavit, it had been Kleinman who had convinced several jurors to change their vote from life imprisonment to the death penalty. The juror, Ed Landrigan, wrote:

Never would I have changed as I did if it had not been for Dan Kleinman, who insisted we should vote for the extreme penalty. Then, he argued, such a verdict would make Mrs. Judd talk, involving the accomplice or accomplices. Dan said he had a good political friend on the Board of Pardons and Paroles and that he would get the sentence commuted if Mrs. Judd would talk.

Furthermore, all of us jurors made an agreement, as a body, that if new evidence came to light subsequently, and Mrs. Judd would talk, we would immediately urge the Board of Pardons and Parole to have the sentence commuted.

If it had not been for the above promise, I would not have come over to the death penalty.

Jurors Ed Gray and Tom Kunze agreed, signed affidavits and told the same story - not realizing that things don't work that way. Dan Kleinman had fooled all three of them and undoubtedly had some influence over jury foreman Stewart Thompson, too. He filed his own affidavit a year after the trial, stating that the death penalty had only been "to make her talk." They never intended that she should actually hang.

It seemed the prosecution had Dan Kleinman to thank for their verdict. Not surprisingly, his actions inside and outside the jury room were labeled "juror misconduct" by the defense attorneys. They requested a new trial two times because of Kleinman, but both appeals were denied.

Even before those other jurors had reported his "make her talk" scheme, Kleinman had been under scrutiny by Herman Lewkowitz. Three different people had come to him and said that before he was sworn in as a juror, Kleinman had been saying that Ruthie was guilty and deserved to hang.

Armed with sworn statements from the three jurors, Lewkowitz charged that Kleinman had lied during jury selection when he claimed to have no set opinions about the defendant's guilt or innocence. He charged that Kleinman was "wholly unqualified and unfit to sit as a juror."

To prove his point, the defense attorney produced other affidavits, including one from a Phoenix man named A.E. Parmer, who said he'd had a conversation with Kleinman in a drug store downtown in mid-January 1932, just days before jury selection began. Parmer quoted him as saying, "This Judd woman is guilty as hell, and if I ever get on that jury, I'll hang the bitch."

An affidavit from B.H. Ward, a potential juror who was not chosen for the trial, was in the courtroom hallway and overheard Kleinman tell a group of men, "This Judd woman is not crazy and should be hung."

Another affidavit - this one from a long-time friend of Kleinman who admitted this "reluctantly" - stated that Kleinman "admitted that he probably had said, before being selected as a Judd juror, that Mrs. Judd was guilty and should hang." The man, J.L. Rodgers, said he had kept quiet about this because "I thought Dan would do something for Mrs. Judd when the right time arrived, as he said he would. Since he hasn't, I honestly feel it is my duty to tell it now."

Kleinman was never called to answer these allegations, even though he faced the possibility of jail time if he was found guilty. Instead, the prosecution presented their own affidavits, which claimed the charges were "wholly false and untrue."

One of those affidavits came from Kleinman's daughter-in-law, who said she'd never heard him say anything about the case.

His main defender was a Tempe, Arizona man named A.N. Smith, who was introduced to the court as simply an old friend present when Kleinman and Parmer were talking at the drug store. Smith maintained that he never heard any comment about "hanging the bitch." But he initially swore the encounter he'd witnessed had occurred in mid-December - a month before the conversation Parmer described. Instead of rejecting Smith's testimony, the court allowed him to "correct" his memory lapse about when the meeting had occurred.

But that wasn't all. Allegedly, Ruthie's supporters later discovered that Smith wasn't just some innocent bystander in a drug store who helped Kleinman avoid charges - Smith was the link between the manipulative juror and Jack Halloran.

In early 1933, these supporters claimed they were approached by Smith, who said he was acting as "an agent for Jack Halloran's powerful and influential friends." According to a sworn affidavit, Smith offered Ruthie's family a deal. The affidavit stated:

If she issues a written statement wherein she would exonerate Jack Halloran of the part he had in the tragedy and publish the said statement in the press, Jack's powerful and influential friends, business and otherwise, would see to it that the Pardons Board would commute her death sentence.

But none of these things moved Judge Speakman - or later, judges on the Arizona Supreme Court - to decide that Ruthie Judd didn't receive a fair trial.

Judge Speakman dismissed the defense claims and denied a motion for a new trial. The date of Ruthie's execution was set for May 11, 1932. It would be on a Wednesday, a departure from the long-standing Arizona tradition of scheduling executions on Friday.

The judge had done it to avoid a hanging on Friday the 13th.

He was trying to avoid the superstitions that already surrounded Ruthie but, in doing so, just gave people something else to talk about.

9. ON DEATH ROW

SOON AFTER THE COURTROOM WAS CLEARED SHORTLY after 8:00 P.M., Ruthie began her journey to the Arizona State Prison in Florence. The trip was made in Sheriff McFadden's car, and they were accompanied by the jail matron, Mrs. Jordan, and others. Ruthie joined in singing popular Mexican folk songs to pass the time over the 67-mile trip.

During the leisurely drive, Sheriff McFadden asked Ruthie about specific details of the crime, and while she declined to answer most of them, she replied to his question about whether she had an accomplice.

"Yes, I had an accomplice," she stated.

Warden William Delbridge and other prison officials met the party when they arrived at the penitentiary. Ruthie was assigned no. 8811, and she was taken to the prison hospital for a complete physical examination. The prison doctor, H.B. Steward, reported her in good condition, although "her heart was pounding from the effects of her emotions." He noted in his report that she was "visibly shaken."

At midnight - even though it had been announced she would be placed on the women's ward -- Ruthie was taken directly to Death Row. She shuddered as she entered that section of the prison. Only four gray, dimly lit cells were located in the small building that also housed the gallows. Only a few steps away from the narrow corridor

The entrance to the Arizona State Prison in Florence

between two sets of cells were the 13 steps leading up to the hangman's noose waiting for Ruthie.

After she was settled in her cell, Sheriff McFadden and the contingent from Phoenix said goodbye. Warden Delbridge then suggested she turn off the light and get some sleep.

The darkness of Death Row brought an end to the harrowing day.

Ruthie was officially registered the following day. Her fingerprints and photographs were taken, and the history of her case was recorded in prison files.

That same day in Phoenix, Governor George W. P. Hunt revealed he had received four appeals in the mail asking him to intervene in Ruthie's execution. These were not the first letters he received, nor would they be the last. Dozens of others had already been received, and scores of others were still to come - although there was nothing he could do about the situation unless he received a recommendation for commutation of sentence from the Arizona Board of Pardons and Paroles.

Ruthie received her first visitors on February 25. "Oh, I'm so glad to see you!" she sobbed as her parents appeared at her cell door for a surprise visit. All three broke into tears, and Warden Delbridge

Prison Warden William Delbridge (far right) in the prison yard with several state officials, including Governor George W.P. Hunt (Second from Left)

ordered a guard to unlock the door. Rev. McKinnell took his daughter into his arms and whispered, "Don't worry. God is with you. He'll take care of you."

Delbridge allowed the McKinnells to stay in the cell for a half hour and assured them they could return for an hour each Sunday if they liked. He knew the couple would be moving to Florence in a few days to be closer to Ruthie. At the end of the visit, the McKinnells knelt with Ruthie and prayed.

Over the next few days, while she adjusted to life on Death Row, Ruthie's attorneys, Herman Lewkowitz and Joseph Zaversack, began preparing their briefs for an appeal to the Arizona Supreme Court for a new trial. At best, they could hope for a retrial; at worst, they might at least gain a stay of execution.

Despite the isolation of Ruthie's cell on Death Row, the prison's "grapevine" hummed with news and rumors about the famous new arrival. The 600-plus inmates showed the same curiosity in the "Trunk Murderer" as those on the outside. The inmates gave her a cat and a bird as pets.

Locked up on Death Row, Ruthie was given meals that were better than the usual prison fare - milk, cream, vegetables, steaks, and other meats. The condemned ate well in Arizona; for Ruthie, she had more access to decent food than she'd had in years.

And then there were the fan letters. According to Warden Delbridge, she received more mail than any other inmate in the institution's history. Letters simply addressed to "Mrs. Judd, Arizona State Prison" were delivered just as promptly as those with complete addresses. The warden reported that she spent a great deal of her time writing, but it didn't seem as though she was replying to the letters she received - none of her writing was ever mailed out.

But Ruthie wasn't the only person getting mail about her case. Lin B. Ormes, chairman of the Arizona Board of Pardons and Appeals, also received stacks of letters. They were all filed away, though, since there had been no application for commutation of the death penalty before the board. That wouldn't happen until the state Supreme Court heard Ruthie's case.

Governor Hunt received two out-of-state applications for the privilege of hanging Arizona's most famous prisoner. They were sent by F.P. Griggs of Iowa and from G. Phil Hanna, the so-called "Humane Hangman" of Illinois. Both men offered to come out of retirement as executioners and hang Ruthie at no cost to the taxpayers of Arizona.

Hanna, in particular, had a reputation as a hangman. He had retired four years earlier after the execution of Charlie Birger, a notorious Southern Illinois gangster. Although admitting "I never hung a woman before," Hanna counted on Mrs. Judd to be the 62nd person to hang "painlessly" by his hand.

The applications were tossed, however. According to state law, the prison warden was in charge of executions at the penitentiary gallows. It was not, he'd admit, his favorite part of the job.

But on March 2, 1932, the warden's grim responsibility was temporarily lifted when attorneys Lewkowitz and Zaversack filed notice of an appeal with the Arizona Supreme Court. The accompanying brief stated that Mrs. Judd was appealing the judgment, conviction, and order denying a motion for a new trial. The brief caused an automatic stay of execution - which meant that Ruthie wouldn't go to the gallows on May 11 after all.

Her attorneys also filed an affidavit that stated that she was "without means and wholly unable to pay" for the appeal. This new announcement required a hearing in the case, and this required the county clerk to assemble documents, which were all ready except for the trial transcript. It would require a month to copy it because it was 2,587 pages long. That meant it would be at least late fall or early winter before the court considered the formal appeal.

Ruthie Judd would live for at least a year longer than everyone expected.

On March 9, County Attorney Andrews began an investigation on behalf of the state to determine Ruthie's financial status. He wanted answers about why she had no money since it was rumored that she'd received large sums for her story from newspapers. If she had, he didn't think it was the responsibility of county taxpayers to pay for her appeal.

There was also speculation that she had been paid to stay quiet about evidence that might incriminate others in the murders, but Andrews didn't mention that.

Ruthie was required to give evidence about her finances in Judge Speakman's courtroom on Monday, March 21. Reporters assumed she'd be asked where she had gotten the money for her defense in the 21-day trial, how much she'd received, what she did with it, and whether any of the money was left. Speculation was evenly divided as to whether Ruthie would use the hearing as an opportunity to make good on her threat to "tell all."

Meanwhile, Dr. Judd was dealing with his own legal problems in Los Angeles. His trial for practicing medicine without a license was postponed when the court learned that he had been admitted to the Fort Whipple Veteran's Hospital after suffering a nervous breakdown. It was, attorney Paul Schneck told the judge in the case, caused by the strain of his wife's murder trial and the subsequent verdict. Officials at the hospital, who stated that the doctor wasn't mentally or physically able to stand trial, hoped to get a suspended sentence for Dr. Judd without him appearing in court.

Even though Dr. Judd was dealing with legal issues of his own, he was subpoenaed to appear at his wife's next hearing.

Despite his status as a mental patient, Dr. Judd was still subpoenaed on March 19 to appear at his wife's hearing two days later in Arizona. Andrews wanted answers from Dr. Judd because he'd reportedly handled Ruthie's finances after her arrest. There were still those rumors of large sums of money paid by L.A. newspapers and national magazines for Ruthie's "confessions" and life story, with her husband handling the financial arrangements. Andrews subpoenaed tellers from every bank in Phoenix to determine if any deposits had been made in Ruthie's name.

Andrews was also looking for the couple's community property. According to Arizona law, anything owned by Dr. Judd had to be shared with his wife, and that property could be used to pay the costs of the death conviction appeal to the state Supreme Court.

Ruthie was escorted to her Monday afternoon hearing by Warden Delbridge and two prison guards. A crowd of over 1,000 people milled about outside the courthouse, hoping to glimpse Ruthie. When they arrived, she was taken directly, despite her protests, to a cell in the county jail, which occupied the upper floors of the courthouse. She had wanted to go straight to the courtroom, even though they were an hour early for the hearing. When she saw Sheriff McFadden, she begged him not to let them put her in the cell. "I don't want to go up

Ruthie signing papers for her attorneys as the hearing began.

there," she said. "They tried to poison me there, and I don't want to be poisoned again."

When the hearing started, Rev. and Mrs. McKinnell quietly took the same seats they'd occupied during the trial. Dr. Judd sat near the defense table, where attorneys Lewkowitz and Zaversack were already seated. When Ruthie walked briskly into the courtroom, Dr. Judd stood up and smiled to greet her. She loudly cried out, "Well, hello, I haven't seen you in a long time." They struck up a conversation that was easily heard all over the courtroom. Judge Speakman pounded his gavel and told them to be quiet. They talked in whispers until it was time for the hearing to start. Ruthie sat down and began twisting a handkerchief around her left hand, as she'd done at the trial.

Lloyd Andrews opened the hearing by explaining why it was taking place. He said the county should not be forced to pay for Ruthie's appeal if she and her husband had the money to pay for it. Lewkowitz then objected to the proceedings on the basis that Andrews had not requested the hearing within the five-day limit he said was required by law. Judge Speakman called for a 10-minute recess to consider the arguments.

During the recess, Dr. Judd told reporters it was untrue that he wanted to stay away from the financial hearing. "I haven't any money," he told them. "Why in the hell would I be in a government hospital if I had any money?"

When the judge returned to the courtroom, he upheld Lewkowitz's argument that Andrews had waited too long before taking action, and that was the end of it. The hearing was over.

But Ruthie was apparently just getting started.

Within minutes, the courtroom was in an uproar caused by her sensational tantrum. She shrieked, screaming accusations at Andrews and shouting almost incoherent cries about her innocence. Dr. Judd slapped her across the face to try and get her under control.

Finally, Sheriff McFadden, with help from a deputy, picked up Ruthie and bodily carried her out of the courtroom. She continued to scream in the middle of the packed hallway. She kept yelling at Andrews: "You're trying to protect a political friend! You're trying to hang me, and I won't have it! I didn't cut up those bodies! I couldn't do it!" In the jail elevator, she told the sheriff she was being framed and wasn't being given an opportunity to talk.

Andrews didn't take this outburst lightly. He immediately announced plans to hold a press conference in Ruthie's cell. Less than an hour later, eight people - including several newsmen and two shorthand recorders - faced Winnie from outside her cell.

Who wasn't there? Ruthie's defense attorneys. They left her on her own to deal with Andrews and the press, and the results were disastrous.

"You said you wanted to talk," said Andrews, "and now we're going to give you an opportunity." He started to say something else, but Ruthie interrupted him.

"When I talk, I'll talk at my second trial or else in the courtroom before people," she said.

Andrews replied, "That won't make a bit of difference if you give us the facts."

"What do you want them for? You want them to go out here and try to hang somebody else?"

"I'm concerned with you personally. If anybody else is involved in this case, I want to know who it is. I've been trying for six months to learn who it is. Now, will you tell me who it is?" Andrews asked her.

Ruthie became unhinged during the hearing, which many believed was to reinforce the claims that she was insane.

"No, I will not - you know!" Ruthie snapped and suddenly began storming around the cell, gesturing wildly and crying incoherently. She shouted at Andrews about the testimony she claimed he'd falsified, which he failed to present at her trial. She claimed the state's witnesses "lied" on the stand to convict her and that Judge Speakman was "unfair" to her.

As we already know, there *was* some truth to what Ruthie was saying. We know the police had other evidence and witness statements that they chose not to use because it might've created reasonable doubt for the jury. They also had information that the defense could have used, but in those days, they weren't obligated to give it to them.

But while Ruthie didn't know about those things, she knew enough to whip her up into a frenzy. She continued to shriek at Andrews, rambling from one subject to another: "You say the shooting was at 10:30. Well, I was at home, in my own home, until 11:30 when a man came over to my house and picked me up in a car! He just wants the glory of hanging another woman! Sammy shot me! You're trying to keep me from a new trial because I have no money! I've been a political football - that's all. It's a little bit of notoriety to hang a woman. They don't do that in most civilized states. You know good and well that I never cut up a body!"

Deputy County Attorney Robert McMurchie, who was also present, then asked, "Are you willing to say anything that will help the country attorney?"

"My God, NO!" Ruthie screamed. "I will do anything to help myself. I'm not helping him!"

She continued to move around her cell in a frenzy. "Judge Speakman said, 'May God have mercy on your soul.' I haven't got a soul! My God, you can't do that anymore! They can't do that to me anymore! My God, you leave me alone! You can't do that anymore!" She continued to scream that last phrase over and over as attorneys and reporters walked away, leaving her there to cry and weep hysterically in her temporary cell.

Hours later, Ruthie was back to being the only occupant on Death Row at the state prison. She remained there until early April when she became hysterical again. Prison authorities sent for her parents.

Ruthie had reportedly placed several lines of string in her cell, warning visitors to beware of them because they were "high-tension wires." She was ranting and raving until her parents arrived, and then she finally calmed down - and left Death Row.

She was quietly moved out of those stark accommodations to the women's wards, a sturdy adobe structure that housed 12 other women convicted of crimes that ranged between misdemeanors and murder.

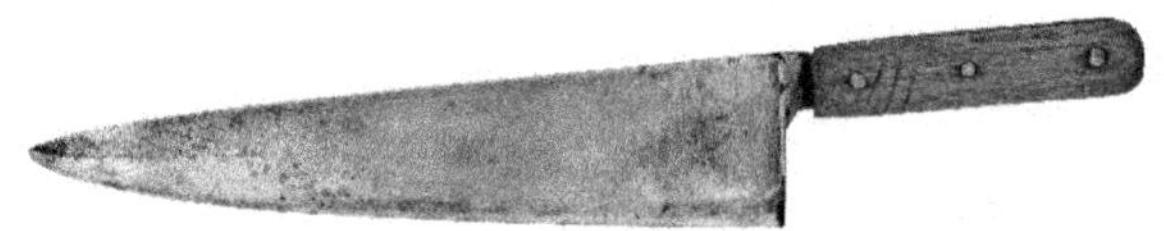

10. "I'M NO MURDERER!"

ON APRIL 5, 1932, A STARTLING ANNOUNCEMENT WAS made in the Winnie Ruth Judd case. Herman Lewkowitz told reporters that he and his associates - Joseph Zaversack and Paul Schneck - were no longer the attorneys of record in the case. They had been dismissed as defense counsel by Dr. and Mrs. Judd. No reasons for the dismissal were given.

The next day, an announcement was made that Phoenix attorneys Edward J. Flanigan - a former Arizona Supreme Court justice - and O.V. Willson were the new defense lawyers for Ruthie Judd.

Flanigan and Willson officially presented Ruthie's appeal to the state Supreme Court on April 7. With the appeal were five volumes of court reporter transcripts and a half dozen affidavits, including one from Ruthie asserting her inability to pay the costs of the appeal. Defense counsel had 30 days to file the briefs supporting the appeal's reason. However, due to the change in attorneys and an upcoming summer release for court, counsel was expected to be allowed to postpone the filing until early fall.

If the Supreme Court decided that Ruthie's conviction should stand, she would still have three chances to escape the gallows. She could appeal to the state Board of Pardons and Paroles for a commutation of the death penalty to life in prison, or the case would be appealed to the U.S. Supreme Court, but there was only a remote possibility it would make it there.

Ruthie could also be judged insane at a sanity trial in Pinal County, where the prison was located. But a sanity trial could only be held if the prison warden filed an affidavit saying that he believed Ruthie was insane. A judgment of insanity would result in her being committed to the Arizona Hospital for the Insane in Phoenix.

Ruthie had quickly adapted to the less restricted life of the women's ward. Warden Delbridge reported that she was much quieter now and apparently more content. But he added that she had reverted to her courtroom habit of continuously winding and unwinding that handkerchief around her left hand. She seemed appreciative of the weekly visits from her parents.

On April 26, Judge Speakman received an unsigned letter purporting to offer a solution to the trunk murder mystery. The letter read, in part: "Just a few lines to tell you that Mrs. Winnie Ruth Judd is not guilty of killing Mrs. Agnes Anne LeRoi and Hedvig Samuelson. The man who did the killing is on his way to Mexico, so please let Mrs. Judd free."

The letter had been written in pencil and was dated March 30 in Phoenix. However, the envelope was postmarked on April 23 in Kennedy, Texas. The judge filed the letter in a box with more than 200 others he'd received since the Judd trial ended.

With both Ruthie and her defense attorneys forced to do nothing but wait until the Supreme Court decided on her appeal, the condemned woman was becoming better adjusted to prison life. In early August, Warden Delbridge stated, "She has become a model prisoner, but she has developed a nervous condition. She doesn't cause any trouble, although at times she gets into a wrangle with other inmates in the ward when they talk about her."

Two of her fellow inmates were Zora Neal Ross, of Prescott, convicted of manslaughter, and Jennie Rutledge, convicted in Phoenix for killing her mother. Although Ruthie was not the only female inmate convicted of murder or manslaughter, she was the only one sentenced to death.

Delbridge reported that Ruthie spent most of her time in a small cell that was used for solitary confinement when disciplinary action was required in the ward. Delbridge explained that she wasn't placed there because she caused trouble, though. It was the cell that had been fixed for her when she was transferred from Death Row. She occasionally strolled in the small exercise yard or chatted with the other women convicts. Ruthie was often visited in the courtyard by her parents but would run from others whose curiosity led to them seeking her out there. She retreated to her solitary cell inside.

Ruthie was often seen sitting on a bench in the courtyard from the windows of the nearby prison administration building. She was observed biting her thumbs and chewing on the ends of her fingers but usually, she was smiling, her hair neatly arranged as though she was expecting a special visitor at any time. The female inmates weren't required to wear uniforms like the male inmates were. Ruthie had a choice of clothing but usually wore a simple white dress.

Warden Delbridge said that moving Ruthie into the women's ward had improved her morale, but her nervous condition was worsening. She worried incessantly about her appeal and her fight to escape the gallows, but the warden wasn't concerned about her trying to escape. A high iron fence surrounded The women's ward on two sides. The prison wall and the administrative building are on the other sides. The courtyard that she enjoyed so much was always under watch.

The one thing Ruthie often asked for was a visit from her husband. She hadn't seen Dr. Judd since the finance hearing. He would've been allowed to visit if he wasn't a patient at Whipple's Veterans' Hospital near Prescott. He was still there on August 31 when he was granted another continuance in his California trial on charges of practicing medicine without a license.

He finally made it to trial on October 31. On the witness stand, he admitted to working for $6 a day as a substitute physician but said he did not write prescriptions and gave only first-aid treatment. He also admitted he did not have a California license. The jury deliberated less than a half hour before finding him "not guilty," and he returned to Fort Whipple.

ON SEPTEMBER 1, RUTHIE'S DEFENSE COUNSEL, which now numbered six attorneys, filed opening briefs for a rehearing in the Arizona Supreme Court. The 300 pages of briefs alleged 12 errors by the Maricopa County Superior Court in the murder trial.

Two major points were presented. One dealt with the interpretation of the term "legal insanity," and the other with the failure of Judge Speakman to instruct the jury on self-defense as a reason for the murders. It was claimed that this was the first time the state Supreme Court had been asked to define legal insanity.

The attorneys declared that the story told by their client in the "Drainpipe Letter" to her husband - which had been read to the jury - was a sufficient reason for the jury to be instructed about self-defense. The trial court, they stated, had erred in failing to do so. In the letter, Ruthie had said she killed in self-defense.

But her attorneys had offered insanity as her defense, and except for the story of a fight between Ruthie and the girls in the "Drainpipe Letter," the record of the case showed no evidence of self-defense. This was admitted by the counsel in the briefs, but they held that the evidence in the letter introduced by the state was obvious enough that the judge should have instructed the jury on the point.

On November 1, J.R. McDougall, Arizona's Assistant Attorney General, filed a 67-page brief with the state Supreme Court. The state claimed the trial court hadn't erred in failing to instruct the jury that it could find a self-defense verdict. There was, the state said, no evidence in the "Drainpipe Letter" that Ruthie shot Anne in self-defense. Instead, the letter seemed to show Ruthie had fired at Anne because she was going to "blackmail me, too, if I went hunting - and would hand me over to the police."

The state added that the Supreme Court had defined insanity many times before, and there was no need to repeat it.

The brief ended with the state asserting that every legal right had been extended to Mrs. Judd during her trial and that the higher court should affirm the judgment.

Oral arguments on the dueling briefs were conducted before the court on Wednesday, November 21.

One attorney anxiously awaiting the decision - expected by mid-December - was Paul Schneck. Although he'd been fired from Ruthie's defense team, he remained deeply interested in her case. In a law practice started in 1899, he had saved 90 men and women accused of murder from the gallows. Ruthie's trial had been the first significant defeat in his career. Unfortunately, he wouldn't live long enough to discover how it all ended up.

LATE IN THE AFTERNOON OF DECEMBER 12, THE STATE Supreme Court announced its decision. Ruthie's conviction had been upheld, and Judge Speakman was found without fault on every point challenged by the defense. The court ruled that Ruthie's death sentence remained in effect, and it set February 17, 1933, as her new execution date.

Warden Delbridge, who knew that Ruthie's parents were visiting, went to see Ruthie. He told her: "I have some unpleasant news for you. The state Supreme Court has denied your appeal for a new trial."

Ruthie burst into tears and cried out, "Oh, Mr. Delbridge, I'm no murderer! I fought for my life when she came at me with that gun."

She then turned to her mother. "Mother, I am a good woman," she wept. "I have never associated with bad, low, or degenerate people. I never cut up those bodies. I could not have done it."

Rev. McKinnell had no words of comfort for her. "Let us pray," he said instead, and the family knelt together, hoping for a miracle.

Warden Delbridge didn't tell Ruthie about the new execution date. He decided not to do that until he received the official notification. And that was not the only small mercy he offered that day. He allowed Carrie McKinnell to spend the night in the cell with her daughter, thinking it might make things a little easier for Ruthie. He might have also feared that Ruthie was suicidal. He'd recently received a report that she had been screaming hysterically in her cell, "I'll never hang!" There were multiple ways to interpret that - including self-harm - but he didn't want to take any chances.

There's a reason that the convicts often referred to the warden as "Uncle Billy."

AFTER THE SUPREME COURT RULING, NEWSPAPERS speculated about whether the "Trunk Murderer" would finally "tell all" and name her accomplices.

Sheriff McFadden, who had talked with Ruthie several times since she'd gone to the state prison, said he believed she might have an ace up her sleeve that she might play at the last moment. He told the press: "I repeatedly told her that if she would only tell the truth, she might benefit by it."

County Attorney Andrews, though, felt differently. He told reporters: "No matter what she says, it will not mitigate the circumstances that she is a cold-blooded murderess. She killed two women, and she can't get away from that fact no matter what her story is."

After Ruthie was notified of her new execution date, she continued to maintain that she would never hang. And it truly began to seem that she might have some sort of plan.

On December 15, a three-hour private meeting was held at the state prison. It included Ruthie, her defense counsel, and Rev. McKinnell. Dr. Judd had requested a special furlough from the Whipple Veterans' Hospital to attend, but the request was denied. He came anyway, however, which caused him to be dropped from the hospital's roll of patients soon after.

Ruthie had been hinting since the beginning that at least one other person had been involved in either the actual murders or in the dismemberment of Sammy's body. Immediately after hearing about the Supreme Court's decision, Dr. Judd reportedly announced, "I am going to do now what I should have done months ago - which is to tell the truth and whole truth about this case. And when I do, there will be another person in a prison cell, and Ruth Judd will stand exonerated of this horrible crime of which she has been accused and convicted."

Warden Delbridge had allowed the meeting to be held in the matron's room, with guards and matrons in the hallway and out of earshot. When the small group emerged from the room, Ruthie appeared highly nervous, wrapping and unwrapping a handkerchief around her left hand. She was very animated and excitedly talking to her husband. The warden overheard only one thing she said.

She said to Dr. Judd, "I'm game if you are."

But what they remark meant, no one would say.

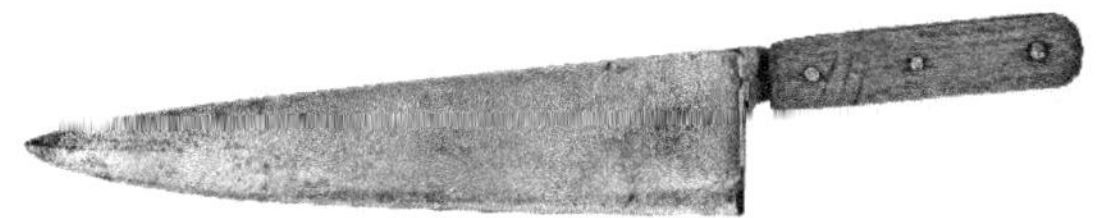

11. RUTHIE "TELLS ALL"

ON DECEMBER 19, A PRIVATE CONFERENCE WAS HELD at the prison at Ruthie's request. She was joined by one of her attorneys, O.V. Willson, Warden Delbridge, and Sheriff McFadden. Dr. Judd also participated in the conversation by telephone, long-distance.

None of the participants would discuss what had transpired, but the sheriff admitted that he and Willson had been accompanied by a shorthand secretary, who took down all the questions asked of Mrs. Judd and her answers.

When asked if Ruthie told a "new story," Sheriff McFadden replied, "She didn't tell me anything about the case that I didn't know before."

But as it turns out, that's not because Ruthie had no new details about the murders; it's because Sheriff McFadden had likely been one of the only people to whom Ruthie had already "told all."

Sheriff John R. McFadden was a big cowboy of a man in 1932. At the time, he was 41 years old and an oversized man with a bit of a paunch and a weakness for Western-style shirts. Some considered him too friendly of a man to hold the highest elected law-enforcement position in Arizona's most populated county, but there's no denying that he was voted into office so often that no one who came after him could match his time as sheriff.

Sheriff John R. McFadden

McFadden had won his first two-year term on the Democratic ticket in 1930. He'd go on to be reelected two more times. Though it would eventually end badly, that was still years off in 1932. At that time, he was a popular law-and-order sheriff. He raised illegal whiskey stills, conducted regular raids on brothels, and hired deputies cut from the same cloth. Six of them would go on to become sheriffs themselves. He was considered a straight arrow, a no-nonsense man who valued honesty above all else.

Of all the law enforcement officials in Arizona, McFadden had the closest view of the case. Not only had he and his deputies helped the Phoenix Police Department investigate the murders, but he'd also personally spent more time with Ruthie than anyone else. He'd brought her back from California in 1931, and he'd first heard Ruthie tell her self-defense story two days after she arrived at the jail. As he later admitted, he begged her to sign a statement to solidify her story, but she refused. She would only tell her story in court, she said.

Ruthie had been in Sheriff McFadden's jail for three months, and the two spoke almost daily. Her attitude toward him fluctuated wildly. One day, she treated him like an old friend; the next, she'd scream that he was trying to hang her like everyone else; the next day, they'd make pleasant small talk. She appreciated the sheriff's strict rules that kept reporters away but was annoyed that the same rules also kept away her husband and limited the time she could spend with her parents.

But McFadden showed her many small kindnesses. Before her trial, he allowed a local dressmaker to bring four garments Ruthie could choose from to the jail. He saw to it that her hair was styled and secretly allowed his 16-year-old daughter, Helen, to visit with Ruthie on Sundays. He even broke all his own rules by allowing Ruthie's mother to spend time with her unsupervised.

McFadden personally escorted her to and from the courtroom each day during the trial. He knew she was waiting for her chance to testify - he wanted her to do it. When it didn't happen, he asked her repeatedly to speak up, but she wouldn't. He knew the most she'd said publicly was when she was in the courtroom for the hearing and made the hysterical outburst that ended when Dr. Judd slapped her across the face.

McFadden had watched over Ruthie during the horrible nights after the death sentence was pronounced, afraid she might try and take her own life. Then, he personally drove her to the prison in Florence.

It was also Sheriff McFadden who calmed her down during her first night in prison when officials placed her on Death Row with the flimsy explanation that it was the only place they could keep her safe from the 12 women in the female ward. It was McFadden who ultimately convinced prison officials that such "protection" was unnecessary.

All that was 10 months before this meeting. It had been nearly a year of legal maneuvering that had kept Ruthie hopeful. A new batch of lawyers - all working for free - took up her cause, filed appeals, and tried to overturn a sentence that had shocked people across the country. Thousands of people wrote to Arizona officials, begging for mercy, including people like automaker Henry Ford and First Lady Eleanor Roosevelt.

But during those 10 months, Ruthie had stayed silent. As much as she complained that her trial attorneys prevented her from testifying, she found that her new attorneys also ordered her to stay silent while her appeals were pending. They were convinced the Supreme Court would overturn the conviction.

But that had been wrong.

And now, seven days after the Supreme Court had decided that she should hang, Ruthie found that she had one hope left - Sheriff John McFadden. When she left her fear and distrust behind, she realized he was the closest thing to an ally she had - the only state official who seemed to care what she had to say and who really wanted to know what happened. Everyone else, including her own defense team, seemed willing to let her go to the gallows.

She had less than two months to live when she decided that it was finally time to "tell all."

Ruthie was brought from her cell to a small room at the Arizona State Prison at 2:15 P.M. that afternoon. She sat down at a table across from Sheriff McFadden, who brought one of his deputies, Jeff Adams, with him. Warden Delbridge had insisted on being present, as had one of her attorneys, O.V. Willson.

McFadden began with a simple, direct statement. It was one that he had said to her many times before. "Now, Ruth, what we want to know is just what happened out there at the house."

On every other occasion, he'd been answered with only silence, but this time, Ruthie spoke: "You want to know about Thursday night. Sure, you do, because it was Thursday night when I introduced Jack Halloran to this girl."

The secretary accompanying Sheriff McFadden to the prison recorded every word spoken over the next four hours. They would eventually be typed up, placed in a cardboard envelope, filed away, and mostly forgotten. They remain preserved today at the Arizona State Archives library, and the document is undoubtedly the most complete version of events that Ruthie Judd ever told about the murders.

Is her story true?

That's an excellent question. There's no real way to verify her account aside from piecing together a clue here and a clue there, a newspaper clipping, a document or two, and frankly, just taking Ruthie at her word - something that doesn't seem all that reliable to me.

Regardless, though, this was what Sheriff McFadden had been waiting for. He'd been asking Ruthie to "tell all" for months. Newspaper reporters had been demanding this story for just as long. This is what all those women who had jammed the courtroom each day had been waiting for, too. They wanted her to defend herself - and now she was.

But would anyone believe it?

The group seated in the prison interview room that day listened intently as Ruthie began to speak. The story poured out of her, and while she sometimes rambled and had to be encouraged to get to the point, she finally had the chance to "tell all" she'd been waiting for.

RUTHIE BEGAN WITH THE NURSE AT THE CLINIC WHO was undergoing treatment for syphilis. The nurse, Lucille Moore, happened to mention to Ruthie that she was going hunting in the White Mountains, and, as luck would have it, Ruthie had friends who were also going to the area on a hunting trip.

"I told her about Jack Halloran, and arrangements were made for her to meet him on Thursday night," Ruthie said.

As the story continued, she stated that Halloran was already drunk on Thursday afternoon when he called her at the clinic and set a time for the meeting. He picked her up, and they drove together to pick up Lucille around 7:00 P.M. They were going back to Ruthie's apartment for supper, but Halloran wanted to stop and see Anne and Sammy.

"I didn't want to go with him," Ruthie said, but then she told Halloran she would. She asked that he not let Anne know she was in the car, and he promised to do that. "I didn't want Anne to know that I had introduced him to this girl - so we drove up in front of the house, and he stopped in the driveway, and I said, 'Don't tell them, don't let them know I am here,' and he said, 'Oh, all right.' I didn't want the, you know, to know that I had introduced him to another woman because he was practically supporting Anne and Sammy - between Jack Halloran and this L.E. Dixon, they were just about supporting them. The books will show it cost them $150, $175, or $200 a month, and the men were helping them, gave them money, and I didn't want to make any trouble."

But, of course, both Anne and Sammy came out of the house. Sammy gave her a hello hug and kiss, and Anne insisted that everyone come inside and join the nice new doctor from next door for supper.

RUTHIE: "Anne ran up to the car, and she said, 'Why don't you come on in, Ruth?' and I said, 'Why, we are going right away, Anne,' and then she saw Lucille Moore, and she turned and said, 'Oh, I got to get back,' and that was all there was to it. I didn't make any introduction, and Anne didn't either."

Two men - and cronies of Halloran's - who had been visiting the girls came out of the house and climbed into Halloran's car. They drove over to Ruth's apartment, where they ate and had a couple of drinks. Around midnight, Halloran drove Lucille home.

RUTHIE: "The next day, Anne came over to my house for lunch. I cashed my paycheck - I had $30. Anne was with me and I went in and paid my landlady $13 on my rent and then we had lunch and Anne was tired and she went in and laid down to sleep while I got lunch.

We weren't mad at each other at all - and then I paid my rent and we went back to the office together and had our arms linked, arms around each other when we got to the clinic."

While walking back to the office, Anne asked Ruthie to come over for dinner that night and play bridge. But Ruthie told her that she couldn't. She had been spending a lot of time looking at houses and was behind typing up her patient notes for the clinic. She just didn't have time, she explained. Anne told her that she was welcome if she changed her mind.

One of the clinic doctors gave Anne a ride home that evening, and Ruthie stayed at the office. She worked until about 6:00 P.M., then stopped on her way home and paid $15 toward her bill at Wade's grocery store. By now, she had only $2 left in her purse. She apologized to Mrs. Wade for not paying her entire bill, but the other woman waved away the apology. She knew Ruthie was good for it and was very attentive to her bill. The women talked about a realtor they both knew who was helping Ruthie find a house big enough for her friends and her parents.

RUTHIE: "Anne and Sammy said that if I got a house that had two rooms off to themselves, or had an entrance to themselves, they would try and move in with me and they would help me pay a little on it, and Anne and I were going to look at some houses on Saturday evening, October 17."

The realtor had promised to leave the back door open on a house that seemed perfect for them on East McDowell, close to the clinic and large enough to accommodate everyone. Anne tried to borrow a car from one of the doctors but couldn't get one. Ruth said she then asked a friend if she could borrow his car on Saturday instead.

"And that is where the dirty low-down policeman was trying to make out a good big lie," she complained to Sheriff McFadden, who didn't need to be reminded that the prosecution had used her request to borrow that car as evidence that she had planned the murders.

After leaving the grocery store, she walked the rest of the way home, arriving around 6:30 P.M. Then she waited - and waited some more. Jack Halloran was supposed to be coming to get her but was very late. Finally, fed up, she decided that if Jack were going to show up late, then he'd find her gone. Ruthie made plans to go to Anne and Sammy's house to spend time with her friends - and, in my opinion, to run into Jack. She had to know that if he wasn't with her then he was almost sure to be at the party bungalow.

She walked part of the way and then caught the trolley for the rest of the trip. She entered through the back door as usual when she arrived at the bungalow. Anne helped her fix up the Davenport in the living room, where Ruthie said she always slept when she was over. It was a little cool that night, she recalled, so they closed the windows in the bedroom.

RUTHIE: "Anne was sitting over on her bed and Sammy was lying on top of her bed and we were talking. Anne said, 'Ruth, how did Jack Halloran ever meet Lucille Moore?' And I said, 'Why, I introduced them,' and she pitched into me for introducing Jack Halloran to a girl who had syphilis. She asked me what in the world I meant by introducing Jack to a girl who knew syphilis, didn't I know any better than that? And we started quarreling over that, and I says - I can't remember every word we quarreled over and you can't when you have a quarrel - but I do know what I said.

"She told me that she was going to tell Jack that I had introduced him to a girl who had syphilis, and I told her she certainly had no right to tell things outside of the clinic. And oh, she threw up a lot of things, and I asked what difference it made to her anyway, and she told me, 'It will make a lot of difference to you,' in a most insinuating way, and she said, 'I know he had been over to your house nearly every night since you have been over there,' and I says, 'What difference does that make to you? I know all about you.'

"They called me some names and I called them some names. She said, 'I could simply kill you for introducing Jack to some girl that has syphilis, really you know better than to do anything like that,' and she said, 'I'm going tell him.' So, I threatened to tell a lot of things that I know.

"I told the girls that 'every doctor in that clinic thinks you and Sammy are in love with each other and Dr. Sweek and Dr. Baldwin have both told me that you were perverts.' That was what I told them - that is the truth. Dr. Sweek did one day when Anne was sick. I told him that Anne didn't have enough money to get home on, and I asked him if the clinic would let her have a month or two salary, because she was sick and broke and he said to me, 'What in the world does she want to sleep with her for, that is love's labor lost.' And I said, 'Dr. Sweek, there is not a single word of truth that is being said about Anne and Sammy. They don't sleep together.' And he said, 'Oh, you can't tell me anything about that, I know all about it. I can't understand why she would want to take care of a tubercular woman, why these two would tie up together.' And then he said, 'Well, the clinic here will let her have $100, and Dr. Grunow won't like it, I will pay out of my own pocket, but that is all we are going to do.' And then Dr. Baldwin at one time told me that he wished I wouldn't live with Anne and Sammy because those two girls would get me in trouble, they were in love with each other, and I said, 'They are not' and he just went off shaking his head.

"When I was living with Anne and Sammy, I told them what the doctors had said, because I thought more of Anne and Sammy than I did about any of them up at the clinic. And when we were quarreling, I said I was going to tell the doctors at the clinic that they were perverts, and when I tell them, they will sure believe it."

At this point, Ruthie wanted to explain some of the issues that Anne had caused at the clinic - issues that Ruthie was not only able to fix, but she also managed to get Anne her job back after she had left for an extended time to receive treatment for her tuberculosis.

While she was away, the doctors at the clinic met and decided they wouldn't take her back when she returned to Phoenix. Anne's boss, Dr. Charles W. Brown, was on leave at the time and had been replaced by a visiting doctor from Oregon named Landsfield. He had taught Anne's assistant how to take x-rays for him, so when Anne returned, he told her that she wouldn't be coming back to work until Dr. Brown was back in the office.

Anne was angry. She had spent a lot of time and her own money learning to be an X-ray technician, and she knew that her former assistant didn't have the knowledge she did. Worse, her replacement's salary was higher than hers had been. Anne had to wait a month before Dr. Brown came back, and thanks to Ruthie, she could return to her position.

But Anne wasn't satisfied with that. She had told Ruthie that she planned to "fix Dr. Landsfield so he would be sorry." She went to the clinic late one night to meet Ruthie at closing time, and she slipped into the x-ray department and adjusted the machine so that the voltage would be extremely high the next time it was used. Her idea was that if Dr. Landsfield or his amateur technician used the machine, the patient would be badly burned.

"If someone would have taken a picture, it would have burned a terrible hole through somebody," Anne explained and while this wasn't accurate, it could have caused problems if the machine had been turned on. "I threatened to tell this on her, to tell that she had done it."

The bickering between the three girls had now transformed into something more serious. It wasn't just a quarrel that would end in tears and promises of forgiveness. It was now a bitter fight, with each side threatening to ruin the other by destroying friendships, causing them to lose their jobs, and perhaps even getting them into legal trouble if these secrets were revealed.

The threat of syphilis has no modern equivalent. In those days, it was the touch of death, worse than the plague and with no cure. Penicillin wasn't available for a decade, and treatments were unreliable. Those who had it were ostracized by society, and newspapers wouldn't even call it by name - referring to it only as "the social disease." And there was no polite way to catch it, which meant that women who had it were shunned even worse than men.

If Halloran knew that Ruthie had exposed him to a woman with syphilis, he would have ended their affair. And what about Dr. Judd? It wasn't hard to miss that Anne also threatened to tell Dr. Judd that his nice young wife was sleeping with another man. An affair was at the top of the list regarding social taboos in 1931. Careers could be ruined, customers might stop coming in, and social standing in the community could be destroyed. It's already been made clear that Phoenix businessmen of the 1930s played around, but they always made sure they didn't get caught.

Ruthie was being threatened with ruin because of a misunderstanding and an overreaction to it. She didn't introduce Lucille to Jack so he could have an affair with her. Ruthie didn't want that, so she was in love with Jack. The introduction was made because Lucille knew about the area where Jack was going on a hunting trip. Anne, though, assumed the worst and lashed out - and Ruthie responded.

Being a lesbian was not medically dangerous like syphilis was, but it was socially fatal in 1931. Newspapers didn't even give that a polite name - they just used the word "pervert." How would doctors at the clinic feel about stories of Anne and Sammy's love nest? And how would Halloran feel about it since he was helping to support the girls and was likely receiving something in return for that help?

It wouldn't sit well, and Anne and Sammy both knew it.

Even more significant, they knew that Ruthie's threat to reveal Anne's sabotage of the x-ray machine would not only cost her a job but also an entire career. She could even be arrested for it. This would be a terrible blow to the only person earning a paycheck in a household during the Depression.

Ruthie described this volatile situation to Sheriff McFadden but told him she tried to escape the fight by entering the kitchen. She had a glass of milk and placed it on the counter. Ruthie claimed that when she turned around, she saw Sammy coming through the breakfast room with a gun in her hand.

RUTHIE: "She had the gun pointed right at my heart. And Sammy used to take spells, and she would look - oh, she didn't look like herself at all and she had the gun pointed right at my heart, and I grabbed the hand with the gun. The table was right there by the door, the kitchen table is right there, and on the table was the bread knife, and I grabbed for the gun and the knife right about the same time she shot me through the hand - just before I stabbed... I stabbed her once in the shoulder and once in the head, and the blade of the knife bent clear around. It was a long knife and had a green handle, and it was blunt, and I stabbed her with that, and it bent double. And then we dropped to the floor, and I grabbed her and pushed her with this arm, and I yelled, 'Give me that gun,' like that, and I grabbed the gun, and her hand was yet on the trigger when that shot went through her chest, and she never relaxed on the gun one bit until after she was shot through the chest.

"And then we both grappled on the floor for the gun, we fell on the floor and fought back and forth, and I yelled, 'Give me the gun,' and then Anne yelled, 'Shoot, Sammy, shoot, Sammy, shoot her!' and she got the ironing board that was right behind the door. When Anne came with the ironing board, she hit me a blow immediately and she said, 'I will brain you!' and she hit me with the ironing board over the head, and I hollered and I yelled, 'Give me that gun!' and she yelled, 'Sammy, shoot!' And she hit me, I don't know how many times it was, but she would knock me flat on the floor with the ironing board, and we rolled around in that way, I don't know how long, until I got the gun, and she had never released hold on the gun at all, not a bit, until we fell, and her hand was on the trigger when she was shot through the chest.

"I kept trying to get up and when I started to get up, when I was rising, Anne knocked me down with the ironing board when I was in a half upright position."

SHERIFF JOHN MCFADDEN: "How many times did you shoot Sammy?"

RUTHIE: "There were at least five or six shots, I know there was that many shots fired because there was but one cartridge that wasn't emptied - all but one. But I didn't see any bullet and I have never loaded a gun in my life, and I have never shot a gun before in my life, in my life before absolutely not, have never shot a gun and I shot to save my life, and now they think they are going to hang me and put my picture in a frame. They are like cannibals - do you know what I mean? Cannibals do that to their victims, eat them and hang their pictures in frames, and that is what this country is doing, hanging innocent people and putting their picture in a frame with a rope that is around their neck, and if you hang innocent me for the betterment of political parasites like Lloyd Andrews and his rotten political friends, this country is no better than cannibals. I fought for my life, and I am going to continue to fight for my life."

O.V. WILLSON: "We are here looking after you, we just want you to tell what happened."

MCFADDEN: "Now, where did Anne's body fall?"

RUTHIE: "It fell backwards toward the stove. Sammy's head was in towards the breakfast room, the feet towards the kitchen door, because she came that way and fell. When we fell, we were both with heads into the breakfast room. I don't know how long I was sitting on the floor - I must have fell too, afterwards, because I was sitting on the floor and Sammy was lying in one place and Anne was in another place...."

WILLSON: "Now, in shooting Anne, were you sitting on the floor?"

RUTHIE: "I started to get up. I was down on the floor and we were rolling back and forth fighting for this gun, and when I started to get up she banged me on the head with the ironing board just as I shot, she hit me on the head. And when I came to, I was sitting between two bodies on the floor. I ran out of that place, I put on my dress and nothing else, just my shoes and dress.

"I went right back to Brill Street to get my pocketbook. I went home and got my black pocketbook and money and started out of the door when Jack Halloran came into the driveway."

Ruthie explained that she was on her way to the Ford Hotel in downtown Phoenix to use their payphone and call her husband in Los Angeles when Halloran arrived.

They went back into the apartment together, and Ruthie said she had told him what had happened at the bungalow. He scoffed at the story, convinced she was lying or confused, so he agreed to go when Ruthie insisted he take her back to the house and see for himself.

On the way to the bungalow, she again recounted the incident with the girls, telling him that she had acted in self-defense.

Ruthie said they parked the car nearby and recalled that the Cunnigham house was lit up. "They had a party at their house and had everything brilliantly lighted up, and he said he was in bed." Gene Cunningham testified that he was asleep and was awakened by three gunshots that Friday night.

Either Cunningham was lying, or Ruthie was.

Ruthie insisted that Cunningham had been over to see Anne himself with Jack Halloran and that once, when she'd ridden on a trolley with Anne, she'd told Ruthie the two men were friends.

She said that when she and Halloran went into the house, he looked over the bloody scene and could hardly believe what he was seeing. And then he did something that would permanently affect the case.

According to Ruthie's newest story, anyway...

RUTHIE: "He picked up Sammy and he carried her in and laid her on Anne's bed. I don't think he knew that she was shot in the head then. I guess she was dead. If they ever find the mattress, a chemical analysis can be made and they can prove that it's Sammy's blood that is on the mattress because the woman was bleeding terribly, but the head was not bleeding at all.

"When he carried her over and laid her on the bed, there was no blood on the clothes in any place. He threw the pillows off and he laid her on Anne's bed, and the covers had been turned down, pulled down, and there was no blood on the covers. If you know what they say about that mattress - I know he took the mattress. Jack Halloran took the mattress out from there."

Ruthie's story - again, if true - might explain what happened to the mattresses, and it also explained how the blood ended up in just one spot in the bedroom. It was also now clear to Sheriff McFadden why Herman Lewkowitz had grilled the blood expert about what might cause a spot of blood in that corner. Even the expert admitted on the stand that the spattering could've been caused by a body that was dropped onto the bed. Unfortunately, Lewkowitz had gotten this admission from the state's witness, but he never pointed it out clearly to the jury. He certainly never suggested that Halloran might have dropped Sammy's corpse onto the bed.

McFadden asked Ruthie what she thought had caused the blood spatters, and she suggested it was from Sammy's hair. Or, she said, maybe Halloran splashed blood there when he was cleaning up - a job he first ordered Ruthie to do but then took over himself when she started crying while trying to operate a mop with her wounded hand.

"Was there any blood in the bathroom?" Ruthie asked the sheriff, and McFadden told her that, yes, some had been discovered right next to the tub. It was unlikely that she remembered the blood expert testified that there had been no blood traces in the bathroom, but Sheriff McFadden knew there were.

But he did he know that a plumber had been to the house and removed blood and hair from the bathtub drain weeks before an official crime scene technician checked it and found nothing?

The sheriff did realize that the search for two bloody mattresses had been pointless - only one had any blood on it. Police officers had found a single mattress in a vacant lot miles from the bungalow but had assumed it was unrelated to the crime because it had no blood on it. McFadden realized that the mattress might have come from the crime scene after all. If it had, it supported the story that Ruthie Judd was now telling.

The sheriff and her attorney wanted her to continue with the chain of events that night, but Ruthie paused for a long time when they began to prod her about what Jack Halloran did next.

RUTHIE: "He said, 'You better let Dr. Brown treat your hand' and I told him I didn't want him to do it. You know, a long time before, he told me he had plenty on Dr. Brown. He told me he had enough on Brown to hang him. He dialed the phone a couple of times and that is when I told you about a fingerprint on the blind."

She reminded McFadden that as Halloran used the telephone, he pulled down the blind in the bedroom, leaving a single bloody fingerprint behind. She knew the fingerprint was there, but she claimed that Lewkowitz had told her not to talk about it during the trial.

McFadden told her, "I cut those out myself."

Ruthie didn't react to this admission. She just continued, "Well, Lewkowitz told me, 'There are fingerprints, but let's not mention it now.'"

But, of course, the fingerprint was never mentioned during the trial.

She was brought back to her story when McFadden asked her what happened next.

RUTHIE: "He wanted me to straighten things around the kitchen and I couldn't do anything with one hand, couldn't do anything, and I wanted to call Dr. Judd, and I was going to tell him about this affair, and he advised me not to do that - he would tend to all this himself. 'If you will let Dr. Brown dress your hand, I will attend to the whole thing myself.' Then he pulled the trunk in from the garage. He told me that he was going to take Anne out in a trunk. He didn't say anything about Sammy."

In response to more questions from Sheriff McFadden, Ruthie explained that Halloran knew Sammy's packing trunk was in the garage because he'd put it there himself after he helped Sammy move into the bungalow. On that Friday night, he dragged it into the kitchen, and Ruthie watched him lift Anne's body and fold her into the trunk. He said that he was going to get rid of the body in the desert.

After that, he mopped the kitchen floor and cleaned up a bit in the kitchen. After that, he took Ruthie home.

RUTHIE: "He advised me to let Dr. Brown treat my hand for me and never say anything to my husband about this, because he would take care of this thing himself and there would be nothing to it. Jack dialed the phone several times in the dark, because he had the lights off in the bedroom and he pulled the blinds down and dialed the phone, and then he took me home because I was getting hysterical. I was raising the dickens. He took me home and told me he would take care of everything and for me not to say a thing to anybody and he would see me later."

WILLSON: (interrupts) "Can you quote the words that Halloran used? You told me that you had come to some kind of decision that you wanted to give yourself up to the police and he said, 'No, that would never do.'"

RUTHIE: "He scared me of the police. He scared me of the state's attorney - I didn't know who the state's attorney was. Why, he scared the life out of me, what it would mean. He told me not to call my husband or call the police, I must not mention this to anyone, that he would take care of this himself, and that he would see me at once and to keep still and that everything would be all right, and to say absolutely nothing."

Ruthie explained that as she and Halloran left the house, she picked up the gun from the kitchen floor and put it in her purse. She didn't sleep at all that night.

Around noon the next day, Halloran called her at the clinic and told her he couldn't "take care of those parties" as he'd planned. He asked Ruthie if she had done anything about her hand yet, and she told him she hadn't, but she had a plan.

RUTHIE: "I told him I wanted to go out to Los Angeles. I want to get this bullet out of my hand, I think it is best. And he said he thought it was a good idea for me to go to Los Angeles. He wanted me to take the trunk to Los Angeles and I said, 'I will not take those to Los Angeles,' and he says, 'I can't do anything about that trunk,' and he wanted me to meet him that night. H wanted me to talk things over with him, so I waited outside and he kept driving around and around the house, and I went inside because it was cool and I was afraid, I didn't know what he was going to do, whether he was going to kill me or not, and then when he stopped the car, why, he went into the house and then trunk was then in the living room, back of the door.

"He told me he had operated on Sammy - Sammy had been operated on. He said Sammy had been operated on, but she was dead. He thinks he is Dr. Buckley, every time he gets drunk, he thinks he is Dr. Buckley from Buckeye."

She recalled to the sheriff how Halloran had gotten into Good Samaritan Hospital one night after visiting hours, claiming he was the imaginary "Dr. Buckley." When he met nurses sometimes, he used the title "He was always wanting me to introduce him to nurses," Ruthie added.

MCFADDEN: "Now, Ruth, on that Saturday night out at the house, relate as near as you can the conversation you had with Halloran and his plans."

RUTHIE: "That dirty, low-down scoundrel! He won't admit what I want him to admit, where he saw the bodies. I don't care what he does, if he will only admit that. He is a coward, and I am telling you that I am going to get justice from the Supreme Judge of the Universe. I fought for my life there, and I got shot in my hand, and that is where the bodies were lying, and this Jack Halloran was there and absolutely bullied me into going to Los Angeles, and he is too big of a coward to admit that.

"I didn't want to hurt anybody. Anne and Sammy were my friends, but I had a fight with them, and I wouldn't hurt them now. Lots of times I think of things I would like to tell them."

MCFADDEN: "This is an important part. What conversation did you have with Halloran and what were the suggestions he made?"

RUTHIE: "These were the suggestions, and that is what he told me - never to tell about it, that I knew what it meant to me and my family and him and his family, that Sammy had been operated on."

DEPUTY JEFF ADAMS: "Did Halloran tell you who done it?"

RUTHIE: "No, he did not tell me who done it, but you know good and well who did it, if he didn't get Dr. Brown to come over and help him, and pronounce her dead, he tried to do something else."

WILLSON: "Ruth, did you ask him to cut up the body of Sammy?"

RUTHIE: "I didn't, and he didn't say, 'cut up,' he said, 'operated on.' He cuts up deer all the time. He had been in a butcher shop himself."

Ruthie then explained that the "talk things over" meeting that Saturday night in the bungalow really only amounted to Halloran giving her instructions. He told Ruthie to take the trunk with her on the late train that night to Los Angeles. He opened his wallet and frowned.

"I'll tell you," he said, "I will have to go back past the office and get more money to get a ticket for you to go on to Los Angeles."

He told her to call the delivery company just before the train departure time and that he'd meet her near the depot to give her money.

RUTHIE: "He wanted me to take the trunk, and he said there would be someone there to meet me and take the trunk in Los Angeles. He had a man, by the name of Williams, or Wilson, who would meet me in Los Angeles.

"And Mrs. McFadden, you can ask anybody in the depot, and they will tell you I was there for two hours looking to see if I could find the man who was to meet me when I got into Los Angeles. I didn't call my brother, I didn't phone my brother, and there are lots of people that can tell you that I walked up and down that place looking for someone."

As Ruthie told the story, it seemed clear that in her mind, on that Saturday night, the plan was going to work. All she had to do was get the trunk to the train station and make the trip to L.A. Halloran's friend would take over after that. She would go and see her husband, and he would remove the bullet from her hand.

One of the men sitting at the table asked her what she was supposed to do if she was caught.

"I didn't expect to get caught," she said simply.

But the plan went awry at the beginning because the trunk was too heavy. Instead of taking the Saturday night train to Los Angeles, she was stuck in her own apartment with the trunk - a trunk that contained the body of one of her best friends.

RUTHIE: "I paced the floor all day and all night. I said to myself, 'My God, my God, what will I do?' all Saturday night. The Lightning Delivery came, and when they told me they couldn't take the trunk. I didn't know what to do, because Jack wanted to get them out of that house right away, and I was afraid to stay there any longer. I wanted to get out of there and he told me to take the trunk, and they told me I couldn't take it, and I didn't know what to do, so I said, 'Take it over to Brill Street then.'"

Ruthie made a startling discovery when she returned to her apartment - realizing she could be caught before she even left town. As the delivery men had carried the trunk out of the bungalow, she had noticed dark spots on the porch - blood, dripping from the trunk.

Leaving it behind at her apartment, she took the trolley back to the bungalow and used the outside hose to wash off the porch. When she finished, she took the trolley back home again.

RUTHIE: "I paced the floor all night long on Saturday night. I paced that floor all that Sunday, and I said, 'My God, my God, what will I do? What will I do?' I went over to the Grimm's house and called up Jack's office. I called and there was no answer, and then I called up a party and asked them if I could borrow some money, that I wanted to go to Los Angeles, because when they coward didn't meet me and give me money for a ticket, I couldn't go - I only had $4 or $5, and I walked the floor and he didn't come and I waited until Sunday and, of course, he told me to go and I didn't know what to do."

Ruthie kept thinking that Halloran would realize something was wrong and would come by her apartment to see what was going on. But he never came. By Sunday, she felt trapped. She knew Halloran wasn't at his office, and she was too scared to call him at home because "I was afraid his wife was there."

When it became clear that she wasn't coming to help, she went from friend to friend, trying to borrow enough money to get out of town. "I was stuck with those bodies in my house," she said, "and all I could think of was to go to Los Angeles."

The men in the room knew that Ruthie was still hiding something. They prodded her more than a dozen times to explain the one thing she didn't want to discuss. Again and again, she evaded the question, nearly becoming hysterical at some points.

But no one was leaving the room until they had an answer - how did the bodies that arrived at her apartment go from one body in a trunk to two bodies, one of which was in several pieces of luggage?

Ruthie continued to dodge the question as the men pressed her about it.

RUTHIE: "What would you do if you had two bodies in your house? I didn't know what to do, and I just paced the floor, and I said, 'My God, what will I do?' I walked the floor, and I walked the floor and my hand throbbed, and my brain was gone, and I waited for him to come, and nobody came, and I didn't know what to do.

"I didn't want to hurt those girls, they were friends of mine, but I had to fight for my life, and I am going to keep on fighting for my life, and if anybody tries to hurt me, because I don't love anyone that just is trying to kill me and I thought more of them than I ever thought of anybody that I ever knew, but they tried to kill me and I am going to fight."

WILLSON: "You told me you used a Turkish towel in transferring the pieces to your little steamer trunk?"

ADAMS: "Did anybody help you change these pieces? Must have been somebody helped you, must have been somebody help you change part of the big trunk into the other one."

RUTHIE: "I told you that I paced the floor and that nobody came there, didn't I? Well, I did. I paced the floor, and nobody came."

MCFADDEN: "Have confidence in us. We are not trying to damage you. Was anybody involved there?"

RUTHIE: "No! I will just go to the Supreme Judge, and he can judge whether I didn't have to fight for my life."

MCFADDEN: "I am confident of that, or I wouldn't have come over here this afternoon. If you want us to help you, you have to tell us a lot of little things that you don't think help you."

RUTHIE: "Yes, but I read in the papers in Los Angeles that you were going to try and hang me and hang Jack Halloran. All I want him to do is tell where he found those bodies."

Found what bodies? At this, Ruthie was starting not to make sense. So, Sheriff McFadden called for a break since they were getting nowhere. Everyone left the room for fresh air and returned after about 15 minutes.

When the men return, it's evident that their patience is wearing thin.

ADAMS: "The thing I can't understand is how this stuff got in one of the smaller packages."

WILLSON: "She lifted them out. Now, Ruth go ahead and tell Mr. Adams how you used the Turkish towel and how you handled it - you had that little steamer trunk in the house there, didn't you?"

Ruthie was not quick to admit the things the men needed to hear. Little by little, over the next 30 minutes or more, they coaxed portions of the story from Ruthie. Every reply seemed to cause her pain.

Eventually, they were able to get her to admit that she had stacked the suitcase on top of her empty steamer trunk, pushing it against the larger trunk that held the bodies.

WARDEN WILLIAM DELBRIDGE: "Tell us what you did, if you opened the big trunk and took parts of them out and put them in the other trunk?"

RUTHIE: "I had to. There wasn't anyone else there to do it and I walked the floor all Sunday and all night Saturday and nobody came."

WILLSON: "You mean that you tumbled the pieces out of the big trunk into the steamer trunk?"

RUTHIE: "I don't know how, I don't know what I did, I don't want to remember. I don't want to know anything about it, because I don't want to remember, because I can't."

WILLSON: "She was in a frenzied state of mind, I think."

DELBRIDGE: "She has told everything, and this part would be very helpful to her to just tell all of it."

RUTHIE: "I think that I walked the floor, and I didn't know what to do, and I said, that I didn't lift it, I pulled it out, and there was something messy that dropped out."

MCFADDEN: "What did you do with that part that dropped out?"

Sammy's internal organs were never found, by the way.

RUTHIE: "It was a dirty, messy towel. I was an awful messy towel stuck inside."

ADAMS: "How many packages did you have when you got ready to go to Los Angeles?"

RUTHIE: "I had the trunk and the suitcase and a bag, and I had a little case. I had a little kit, and it had tiny, little probes - it was the doctor's that he used to pick our splinters - and that was to cut the bullet out of this hand, and I had a couple of bandages and material, and they tried to say I had a big knife, and I didn't. I didn't have a big knife they operated on Sammy with, because this was a little surgical kit that my husband used - no bigger than a lead pencil, a little tiny, tiny knife."

WILLSON: "You didn't see what was in the bottom of this trunk?"

RUTHIE: "I didn't ever find out what was in the bottom of the trunk except what they said in the courtroom. I listened and I couldn't hear what they said was in the trunk and I don't want to remember, don't want to know about it, because I don't want to. I don't know what was in it."

WILLSON: "Well, did you pull the pieces out and let them dump into the other luggage?"

RUTHIE: "I don't know if I did, because I said I walked the floor all the time and said, 'My God, what will I do,' and I told you there was no one there."

DELBRIDGE: "I can't understand why she doesn't tell you how she opened the trunk."

MCFADDEN: "This is very important that you tell us as near as you can recall how you transferred Sammy's body from the trunk into the steamer trunk and suitcase. Wasn't there a black bag?"

RUTHIE: "That had dirty towels in it. Listen... Anne and I had on pajamas that were alike, and I asked her to put one of those pairs on that night when we had our fight. And they were torn. And I opened the train window, and I threw them out the window. "

MCFADDEN: "Now, in these towels, could there have been anything wrapped in them?"

RUTHIE: "No, they came out of the trunk, they fell on the floor. I threw them out with the other pajamas - the two towels and the pajamas, and I threw them out the window."

As the transcript continued, the discussion wandered all over the place. The men realized that Ruthie was upset and didn't plan to give them a straight answer about Sammy's body. Even so, they eventually came back to the issue.

ADAMS: "What was the idea, Mrs. Judd, in changing the bodies into another package?"

RUTHIE: "Because I had to. Because the trunk was too heavy to go by express and I didn't know what to do."

WILLSON: "Tell us how you lifted those pieces."

RUTHIE: "I said I didn't lift them. I lowered them. Over the edge and they fell into the lower trunk. The piece I lowered, it was on top. I pulled it over the edge into the trunk at the side of it. I had the big trunk and the little trunk at the side, and I pulled them over to the edge and lowered it into the other - you can't lift that big trunk."

DELBRIDGE: "How did you get the pieces in the suitcase?"

RUTHIE: "By putting the suitcase on top of the steamer trunk, it made it almost as high as the big trunk."

ADAMS: "You just reached down and pulled it over?"

RUTHIE: "Just pulled it over."

WILLSON: "Was there any blood spilled as you transferred the pieces?"

RUTHIE: "There was no blood at all, not a drop of blood ever dropped in my apartment, that I know of. I don't know of any because that body had been cut up over there, and there was no blood on the body."

DELBRIDGE: "About what time was it when you unlocked the big trunk?"

RUTHIE: "It must have been at least 3:00, it was late."

DELBRIDGE: "You just made up your mind you had to do something to unlock the trunk?"

RUTHIE: "I had to, I didn't know what to do."

DELBRIDGE: "Well, coming back to that again, what did you take out of there?"

RUTHIE: "I didn't have any idea what I was going to take out and that was on top."

WILLSON: "What was on top?"

RUTHIE: "Portions of a body."

It had been a long afternoon, and Ruthie had told the four men a story she should have told months before. Why did she keep silent for so long? Why didn't she tell the truth to her first attorneys in Los Angeles?

She had a quick answer for that one. "Because I wanted to talk to Jack Halloran before I made any statements. The first thing I done was to tell them to get in touch with Jack Halloran and they told me, no, that would not be advisable for him to come over here."

It wasn't until she had been in the county jail in Phoenix for two weeks, Ruthie admitted, that she told her attorneys the same story she was telling now. She said that Joseph Zaversack took down a full account of the story, and later, he told her that he gave it to Judge Speakman. He also told her that was all she needed to say and that she should now "keep still."

One of the men asked her if she was instructed not to talk.

RUTHIE: "Absolutely - all they told me, they said, 'Listen, the state is subpoenaing Jack Halloran, and when we get him on the witness stand, we will tear him to pieces on cross-examination, and you will be cleared.'

"Jack Halloran came in with about 30 people, and he held up his hand when they were all there, but his name was never read off, his name never was. Then they told me, 'All right, we will call him if the state does not and use him. We will call him. It will be all right, you just keep still, we will put Jack Halloran on the stand ourselves if the state doesn't.'

"All right, they didn't put him on but they said, 'If we put him on, then he will claim his constitutional rights to say nothing which would incriminate him and then that is all we can question him about.' And finally, Zaversack said, 'If they don't put him on, I will go on the witness stand myself, Mrs. Judd, and tell the whole story, I will do that.'

"And until the last day I thought I was going to the witness stand myself, and when I didn't - I wrote Judge Speakman the whole story, or Zaversack has it in his possession, and that is the truth, and he told me that he went to Judge Speakman's house and read it to him."

No one in the room believed that Judge Speakman was ever given a private account of Ruthie's version of events. And I don't believe he ever heard the story, either.

But everyone in the room did have some new insight into what happened that night at the bungalow. Much of what Ruthie said matched the evidence - or at least one version of it.

I think that some of what Ruthie told the men that day was true - but not the whole truth. Anyone who puts much thought into the story she told knows there are some missing pieces.

But there was enough truth to what Ruthie said that day that the men who had gathered to hear her story did believe that, if it had been presented at her trial, it might have been enough to raise reasonable doubt with the jury.

More to the story needed to be revealed, but they knew that couldn't be done if Ruthie Judd was dead. The goal now, it seemed, was to find a way to save her life.

12. "HAPPY JACK" ON THE HOT SEAT

DURING THE LAST WEEK OF 1932, THE ARIZONA SUPREME Court denied the defense counsel's petition for rehearing Ruthie's case. But before Ruthie and her attorneys could focus on this potential disaster, a lifeline appeared - a subpoena was delivered that required Ruthie to testify before the Maricopa County Grand Jury on Wednesday, December 28, in Phoenix.

Ruthie was finally getting a chance to "tell all" outside of a tiny interview room at the state prison.

That morning, Ruthie was transported to Phoenix for the closed grand jury session. County Attorney Lloyd Andrews and 20 grand jury members would hear her new version of events.

Andrews briefed the jury members before the session began. He was now finishing out the last days of his term after being defeated in the fall primary. In fact, this hearing would be his last official act.

He explained that Mrs. Judd would finally tell the story she didn't tell at her trial. He reminded them that he had tried to get her to talk, but she refused. He even mentioned the time he herded a group of reporters to her cell and tried to browbeat her into telling the truth, but she only wanted to talk in a court of law. He used these attempts as "proof" that he had tried many times to get her side of the story made public.

On this day, Andrews told the jury, she was having her day in court, even though reporters were banned from the session and everything said had to be kept secret by law.

But Andrews' self-serving introduction didn't end there. He went on to warn the jury that Ruthie might fly off the handle and might even throw things at them - be on your guard!

While there's no way to know what Andrews was thinking with this warning, he likely hoped Ruthie's story would be discredited. An insane Ruthie Judd was likely to say anything - even implicate one of the city's most prominent businessmen - but no one would take her seriously if she were nuts.

But whatever Andrews' motivation, it was clear that he had been forced into the hearing by Sheriff McFadden, who was also present that day. He had taken the transcript of his December 19 prison meeting and demanded that the information be presented to a grand jury.

His daughter, Helen, never knew how he managed this - whether he threatened to go public with it if Andrews didn't act or threatened to arrest Halloran himself - but however he did it, the sheriff was the driving force behind it.

And he paid for it. Helen later said her father's political aspirations were destroyed because he championed Ruthie Judd's cause. He was later linked to a real estate scandal, and while he was cleared of any wrongdoing, his association with it turned off voters. When he died in 1940, he was so poor that his friends had to raise the money to pay for his funeral.

McFadden had to have known what he was doing would cost him dearly, but he plowed ahead anyway. Why? His daughter knew exactly why he did it. "He was an honest man," she said. "He couldn't just let it drop."

THE GRAND JURY LISTENED INTENTLY AS ANDREWS asked questions, and Ruthie calmly told her story, quickly dispelling the idea that she was dangerous or insane. They heard about the fight, about Halloran's actions, the "operation" on Sammy, Ruthie's horrifying night with the two corpses, and her desperate search for money to get out of town.

The grand jury heard the story that Ruthie had told to the four men at the state prison and formed their own ideas about the murders. They decided that she had been involved in the crime but that it was not a cold-blooded murder. She had not acted alone. They didn't believe she could have cut up a body. They were convinced it would have required a professional. As they listened to her story, they formed the opinion that she wasn't insane and wasn't guilty of anything other than getting into a jealous fight.

And they shocked the nation by making that opinion public. They believed Ruthie's story of killing in self-defense. On Friday, the grand jury petitioned the state Board of Pardons and Paroles to grant Ruthie an immediate commutation of her death sentence to life imprisonment.

And there was more. Not only did they believe Ruthie had acted in self-defense, but they also indicted Jack Halloran as her accomplice. He was formally charged as "an accessory to the crime of murder."

The indictment made big news across the country. The *New York Times* reported the next day that a secret indictment had been issued for Halloran. However, Sheriff McFadden notified him about the grand jury's decision over the telephone. He had shown up in Judge Speakman's courtroom, posted a cashier's check for $3,000 as bond, and demanded the earliest possible arraignment. It was set for January 4.

The Hearst newspapers had a field day with the indictment against "Happy Jack." They called him a playboy - a derogatory term in those days - or the "millionaire clubman" and the "rich sportsman."

The International News Service printed Halloran's cockier statements to the press: "We'll take our medicine - there's no yellow streak up our spine," he said with a grin, as the International News

Service reported. "I'm glad that it's all coming out. It will clear the air, and people will not have so much to talk about."

Jack Halloran leaving the courthouse after posting his $3,000 bond. He insisted that he wasn't worried about the allegations that had been made about him.

The press in Phoenix, though, used a statement released by his attorneys, in which Halloran reportedly said, "There is no basis of truth in the charge, not in any statement that produced it. That it is absolutely false and a grave injustice to me will be proved at the proper time."

In another story, Halloran's attorneys quickly pointed out what they called a major flaw in the indictment. If the grand jury was convinced that Mrs. Judd killed in self-defense, then there was no murder. And if no murder was committed, then Mr. Halloran should not have been indicted as an "accessory to a crime." If there was no murder committed, then there was no crime, the attorneys stated.

The local papers also publicized attacks on the grand jury, including a stinging criticism from Judge Speakman: "According to their statement - which they had no business to make - all they say is that she acted in self-defense. They don't know any more about it than the trial jury did. In fact, virtually all they had was her own story."

Speakman added that by appealing to the parole board, the grand jurors had "violated the law and their oaths."

County Attorney Renz Jennings took over from Lloyd Andrews. This photo was taken later in his life.

Lloyd Andrews was no longer in office by the time Jack Halloran's preliminary hearing took place, and the new county attorney, Renz Jennings, was thrown into the middle of the complex case on his first day.

The preliminary hearing was held on January 4, 1933, in Judge Speakman's courtroom. Halloran's attorney, Frank O. Smith, filed a motion to quash the indictment, and County Attorney Jennings was given a 24-hour continuance so he could prepare his case.

Meanwhile, Judge Speakman was in the newspapers again, blustering about how the grand jury had broken the law by revealing Ruthie's "secret" testimony. He also blasted them for filing the indictment in Superior Court because the state Supreme Court had taken the matter out of his hands when they affirmed the court's actions during Mrs. Judd's murder trial.

"The grand jury has a right to recommend to the Parole Board," he said, "but no right to return any such thing as that into this court because this court now has nothing to do with the case of Winnie Ruth Judd."

Speakman wanted nothing more to do with Ruthie Judd or her case, and who can blame him? Anyone who hoped to be reelected in Phoenix in those days didn't want to do anything that might upset the most important men in the city.

It likely comes as no surprise then that on Friday, Judge Speakman ruled the indictment was defective. He declined to squash the charge, though, and ordered Jennings to resubmit the case to a Justice of the Peace Court. Halloran's $3,000 bond remained in effect until the new complaint was settled.

Judge Speakman had finally gotten rid of the Judd case once and for all.

As it turned out, Judge Speakman wasn't the only official embroiled in the Judd case who wanted to offer opinions about the new indictment. While County Attorney Jennings was preparing the complaint, former County Attorney Andrews spoke to the press: "I don't believe her story, and I wouldn't consider going to the Parole Board on her behalf. Mrs. Judd has told too many stories - five or six in all, and there are discrepancies in each of them. Too many things would have to be explained before I could believe any of her stories. She first sold her "true story" to the Los Angeles Examiner for $5,000. This woman has consistently sought to commercialize this atrocious crime. Every story I've heard of the deaths of Agnes LeRoi and Hedvig Samuelson - and each was reputed to come from Mrs. Judd - has been different."

Honestly, Andrews did have a point here. There were a lot of versions of the "true story" of the murders told by Ruthie Judd, and it's not out of line to ask some questions about all of them.

But then again, of course, Andrews had to make sure that he came across looking as though he was a dedicated public servant who'd only ever been looking for the truth. He told a reporter:

I tried to get Mrs. Judd to tell me what actually happened when I first saw her in the office of Chief of Detectives Joe Taylor in Los Angeles. She refused to talk on the advice of counsel. Then I tried to get from her the real store when she was brought from the county jail to my office for a conference after our return to Phoenix. Her answer was the same.

After she was convicted - in the presence of newspapermen - I gave her the chance to talk, for which she had been clamoring. She didn't tell the story then that she how tells, though the press was only too anxious to record it.

Now that her avenues of escape are closing, she comes forward with this story involving Halloran. Before I believe her story, the location of the wounds in the women's heads must be reconciled.

Blood spots on the window shade next to Mrs. LeRoi's bed and underneath her bed must be explained. The fact that Mrs. Judd's own gun was used in the slayings - the shell found in Mrs. Judd's apartment, and the clever acting in court of the blond woman slayer also need some explaining.

So, emphatically, no! I do not believe her story.

The new complaint against Halloran was filed late on Saturday afternoon in the West Phoenix Court of Judge Nat T. McKee. It charged Halloran as an "accessory to the crime of murder" in that he "aided and assisted" Winnie Ruth Judd in disposing of, and concealing the body of, Agnes Anne LeRoi; advised and directed her "to not reveal or disclose that she had committed the crime of murder;" and further abetted her crime by "aiding, assisting, and advising her" to escape from Maricopa County and Arizona to California.

On Monday, January 9, Halloran's defense counsel filed a motion with Judge Speakman's court seeking a transcript of Ruthie's testimony before the grand jury. The motion was denied.

That same day, County Attorney Jennings' office prepared an affidavit and court order directing that Ruthie be brought to testify for the state at the preliminary hearing, which was scheduled to begin in two days.

This was going to be Ruthie's big moment. Her attorneys had already petitioned the Board of Pardons and Parole to commute her death sentence based on the grand jury's recommendation. Ruthie was even heard to wonder if she might not win a "full pardon" when everyone realized she had acted in self-defense. In her mind, everything would be cleared up when she finally got to testify publicly in court.

The board didn't commute her death sentence, but to allow time for the new court proceedings, they did reschedule her execution date for April 14.

And yes, that date fell on a Friday.

HALLORAN'S PRELIMINARY HEARING WAS SUPPOSED TO begin on January 11, but delays began almost immediately. First, it was announced that Judge McKee was very ill with pneumonia and would be unable to hear the case. A few days later, Judge J.C. Niles was substituted to serve as the magistrate.

On Monday, January 16, Judge Niles reversed the ruling by Judge Speakman and allowed Halloran's defense attorneys access to Ruthie's grand jury testimony. This was a significant victory for the defense - Ruthie would have to be extremely careful to avoid changing anything about her story.

The delays finally ended on January 17, when the hearing began. Once again, the courtroom was overflowing, and reporters from around the country elbowed through the crowds to record everything Ruthie said over the next eight days.

No one was disappointed by the show - except for anyone who was there for a clear narrative of events.

Time after time, Ruthie electrified the courtroom audience with startling revelations, hysterical outbursts, and verbal attacks on Jack Halloran. She screamed. She cried. Her story wandered all over the place, and while she kept her promise to "tell all," her story was interrupted by what the press dubbed "wild cries" and "angry outbursts."

Halloran's attorney, Frank Smith, used her outburst to argue that she was insane and incompetent to testify. "It is simply plain she is wild," he declared, asking the court to dismiss the case. Judge Niles disagreed, and the hearing continued.

But there was more drama in the hearing than just Ruthie. It began with a considerable argument about whether Ruthie should remain in the custody of Sheriff McFadden, who was also subpoenaed as a witness. Judge Niles ruled that he could remain in the courtroom since he was officially responsible for Ruthie during the hearing.

McFadden was questioned ruthlessly by Frank Smith during a break during the three hours of the opening-day testimony given by Ruthie. Smith quizzed the sheriff about the ironing board that Ruthie alleged had been used in the attack on her by Anne. The attorney wanted the ironing board introduced as an exhibit. McFadden testified he had brought the ironing board into the sheriff's office and had locked it in an evidence vault - but it had vanished.

When asked what was in the vault now, McFadden replied, "Most everything you'd look for - except the ironing board."

Asked how exhibits in some instances were recorded when stored, McFadden replied, "I don't keep the records myself."

"There is no reason why you should?"

"No, sir."

"But you would expect a deputy to do so?"

"Yes, sir. I don't bother with little things like that. I have too much else to do."

"You call that a little thing?"

"I mean the records."

"I'm taken completely by surprise here," Smith announced. "I need this ironing board. It's an important piece of evidence."

Earlier, Smith had elicited from McFadden that he had once questioned Ruthie for 30 hours in one stretch, establishing that McFadden knew something about the ironing board. Since the board was now missing, Smith asked him to describe it: how long was it? How tall was it? What color was it?

McFadden snapped, "I don't know. I never ironed with it."

McFadden's time on the witness stand turned out to be a calm between Ruthie's storms. When her turn came, she was determined that she would not be gagged - no matter what questions were asked or how painful it was to recount her story of that awful night.

But things quickly went off the rails.

And Jack Halloran was largely responsible for it. He smiled at Ruthie when she became upset and laughed aloud when she screamed, "I am going to be hanged for something Jack Halloran is responsible for. I was convicted of murder, but I shot in self-defense. Jack Halloran removed every bit of evidence. He is responsible for me going through all this. He is guilty of anything I am guilty of."

Another time, after accusing Halloran of trying to signal answers to her, Ruthie shouted, "I don't want him to talk to me! He's talked to me too much already! He told me not to tell anyone what had happened - not even my husband. He said to me, 'For God's sake, do you want to hang?' He bullied me that night, and now he is too big of a coward to tell everything!"

At one point, when she was crying hysterically, Smith asked the judge to clear the courtroom of spectators. "It might be easier for Mrs. Judd if we did so. I am not trying to shield Mr. Halloran when I suggest this, for he is as innocent as anyone ---"

"He is not!" Ruthie screamed from the witness stand. "He is responsible for the deaths of three girls. Anne is dead. Sammy is dead, and I'm going to die!"

She jumped up from her chair and charged across the courtroom to where Halloran was seated, facing him directly. As a ripple of fear and excitement went through the crowd, Ruthie bawled, "You don't care what happened to Sammy - that she's dead, and that Anne's dead, and I'm going to die! You sit there and laugh. You still play around. I hope you suffer everything Anne's mother has suffered, and my mother and Sammy's mother has suffered."

A reporter from the *New York Journal* reported that this outburst from Ruthie "brought tears to the eyes of the spectators and even the judge."

Ruthie told the court that there had been so much proof to back up her story, but Halloran had moved it, or stolen it, or rearranged it. "I wish that mattress would be brought in here and it was shown that no one was shot in bed, and I would have been cleared in my trial."

When Smith asked how she could claim that Halloran had taken the mattress away, she replied that everyone knew he had done it.

"Who do you mean by 'everybody?" Smith asked.

"Everybody with common sense," Ruthie said. "I am not accusing him of murdering anyone, but only of operating on Sammy or having her operated on and obliterating the evidence."

While this was going on, it was clear that Halloran was still enjoying the show. He never once seemed nervous that his case might go to trial after the hearing. His wife accompanied him to court daily, and his mother had flown in from Oakland, California, to be with the family. One morning, when he had to push through the crowd to get into the courtroom, he told them to let him pass because he was the "head man in the show."

Ruthie electrified the courtroom with startling revelations, hysterical outbursts, and verbal attacks on Jack Halloran. She screamed. She cried. Her story wandered all over the place and was interrupted by what the press dubbed "wild cries" and "angry outbursts."

He continued to smile as Ruthie testified, sometimes shaking his head at her version of events, and more than once, he laughed out loud. His actions kept stirring her up. Each time he showed some outward sign of mocking her, she would blow up.

It took nearly three days for Ruthie to tell the whole story. The judge had to admonish her repeatedly to answer the question, not give a speech. She paid little attention to those directions, though. "I'm not here for the purpose of clearing Jack Halloran!" she shouted at one point. "He had an opportunity to clear me at my trial, but he didn't!"

Almost every question led to her launching another attack on Halloran, whom the local press called "her former friend." Over and over, her outbursts were stricken from the record as being "unresponsive to the question."

Once, when Smith objected to her testimony, she screamed, "I expect Mr. Halloran would be able to tell it more accurately!"

Most of Ruthie's story followed exactly what she had offered in her rambling story at the state prison in December. There were a few variations and differences, however. I don't think it's necessary to transcribe her testimony again, but I think it's worth looking at some of the additions and changes she made at the preliminary hearing - in between her screams, rants, and insults, of course.

RUTHIE: "I told him that Anne and Sammy were lying on the floor. Jack said, 'What in the world is the matter with you?' I told him I was on my way to call my husband on long distance and tell him Anne and Sammy and I had had a fight. I told him I was shot. I told him Anne and Sammy were shot. I told him about the quarrel. Jack then dragged me out to the car and we went to the Second Street house. We went in through the kitchen door - Jack preceded me. When we got inside the door, he stopped and said, 'My God! Sammy!' and he ran over and stooped at the side of Sammy, checked her pulse and examined her chest wound."

Aside from some additional conversation, her narrative mainly stayed the same, detailing how Halloran had placed Anne's body in the trunk and how he had taken Ruthie back to her apartment while Sammy's body was still lying on Anne's bed.

The next day, he called her at the clinic and convinced her to take the trunk - which he first told her contained both bodies - to Los Angeles so that she could have her husband patch up the bullet wound in her hand. Halloran was supposed to bring money to her at the train station for her escape, but he never showed up.

She recounted that the trunk had been too heavy to lift, so it was taken to her apartment.

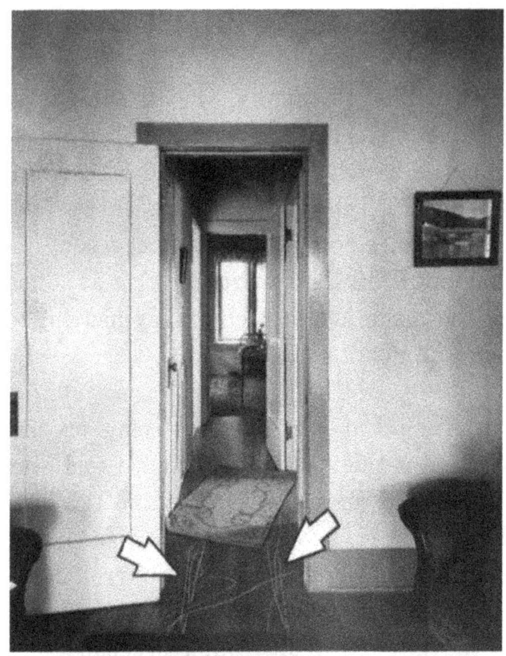

The hallway at Ruthie's Brill Street apartment, The arrows show the scratches that were made on the floor by the trunk. Too heavy to move with Sammy's entire body inside, Ruthie admitted to separating the parts into separate cases.

RUTHIE: "I waited all Saturday night for Jack, and I was in a terrible frame of mind. I do know this - when they carried the trunk out of the Second Street house, I noticed something spilled on the porch. When they left the trunk at the Brill Street house, I went back to the Second Street house and turned the hose on the porch. I took the last car out and caught the same car back."

She testified that she didn't see Halloran again after Saturday night "until he came into the courtroom at my trial and raised his hand as a state witness."

Asked by County Attorney Jennings if a mattress was missing that night from the bedroom at the bungalow, Ruthie said, "The beds were made up, but Jack had taken the mattress off the bed."

During Smith's cross-examination, Ruthie talked about having worked at various times for the Ford family and Dr. Charles Brown. She described working at the Grunow Clinic and meeting Anne and Sammy in January 1931.

After asking Ruthie how many times Halloran had driven around the bungalow on Saturday night, Smith suddenly jumped to his feet and demanded, "Whom are you watching and communicating with back there in the courtroom?"

"I'll turn then and face this way," she replied, turning toward the reporters seated in the jury box.

After suggesting she turn back and face Judge Niles, Smith remarked, "He is the one who will decide whether or not you're telling the truth."

It was a rare bit of unusual behavior during the hearing that Ruthie didn't cause. But don't worry, her strange behavior was the main attraction for courtroom spectators.

Ruthie's strange behavior in the courtroom didn't help her situation, but it did provide many hours of entertainment for the audience.

She almost became hysterical when Smith pointedly asked her how she knew that Halloran had disposed of the mattress. Ruthie shrieked, "Well, he's done some trick about that mattress! You're trying to trick me now and I'm telling God's truth! I'm telling you what I intend to write when I commit suicide!"

A few moments later, she'd turned eerily calm. She added, "I am not accusing him of murdering anyone but only of operating on Sammy or having her operated upon and obliterating the evidence - and there were some organs missing, too."

"How do you know an operation was performed?" Smith asked.

"He told me Sammy had been - I do know that when he is drunk, he calls himself 'Dr. Buckley.'"

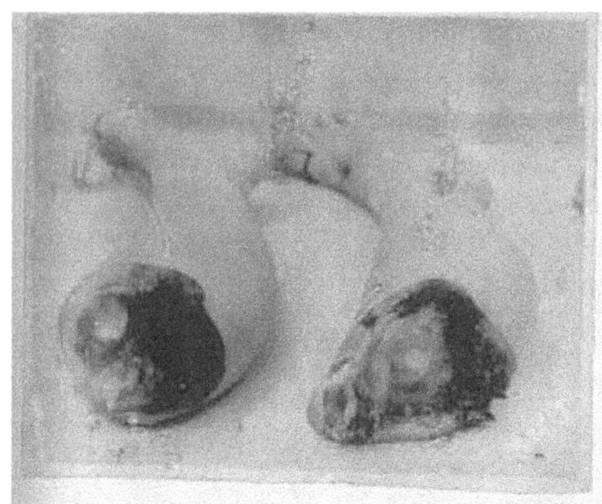

One of the claims that Ruthie made was that Halloran had dismembered Sammy or had gotten someone else to do it.

Sammy's severed legs are above. Below is the suitcase that was found containing parts of her body.

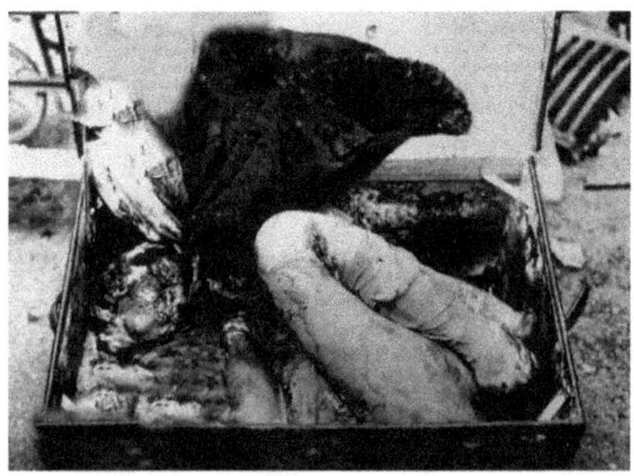

Smith objected to further testimony from Ruthie on the grounds that it was irrelevant and not responsible. Court was then recessed until the following morning.

After court resumed on Wednesday at 9:00 A.M., Ruthie was 40 minutes into her testimony when she began a dramatic recital that kept the crowded courtroom in deep silence. It was the first time she'd ever publicly offered details about the double murder. Smith carefully led her through the events leading to the fight.

Again, I won't go over Ruthie's story about the quarrel and how things turned physical. Her story stayed the same from the December 19 meeting.

At one point, though, Smith said to the court, "It is unfortunate that this testimony involves so many people. It is exceedingly unfortunate that the name of this nurse, and of other citizens, should be dragged into this. I regret it deeply. I am perfectly willing to exclude the public from this hearing if it is so desired."

County Attorney Jennings countered by saying he was "not responsible as county attorney for what her testimony may be."

Smith then asked, because of the importance of the testimony, that it be continued. He added, "Jack Halloran is just as innocent of these charges as any man in this state."

"He is not!" Ruthie screamed. Women in the audience applauded as Judge Niles pounded his gavel, trying to restore order. But Ruthie continued, "He is responsible for the deaths of three girls in this state! Anne and Sammy are dead - and I only have four more weeks to live!"

After order was finally restored, Ruthie's accusations were ordered stricken from the record. Once she calmed down, she continued her narrative but added a little more detail - and a lot more melodrama -- to her initial encounter with Sammy after the argument in the bedroom.

RUTHIE: "At that time, I went out and took my glass of milk from the icebox and went out into the kitchen and set it on the sink. Sammy came running around through the hallway, through the living room, and back into the breakfast room there. As I turned around, she faced me with a gun. She said, 'If you dare telling anything on Anne, I will kill you sure.'

"She had the gun in her hands. I grabbed the gun with this hand ffiindicating her left handffl and she shot, and as I grabbed the gun, I grabbed toward the knife. I grabbed the bread knife off the kitchen table there. It was a blunt-end knife, and I grabbed the knife, and as I grabbed for the gun and knife - I don't know at the same time or not - but I grabbed them right there, and as I grabbed towards the gun, she had it pointed at my heart.

"She shot me through the hand this way. I had the bread knife this way, and I stabbed her twice in the shoulder. At that, Anne came yelling into the kitchen, and I said, 'Give me that gun' to Sammy, 'Give me that gun!'

"And Anne yelled, 'Shoot, Sammy, shoot!'

"The bread knife bent double like that. It was a green-handled knife, and it bent completely double. I then grabbed with this hand toward the gun. This hand was shot ffileft hand againffl and I grabbed toward the gun with this hand ffiindicating her right handffl and only with the back of my arm tried to get the gun out of her hand, and twisted like this the gun in her hand, and this finger was torn and this figure torn wrenching for the gun.

"Her finger was yet on the trigger when that shot went through her chest, Anne grabbed up the ironing board that was behind the water heater there, and when Sammy and I fell on the floor - when they shot went through her chest as we fell on the floor. I don't know how we tripped, but we fell on the floor, and Anne came over and beat me with the ironing board and yelled at Sammy, 'Shoot, Sammy, shoot!'

"She beat me over the head, and she beat with the ironing board as we rolled there back and forth in the doorway fighting for the gun. We rolled back and forth in the doorway and fought.

"I fought for my life. I fought for every ounce of strength that I had for that gun there in the doorway rolled back and forth, and Anne beat me with the ironing board all the time she was there, and said, 'Get her, Sammy! Get her, Sammy! Shoot! Shoot! Get her!'

"And I said, 'Sammy, give me that gun! Give me that! Let go of the gun! You give me that gun!'"

At this point, Ruthie became hysterical again, weeping and screaming. She cried out, "If anyone thinks they are going to hang me for killing in self-defense, I'll write it all out and take it to God - he's the Supreme Judge - Jack just wants to play around. I am convicted of murder. There was no murder. I shot in self-defense. Jack Halloran made me the goat for all this.

The references to Halloran were ordered stricken from the record.

Ruthie finally finished her story about the argument, which ended with the deaths of both women. She broke down and sobbed on the witness stand. "He don't care that Anne is dead, or Sammy is dead, or that I'm going to die. He just sits there and laughs about."

She pointed a wavering finger at Jack Halloran, who smiled at her.

Finally, Ruthie - now a shuddering and seemingly broken woman with her face covered in tears - was taken from the courtroom. It took Jewel Jordan and another jail matron more than two hours to calm her down.

Ruthie's frequent outbursts and crying spells led to her being escorted in and out of the courtroom several times.

AFTER RUTHIE WAS RETURNED TO THE COURTROOM, Smith again tried unsuccessfully to have Sheriff McFadden removed from the room during Ruthie's testimony because he was a witness and - Smith insinuated - he might have been the person who was coaching Ruthie from the spectator's seats. County Attorney Jennings objected, and while the sheriff wasn't banished to the hallway, he was moved to a side of the room out of Ruthie's line of sight - just in case.

With Ruthie back on the stand, Smith produced an ironing board that was allegedly the one mysteriously missing from the evidence vault at the sheriff's office. But when Ruthie was asked to identify the board as the one used in the fight, she would only say it was "similar to that one."

During later testimony, Smith asked Ruthie if she had requested permission from her attorneys to testify during her murder trial.

"Certainly," she told him.

"And you were refused permission?"

"No, I was led to believe I would be allowed to tell later on."

"That you would be allowed after the trial?"

"No, during the trial," Ruthie insisted. "I was led to believe I would be allowed to take the stand after Jack Halloran. I begged to take the witness stand and tell everything in my defense - I prayed that Jack Halloran would take the stand and tell everything."

Although Halloran spent most of the hearing alternating between looking annoyed and amused, there was one moment during the second day of Ruthie's testimony - and after one of her outbursts - that Halloran got angry and started to stand up from the defense table. He was restrained by one of his attorneys. It was the first - and only time - during the hearing that he reacted to what Ruthie was saying about him.

A surprise motion and some slick legal maneuvers - by both Ruthie's and by Halloran's defense - highlighted the third day of the hearing.

After more difficult cross-examination of Ruthie - which only included a handful of evasive answers - Frank Smith made a motion that challenged her competency as a witness. He asked that all her testimony be stricken from the record. Judge Niles took the matter under advisement, indicating that he would rule on it pending further developments during the hearing.

There was a lot of speculation surrounding the motion. If sustained, the hearing would end, and the charges against Halloran would be dismissed. Ruthie was the only person to incriminate him; if incompetent, there was no case. But if the judge denied the motion, it was believed that Ruthie would have trouble winning any insanity hearing she asked for before her execution. If he denied the motion, Judge Niles would essentially be saying that Ruthie was a competent witness and, therefore, sane.

While Smith's motion caught County Attorney Jennings by surprise, some of his other legal shenanigans angered Ruthie's personal attorneys. Prior to the hearing, Smith had subpoenaed all her lawyers as witnesses. He then successfully got them banned from the courtroom under the witness rule, even though he never actually planned to call them to the stand.

On Thursday morning, after Ruthie had been on the stand for more than two days, Smith withdrew the ban that kept them from the courtroom. But not until after he'd announced to the courtroom audience, "I have a duty to perform for Jack Halloran. I am not representing her - but God knows she needs counsel!"

Smith claimed that all of Ruthie's testimony was "under compulsion" and without advice from her lawyers, which had been her right. The audacity of this statement amazed the crowd. It was now clear why Smith had gotten her attorneys kicked out of the courtroom.

Jacob Morgan, one of Ruthie's attorneys, was angry when he was allowed back into the courtroom. "We were barred for two days on fake subpoenas! We resent the pitfalls that are being dug for us purposely - and these attempts to push us into them."

Smith snorted. "Those subpoenas were issued under due process of law. If anything was wrong with them, I don't know it."

"I challenge the sincerity of them," Morgan snapped.

Later in the day, still upset after Smith's claim that she was "physically and mentally diseased to the extent that she is incompetent to testify," Ruthie proved that she had some legal skills of her own. When Smith ordered her to relate in detail how she had repacked the bodies in the two trunks in her apartment on the night of the murders, Ruthie became irritated. "Now listen," she said to Smith, "the other day you tried to stop me when I tried to tell you what Halloran did to Sammy, and now I don't have to tell..."

Judge Niles cut her off. He directed her to respond to Smith's question. Winnie gave a snippy reply: "May I then ask for my constitutional rights to say nothing about another case that may be incriminating to myself?"

She explained that she was referring to Sammy's murder, for which she had not been brought to trial. The judge agreed with her - Ruthie did not have to answer the question. It really didn't do anything to help her, but since she managed to spite Frank Smith, she was undoubtedly pleased.

Ruthie got the better of Smith again that afternoon when he asked her about the two letters she had purportedly written to her husband on the day after the murders. She refused to answer on the grounds that the letters were privileged communications between husband and wife. The judge agreed with her once again.

Twice during the day, Smith abruptly dropped the subject while cross-examining Ruthie. The first time came after he asked, "Mrs. Judd, you state a criminal operation was performed on Miss Samuelson..."

Ruthie interrupted him. "I just know that an operation was performed. Mr. Halloran told me Sammy was operated on Saturday night.

Smith then abruptly changed his line of questioning after asking if she thought there was a good reason for Halloran to go to her apartment Saturday night after delivery men had taken the trunk. She said, "There certainly was a reason for him coming, a terrible reason for him coming..."

But Smith cut her off.

Smith had also questioned her about how close the gun had been to Ruthie's two victims. "How far away was the gun when the shot was fired that went into Miss Samuelson's head?"

"We were yet on the floor grappling for the gun. We were clinching. We were rolling on the floor. We were fighting for the gun."

Judge Niles asked her to respond to the question.

Ruthie added, "We were in each other's arms - it was that close."

"How close?"

"It was just as close as the doorway..."

"Three feet away?" Smith interrupted.

"It was not - we were both in the doorway."

"How close was it then?"

"She was trying to get the gun, and I was trying to keep the gun, but..." Ruthie suddenly cut herself off and retorted, "I am not on trial here now!"

Again, Smith asked her, "How close?"

"I don't know. I can't say how many inches because I was in a wild, wild fight - the most wild fight any human being has ever been in."

Unable To get a straight answer, Smith then asked how far away the gun was when Anne was shot. Again, after asking repeatedly, "How close?" Ruthie said, "As I started to get up, she hit me again with the ironing board. I was in a half-rising position - she had the ironing board raised in her hands. I started to rise. I fired at her as she hit me with the ironing board, and we both fell at the same time. I fired in the left side of her head."

It still wasn't really a straight answer, but it's thought that Smith didn't care. It's been theorized that this line of questioning was an effort to substantiate Ruthie's claim of self-defense, which supported the contention that Halloran's attorney had been making all along. If it was self-defense, there was no murder, and so Halloran couldn't be charged as an accomplice.

At another time during Ruthie's testimony, Smith accused her of simply memorizing what she planned to say. He said to the court, "Why, when she relates the story of those killings, she pitches right in and tells a connected story. It must be memorized. She wanders off once or twice but comes right back in again. And the story she told to the grand jury is like that she told in the courtroom. She had 14 months to figure these things out. But when she drops out of that story - the 'magic carpet' on which she rides - she is lost."

This is a rather ridiculous accusation, especially with all of Ruthie's unhinged outbursts that were unlikely rehearsed - but if her story had been any different than what she told the grand jury, Smith would have undoubtedly accused her of embellishing her tale. It was a typical defense attorney strategy, and there was no way for whoever was on the witness stand to come out ahead.

Testimony eventually came around to the bloody fingerprint that had been found on the window shade in the bungalow's bedroom. Sheriff's office fingerprint expert B.O. Smith testified for the state on Thursday. He described visiting the duplex about two weeks after the murders to look for fingerprints and take photos of the bedroom.

And no, no one asked him why he waited two weeks to investigate the scene.

He testified that he had found a "bloody print" of what he believed "was the print of a left thumb" on the bedroom window shade - the same print that had been seen on the night of the murders, by the way. The forensic expert said it was smudged and couldn't be identified, which is no surprise considering how many people had traipsed through the house in those two weeks. This testimony was supposed to substantiate Ruthie's testimony from the first day of the hearing that Halloran, with blood on his hands, had pulled down the shade.

It failed to do so.

However, the "bloody print" testimony became a bigger issue on Friday. Over strenuous objections from the defense, B.O. Smith and Sheriff McFadden were both put on the stand by Jennings to discuss the matter further. Jennings produced the window shade, and both witnesses identified what they believed were blood smudges.

During cross-examination, Frank Smith asked the fingerprint expert, "It is possible, isn't it, that those smudges were placed there by Winnie Ruth Judd?"

"Yes, it is possible."

"It's reasonable, isn't it, that she did it?"

"It's reasonable that *someone* did it."

"Can you tell whether a man or a woman did it?"

"No, I can't."

"Might not these spots be from a spurting wound?"

"On no, I believe they were caused by fingers."

"Then it is a matter of speculation as to what made two of these spots?"

"Somewhat."

"One theory is just as reasonable as the other?"

"Yes."

Smith then moved to have B.O. Smith's testimony stricken from the record, stating that it had no connection to the defendant. Judge Niles disagreed. He ruled that the testimony corroborated the narrative from Ruthie about Harris pulling down the shade with his bloody hand after carrying Sammy to the bed.

The fingerprint expert and Sheriff McFadden were two of the 15 witnesses Jennings called to the stand during the day as he tried to build on portions of Ruthie's testimony.

Sheriff McFadden was asked if he had checked a license number at the request of one of Ruthie's neighbors. He said that he had and that it was a car registered to the Halloran Lumber Company. The car, a tan Packard, had reportedly been seen near Ruthie's apartment on the night after the murders.

Most of the testimony from the other witnesses was similar to what was given during Ruthie's murder trial. An exception was the testimony of Marvin Hicks, who worked at the train station in Phoenix. He said he had seen Jack Halloran at the station "right after the departure of a westbound train." Hicks, though, couldn't be sure if he'd seen Halloran on Saturday night or Sunday night.

The defense attorneys objected strongly to Hicks' testimony, interrupting the prosecutor as he tried to question the witness. When the county attorney snapped back at Smith for interrupting, the audience applauded for the second time during the hearing. Judge Niles threatened to clear the courtroom, and the spectators quieted again.

The state rested its case shortly before 5:00 P.M. Halloran's attorney was on his feet right away, introducing a motion to dismiss the charges against his client.

Smith stated to the judge, "Her own testimony is a moving account of self-defense, one that affected all of us, including the court. It is a clear case of self-defense. There could have been no crime."

Judge Niles gave Jennings overnight to prepare for what were expected to be the final arguments of the hearing on Saturday morning.

Jack Halloran was sitting with his wife in the courtroom when the judge called the proceedings to order the next day at 10:00 A.M. The state opened by asking for additional time to prepare arguments against the defense counsel's motion.

But before the judge could respond, Frank Smith quickly spoke up with another surprise motion. He told the court, "We are prepared to prove that on October 25, 26, and 27, 1931, Winnie Ruth Judd published in the *Los Angeles Times* of Los Angeles, California, her confession, and that confession so published is a complete refutation of all charges against Jack Halloran. We move that the case be reopened for the one purpose of questioning Winnie Ruth Judd, the accusing witness, with reference to her story upon evidence impeaching her story."

Jennings immediately objected, but Smith continued. "I first learned of this situation this morning at 6:00, Your Honor. I have been convinced from the first that if we could find her first statement before she received various theories from other persons and newspapers, we would get to the bottom of this. But it has been difficult to find it."

Smith pointed out that the *Los Angeles Times* articles appeared with a certificate that read: "This is to certify that the articles appearing in the *Los Angeles Times* are correct and authorized by me ﬃsignedﬄ Winnie Ruth Judd."

The attorney then read part of the alleged "confession":

By Winnie Ruth Judd.

This is my own story - the whole truth of the double tragedy that ended the lives of Agnes Anne LeRoi and Hedvig Samuelson in Phoenix, Arizona, on Friday, October 16, 1931.

I have given it to my husband, William C. Judd, to dispose of as he sees fit and in order that the world may know the exact facts of the whole terrible affair.

It has been charged that I had an accomplice either before, during, or after the actual tragedy. This is not true. I alone shot and killed both women who were once my friends. I did it in self-defense - to save my own life - and for no other reason. I alone disposed of the bodies in a manner which I shall describe in more detail later. I had no help of any kind from anyone. It seemed to me the only thing to do was to hide - hide everything and myself.

I was mistaken but that is what I did in my blind terror.

Smith said he would seek to impeach Mrs. Judd's testimony in court by her purported true confession, published in the *Los Angeles Times.*

Judge Niles decided to allow it. He told the attorneys before him, "The court is disposed to know the whole truth about this matter, if it is possible. Therefore, I will permit the reopening of the cross-examination of Mrs. Judd."

Ruthie was brought back to the courtroom from her county jail cell and took the seat on the witness stand again. Smith spent most of the next hour reading the story that claimed to be Ruthie's confession. When he was finished, Ruthie spoke up, "There have been about 50 stories out, supposed to have been written by me. This is the time I've ever heard this one."

Ruthie and Smith began to bicker about the story. Ruthie repeatedly and angrily asserted the articles were "not in my language - I did not make that statement" and "I was delirious, and don't know what I did." As Smith grilled her, though, she admitted many portions of the statements were partially, even mostly, true. She said that some were "in substance" what she had told her husband. But some portions of the statement -- she made very clear -- were not true.

During redirect examination by County Attorney Jennings, Ruthie pointed out the untrue portions of the "confession."

"Where is says 'This is my own story' - that is not true. The part that says 'The Whole Truth' - that part is not true. October 16 - that is the correct date of the fight. Where it says 'I have given it to my husband so the whole world would know' - I must say this article was published before I knew it was to be published. Where it says 'It is not true I had an accomplice' is not true. It is true that I had an accomplice."

Jennings asked, "Why did you say at that time, if you ever did say it, that Mr. Halloran had nothing to do with it?"

Ruthie replied quietly, "I'd have rather died than let my husband know about him."

The day's most dramatic moment came just before the end of the afternoon session. Smith had been pressing Ruthie to discuss the repacking of the bodies, which had been mentioned in the newspaper "confession."

"Did you lift Sammy from the trunk?" Smith asked.

"No! I didn't lift Sammy - I lifted a part... a portion..."

Smith cut her off. "And you lifted other portions and changed them?"

'Yes."

Smith then abruptly ended the cross-examination.

Ruthie had managed to avoid all discussion of the situation with the bodies during the first four days of the hearing. She had earlier demanded and been granted constitutional privilege to refuse to reveal what took place in her apartment before the bodies were prepared for shipment. It was Ruthie's first public admission of personal involvement in the actual repacking of the large trunk, smaller trunk, and other luggage.

At the close of that day's session, Judge Niles granted a continuance of the hearing until Monday. Ruthie was returned to the Arizona State Prison in Florence on Saturday afternoon.

On Monday morning, County Attorney Jennings was granted a further continuance until Tuesday. The prosecutors were now in the position of having to tear down the testimony of their own star witness - Winnie Ruth Judd - if they were going to have any hope of bringing Jack Halloran to trial.

The defense and the prosecution argued for four hours on Tuesday - Halloran's attorneys insisting that Ruthie's self-defense story meant the case against their client should be dismissed, while the prosecution argued that Ruthie's testimony was "all wrong" and that she had committed murder.

It was all in the hands of Judge Niles, who sighed as he looked at the prosecution team. "We have here a situation where you have proven a prima facie case by the record and your very own witness,

Mrs. Judd. You have proven self-defense. The state itself proved self-defense. I do not believe there is a court in Arizona that would review this on habeas corpus and say there is anything here for the court to weigh."

Deputy County Attorney Latham spoke up, "This is a very unusual situation. I don't suppose you could find in any case in the United States a situation which brings up the questions involved in this."

Judge Niles nodded his head. "I agree these circumstances are unique - that there probably has never been a case presented to a court where the state is in the position first of proving a crime committed, and then in the same proceedings proving it justifiable. I want you to have all the time necessary - but I am not satisfied with this showing."

The court gave the prosecutors until 9:00 A.M. the next day to produce sufficient evidence to hold Halloran for a Superior Court Trial.

They couldn't do it.

Halloran could not be an accessory to a crime if no crime had been committed.

"By your own witness, you proved self-defense," Judge Niles reiterated." If you can show me any law that will give me anything to weight here - and question of fact or any question upon which reasonable men might differ - I will feel it my duty to overcome this motion for dismissal.

But Jennings had nothing. As he would recall years later in his autobiography: "I previously had some experience with the judge who tried the case and I felt that this 'stinger' was out for me. In addition, before the trial was over, I felt that he had some kind of a close relationship with the so-called conspirator."

On January 25, 1933, Judge Niles set Halloran free. He jumped up, kissed his wife, and, smiling, they walked out of the courtroom together.

For Halloran, it was over. The law had exonerated him - he'd been found not guilty, but that didn't mean he was innocent. And the people of Phoenix knew it. His secret business partners, the powerful O'Malleys, forced the sale of his lumber company. The lumberyard he'd opened on his own on the south side of town had never been very busy. The case dirtied his family name, and the home he owned in the upscale part of town would still be his home years after the neighborhood had fallen into disrepair.

Halloran walked out of court that day a free man, but his glory days as a prominent citizen of Phoenix were over. Within a few years, his name was mostly lost to history. A television documentary made about the Judd case in 1969 censored his name. A book written in the 1970s gave him the fictitious name of "Carl Harris." Some newspapers referred to him only as "Mr. X." Even people involved in the case in the 1930s forgot he was ever charged.

Halloran - who was possibly just as involved as Ruthie in the murders - was never brought to justice and has largely been forgotten over the years.

But we're not quite finished with him yet.

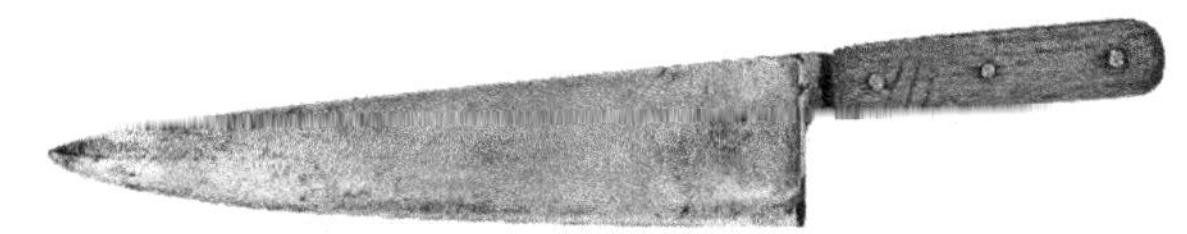

13. A CRY FOR MERCY

WHEN RUTHIE JUDD LEFT THE COURTROOM ON JANUARY 25, she was not set free. She returned to Death Row to wait for her date with the hangman.

But the bizarre twists and turns of the case had gotten her more attention - most of it good. As the *Los Angeles Examiner* put it, "It leaves Mrs. Judd convicted of murder and sentenced to be hanged and yet virtually exonerated of the crime by another court, before which she told the story she was not permitted by her previous counsel to tell at her own trial."

It gave hope to everyone who saw Ruthie as a victim. Her attorneys quickly took advantage of the situation. On the same day the hearing ended, one of her attorneys, Arthur Verge, told the press, "Based on the findings of the Maricopa County grand jury that it believed she killed Agnes LeRoi and Hedvig Samuelson in self-defense, and upon the decision of Judge Niles in the Halloran action, we are confidently hopeful that the Arizona Board of Pardons and Paroles will grant Mrs. Judd a full parole at her hearing to be set next week."

Verge interpreted Judge Niles' decision to release Jack Halloran as proof that Ruthie was innocent of committing murder. And he may have been right about that. Judge Niles spoke up to add, "If they summon me as a witness, the same as anyone else, I'll go." He didn't reveal what his testimony would be, but Ruthie's attorneys had high hopes.

Judge Niles would not be the only new name to be added to her list of supporters. That list had grown spectacularly.

More than one-third of the Arizona state legislature - 30 lawmakers in all - signed a petition for the parole board on her behalf. Citing both the grand jury and Judge Niles, the legislators told the board, "Since the state of Arizona itself has proved that Mrs. Judd acted in self-defense, we feel that it is highly offensive to our sense of justice to allow our fair and sovereign state of Arizona to hang Mrs. Winnie Ruth Judd."

A second impressive petition for justice came from a group of 34 ministers and priests, which was an unusual union in the days when churches seldom joined together, and there was a general dislike between Protestants and Catholics. But they put aside their differences in what they believed was a worthy cause, uniting 27 different parishes and congregations and the state leaders of the Episcopal Church and Free Methodist Church. The chaplain from the state prison in Florence also joined the group, as did various Baptists, Methodists, Lutherans, and even the Salvation Army.

The clergymen gave the parole board two ways out - either follow the lead of the grand jury and Judge Niles and commute the death sentences or give Ruthie an "indefinite reprieve" until she could be tried for the death of Hedvig Samuelson. They reminded the parole board that three arrest warrants had been issued in the Samuelson case - Mrs. Judd and two unnamed "John Doe" accomplices. The clergymen demanded that all three of them be brought to trial with Ruth Judd's punishment based on its outcome.

"If a trial jury on the Samuelson charge finds that Mrs. Judd acted in self-defense and their verdict is not guilty, then a full pardon should be issued on the LeRoi charge," the petition stated. "If the trial just on the Samuelson case determines Mrs. Judd is guilty to the extent of manslaughter, then a commutation of the death penalty should be made to that of manslaughter on the LeRoi charge."

Waiting in her cell for the parole board to act, Ruthie was being reminded about what happiness was like. Her parents, who'd moved to Florence to be near her, were allowed to spend most days and evenings with their daughter. Ruthie told her parents she wanted to return to Indiana, where she'd grown up. The McKinnells were just as anxious to return to Darlington, to retire in the community they'd served for so many years.

In Florence, they were nearly penniless and forced to rely on the generosity of the strangers who had entered their lives. During the trial in Phoenix, they had been looked after by various ministers who took them into their homes and provided their meals. That was to be expected - the McKinnells would have done the same thing.

Ruthie will her cat, Egypt, who soon gave birth to kittens, which she was allowed to care for.

They were both surprised and grateful to find that the people of Florence were just as kind to them. The residents of the little town, where the prison was the largest employer, befriended the older couple. Many shops in town put donation cans at their checkout counters to support them, and the town's two cafes filled up pails each night with soup and leftovers so the couple would have plenty to eat.

Someone in Florence gave Ruthie a pregnant black cat she named Egypt and kept with her in her cell. As the hearing in front of the parole board neared - the last formality, as her attorneys called it, or "her last chance to cheat the gallows," as the Phoenix Gazette called it - Ruthie wondered if she would be free before the kittens were born.

Visits from her attorneys and Dr. Judd broke Ruthie's prison routine as the days and weeks passed. Originally, her hearing with the parole board had been set for March 6, but citing "pressing business matters," it was rescheduled for March 14. The public would not be allowed to attend, and following Ruthie's appearance, the hearing would continue at the state capital building in Phoenix.

The hearing finally began at 2:25 P.M., and Ruthie was again allowed to "tell all" to the three men with authority over the pardons and paroles of all inmates in Arizona. In her application for a hearing, mercy had been sought in one of three ways - a full pardon, parole, or commutation of death sentence.

Wearing a blue and white gingham dress with pansies pinned to it, Ruthie sat across a table from the board members. Her attorneys were next to her, and around the small parole clerk's room in the prison administration building were Warden A.G. Walker, several other prison officials, and six reporters who were allowed to attend as "representatives of the public."

Her testimony took three hours, including the two recesses that were called when Ruthie broke down in tears and needed a break before she could continue. She told essentially the same story of self-defense that she'd told during the Halloran hearing, describing in detail her life, her husband, and her friends after she arrived in Phoenix.

Often speaking through tears, she gestured with a clenched fist to show how she had fought back to protect herself, how she had stabbed Sammy with the bread knife, and how she had tried to get the automatic pistol after being shot in the hand as they wrestled on the kitchen floor. Ruthie got on her knees to demonstrate how she had attempted to rise when Anne struck her with the ironing board. She then slumped back into her chair, sobbing hysterically and saying once again that she'd only fought to save her life.

Ruthie shocked her small audience with an allegation she claimed was told by her attorneys during the murder trial that the jury was "fixed." She said she was told that among the jurors, there was a man who would "hang up the jury," and she would not be convicted. Then she accused parole board members of trying to "influence" her to tell an untrue story on the promise that her sentence would be commuted if she exonerated others allegedly to blame and that she would be hanged if she didn't go along with it.

Ruthie did all she could to make a good appearance for the Parole and Pardon Board, but her testimony was frequently interrupted by tears and conflicting statements.

She then asked to be tried for Sammy's murder "so I can take the stand." Ruthie said she would tell the same tale of self-defense if granted a trial. She claimed again that her trial attorneys had prevented her from testifying. "They wanted the insanity defense. I did not want it, and I did not like some of the things they said about me." She also stated that she'd been promised she would be sent to the state hospital for the insane for a year or two and then paroled into her husband's custody.

Reporters, as well as Ruthie's lawyers, were excluded from the secret session that involved the condemned woman and the parole board. They stayed behind locked doors with Ruthie for nearly four hours.

During a brief - and very heated - meeting afterward, Ruthie's lawyer, O.V. Willson, repeatedly demanded a transcript of the testimony given during that secret meeting. His requests were denied.

Ruthie wasn't present for Willson's arguments to the board. He charged that the jury that convicted Mrs. Judd of murder made a "deal to impose capital punishment only for the purpose of making her talk." Willson said the jury was influenced by four of the members to believe that the Board of Pardons and Parole would commute the death penalty, and the threat of death would force Mrs. Judd to expose others the jurors believed were involved in the murders.

Willson urged the board to hear more witnesses, including some of the jurors, who had since made it known that if they'd heard the testimony that Ruthie gave at the Halloran hearing, they wouldn't have returned with a capital punishment verdict.

After more heated debate, the board made it clear that they weren't interested in the jurors' testimony. "I wouldn't believe them if they said they did it with an ulterior motive," said board member and state attorney general Arthur T. La Prade. "So, there's no use bringing them before me. Take those jurors to the Superior Court and let them 'confess their sins' and let the Superior Court prosecute."

Willson abandoned this argument and turned to the question of Ruthie's mental condition. "Now this woman - if she is not legally insane, she is medically insane. Her conflicting and various stories, to my mind, are expressive indications of insanity."

Board chairman Lin B. Orme waved this away. "There are so many conflicting things which you try to reconcile, and you meet with disappointment each time."

The hearing would resume, it was decided, on Monday, March 20, in Phoenix. Willson submitted a list of 12 witnesses, which the board - for no clear reason - promptly cut in half. The names of Judge Niles and court clerk Walter S. Wilson, plus the four jurors alleged to have made a deal, were eliminated from the list over the protests of Ruthie's attorneys. "I don't see why the board is so anxious to limit us," Willson shook his head.

Attorney General La Prade asked why Judge Niles was wanted as a witness. Willson explained, "We want to show that Judge Niles believed Mrs. Judd during the course of the testimony at the Halloran hearing."

But La Prade scoffed. "His opinion isn't any more valuable than that of anyone else!"

On the Sunday evening before the next stage of the hearing, it was announced that Ruthie would not be brought to Phoenix for it. Her attorneys had requested that she be allowed to attend, and Ruthie herself wanted to be there to face one of the witnesses the board had called - Jack Halloran - but she was out of luck.

Between those requested by the defense and those called by the board, 13 witnesses testified for the hearing. A few of them had new information to add, like Kenneth Grimm, the 20-year-old son of Ruthie's former landlords. He discussed his part in helping Ruthie move out of the bungalow and into the Brill Street apartment that his parents owned. He said that Mrs. Judd had asked him to take her back to the bungalow because she had "forgot something." He said he waited outside in his car and, through an open window, he heard her say to someone, "I went off and forgot my gun. I always keep it with me when I'm alone, so I came back for it." If anyone replied to her statement, Kenneth didn't hear it.

Two witnesses - a middle-school student and her mother - refuted Ruthie's claim that she had been at the Grunow Clinic throughout the afternoon of Saturday, October 17, the day after the murders.

The seventh grader said that she had seen Ruthie "about 3:00 P.M." near the bungalow and that she later ordered her and her friends away from a pile of bricks on which they were playing in a nearby vacant lot. The girl's mother corroborated her daughter's statement and added that she, her husband, and her brother-in-law "smelled something burning" near their home late that night and on Sunday morning.

The board was apparently trying to do a little sleuthing on its own, likely trying to determine if the burning smell might have been linked to the missing mattress, which was never found.

Attorney General La Prade, who was one of the three men on the parole board who was supposed to be taking an unbiased look at Ruthie's case, was prejudiced against her from the beginning.

Former Judge Louis P. Russell, Ruthie's first attorney in L.A., testified that she had given a statement to him and a shorthand recorder in the presence of Dr. Judd before she surrendered to the police. He said the statement was not used because the Judds had hired a new lawyer before her trial. He said he would reveal that statement to the board only if Mrs. Judd approved it.

Sheriff McFadden was the last witness of the day. Stating that he believed Mrs. Judd, he strongly substantiated portions of her self-defense story - and made some startling disclosures. For the first time in front of the press, the sheriff explained what had happened to the missing parts of Sammy's dismembered body. He said Ruthie told him they "fell out" while she was repacking the bodies in trunks and other cases at her apartment and that she had thrown them out of a window during the train trip to Los Angeles. McFadden said she told him she "didn't know" where she had thrown out the towels containing the body's organs.

McFadden said that Ruthie had first told her self-defense story to him on the second day after she returned to Phoenix for trial but said she wouldn't sign a written statement about her claims.

He admitted that he had personally found considerable evidence of blood in the breakfast room and kitchen of the bungalow but that the amount of blood he'd seen wasn't reflected in the final police reports.

He also talked about a hotel night clerk who told him Jack Halloran and two other men were in the hotel around 10:00 P.M. on the night of the murders. He said the clerk told him that he "had a drink with them" and that they left about 10:20 P.M., returning later very excited about something.

After the witnesses had testified, Ruthie's attorneys renewed their efforts to get the board to consider affidavits from jurors who confessed to participating in the "deal" to get Ruthie to talk with the death penalty hanging over her head. The board said it would rule on the matter the next day. However, they quickly denied the request to have Ruthie brought to Phoenix "for the purpose of advising her counsel when they questioned Jack Halloran."

The following day - even though she was miles away in her prison cell - Ruthie still had a dramatic effect on the hearing. Through a written statement, she refused to permit three of her former attorneys - Herman Lewkowitz, Joseph Zaversack, and Louis Russell - from telling the board anything about her case that she had revealed to them. Her current attorney, O.V. Wilson, explained that she feared they might not remember exactly what she'd told them, and she didn't want to take a chance they might get things wrong. Attorneys following the case called this "unprecedented before a parole board" since she was making her final plea for life.

The board accepted the statement and then ruled against the jurors who had come forward about the "make her talk" scheme. The board was unmoved by their affidavits and refused to allow them into evidence.

And that wasn't the only hint of bias the board displayed that day. Attorney General La Prade - one of the three men who were supposed to be examining Ruthie's plea in an unbiased way - admitted that he had his own theory about the murders. In fact, he'd revealed that theory to Ruthie herself during that secret session at the prison that her lawyers weren't allowed to attend. He said it was his theory that Ruth had shot and killed Anne in bed and then had wounded Sammy as she came out of the bathroom, then killed her in a struggle in the kitchen. La Prade also told Ruthie that he believed she had dismembered Sammy's body.

So, that should give you a good idea about how this hearing would go.

Shortly after this confession, a vital witness began to be questioned - Jack Halloran.

After sitting down in the witness chair, he addressed the board:

Jack Halloran was forced to return to give more testimony in front of the board. He insisted that he'd had nothing to do with he murders or with covering up the crime.

I want to get this on record. I have been subpoenaed here, and I am not a voluntary witness in answering the subpoena - but I am not a hostile witness. Under no conditions can it be understood that my appearance here indicates any bitterness in my mind toward anyone. I was subpoenaed at the trial. I reported there and I attended the trial every day, but I was never called. My name has been blazoned throughout the land, in an untruthful manner - whether vindictively or not, I am not judging. I am here to tell the truth - to answer truthfully all questions involving my alleged appearance at either of the houses mentioned, or of having seen or talked with Mrs. Judd after Thursday night, October 15, 1931.

Halloran, under examination by La Prade and Willson, categorically denied he had any knowledge of the slayings or that he helped or arranged for someone else to help Ruth Judd with the disposal of the bodies.

"The board is desirous of knowing," La Prade began, "whether or not you went to the Brill Street house on Friday, October 16, at any time."

"I did not."

"Did you see Mrs. Judd there about 11:00 or 12:00?"

"I did not."

"Did she convey to you the information she had killed Mrs. LeRoi and Miss Samuelson?"

"I never saw Mrs. Judd after Thursday night, and I was not the last to see her at that time. She was escorted to the door by another man as I sat in the car outside."

"Did you go with her to the Second Street house?"

"I did not."

"Did you ever see any bodies there?"

"I did not."

"Did you know Miss LeRoi and Miss Samuelson?"

"I did know them."

"Did you cut up a body?"

"I certainly did not."

"Did you arrange to have it done?"

"I did not."

"On Friday night - the supposed night of the slayings - were you in Phoenix?"

"I was."

"Where were you?"

"At home."

La Prade asked Halloran to detail his movements after 6:00 P.M. on Thursday, October 15. Halloran said he went to the girls' bungalow with two other men, arriving around 7:00 P.M. He said they remained there for about 20 minutes and then went to Ruthie's apartment on Brill Street.

Halloran continued: "We sat and talked and had something to eat and then took a ride for about 20 minutes." He said they took home another woman who had been at Ruthie's apartment, and then he immediately took Ruthie home. He said he then stopped by his own home for about 10 minutes and then took the men to their hotel. After that, he claimed, he went home and stayed there.

Halloran criticized testimony from other witnesses that claimed he'd been seen in a hotel on or about the night of the murders and that he and his party seemed excited about something. "I don't care who made the statements, they are positively untrue - I was not out of my house on Friday night."

La Prade asked, "Who was at your home?"

"My wife. My daughter was at a show, and my son was out and returned at about 11:00 P.M. I had planned to go to a football game with my son at the stadium, but he had another engagement, so I stayed home and heard the game on the radio."

"Did you call Mrs. Judd on Saturday morning?"

"I did not."

"Did she communicate with you?"

"She did not."

"Did you see her Saturday night?"

"I did not."

"What did you do Saturday morning?"

"I was at my office." He added that he left there around noon, had lunch at home, and went to the Phoenix Country Club for a round of golf. He said it was a regular thing for him to play golf on Saturday afternoon with the same group of friends.

"Do any of these men remember whether they played golf with you that Saturday?"

"I haven't asked them."

Halloran said he left the club between 5:30 and 6:00 P.M., had dinner at home, went to the office of a business acquaintance, where he stayed until 9:00, then went home and entertained visitors until 10:00 P.M.

"What did you do then?"

"I went to bed."

Halloran said that he played golf again on Sunday morning, went to a show with his wife in the afternoon, and went to dinner downtown with his son and two daughters in the evening. He was home between 7:00 and 8:00 P.M. and didn't leave again.

He'd first learned of the murders, he said, when a doctor he was acquainted with telephoned him on Monday night after the bodies had been discovered in Los Angeles. He was "shocked," he told the board.

Halloran was asked if he had been contacted by attorneys or anyone else about Ruth Judd. He said that, before her return from Los Angeles, he received a phone call from a Phoenix attorney who asked if he "knew anyone connected with the case," saying that he'd received a call from Los Angeles and "presumed it was a case of money."

Halloran said, "I told him that if that was the situation, I was not interested."

He added that he'd received a second call from an L.A. lawyer who asked about the whereabouts of another man - someone he knew. And then later, he had another call from a man, he said, "who had some story about knowing the McKinnells. I just figured it was another one of those mysterious calls or letters I had been receiving and paid no attention to it."

"Did you ever have a conversation with Rev. McKinnell?"

"No."

"Any conversation with her brother?"

"Yes," Halloran replied. He said that Ruthie's brother, Burton, had called him, saying he was "interested in saving his sister's life." He asked to see Halloran and was told to come to his office, but Burton refused, asking him to meet elsewhere. But Halloran was adamant - at his office, or not at all. Halloran said that Burton replied, "I'll phone you again tomorrow - you think it over - maybe you'll change your mind." But when Burton called back, Halloran hadn't changed his mind.

La Prade asked, "Did he ask you to aid or assist his sister?"

"No, he did not."

"Did he say anything about money?"

"No."

Halloran said Dr. Judd had called him once during the trial and asked to see him. He invited him to his office.

"Did he come?"

"He phoned again in about 30 minutes, said he had decided not to come, that detectives might be following him, and his visit might be misunderstood. I said he was probably right."

"Have you any letters from Ruth Judd?"

"No."

"From Dr. Judd?"

'No."

"From the brother?"

"No."

"From the mother?"

"No."

Halloran reported receiving a letter - dated December 16, 1932 - from a Los Angeles attorney who said he had recently been in Phoenix but had not called on him then. He said the letter outlined plans for gaining clemency for Ruthie and said in part, "I feel if I should come to Phoenix again, you would be willing to offer aid."

"Did you answer it?"

"I did not."

"Did you receive any other letters from any lawyers?"

"None."

Turning to Ruthie's self-defense story, La Prade asked, "Can you give us any information as to why she says those things?"

"I cannot."

"Can you give us any lead to develop any reason?"

"No, I cannot. It's a mystery to me why, after a year and a half, my name has been brought into this case in this way. If I had been connected with the case, Mrs. Judd certainly would have brought to the charges originally."

DURING THE CROSS-EXAMINATION THAT FOLLOWED, Willson tried unsuccessfully to get Halloran to discuss his relationship with Ruthie and the two murdered girls. Halloran would only say that what had happened before the murders was not relevant to the hearing and demanded that Willson "stick to the issue." He accused the attorney of trying to connect Halloran to "something that does not involve me."

Willson pointed out to him, "You haven't attempted to clear your name from the time of this tragedy until this hour, except for a statement in the *Arizona Republic*."

Halloran replied with a shrug. "I saw no necessity for rushing in for print. I made one statement. Your question is not properly put and has no bearing on the issue at hand. I have sat calmly by and suffered, knowing the truth with come out."

He then turned toward the handful of reporters that were present. "I am making no refusal to answer any question directly bearing on charges against me," he made sure to point out to them.

The next day, Dr. Judd took the witness chair to tell why he believed his wife had killed in self-defense, and he was convinced she hadn't dismembered Sammy's body. He admitted that for more than three weeks after her surrender, Ruthie concealed from him what he now believed to be the true story - that she had help in disposing of the bodies. He told Willson, "Her second story to me was very similar to what she told the board. I have never been able to forget or disbelieve her because of the wealth of detail. If one were composing

Dr. Judd returned to testify again about his belief that his wife had acted in self-defense.

a lie, why would one put so many improbable things in it?

Despite this, Dr. Judd said, "There is no use denying she has contradicted herself time after time. I don't know when she will do it again. Conflicting stories she would tell us graphically with a wealth of detail. Perhaps the next day she would deny it and tell us she was alone. We never knew for 24 hours what she would say. Once she let me write out a story for her to sign - but she wouldn't sign it. The thing that struck me first so strange was the emphasis she placed on being alone. Without being asked a question, repeatedly and emphatically she volunteered, 'I was alone.'"

He said he had told one of Ruthie's attorneys about her "second story" and that she then denied to the lawyer that she had said any such thing. He said she later advised him she had told it to him "privately."

Dr. Judd discussed his wife's movements before her surrender. "The newspapers remarked on the resourcefulness she had shown in concealing herself. It was not that. Remember her actions in Los Angeles - she gets out of her brother's car, so where does she go and hide? She had worked once at the Broadway Department Store. She goes to one of the few places she might be recognized - that store - and hides for the night. She met a buyer she once knew in the elevator. He didn't recognize her, but it frightened her. She knew she couldn't stay long in the store, so then where does she go? To the sanitarium where she had once been a patient - another of the few places she might have been recognized. Where does she go the next day to do her telephoning? Back to the Broadway store. It is interesting to show her state of mind during that period of stress and her complete lack of planning."

Dr. Judd related various methods he said Ruthie claimed she had used to cut up Sammy's body in a bathtub. He said that each time he objected to her stories on the grounds of impossibility, she would think for a few moments and then come up with another method. He was clear about the fact that his wife had no understanding of how to dismember a body.

He added that she had never had any experience with surgical operations. "I tried many times when I was in Mexico to get her to help me with dressings, but she would never do it."

As Dr. Judd neared the end of his testimony, Ruthie's father, Rev. McKinnell, interrupted to ask permission to ask his son-in-law a question. Chairman Lin Orme agreed to allow it.

Rev. McKinnell asked, "As a physician experienced in mental cases, do you believe that our Ruth is a woman of sound reason?"

"No," Dr. Judd replied. "I do not."

A handful of other witnesses appeared, testifying similar to what they'd offered at her trial, including a grocery store manager who agreed with Dr. Judd about whether Ruthie could dismember a body. He said she never bought a chicken that wasn't already cut up and ready for cooking.

On Thursday, Dr. Judd was back in the witness chair for cross-examination. His only sign of nervousness was his chain-smoking, lighting each cigarette from the stub of its predecessor. He stuck with his testimony from the previous day, which actually earned him praise from Attorney General La Prade.

"We appreciate very much the candor and frankness with which Dr. Judd spoke. There was no holding back nor attempts to parry on his part. He is worth listening to and we want to talk to him some more," the attorney general said and indicated that the board would be meeting with Dr. Judd in private.

Rev. McKinnell was allowed to make a plea for mercy for his daughter. His voice, which had served him from his church pulpit for decades, was firm and dramatic:

"I do not wish to appear as courting personal sympathy. My wife and I are not entitled to any more consideration than the parents of Anne LeRoi and Hedvig Samuelson. I may bring no new evidence, for many angles in this case are fictitious. Who mutilated a human body and shipped certain bodies is not in legitimate consideration, for the state never charged Ruth with doing either. There are but three things to weigh - did Ruth Judd kill Anne LeRoi, which is confessed;

Rev. McKinnell was allowed to appear before the board to make a plea for mercy for his daughter.

was it malice aforethought or was it in a fight, and if in a fight, may it be a defensive fight; and, if punishment be deserved, what should that punishment be?

"Granted that I am supposed to be prejudiced on my child's side, which I do not want her considered as a paragon of perfection, yet in view of the judgment at which I must shortly appear, in considering her life from the dawn of responsibility to the present hour, I brand the assaults on her chastity and veracity as false... "

As he stumbled over his final words, his voice finally faltered, and he began to weep for his daughter.

In summing up for Ruthie's counsel, H.G. Richardson begged the board to consider itself, in fact as well as theory, the court of last resort so far as the life and death of Ruthie was concerned. He spoke to the three-person board, "There has been a lot of talk about going before the Supreme Court of the United States, but for the life of me, I don't see how we can go there. We have no money. I think you gentlemen will say the last word. You might say I am asking for mercy - well, gentlemen, you are sitting here in a capacity to be merciful."

The hearing lasted for nearly two weeks of testimony, including closed and secret sessions, and ended on Thursday, March 23, 1933. Within a few days, rumors were running rampant that Ruthie would soon be tried for Sammy's murder, giving her the chance to use the plea of self-defense that hadn't been introduced in her first trial. Those rumors stopped on March 29 when Judge Howard Speakman refused to grant another trial, saying it would be a waste of time.

Then, on March 30, the Arizona Board of Pardons and Paroles finally announced their "last word." They had not been moved by the testimony, by Judge Niles' ruling, by the jurors who came forward about the "make her talk" plan, by the Arizona lawmakers who spoke on Ruthie's behalf, by the impressive list of clergymen, or even by the thousands of letters from across the country begging for mercy.

The board declared that Ruth Judd was a cold-blooded killer who had shot Anne in her bed as she slept - and she would be punished for it by hanging from the neck until she was dead. The board set a new execution date for April 21.

It was a Friday.

14. THE HANGMAN COMETH

THE NEWS OF THE DECISION BY THE BOARD DIDN'T SHAKE Ruthie up visibly - not at first. She went through the next day in what seemed a peaceful mood, often smiling. Her attitude puzzled not only prison officials but also pretty much everyone who knew her. She was known for her temper and her moods and had vowed many times that she'd either escape or commit suicide rather than be hanged.

No one could explain her behavior, although her father gave the credit to God. He had tried to bolster his daughter's hope with his religious faith. Rev. McKinnell assured Ruthie - and the press - that he didn't believe it was God's will that she should die on the gallows.

Her attorneys made their own statements, saying Ruthie was "very hopeful. She does not feel she has been given a fair chance, but she has not lost hope that she will be saved. Her attorneys will stick by her to the end."

It was as though Ruthie just simply refused to believe that she would be hanged - and she wasn't the only one. People across the country couldn't believe Arizona was serious about stringing up Ruthie Judd with the hangman's rope.

While the death penalty was still going strong in the 1930s, the debate over its morality was just as heated then as it is today. And Ruthie's case was the perfect example of justice denied for those who argued that legalized murder was barbaric.

Church leaders in Phoenix - the same ones who had sent that letter to the parole board - wrote and spoke extensively on Ruthie's behalf, making some very strong points. "Here is a case shrouded in mystery," Rev. W.C. Reynolds said." The more we study its various angles, the more the mystery deepens. To hang any person under such conditions is a monstrous crime against civilization and a blot on the state that does it."

Public opinion across the nation seemed to side with Ruthie. Thousands of letters continued to arrive on her behalf, including one from Eleanor Roosevelt, who received national recognition for bringing the case to the attention of the President. Editorials were written about the strange twists and turns of the case, and some even argued that if her accomplice were ever charged, Ruthie's testimony would be needed against them. Some maintained that it was impossible to believe the state would execute a woman, while others begged that she be spared for the sake of her elderly parents.

On Monday, April 3, Warden Walker gave the governor an anonymous letter that had been sent to the prison threatening to bomb the state capitol building unless Ruthie was released to her mother. The writer of the letter, which was mailed from Los Angeles, threatened to place enough explosives to kill everyone in Phoenix and shake the buildings "worse than the recent Pacific Coast earthquake."

More ominous letters followed from other mysterious writers. Several threatened to assassinate state officials unless Ruthie was released or to blow up the state prison and rescue Ruthie from the ruins.

The Board of Pardons and Paroles met again on April 6 to reconsider its ruling or grant a delay in Ruthie's execution of 42 days, allowing time for a possible appeal to the U.S. Supreme Court. The board wasn't interested in either option and quickly issued a 28-word statement of refusal.

Ruthie's attorneys were forced to bring her the bad news that they had been unable to stop her trip to the gallows.

Ruthie Judd was still set to hang on April 21.

Attorney H.G. Richardson brought the bad news to Ruthie, and it finally seemed to sink in that she was in serious trouble. She broke into tears, becoming hysterical. Richardson later recalled, "She seemed to read in my face that I had bad news for her. We feel that Mrs. Judd has suffered a living death already, and that if the Board of Pardons and Paroles could see fit to grant her a new lease on life, even if it erred, it would be erring on the side of mercy, and in the face of great doubt."

Ruthie's attorneys almost immediately filed a motion for a new trial in Maricopa County Superior Court, contending that the jury "had no intention that the defendant should suffer the death penalty, as appears by affidavits of said members to be presented to the court on the hearing of the motion." By now, two additional jurors had come forward, agreeing that the jury had been tricked into voting for the death penalty to "make her talk."

On Friday, the day after the motion was filed, Warden Walker released a statement that said Ruthie had begun to break, with fits of nervousness and hysteria. "It's surprising that she has not let down sooner - she has an iron nerve."

Ruthie had finally been placed on suicide watch. Her cell was stripped of everything she might use to kill herself. A guard was placed on duty around the clock, and hers became the only cell in the women's ward to be locked at night.

In preparing to argue the motion, Ruthie's attorneys subpoenaed all 13 jurors from her trial, as well as Herman Lewkowitz and Joseph Zaversack. They gathered everything they believed they needed to save their client's life.

Unfortunately, when they presented the motion to the Superior Court - they found themselves before Judge Howard Speakman again. He ended the proceedings in just five minutes.

As he took his seat on the bench, he spoke, "The Supreme Court of this state has spoken on this matter repeatedly, so there is no question but what the lower court is absolutely powerless to reverse or interfere with any decision made by the Supreme Court."

O.V. Willson interrupted, "Do I understand that I am to be deprived on behalf of Ruth Judd...."

The judge angrily cut him off. "I am not depriving you of one thing. I am following the law. The people of this county elected me to interpret the laws of the state. This is exactly what I am doing. I have never deprived Winnie Ruth Judd of anything, and I ask you not to insinuate anything like that. Ruth Judd had a fair trial as far as this court is concerned."

"May I offer my original affidavits?"

"This court has no jurisdiction. If you want to go to the Supreme Court and have them set aside their judgment, I will more than welcome it."

On Wednesday, Ruthie's attorneys appeared before Supreme Court Chief Justice Henry D. Ross, but a request to place a petition before the high court was denied, closing off the Arizona Supreme Court as a way for Ruthie to escape the gallows.

The date for the execution was ticking closer.

AS THE DELUGE OF LETTERS WRITTEN ON RUTHIE'S behalf continued to arrive, it was becoming painfully clear to Arizona business leaders, politicians, and residents that the negative publicity from the case was the last thing the state needed. Arizona's booster campaigns declared it a place where good people raised healthy

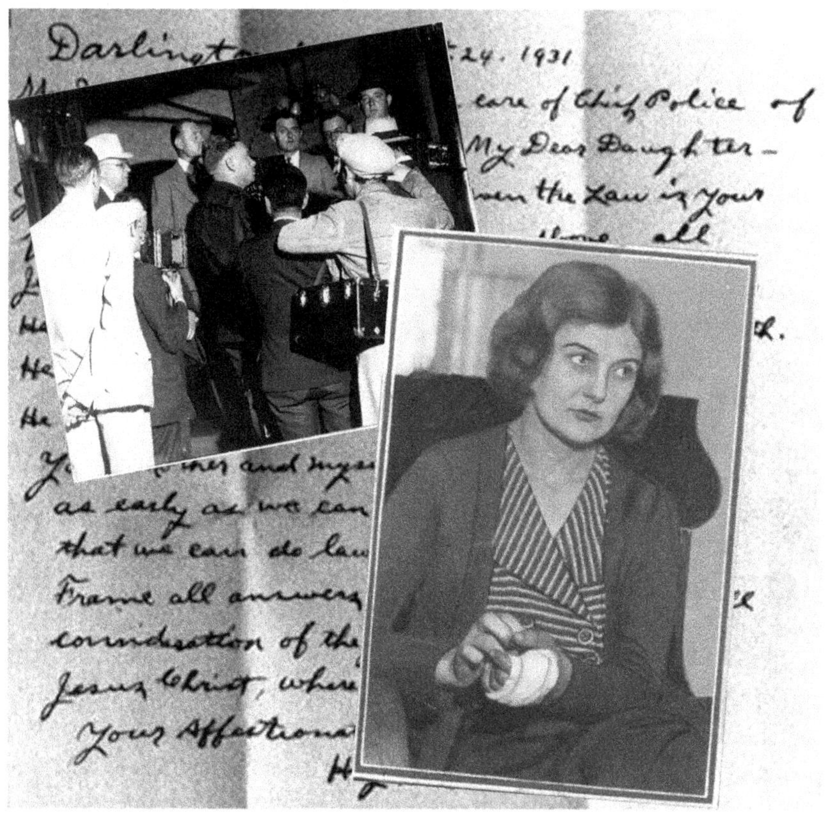
Darlington ... 24. 1931
care of Chief Police of
My Dear Daughter -
the Law in your
all
as early as we can
that we can do law
Frame all answers
consideration of the
Jesus Christ, where
Your Affectiona

Letters of support for Ruthie poured in from all over the country, hoping they can convince the state of Arizona of the bad press they would receive if Ruthie was executed.

families in a warm climate. How could they explain executing a woman who had so much public support?

But there seemed to be little that could be done. State law placed the final word in the hands of the parole board. The governor of the state was prohibited from acting without a recommendation from the board - and they'd already decided that Ruthie needed to hang.

There was only one unlikely option that remained. At that time, Arizona law allowed the state prison warden - appointed by the governor - to call for a sanity hearing for a death row inmate. However, since two different courts had declared that Ruthie was sane, it was political suicide for the new warden, A.G. Walker, to use this option.

But he did it anyway - likely with some reassurance from the governor that he'd keep his job.

On April 12 - nine days before her scheduled execution - Warden Walker petitioned the Pinal County Superior Court, noting: "There is good reason to believe that Winnie Ruth Judd has become insane after the delivery of the said Winnie Ruth Judd to the Superintendent of the Arizona State Pison for execution."

The request set in motion the legal machinery for determining Ruthie's mental condition. Within 45 minutes after the petition was received, Judge E. L. Green granted it and set 9:30 A.M. on April 14 for the hearing.

H.G. Richardson quickly assembled a new batch of attorneys for Ruthie. O.V. Willson had retired and was suffering health problems, but he was the first to return. He was assisted by young law partners who would both become important men in Arizona politics. They were Tom Fulbright, who later became a judge, and Ernest McFarland, who had a 35-year career in public service as a U.S. senator, governor, and chief justice of the Arizona Supreme Court.

Neither of the younger men had volunteered, but believing they had, Ruthie's father came to their office one day to tell them how grateful he was to have them on the team. McFarland later said, "We didn't have the heart to turn him down."

Fulbright later recalled that none of the lawyers were paid, besides getting the experience of handling one of the most watched trials in America.

With only days to present their case, they scrambled to find experts willing to say that Ruthie was insane. Among them was Dr. George Stephens - the asylum doctor who had testified at Ruthie's murder trial - and Dr. Wynn Wylie, a Phoenix psychiatrist. The mind of Dr. Stephens hadn't changed since the trial. He noted, "I made a diagnosis of dementia praecox when I went to the witness stand as the first alienist at her trial. That diagnosis still stands, and there has been no improvement in her mental condition during the past year, though there has been some physical improvement."

O.V. Willson said that Ruthie would not be placed on the witness stand during her sanity hearing. He told the press, "She is not a competent witness; hence, we will not send her to the stand, though such action is discretionary with us."

The defense experts would have a tough time on the stand since the county attorney had already announced that they planned to use Dr. Joseph Catton from San Francisco - who was very familiar with the case - to shoot down any arguments Ruthie's doctors might come up with.

On the night before the hearing, Ruthie cowered, weeping and incoherent in her cell in the women's ward. Not even her cat, Egypt, and her kittens could distract her.

The sanity hearing began at 9:40 A.M. on April 14 - Good Friday - and anyone who had expected officials to move quickly with the hearing soon realized that wouldn't happen. There wasn't enough time before the execution to hear from all the witnesses, and Ruthie's attorneys argued it was ludicrous for the state to execute her while her insanity hearing was still taking place.

On April 18 - even though the hearing was already in motion - the parole board delayed the execution until April 28 to give the hearing some "breathing room."

As had been stated at her murder trial, Ruthie's parents said there was a long history of family insanity that stretched back for generations. Ruthie willingly put on a good show for the court, pulling her hair, tearing at her clothing, and staring into space as she muttered in response to voices that only she could hear. From the first day of the hearing to the last, she was as crazy as a loon.

On the first day, she mainly seemed bored during the many hours it took to question prospective jurors. She again twisted a handkerchief around her left hand, often bending forward to rest her head on her hands. Once, she scolded a news photographer who tried to take a picture of her. She seldom spoke; when she did, it was only to the jail matrons. Once, when one of them got up to leave the courtroom, Ruthie got up too but was pulled back into her chair by the other matron. When someone spoke to her late in the afternoon, she responded, "I've been tormented enough, and I'm tired of it."

Psychiatrists for the state and defense observed Ruthie during the day, jotting down notes for the testimony they'd give later in the hearing. They were allowed brief visits with her during the noon hour at the nearby state prison.

Dr. Catton became the spokesman for the state experts. He told reporters, "We are here, not as persecutors, but to express our views in accordance with justice. The Arizona law under which this hearing is being held provided substantially that if Mrs. Judd has appreciation of her circumstances and the mental capacity to comprehend the fate awaiting her, she must hang. We, no more than the great state of Arizona, desire to be charged with the responsibility of hanging anyone whose mentality is so diseased that she goes to the execution chamber unknowingly."

He added that he would be glad to testify on behalf of Mrs. Judd if his observations convinced him that she was mentally incompetent under the tests provided - but it's safe to say that had a snowball's chance in hell of ever happening.

Another well-known California psychiatrist, Dr. Edward Williams - who had testified for the defense at the murder trial - commented in Los Angeles that he was unable to make the trip but said he was more convinced than ever that Mrs. Judd was "absolutely crazy."

That seems very unprofessional, but hey, I'm no doctor.

Williams explained this by recounting an incident that hadn't been officially disclosed before. He told the press: "Two weeks before Mrs. Judd's trial in Phoenix, an insane woman was placed in the same jail tank with her. Mrs. Judd became infuriated until her attorney, Herman Lewkowitz, was called to calm her. He discovered that Mrs. Judd had obtained a butcher knife and was concealing it beneath her armpit. When he took the knife from her, Mrs. Judd screamed that she wished to 'cut that woman's heart out because I can't stand her.'"

Dr. Williams said that he had wired Ruthie's attorneys in Arizona and advised them to bring attention to the "knife incident."

County Attorney Will C. Truman and his assistant, Charles Reed, questioned prospective jurors that first day, admonishing several of them, "You must arrive at a verdict exactly as though some person not under a death sentence were before you."

The first day of the hearing closed with Judge Green denying a request from the state to hold a night session to speed things along - because the state had no plans to halt the execution unless they were forced to do so.

Preparations were still being made. Warden Walker had already sent 50 small white, black-bordered pasteboard invitations to Ruthie's execution. They read: "You are invited to be present at the state prison in Florence for the execution of Winnie Ruth Judd."

The first batch had already been sent when the parole board changed the date to April 28, making them worthless.

On April 14, though, the rope for the hangman's noose began to be soaked and stretched to hold the weight of 300 pounds. The processing of the rope always began about seven days before the execution date.

TESTIMONY BEGAN ON APRIL 15, JUST AFTER THE JURY WAS sworn in. It was made up primarily of ranchers and highway department employees, so obviously, it was a group of women's mental health experts.

Marjorie Driscoll of the Universal News Service wrote about Ruthie that day:

Her hands clutching her hair, her body rocking back and forth, and her almost continuous laughter or tears made Mrs. Judd a pitiful sight at today's session. She stared into space and laughed or sobbed while her husband now and then, took her groping hands into his own and endeavored to calm her. Occasionally, she relaxed a little, but her lips moved as she muttered incoherent sentences. Once she turned to her husband and pleaded with him to permit her to throw herself from a nearby second-story window of the courtroom. At another point, she threw the court into an uproar when she jumped to her feet

A newspaper used this arrow to point out Ruthie in this image from her sanity hearing. As the Universal News Service correspondent wrote about her: "Her hands clutching her hair, her body rocking back and forth, and her almost continuous laughter or tears made Mrs. Judd a pitiful sight at today's session."

and shouted to the jury: 'You're all a bunch of degenerates - gangsters. You're just here to see me suffer. You're all crazier than I am!'

Two days later, the Associated Press reported:

Shrieking imprecations in a wild voice, Winnie Ruth Judd was removed forcibly today to her state prison cell from the courtroom, where a hearing was in progress to determine her sanity. After a drive around country roads in the custody of Warden Walker, the convicted 'trunk slayer' returned to the courtroom meekly, sat down, placed her chin on her hands, and stared at the floor. The outburst, her most violent since the hearing began last week, came while her husband was on the stand testifying to a belief that she was insane.

One of her attorneys, Tom Fulbright, later recalled her blank stare, the monotonous twisting of the handkerchief, her inattention, and her outbursts, including one he called a "lulu." He said, "When the name of the Phoenix playboy was mentioned, she jumped to her feet screaming and said, 'That damn Jack Halloran! I would like to take his head and break it against the ceiling and splatter his brains like a dish of oatmeal!'"

Ruthie railed about the psychiatrists - both those who were there to help her and those who were not. She swore at her brother for not being there - but then realized he was, although Burton had chosen an odd disguise of "false red whiskers, a wig, and dark glasses."

And it went on like this for the entire 10 days.

The testimony began with the prison officials who had overseen Ruthie for months, including Warden Walker, Assistant Warden Shute, and four matrons - Ella Heath, Laura Rossiter, Mary Devore, and Nora Stephenson.

Warden Walker said he had become convinced that Ruthie was insane after conferring with the prison physician, Dr. Berends. He had reached his final decision about her just two days before the hearing.

One of Ruthie's attorneys. H.G. Richardson asked the warden, "In your opinion, does she understand all the facts of the crime of which she was convicted?"

"I don't think so," Walker answered.

Assistant County Attorney Reed cross-examined the warden. He asked how long Walker thought Mrs. Judd had been insane. Walker replied that he believed she'd been insane all the time that she had been in his custody.

"Why then did you wait until this late date to call this hearing?" Reed demanded.

"Because I wanted to be sure."

"You dread the responsibility for the execution, don't you?"

"Yes, I do dread it."

"Well, then, your attitude is about this, isn't it? You feel that instead of one man bearing so much responsibility, it should be placed on the shoulders of 12?"

"No, I would not say that."

On the stand, Assistant Warden Shute said, "Mrs. Judd is absolutely indifferent. I have gone so far as to ask if she realized a noose was around her neck. She shrugged her shoulders and laughed and passed on to some other conversation."

Shute had noticed her gathering stones in the yard of the women's ward one day, then laying them in rows across the floor of her cell. Once, he said, she hid under the bed and pulled the blankets down on the sides so the matron in charge thought she had escaped. About six weeks earlier, Ruthie had convinced her mother she had a razor blade in her mouth and was going to swallow it. Her mother had forced her lips apart - there was no razor blade.

The head matron, Ella Heath, told the jury that she thought Ruthie was "absolutely insane." She said that the other female inmates in the state prison were "all afraid of her." Mrs. Heath described how Ruthie had beaten herself on the head with a shoe, thrown herself on the floor, and torn at her hair many times without apparent reasons except that some word or incident had excited her. A minute later, she said, Mrs. Judd would be laughing.

Mrs. Heath added that Ruthie "didn't seem to realize the seriousness of her situation. She believes she is being persecuted. She says over and over that the doctors want to kill her so they can examine her brain. She doesn't speak of it as punishment for anything she has done, but she thinks someone wants to hurt her for their own satisfaction."

Laura Rossiter recalled that Ruthie "sings a lot - climbs in the window, climbs down again - slaps her hands - one minute she laughs and the next she cries - she takes her slipper off and beats herself on the back of the neck with it."

All the matrons testified that she did not appear to have prepared herself for death but had made plans for the future, including extended trips to Alaska and Latin America.

Dr. Joseph Catton, who was determined to make sure that Ruthie was executed, testified during her sanity hearing and told reporters that he was convinced she was faking her mental illness.

When not testifying, Ruthie kept the matrons busy in the courtroom with bursts of anger, outrage, and weeping. It often took two matrons and Dr. Judd to quiet her down. At other times, she alternated between chuckling and softly sobbing.

After the hearing ended for the day, Dr. Catton expressed to reporters that he believed Ruthie was partially faking her courtroom hysteria. "One under sentence of death must necessarily be in such a highly string nervous state that hysteria, at first feigned, could readily become actual."

There was nothing that Catton could find that would change his previous opinion that Ruthie was legally sane. He told reporters, "Something may develop to cause us to change our view between now and the time we take the witness stand, but so far, no developments have appeared."

The hearing was suspended on Easter Sunday, and while most of those involved with the case enjoyed a relaxing day with their family, for Ruthie, it was one of the few days she had left to live. The clock was ticking closer to her execution date.

On Monday, Dr. Berends and Dr. Judd took the stand, offering testimony from physicians with many years of experience with psychiatric treatment. Dr. Judd - speaking as a doctor and not a husband - declared, as he had in the previous trial, that his wife had a mental illness. "God himself," he said, "could not coach that woman to act insane - all she has to do is act natural." Describing her mental state as "entirely inconsistent," he said, "At one moment she is in a state of exultation, in another moment she is quiet - from intense dejection, she rises to the most supreme exhilaration."

While Dr. Judd was on the witness stand, Ruthie suddenly started screaming wildly, her head spinning around the courtroom, "You bullies! You cowards! You gangsters! Quit torturing me! Quit taunting me!" When one of the matrons put a hand over her mouth, Ruthie bit her and continued to scream.

"Where is the warden of the penitentiary?" Judge Green shouted.

Warden Walker hurried over to Ruthie, lifted her from her chair, and carried her bodily from the courtroom, one foot dragging behind her along the floor.

"Let me alone! Let me alone! Quit torturing me!" she wailed as spectators scrambled to get out of the way. Her arms waved wildly in the air, and she kept screaming after Walker and a matron put her down on the courthouse lawn and tried to quiet her. But her screams were so loud they continued to filter through the windows of the courtroom.

Judge Green angrily banged his gavel and ordered the bailiff, "Tell the warden he must take the alleged insane person out of the hearing of this jury!"

Ruthie was lying on the ground, beating her heels on the ground and still screaming when Walker took her to the car. After a half-hour ride around the area, she finally quieted down and was returned to the courtroom. She was smiling when she first sat down but then became somber and quiet.

Testimony had continued in Ruthie's absence. Dr. Berends agreed with Dr. Judd that she was insane. He testified, "She is lacking in judgment, lacking in reason and insight, and apparently suffering from illusion. She is unable to take care of herself, is a menace to herself and others is unable to concentrate, and lacks attention. Her speech is abnormal, irrelevant, and delivered under great pressure." He insisted that Ruthie was not malingering.

Ruthie's mother also took the stand that afternoon. As she had testified in the past, she presented many instances of insanity in Ruthie's family. Carrie McKinnell proved to be a spirited witness, sparring with the attorneys on both sides.

"He knows she's insane," she said, narrowing her eyes at Assistant County Attorney Reed, "but he wants to hang her!"

Once, when O.V. Wilson interrupted her, she snapped, "And he's a pill, too!"

She told the jury, "There is insanity on both sides of my family. I have always felt that insanity was on me to some extent and on Ruth even more. I want you to know that girl is insane and has been more or less insane all her life."

When the hearing ended on Monday, it seemed no closer to being complete, which was concerning since Ruthie was scheduled to hang in just over a week. The defense attorneys announced they had sent a petition for a three-week reprieve to the parole board but had received no reply. They also sent telegrams to U.S. Senators Carl Hayden and Henry Amhurst of Arizona, urging them "in the interest of justice to Winnie Ruth Judd and the fair name of Arizona" to lend their "full support and influence for an immediate reprieve."

In the meantime, a telegram had been received by the defense from Ernest Whitehouse Cortis, secretary of the Men's League of Mercy of the United States, organized to prevent the execution of women in the United States. It read: "Please notify Mrs. Judd I am leaving Tuesday at daybreak for Washington to personally plead with President Roosevelt on her behalf. Ask her to pray for my success. Tell her to trust in God."

ON TUESDAY, MORE TESTIMONY WAS HEARD FROM defense psychiatrists, including Dr. George Stephens, who had appeared for Ruthie's murder trial. He believed she was insane at that time and had continued to deteriorate since then. "She is unstable," he told the jury. "I am making my diagnosis in this case now purely on the fact that this woman is delusional. She has a persecution complex - she dislikes people without rhyme or reason - she dislikes officials. I have a letter in my pocket that she wrote to her husband. That letter shows a paranoid trend regarding the prison warden, her mother, her father, her attorneys. She speaks of 'John Robert' and says she is going to see him when she dies."

"John Robert," be the way, was her name for the child that never existed.

Two additional psychiatrists, Dr. John Huffman and Dr. Harry Pinkert, followed Dr. Stephens on the stand. Both men agreed that Ruthie was not faking her insanity. Dr. Pinkert added that a picture of a genuinely insane person "is just like a jigsaw puzzle - you can't see the picture unless all the pieces fit. The ordinary person knows of and feigns only two kinds of insanity. One is your gibbering, drooling idiot, the other is your raving maniac. They attempt to feign one or the other, and they jump right into the last stages." He blamed Ruthie's outbursts on "the same emotional pressure that prevents her from telling a connected story - that pressure piles up until the emotions break under the stress."

During cross-examination, County Attorney Reed attacked Dr. Pinkert's statement, saying that he had received no compensation - nor expected any - for his services during the hearing. "Don't you know as a matter of fact, Dr. Pinkert, that the expenses on behalf of Mrs. Judd are being financed by the Hearst newspapers?"

O'V. Willson was immediately on his feet. "Now here... wait! I object to that! And I charge this counsel with misconduct and ask the jury to be instructed to disregard the remarks of counsel. I want to announce right now in open court that this is absolutely false!"

But Reed insisted, "We intend to prove the fact."

"You can't prove it!" Willson scoffed.

"If you take the stand, I can prove it."

"I will take the stand any minute you want me to."

Judge Green turned to Reed. "Do you want to show the witness is interested in this case?"

"I want to show who is financing this case."

"Are you going to show he is getting compensation?"

"I expect to."

Willson again interrupted, "Now that this is before the jury, let's have it out right now. I want to take the witness stand, as will any lawyer or physician engaged here, and we will show that not a dollar has been received in this case in the way of a fee for medical or legal men here since the commencement of it, our taking hold of it, a year ago."

The discussion finally ended when Dr. Pinkert said, "This is the first I've heard of it."

And he wouldn't have heard of it. All the doctors and attorneys working to save Ruthie's life were working for free. It was true that William Randolph Hearst had footed the bill for Ruthie's murder defense, but the money had stopped coming in a long time ago.

Attorneys for the state and the defense became embroiled in another heated debate just after Judge Green announced a recess until Wednesday morning. He informed the jurors, "You are to be placed in the custody of the bailiff and kept together for the remainder of this trial." Reports had been brought to the attention of the judge that jurors had been reading newspaper articles about the hearing.

But County Attorney Truman chimed in, "May it please the court, but we wish the record to show that it was the defense counsel who requested this action and that we did not desire it."

The state wanted the unhappy jury to know that it wasn't their fault they were going to be sequestered - blame it on the defense attorneys.

One of Ruthie's attorneys, E.W. MacFarland, shot to his feet. "I object! That is the most gross error I ever saw committed in a court of law."

Judge Green concurred. "It is an error, but it's done now. I think the jury understands it is not to allow any such things to affect its judgment. The order was agreed upon between counsel. The state did not oppose."

After testimony from the defense psychiatrists, one of the state's experts, Dr. Paul Bowers, got into a lively discussion with reporters. He continued to maintain that Ruthie was not insane. "She is suffering from a state of great fear and is thoroughly frightened, but wouldn't you be if death were as near for you as it is for her? Her actions in the courtroom yesterday afternoon were an emotional outburst, not uncommon for a woman. Many women whose minds are not mentally unbalanced have such outbursts over trivial matters, but it only goes to show that she is under a highly nervous strain."

The reporters had questions - although no comments on the wildly misogynistic statements the doctor had just made. "But Dr. Bowers, what about Mrs. Judd's blank stare during the proceedings here?" one newsman asked.

"Look here," he replied, imitating Ruthie's stare for what one report stated was "several minutes."

"Then, should Mrs. Judd be shamming insanity, what do you think of her ability as an actress?"

"She has great histrionic ability," he quipped with a self-satisfied smirk.

That evening, Dr. Bowers and Dr. Catton interviewed Ruthie in her cell - or they tried to anyway. She refused to answer questions, chatted about nonsensical things, or played with her kittens.

That night, the twelve jurors bunked down on cots in the courtroom that was being used for the hearing during the day. A cold rainstorm had settled in over Florence, so wood fires were lit in the stoves along two of the walls to chase the chill and damp from the big, drafty room.

The men drifted off to sleep to the sound of rain falling on the courthouse's roof, providing a peaceful soundtrack to the ending of an upsetting day.

THE HEARING OPENED AGAIN ON WEDNESDAY WITH more testimony from defense psychiatrists. Dr. Stephens and Dr. Winn Wylie, a Phoenix psychiatrist, both testified briefly, and then the defense counsel abruptly rested their case, catching the county attorneys off guard. Despite protests from the defense, County Attorney Truman and his assistant, Reed, asked for and were granted a four-hour delay to summon and confer with witnesses.

When the hearing resumed after lunch, the state brought a parade of witnesses to the stand, including a court clerk who said that Ruthie seemed sane when she appeared at the preliminary hearing for Jack Halloran and a prison parole clerk who described Ruthie's testimony before the board as connected and intelligent. A Maricopa County grand jury member said the same thing, as did Pardon and Parole Board Chairman Lin Orme and fellow board member Herman Hendrix. Each man said that he believed Mrs. Judd knew she was going to be hanged when they saw her. When pressed for an opinion about her current medical condition, Hendrix declined to answer, saying he hadn't observed her long enough to know.

During Lin Orme's testimony, Ruthie exploded when he stated that she'd revealed to the board during that secret session at the prison that she would attempt to get pregnant if the board ignored her plea for a life sentence. "She said that she wanted to save her life, and she wanted us to commute her..."

Ruthie screamed aloud and began shouting at Orme. She pointed at him, her face red with anger, "You told me that if I would not exonerate Jack Halloran, you would kill me! I said, 'Please don't kill me because I'm going to have a baby.' You said if I exonerate Jack Halloran, you would not kill me. That's all I said! Jack Halloran... where is he? Where is Jack Halloran? Make him come up here! He said Jack Halloran, and unless I exonerate Jack Halloran, he would kill me, and I said you won't! Where is Jack Halloran? Get him! Mash his brains over the ceiling like a dish of oatmeal! I said, get Jack Halloran! Because he said Jack Halloran, if I exonerate Jack Halloran, 'we won't kill you.' 'If you don't exonerate Jack Halloran, I will kill you!' I said, 'Don't kill my baby!'"

While this outburst from Ruthie was certainly unhinged, we'll never know for sure what was said inside that "secret session" that took place at the prison. It was all totally off the record, and no notes from the session were ever found. Is it likely this is what Orme said to her behind closed doors? It's not, but on the other hand, I'm not convinced that what Orme claimed was said was accurate either.

None of it mattered anyway because, once again, Warden Walker and the prison matrons forcibly removed Ruthie from the courtroom. They took her on a walk around the courthouse grounds, and then she returned to the hearing. Back in her chair, she sat sullenly, ignoring what was happening around her.

On cross-examination, Willson asked Herman Hendrix if he hadn't seen Mrs. Judd "in hysteria, wailing and crying."

"Yes."

"Did you consider that the manifestation of merely a nervous woman?"

"I've seen high school girls act worse."

"Would you say she is sane today?"

"Me? I have made no observation."

"You don't know now, then, whether Ruth Judd comprehends her surroundings?"

"Well, I think she did Saturday."

"What makes you think so?"

"Orme and I were sitting in the rear of the room while the jury was out. I said to Orme, 'I would like to see Mrs. Judd face to face again.' She looked around, then turned her eyes away - and called us four names."

"Oh, so that's why you think she is sane?" Willson snorted, implying that Hendrix believed Ruthie was sane because she recognized the two men were the "four names" she called them.

After that, the state asked for and was granted an early halt to the proceedings on Wednesday afternoon. The defense protested again, but the judge overruled their objections.

Willson, Fulbright, and the others were getting more nervous with each passing day as the execution date drew closer.

THE STATE WAS READY TO PROCEED ON THURSDAY morning. Now, they were really to bring out their heaviest hitters - the psychiatric experts they were sure would send Ruthie to the gallows.

The previous day, at 3:00 P.M., a gathering of Winnie Ruth Judd sympathizers had held a mass meeting at the Free Methodist Church in Phoenix. An evangelist and several state legislators were on hand as special guests, putting pressure on the county attorneys to wrap things up as quickly as possible.

Although several Arizona psychiatrists and doctors attested to their belief in Ruthie's sanity that morning, the testimony from Dr. Bowers and Dr. Catton brought an overflow crowd of spectators to the courtroom.

Dr. Bowers was up first. Predictably, he told the jury that he found "no evidence of insanity, or any delusions - no hallucinations, no illusions - no evidence of any behavior belonging to the category of insanity. I saw none of the behavior that goes with dementia praecox - I saw behavior that goes with deliberation; behavior that goes with a self-serving attitude of mind. I reached the conclusion -- she didn't because she chose deliberately not to talk."

Bowers glanced at Ruthie and frowned, like a disapproving teacher looking at a problem student. "She is disagreeable to her parents. She treats them miserably. I was not particularly impressed by that. When a person has a particular purpose in mind, they carry out that purpose - and what greater purpose than to save one's life?"

He added, "I considered her family history and felt it possibly is a bit tainted - but knowing many sane individuals have insane relatives and knowing I had examined such patients of tainted heredity, it did not count for much."

But then Dr. Bowers softened a little. "I feel this lady is in a nervous condition. I feel she is under great strain. She is depressed - seeking refuge from a terrible situation. She stands the strain better than I could, if I were in the same situation. I think the woman is in a neurotic state. I think she is nervous - and she is scared to death almost - but I think the reaction to save herself is perfectly normal."

When Dr. Catton took the stand, he showed no gentle side toward Ruthie. He had been exasperated from the start, going all the way back to when he first interviewed her and found her disagreeable.

He'd immediately assumed she was a fraud, and his opinion refused to be changed. Ruthie could expect no softening from the doctor.

He immediately went to work, trying to dismantle the defense's claims. "Family history helps explain insanity in an individual," he said, "but it does not help you to say an individual is insane."

Ruthie watching testimony from Dr. Catton in the courtroom. When he insisted that she was faking her illness, Ruthie hurled herself into the arms of the matron next to her.

He crossed his legs, relaxing into the witness chair. "I know Mrs. Judd does not talk in certain instances, but whether or not she is able to talk on those occasions, frankly, I do not know. I am not so smart I cannot be fooled. I believe about 60 percent that this woman has a definite prison psychosis. I believe with the other 40 percent that the picture she presents may be fraudulent."

Dr. Catton went on to repeat much of what he'd said at the murder trial, reinforcing his belief that Ruthie was sane according to the legal definition. He did say, though, "beyond a doubt, she is suffering from a condition that I would term 'neurosis of the condemned.' It is my belief this neurosis is made up in part of simulated symptoms."

He told the jury that Ruthie was faking her insanity. He said that he'd found Ruthie perfectly capable of understanding what was happening and was putting on an act to save herself.

"It is my opinion that Mrs. Judd's symptoms," he stated with the kind of certainty that only a person with the belief that he is the smartest person in a room can do, "will disappear if commutation be granted, within a period of weeks, or months, at most."

Catton told the jury that he should know "because he was a trained psychologist."

Defense attorney Tom Fulbright later wondered if Dr. Catton himself wasn't a little unbalanced. In his memoirs, he recounted a story that he was told after the hearing by Assistant County Attorney Charlie Reed: "Every damn night, Dr. Catton insisted on sleeping at a different place. Then he would lock the door behind him and crawl under the bed."

DR. CATTON WAS THE LAST STATE WITNESS TO APPEAR. Both sides were given time to prepare their closing arguments, which took place on Saturday morning.

Ernest McFarland gave the closing argument for the defense. In his own autobiography, he recalled that morning: I told the jury we had just passed through the Easter season and reminded them that the thief had asked forgiveness of Christ while they were on the cross. I said that was what we were asking for Ruth Judd. If she were to be executed, it would be at a time when she was sane and was able to ask for forgiveness. A reporter from the *Los Angeles Times* told me my speech to the jury won the case."

The jury deliberated for one hour and 57 minutes before they returned to the courtroom with a verdict. By agreement from both sides - and who can blame them? - the verdict was to be read before Ruthie was brought into the courtroom. The court clerk read the introductory remarks, and when he hesitated, the courtroom became very still. Finally, he read the final words - Ruth Judd had been found insane.

The silence was broken by applause from the spectators. O'V. Willson physically slumped against the jury box, visibly affected by the verdict. His fellow attorneys hurried to his side, offering congratulations.

At the moment the verdict was being read, Ruthie was getting out of the car from the prison. She was just outside the courtroom when the applause from inside spelled out a message that the matrons with her clearly understood - but Ruthie showed no sign of celebrating the victory.

When Ruthie was brought into the courtroom, she took her chair. His face flushed with emotion, Dr. Judd took her hand and placed his arm around her shoulders. "You will not be hanged!" he said excitedly. "Everything is all right. Do you hear? You are going to the hospital."

But Ruthie showed no sign that she heard him. She stared blankly across the defense table. Several female spectators rushed to Ruthie, hugging her, even kissing her, but she had no reaction. She just stared.

Her only reaction was when Dr. Stephens came to see her. She recognized him and took his hand. "I'd like one of your kittens," he said to her.

Ruthie heard him and even smiled a little. "I'll give you one of them, although I only have three left. I'll give you Tom, but you can't have Angel."

Ruthie's eyes glazed over again, but then she uttered one more thing. "Lin Orme can't have any of my kittens."

Then she was led out of the courtroom and back to her prison cell.

NOT SURPRISINGLY, MANY IN THE PRESS REPORTED the jury's decision as Ruthie "cheating the hangman." For others, it meant that justice had prevailed.

What really happened is that the state of Arizona managed to get itself out of a sticky situation. By now, no one really wanted to see Ruthie hang - not with all the suspicion circulating about what really happened on the night of the murders. If she were executed, it would not only provide ammunition for the opponents of capital punishment, but it would make Arizona look barbaric in light of the support that had come in for Ruthie from all over the country.

But at the same time, officials were tired of what the Winnie Ruth Judd case represented - Phoenix playboys, corruption, police incompetence, lesbians, syphilis, infidelity, and body parts stuffed into trunks. They wanted the case to be over and done with, and they wanted to silence Ruthie once and for all.

The insanity verdict did both those things: It ended the case, and it shut Ruthie up by locking her away in a mental institution. She's crazy, they could now say, you can't possibly believe anything she says.

Ruthie was spared the noose, but she was sentenced to lifetime confinement in the Arizona State Mental Hospital - "unless her reason was restored." If she recovered, the state would then see to it that she was hanged for the murder of Anne LeRoi.

She was greeted at the asylum gates by photographers and reporters. She was escorted through the crowd, glancing back over her shoulder once before the doors closed behind her. She let out a hiss, "I never saw such a bunch of morbids!"

After that, no one heard much about Winnie Ruth Judd for the next six years, but with a story this bizarre - this isn't the end.

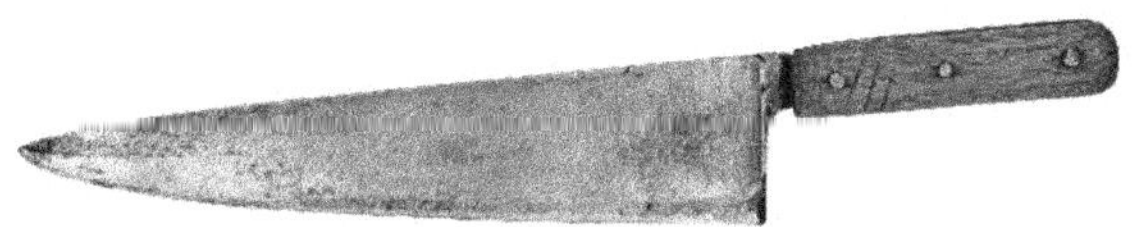

15. ASYLUM

AFTER THOSE ASYLUM DOORS SWUNG CLOSED, RUTHIE was placed in a small room on Ward D, where she remained under observation for the next 30 days - just like any ordinary patient.

Ruthie, of course, wasn't ordinary, however.

She did adjust quickly to hospital life. Within a few months, she gained a reputation as a docile, cooperative inmate who did anything the doctors, nurses, and attendants asked her to do. She was quiet, got along fine with the other inmates, and spent a lot of time with her cat, Egypt, who she'd been allowed to bring with her from the state prison.

But Ruthie was lonely. During those early months of transition, her parents were her only authorized visitors. The McKinnells had moved to Phoenix after the sanity hearing to be closer to the hospital. They had joined Ruthie's brother, Burton, in his campaign to fight for their daughter's complete freedom.

Rev. McKinnell was already a seasoned campaigner for Ruthie. After her murder trial, he'd walked the streets of Phoenix soliciting signatures on a petition requesting a new trial. Before the parole board turned down a plea for clemency in early April 1933, he sent dozens of letters to Arizona Governor Bakin Moeur asking for help. In July, he submitted a petition for a full pardon for Ruthie, basing his plea on Ruthie's self-defense claims. None of his campaigns - or those started by Ruthie's growing legion of supporters - were successful.

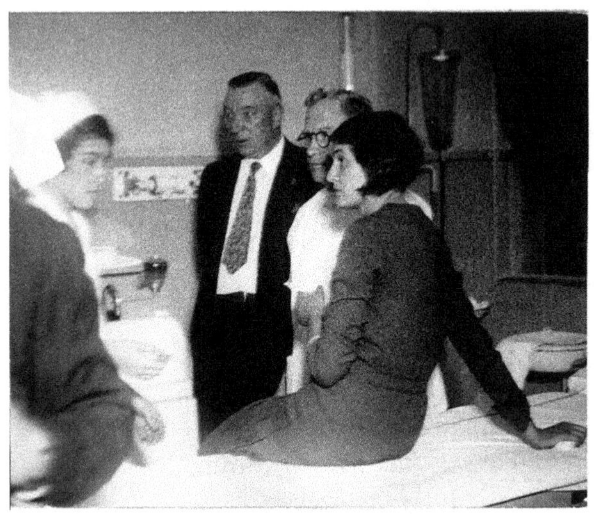

Ruthie adapted quickly to life at the state hospital, spending most of her time out of the public spotlight for the first several years.

Ruthie herself managed to stir up some controversy in 1939. For several years, she had done all she could to stay busy in the asylum. While housed with the elderly patients, she planted flowers, cooked their favorite meals, and read to them. She cared for six babies and a handful of toddlers when the children's wing overflowed. She washed, ironed, and pitched in to clean whenever possible.

She was placed in the young women's wing, and thanks to donations of used clothing, she washed, ironed, and altered dresses so the young women could attend dances and programs arranged by the therapy department at the hospital.

Ruthie also learned how to style and cut hair and used her skills as therapy for the patients, giving many of them the first feeling of pride they'd had in years.

And that's where the trouble started.

In April 1939, Ruthie's beauty parlor became a political issue. After a series of complaints by beauty shop operators in the area, the superintendent of the hospital, Dr. Louis J. Saxe, reluctantly ordered that Ruthie's beauty parlor equipment be removed and her appointments for patients, staff members, and "a few outsides drawn by curiosity" be stopped. It had reportedly become fashionable in local society to announce, "I had my hair done by Ruth Judd."

The Arizona State Asylum in Phoenix

Dr. Saxe's directive followed newspaper publicity that was given to letters written to the governor and other state officials by the Arizona State Board of Beauty Culturist Examiners, claiming "unfair competition" because of Ruthie's low prices.

Governor Robert T. Jones met with three members of the Board of Beauty Culturist Examiners, who were accompanied by 11 beauty shop operators. It didn't go well - mostly because he felt that their complaints unfairly targeted Ruthie.

Governor Jones had zero interest in listening to the beauty shop operators. "I'm not interested," he said bluntly, gesturing to the state employees who were also in the room for the meeting. "These people are all being paid with public funds and cannot take any more time than is necessary with this."

Mrs. Ware, the chairman of the examiners' board, interrupted in defense of the beauty shop owners. "They are the public that supplies the funds."

"I didn't call those women."

"It'll make it tough on you not to see them."

The governor scoffed. "I'm not running for office, and you can go out and tell them that. I'm trying to protect those poor helpless people in the hospital and I'm going to do it, so good day."

But there was little the governor could do for Ruthie at that moment. A few days after her "shop" was closed. Ruthie took an overdose of sleeping tablets and was in a coma for two days.

While still agitated about losing her beauty shop, she recovered and started a "laundry business," washing uniforms for the hospital attendants, who paid her 10 cents each.

By the fall of 1939, Ruthie had managed to earn over $30. She continued her business despite friends' warnings that Phoenix laundries would be the next to complain if word got outside the hospital walls.

In early October, Ruthie sent $20 from her savings to Dr. Judd, now a resident at the government hospital in Sawtelle, California. She had not seen him at all during her confinement at the asylum. Her only communication had been in the form of lengthy letters, which he always answered.

Two weeks later, Ruthie asked one of the staff members she was particularly close with to buy her some new clothes with the rest of her money. She said she was expecting a visit from her husband the following Sunday. The woman bought a purple dress, a pair of black shoes, and tan stockings and used her money to purchase six bottles of a soft drink so Ruthie could entertain her husband.

But to the surprise of everyone, Dr. Judd didn't show up.

Ruthie seemed disheartened and sad for the next two days but seemed to rally a little on Tuesday, which is why it seemed so strange when she didn't attend the dance arranged by the therapy department that night.

Ruthie had been too busy. She had skipped the dance to stay in her room, where she carefully arranged an assortment of boxes, towels, and blankets to make it appear that she was asleep in bed.

And then Ruthie Judd walked out of the hospital and vanished on October 24, 1939 - eight years to the day after she surrendered to the police at that Los Angeles funeral parlor.

Staff members at the Arizona State Hospital

THAT WAS RUTHIE'S FIRST ESCAPE FROM THE HOSPITAL.

There would be more. She did it again and again - for a total of seven times. She became not only a convicted killer but Arizona's number-one escape artist, too.

She escaped again on December 3, 1939.

She did it again on May 11, 1947.

Again on November 29, 1951.

Again on February 2, 1952.

Once more on Thanksgiving Day 1952.

And the last time was on October 8, 1962, when she stayed on the loose for the next seven years.

By that time, news of her disappearances had become a familiar story across the country. Along the way, another generation learned the story of Winnie Ruth Judd, the "Trunk Murderess," and, of course, her story began to be twisted, retold, reimagined, and filled with legends and lore.

When Ruthie escaped the first time - well, more than just the first time, but we'll start there - the newspapers were filled with hysterical stories. Bloodhounds were brought to Phoenix from the state prison to track her down. Manhunts were launched across the West, especially along the border with Mexico. She was fluent in the language and knew the country, thanks to the years she'd spent there with her husband. Most expected that Ruthie would vanish into the desert and pop up again south of the border, out of the reach of the law.

But Ruthie didn't even try to get that far - so why bother to escape in the first place? And how did she do it, over and over again?

Ruthie hadn't been out of the headlines for so long that rumors about her had stopped. People were still talking about the case. Local children had adopted her as a sort of "boogeyman," warned that the "trunk murderess" would get them if they didn't behave. Among the rumors were those that claimed Ruthie had "powerful friends" who helped her escape. Wilder versions of the story had a limousine picking her up at the hospital. Some people in town believed that she spent as many nights outside the hospital as she did locked up, going to parties, dinners, and movies.

Many of those who repeated such stories laughed and cheered her on, chuckling about her getting one over on the law - but not everyone was happy about it. The Phoenix newspapers, in particular, were unhappy that Ruthie had avoided the gallows, and after she escaped, angry editorials demanded that the authorities get tough about keeping Ruthie locked away. They called for investigations to discover the identities of whoever helped her and suggested that if hospital officials were involved, they should be fired. It was an embarrassment to the city and the state that this murderess was allowed to make a mockery of her incarceration.

As it turned out, the investigations led nowhere because Ruthie's escapes were much easier than anyone ever imagined they could be - Ruthie had a key.

Decades after her first escape, an elderly Ruthie still had her key to the Arizona State Hospital. She admitted in an interview that it hadn't just ended up in her hands by accident. But it wasn't a conspiracy and didn't involve "powerful friends." It was given to her by a nurse whose identity was never revealed.

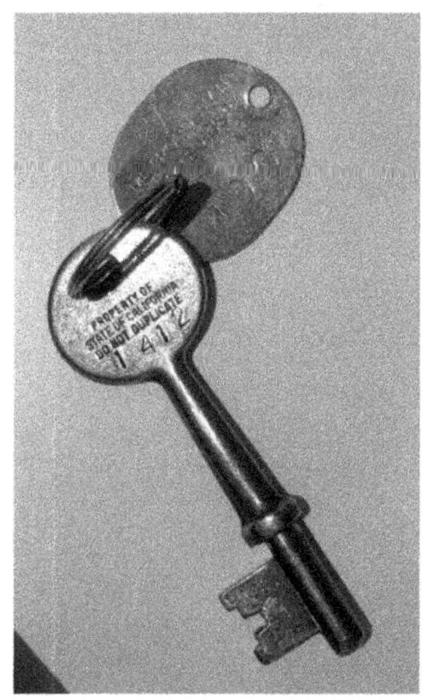

Ruthie took that secret - one of her many -to the grave.

Ruthie kept that key inside a small box next to her bed. Inside was also a portable radio - which she got in the 1950s to listen to news broadcasts about her escapes - and a small purse in which she kept her money. Whenever she cut a staff member's hair or washed their uniform, they handed over coins or bills, which Ruthie placed in the purse and closed back in the small box. No one ever realized that they'd find a hospital door key inside if they had pried the lid open.

As it turned out, Ruthie's many escapes from the hospital had a (possibly) unintended side effect - they highlighted the terrible conditions at the Arizona State Hospital in the 1930s.

The asylum - just like every other facility that fell to ruin in the early twentieth century - was started with good intentions, but it became overcrowded, understaffed, dirty, corrupt, and a soul-crushing place to be. It was also a pawn in a political game since patronage jobs and supply contracts were handed out directly from the governor's office.

There was little pretense of "treatment" at the hospital. By the 1930s, it had become less of a hospital and more of a warehouse for orphans, people with epilepsy, alcoholics, and older people who were unable to care for themselves. In a town with no nursing homes, facilities for people with disabilities, and hospital beds only for those who might get well, the state hospital was a place of last resort.

It would be years after Ruthie's first escape that attempts were made to clean things up. By the 1940s, the hospital's rotting pipes had led to outbreaks of typhoid, and its rotten politics had become so entrenched that a new board demanded the resignation of every single staff member. But change was slow to come for a facility that most people in Phoenix pretended didn't exist, which is illustrated by the fact that in the early 1950s - around the time Ruthie escaped three more times - the Arizona State Hospital was nationally recognized as the most overcrowded public asylum in the country.

By the time Ruthie arrived at the hospital, there were 277 people confined there. The state was then spending less than 62 cents a day to house, feed, and care for each of them. Even by 1932 dollars, that was bordering on pathetic.

Officials, however, claimed so little was spent because the institution was supposed to be self-sufficient. The state hospital had its own ice plant, laundry, bakery, cannery, and shoe repair shop. It had a sewing room for patient uniforms, a mattress factory, and a carpentry shop. The acres surrounding the hospital were used for farming wheat, barley, corn, and alfalfa, and 15 acres were devoted to growing oranges and grapefruit. There was a 20-acre garden for the kitchen and a dairy herd of 100 cows, a few mules, and some hogs.

It also had a poorly trained staff that neither understood nor could deal with the assortment of people they were supposed to be caring for. Patients were often abused, but more commonly, they were neglected and ignored.

Ruthie was a different sort of patient for the state hospital. She was not helpless, bedridden, or mentally incompetent. She was a young woman who was used to taking care of herself, and ironically, behind the locked doors of the asylum, she found a whole community of people who needed her.

She helped with patients, made beds, washed clothes, swept and mopped the floors, and gave baths to those unable to do so. Later, of course, she started her own beauty salon inside the hospital, and initially, beauticians from Phoenix donated shampoo, hairpins, and combs to assist with her efforts. She never charged the patients to have their hair styled, but when the nurses came in and wanted her to do their hair, they always left money in a saucer she kept on the counter. Soon, women from town started arriving, along with their daughters, to have their hair styled by Winnie Ruth Judd.

At first, Ruthie's helpfulness and popularity earned her praise from local newspapers. The *Phoenix Gazette* reported, "She lavishes her love on the other patients" and noted that they adored her for it.

Kindness came easy for Ruthie. Her mother had instilled in her a duty to care for those who were less fortunate, but that wasn't the only reason she found it easy to be kind. According to Ruthie - and she revealed this many years later - she wasn't going to be locked up in the hospital for long. She was just biding her time, and during those first six years, she never thought about escaping because she thought she had a deal.

These stories are, of course, impossible to verify. Everyone involved in her case died years ago, but Ruthie maintained until the end of her life that she was told that she would be released from the hospital after a short time if she behaved herself.

According to her story, she had been at the hospital for just over a year when she was visited by Attorney General Arthur La Prade and Herman Hendrix, who was now Superintendent of Public Instruction.

"We're your friends," La Prade reportedly told her.

"No, you're not," she replied.

But the two men insisted that she could trust them and that they planned to take care of her. They told Ruthie that a man named Janavitch - who had also been judged insane and locked up - had recently had his sentence commuted. They assured Ruthie they were going to do the same for her. Janavitch had been deported to Syria, where he was originally from, but Ruthie would be set free just as soon as public sentiment about her case died down.

Again, there's no way to verify if this meeting happened, but Arizona Department of Corrections records do have a listing for George Janavitch, a convicted murderer who was judged insane and was deported to Syria on July 17, 1934.

But "soon" never came for Ruthie. She continued to behave herself year after year, wondering if she would ever get the freedom she'd been promised.

Life moved on at the hospital, where Ruthie enjoyed privileges that few other inmates had. She could leave the hospital grounds and go to a store across the street. Someone, either a nurse or a doctor, would take her to see her father once a week after he suffered a stroke.

The visits were unsupervised. Ruthie was dropped off at her parents' home and picked up in the evening. While she was there, they talked about many things, but one thing that Ruthie would not discuss was her case. She continually reassured her parents that her days at the hospital would soon be over, and they needed to be patient.

The McKinnells, though, were never as trusting as Ruthie was. If her parents or her brother believed the authorities had a secret plan to free her, nothing about their actions showed it. They continued to work to see that Ruthie got justice. Burton continued his investigations - and campaigns of harassment - for years after Ruthie was sent to the hospital. Until a stroke incapacitated him, Rev. McKinnell wrote almost daily to state officials - passionate letters filled with the pain of a parent who believed his child had been mistreated.

The controversy over the beauty salon occurred through no fault of Ruthie's. The uproar was orchestrated by a society woman in town who was active on the Board of Beauty Culturist Examiners. The woman complained that she was stealing business from licensed beauticians, ignoring the fact that Ruthie's services were usually free or, at most, 25 cents.

Ruthie later claimed that Governor Jones was so angry about the mess that he came to the hospital to see her, telling her that the complaints were a way of criticizing him - not her. He assured her she'd soon get her beauty parlor back, but she never did. Years later, she recalled, "Everybody told me I was doing good work. And then for them to come in and take it all away from me just broke my heart."

Ruthie also said that in addition to losing her beauty parlor, she lost most of her privileges, including visits with her parents. So, after arranging for the new clothes that she'd convinced a staff member to buy for her and pretending Dr. Judd was coming to visit, Ruthie took her key and went to see her father - on October 24, 1939.

No one even noticed that she was gone for 12 hours after she arranged a dummy in her bed and slipped out a side door. However, when they did, a banner headline in the *Arizona Republic* read, "RUTH JUDD FLEES ASYLUM." She was once again the most widely hunted woman in the West.

From Sawtelle, California, Dr. Judd issued a plea for his wife to surrender. "If my words can reach her, this is what I say to my wife: 'Surrender to the nearest officers of the law, wherever you are, for only disaster awaits you if you attempt to remain in hiding or to continue your flight.'" Dr. Judd said he had fervent hope that Ruthie would give herself up. "She can gain nothing by her escape," he added.

When Ruthie fled from the hospital, her parents' house was the first place she'd gone. Her mother urged her to stay there for the night and return to the hospital in the morning, but Ruthie refused. After writing a letter to Governor Jones - which she asked her mother to deliver - she walked out into the night.

This was the letter she wrote to the governor:

I am only going to see my father and husband. I have a right to.

My husband coaxed me to surrender to the police. I did and look what happened. Dr. Saxe tortures me. Even Hitler would not torture his prisoners when they surrender. I was not overcover, so I had to surrender. Only a coward would torture one so helpless.

I am helpless because I trusted fairness. I do not get it. Dr. Saxe says I have no privileges. I did have until he came here. He took them away. For 18 months I had yard parole, could sit in the yard alone or with my family. I never abused a privilege or broke a trust. Dr. Saxe took away my privileges because he hates me. I am persecuted by the Catholics.

When Ruthie escaped, she desperately wanted to see her sick father. Her mother urged her to stay the night and return to the hospital, but she refused.

A portion of the letter at this point is missing, but it continues:

... him $20 to come on. But he can only stay one day. $20 just to see him two or three hours. 200 hours' work to see him two or three hours, and now they have ordered him I have to visit him in Mrs. Lassiter's presence, my bitter enemy.

Bertha Lassiter was a matron at the hospital.

I will not.

Tonight, I am running away. I hate everyone who has forced me to do it. May God punish them. I want to be a good patient. I like you. I hope you may be governor again. You have been kind to me, and I do not want to do anything to ever hurt you.

I am desperate to see my father. I am going to see him tonight, then somehow see my husband and I will surrender to you on condition you promise me Dr. Saxe will be forced to leave me alone.

I will not run away. I do not want my freedom illegal.

The letter was unsigned.

Ruthie had obviously devised a plan for her escape, and everyone thought so, but did she? It seems just as likely that Ruthie genuinely believed that Dr. Judd was coming to see her on Sunday. She had sent him $20 so that he could make the trip, but, as usual, he had disappointed her. When he didn't come, Ruthie put on her new outfit and walked out the door, determined to see her father and husband.

To me, her escape seemed to be a spur-of-the-moment thing with no more than a day's worth of planning. I'm not convinced - based on the strange letter to the governor and my own theories about the case, which I'll get into later - Ruthie was in the right frame of mind to make any detailed plans.

Regardless, she was out, and the law was looking for her again. The McKinnell home was searched "as a precautionary measure." Sheriff's deputies found no clues, but they did upset Rev. McKinnell so much that his condition spiraled, and a doctor had to be called.

A reward of $100 was posted for information, and the newspapers rapidly filled with alleged sightings of Ruthie all over Arizona, California, Mexico, and beyond. Ruthie was spotted in a tourist court in Los Angeles. No, she was in Austin, Texas. But wait, she'd been seen in Eagle Pass, Texas, just 90 miles from where she'd lived with Dr. Judd in Mexico. That wasn't her -- she was in Tempe, Arizona, where a minister approached her and was scared off when she threatened to cut his throat with a razor.

Every sighting was investigated and dismissed.

Ruthie remained on the loose for six days and spent most of that time hiding, she claimed, in a cornfield on the hospital grounds. She was "recaptured" when she showed up at the back door of the hospital and knocked. Her most recent stop had been at a nearby home, which she'd entered to find food, and believing she'd been spotted, she headed straight for the hospital.

She was shoeless when she got there, her stockings were ripped, her legs were scratched and bruised, and she had a sprained ankle. Attendants took her to Dr. Saxe's office and when she walked in, she announced, "Well, here I am!"

When Dr. Saxe pressed her for details of how she had eluded searchers, she "just became more and more hysterical." She was given sedatives and spoke briefly with Governor Jones. "I told you I would come back and give myself up, and I did," she told the governor. "I kept my word to you. I wanted to see my father, I saw him and talked to him, then I came back and gave myself up like I said I would."

While Ruthie had been on the lam, a reporter had asked Dr. Saxe if she would be punished when she returned and the doctor seemed offended by the question. "Of course not!" He exclaimed. "This is not an institution for punishment. She will be treated as she has always been."

But it's unclear what Dr. Saxe considered "treated as she has always been." Ruthie was kept in solitary confinement for the next four weeks. That was known to the public. But Ruthie claimed years later that she was placed in a straitjacket, beaten, and strapped down to a bed. She was eventually released back into the general population, but her earlier privileges were things of the past. There would be no more trips to see her parents or leaving the hospital grounds.

This is likely why, on December 3, 1939 - 34 days after she returned - Ruthie decided to escape again. She apparently walked through the same "locked" door she had used during her first escape.

Investigators soon learned that Ruthie had last been seen at 6:30 P.M., sitting on the edge of her bed, acting nervous and distraught. She was gone when a nurse came by her room again at 7:00 P.M. She did not attempt to hide her disappearance with a dummy in the bed this time.

Two dozen staff members scoured the hospital grounds, remembering that she'd hidden in a cornfield last time, but found no trace of her. Highway patrolmen and sheriff's deputies were sent to strategic points to cut off her escape, but she was nowhere to be found.

Other officers were stationed at the McKinnell home, but Ruthie wasn't there either. Her parents asked that the arresting officers "be gentlemen" with their daughter, and the ailing reverend expressed annoyance that neither he nor his wife had been allowed to see their daughter since her first escape.

Failing to turn up any clues, investigators again advanced the theory that Ruthie must have had some help. Her vanishing seemed too complete for only a half-hour's head start. Hospital attendants said only her wine-colored dress and brown shoes were missing from her wardrobe - she'd gone out into the chilly night without a coat or hat.

Another banner headline in the local papers - "RUTH JUDD AGAIN ESCAPES!" - was followed by another round of hysteria. Numerous tips flooded the sheriff's office, but none led anywhere. A deputy sheriff told the press they were busy following up on the tips but felt most came from people with "Judd jitters."

Bloodhounds from the state prison in Florence were put on Ruthie's trail but lost the scent when they reached the pavement of Van Buren Street.

A few hours later, it was learned that Ruthie had broken into the home of a local minister. She took a coat and a sweater and helped herself to some crackers and a half-filled carton of milk. She left behind a note, expressing regret about the theft, and promised that her mother would pay for what she'd taken. The note also contained a grim postscript about her treatment at the hospital. "It's either this or suicide," she wrote.

The bloodhounds were taken to the minister's residence, but they lost the trail again just one block away.

On Wednesday - three days after Ruthie had vanished - Dr. Judd arrived in Phoenix. It was hoped that his presence in the city would convince Ruthie to turn herself in - but there was no sign of her.

Ruthie's escape once again brought attention to the Arizona State Hospital. On Thursday, Dr. Andrew F. Tombs, one of the staff physicians, handed in his resignation. He was the fourth doctor to resign in as many months. There was now only one staff physician to provide care for 900 patients. Rumors spread that the governor would replace Dr. Saxe, but that was quickly quashed. Governor Jones only said that immediate action would be taken to hire a competent staff, and Dr. Saxe still had his complete confidence.

The hunt for Ruthie continued, but she had no trouble eluding the police in Phoenix because she wasn't there. She was 180 miles away in the town of Yuma.

On December 15, 1939, shortly after noon, Sergeant James Stahl of the Yuma Police Department noticed a woman sitting on the steps

Ruthie was recaptured (this time) in Yuma, Arizona. She was soon returned to the state hospital. She had walked at least 24 of the 180 miles to Yuma.

of the courthouse drinking milk. He was convinced the woman was Ruth Judd. He followed her to a drugstore, where she used the payphone to call her husband's friends in California, hoping he would come and help her. She had no idea that he had traveled to Phoenix to find her. When she left the store, she was approached by Sergeant Stahl, who asked her to accompany him to his car. He had some questions for her, he said.

At first, Ruthie declined. She told him her name was "Marian Burke," and she was just passing through town, but eventually, she relented and was taken to the police station. She was finally identified as Ruth Judd by the mayor's wife, who had been a friend when she had lived in Yuma a decade earlier.

Ruthie was in bad shape. She was filthy, her stockings were torn, and her shoes were scuffed and falling apart. She said she'd walked at least 24 of the 180 miles to Yuma.

A local doctor was called to examine her, and he stated that she was "badly bruised" from her ordeal, "almost to the waist." He also made a more shocking discovery. Twisted into the back of her hair - knotted in place with chewing gum - he found a concealed razor blade. She told Yuma County Sheriff T.H. Newman that she kept it so she could commit suicide "if I felt I had to do it."

Before Ruthie was returned to Phoenix, she was allowed to go to the mayor's home. His wife, Ruthie's old friend, made sure she took a hot bath, cleaned up as best she could, ate lunch, and then left about 3:00 P.M. with Sheriff Newman, Sergeant Stahl, and two jail matrons.

Sheriff Newman stopped in Gila Bend to have a tire repaired, and while there, a truck driver was surprised to see Ruthie. He told the sheriff he'd met her the week before and gave her a ride to Theba, not realizing who she was.

It was in Gila Bend that Ruthie first saw reporters who had driven out from Phoenix to meet her car. She spoke candidly with the newsmen and gave them a 12-page statement carefully written in longhand. In the letter, Ruthie once again repeated her self-defense story and pleaded to be tried for Sammy's murder. She elaborated on the points in her letter and other things about her case in Gila Bend and later at Buckeye, where the party stopped for dinner.

One of the reporters asked Ruthie if she believed she was sane, to which she replied, "I should either be given the chance to testify in court or should be given the proper treatments for insanity." She said she'd received no medical care at the hospital - only "mistreatment."

She expressed a deep desire to be allowed to talk alone with Governor Jones. "When I got back last time," she said, "they shot me full of hypodermics. The attendant told me, 'I lost 36 hours' of sleep because of you,' and he put a knee in my back and shot me with the hypo and said, 'I guess you know why you're getting this. You talk too much.' When Governor Jones came to see me, I wasn't able to talk to him. That stuff constricts your throat, so you aren't able to talk. I was hazy. I just vaguely remember him being there."

She added that she had been promised the opportunity to see her parents, but she wasn't allowed to do so. "They put me in a straitjacket instead."

When Sheriff Newman's car reached the outskirts of Phoenix, Ruthie began to cry and gradually became more hysterical the closer they got to the hospital. Her 12-day absence ended at 8:15 P.M. when the car passed through the gate and onto the asylum grounds.

Officially, she was moved to a new ward - one deemed "escape-proof" - but according to Ruthie, she went back to solitary confinement. "They kept me in solitary confinement for two years," she later said. "In a little tiny cell, and the bed was soldered to the floor. I had no shoes. Barefooted and in pajamas for two years."

DURING THOSE TWO YEARS, RUTHIE FADED FROM THE public eye. It wasn't until July 1941 that she was briefly mentioned in the newspapers again. At that time, a self-appointed "Committee of Nine" asked the Arizona Board of Pardons and Paroles to reconsider her case. The committee asked the board to hold a public hearing to determine if the death sentence that was hanging over Ruthie was an obstacle to her treatment for mental illness. Predictably, the parole board ignored them, and the committee's efforts quickly died out.

However, her father never gave up on his letter-writing campaign. He died on July 1, 1942, but even during the last few months of his life, he wrote at least one or two letters each week to Governor Sydney P. Osborn - despite the paralysis of his right hand. Through great effort, he learned to write with his left hand to continue trying to help his daughter.

By the time of Rev. McKinnell's death, Ruthie had been released from solitary confinement, and she was allowed to occasionally visit her father before he passed away. It would have been easy for her to simply walk away from the house, but she never did. She had promised never to try and escape when allowed to visit her father, and she kept her word.

Even with her husband gone, Carrie McKinnell never gave up on the belief that someday her daughter would be cleared. In 1946, Ruthie had the chance to repay her mother for her years of support. Carrie, now 80 years old and senile, was committed to the Arizona State Hospital because she had nowhere else to go. Burton now lived in California with his family, and Dr. Judd died in October 1945. The two McKinnell women had no one left but each other.

Ruthie took over most of the daily care of her mother and, for a while, was allowed to sleep in the same room with her. The superintendent of the hospital at that time was Dr. Jeremiah Metzger, who had recently recommended to the parole board that Ruthie's sentence be commuted to life in prison. He said this action would clear the way for effective treatment, leading to the possible recovery of her sanity. Once again, though, the board took no action. But Dr. Metzger had tried, and he believed that giving Ruthie more access to her mother would be of great relief to her.

But something happened to change this. Ruthie believed it was because the new hospital administrator, Dr. John A. Larson, didn't like her. There's no way to know if that was the case, but what happened next occurred soon after Dr. Larson took over at the hospital.

With no warning, Ruthie's access to her mother was sharply restricted. She was only allowed to spend a few hours with her on some days, and on other days, she didn't see her at all. Ruthie became obsessed with the idea that Carrie wasn't getting proper care, enough food to eat, or, worst of all, that her mother would think she abandoned her.

On May 11, 1947 - Mother's Day - Ruthie begged to spend the day with Carrie. Word was passed that she could visit - but only for five minutes and with guards present. She waited all day for the brief visit, but it never happened.

In her anger, she escaped once again. She left her room at about 9:00 P.M. and passed through two sets of "locked" doors and the front gate without anyone sounding an alarm.

This time, though, she didn't go far. At 8:15 the next morning, she was found asleep in a grapefruit orchard but slipped away before the farmer recognized her as Ruth Judd. Finally, the police caught up with her two hours later in a pasture near the Arizona Biltmore Hotel. It was only three miles from the grapefruit orchard.

"They took my mother away," Ruthie explained to reporters after her capture. "She is all I have now that my father and husband are dead. Yesterday was Mother's Day. I didn't see her all day. My mother is all I have. She needs me. She is just like a baby. You have a mother, don't you?"

Ruthie was taken to the sheriff's office for processing, and Dr. Larson came to escort her back to the asylum.

As they were leaving, Ruthie spoke to him crisply, "I hope you won't be there long."

"I know you do," he replied - probably hoping the same thing.

AFTER HER RETURN TO THE HOSPITAL, Ruthie's mother was moved to Ward B in a room that adjoined that of her daughter. Ruthie was allowed to care for her again, and once more, she became a "model inmate."

Then, on November 1, 1951, Dr. M.W. Conway took over as the new superintendent. Ruthie heard rumors that she might be moved to a ward away from her mother. Some of the other inmates taunted her, saying she was going to be transferred to the new "criminal ward," which was segregated from the rest of the hospital. Although staff members tried to convince her this was untrue, she refused to believe them.

She became convinced she would never see her mother again.

On November 29, Ruthie was reportedly in her mother's room, giving her some fruit juice. Carrie, now 85, could not talk or do much of anything else for herself. After the attendants returned from dealing with a violently disturbed patient, they rechecked the room at 10:30 P.M. and saw that Ruthie was gone. When they saw a rope and an open window, they first thought that Ruthie had made good on a recent threat she'd made - if she and her mother were separated, she'd kill herself.

Instead of finding her dangling body, though, they found a makeshift ladder anchored to Carrie's bed and reaching most of the way to the ground. The ladder had been woven from yarn, cloth, and pieces of electric cord. Ruthie had used a screwdriver and pliers to remove a heavy steel screen from the window, scampered to the ground, and vanished through another "locked" gate.

Ruthie had planned her escape much better this time. Remembering the bloodhounds that had tracked her before, she'd spent the previous few days in the laundry room. She washed uniforms for the nurses and gowns for the patients, but she was also secretly laundering over and over the bedding and clothing she was leaving behind. The only scent the dogs could pick up this time was laundry soap, and they never even left the hospital grounds.

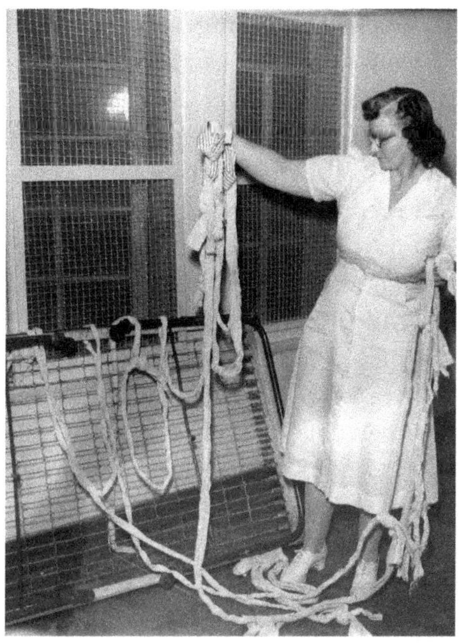

A ward nurse at the hospital displayed the makeshift rope that it was assumed Ruthie used to escape from the asylum.

A notice went out throughout the west for people to be on the lookout for the infamous Ruth Judd, but by the following afternoon, only two calls came in from people who thought they'd seen her. The radio dispatcher at the sheriff's office said the lack of public reaction was "amazing. Ordinarily, when someone as notorious as Mrs. Judd is at large, we get hundreds of reporters from people who think they have valuable information."

The sheriff said it was "anybody's guess" where she might appear next, so no organized search was made - everyone was too uncertain about where she might go.

Were the authorities and the public finally bored of Ruth Judd? Didn't anyone care that she escaped? They cared, but they had no idea where to look because, this time, Ruthie had never left Phoenix.

During her few hours of freedom, she hid in the empty house of a nurse at the state hospital named Ellen Evans, who was at work. She ate food from the kitchen and wrote letters she mailed from a box in front of the federal building downtown. When she left the house, she took a fur coat, a sports jacket, a pair of stockings, a purse, and a flowered scarf.

She was wearing the coat when she was spotted by two police officers a few blocks away from Ellen's house. She'd only been away from the hospital for 23 hours.

"Why did you have to pick me up?" she asked the officers. "I've served 20 years out there, and I think I should be turned loose. I had a tragedy 20 years ago that I wasn't wholly responsible for. I wish you boys would turn me loose. I'm awfully tired. I've walked all day, and I'd like to sit down."

Ellen Evans refused to press burglary charges, and she later told the police, "If I had known Ruth had taken my clothes, I never would have reported her. She wouldn't steal anything from me. I would give it to her. She took care of me when I was ill, when no one else paid any attention to me. Besides, a lot of people do not realize what good she has done at the hospital. She has helped many of the inmates."

When Ruthie was taken to the police station, she was greeted by reporters and photographers. She cried out, "I don't want anything to do with newspapers. I'm a very sick woman and I don't want my picture taken. If you were sick, you wouldn't want your picture taken, would you?" But then she changed her mind and allowed them to take photos. "Well, okay," she said, "but I won't smile. I don't feel like smiling, would you?"

Ruthie tried to explain to the police and the press why she had escaped this time. "I became seized with panic and fear at the coming of the new superintendent and I heard he was going to call a criminal board. I was afraid they'd transfer me to a criminal ward away from my mother. I'm not really a criminal. I'm not like those gangsters. I've never hurt anyone."

Two hospital staff members took Ruthie back to the asylum. Her room was stripped of all but necessities. She was going to have to earn back her privileges - again.

An editorial in the *Phoenix Gazette* appeared soon after Ruthie's latest escapade, discussing the hospital's apparent inability to keep its inmates confined. The editorial concluded: "Whether or not Winnie Ruth Judd should have cheated the hangman in 1931 is pretty much beside the point today. The important thing is that people like Winnie

Ruth Judd should not be permitted to roam at large. Now that she has been recaptured, Dr. Conway should see to it that she has no opportunity to repeat her frequent walkouts. When an insane murderess can pry her way out of the state mental hospital with a pair of pliers and a screwdriver, it's obvious that changes need to be made."

Honestly, it's a fair point. Whether you believe Ruthie should've been locked up in the state hospital or not, it probably should've been a little harder to escape that she continued to find it.

Feeling the pressure, Dr. Conway had no choice but to act. He began by suspending the attendant who had been on duty at the time of her escape and announced it was "the first step to cleaning house." He also added that her escape was "not the fault of any one attendant. You have to go up higher than a ward attendant when you blame someone for bad administration. In this case, blame can be put on the unskilled administration which this hospital has been under for many years." Dr. Conway added that Ruthie "has had entirely too many privileges in the past and has been treated as a private patient. In the future, she'll have the same status as other patients."

He also stressed that she would not have any more opportunities to "make an escape ladder from articles in her room."

In the meantime. Dr. Conway ordered a hospital shakedown. A half-dozen knives were found hidden in the men's ward, and a man convicted of murder was discovered to be working in the butcher shop with full access to knives and cleavers.

And then he took one more step - the one that Ruthie had feared the most. He ordered Carrie to be transferred to another building.

Ruthie had now been completely cut off from her mother.

Nurses and attendants crowded 94 patients into the dimly lit television viewing room on the evening of February 2, 1952. It was standard practice to "warehouse" as many patients as possible into one place. Drug them and put them in a chair was usually how things were done. The hospital was overcrowded and understaffed, and this

Winnie Ruth Judd Vanishes in Desert After New Escape

Posse to Hunt Her with Bloodhounds

Trunk Slayer Walks Away from Asylum in Southwest

Crowded Conditions in Institution Blamed

PHOENIX, Ariz., Dec 3—(U.P.) —Winnie Ruth Judd, the trunk murderess, walked out of the Insane

Loose Again

Senator U Delay in of Child

Governor Is to Wait fo of Fee

Baldwin Is to Any Ha

ALBION, Dec. Joseph A. Bald Gov. Dickinson S action on his re tions of the five Michigan Crippl mission, pendin Four member sion, Emmet R Mrs. Eleonore Pointe, and Ch DeWalker and both of Detro to appear bef day to give th

was an easy way for a limited number of staff members to watch over a lot of the patients at one time.

But one or two attendants were sometimes not enough to watch over a group that size, even if most patients were slumped over in a chair, staring at the lighted television screen with a string of drool running down their chins.

That night, it only took one moment when an attendant looked away for one of those patients to slip out of her chair, get through a "locked" door to a stairway, and hustle upstairs to a third-floor storeroom. In the darkened room, she put the finishing touches on a 48-foot-long rope fashioned out of patient restraints. She anchored one end of the rope to some bedsprings, removed the screens from the wire over the window, and tossed the rope out into the darkness. Then she eased herself out of the window and slid down the rope, dropping the last 15 feet to the ground. The woman quickly got up and ran to the fence, now nine feet tall and topped with barbed wire. She quickly scaled the fence and disappeared.

Ruthie Judd had escaped for the fifth time.

Later, the police would find four different witnesses who spotted a black 1948 Hudson sedan with California plates parked near the hospital's west gate. They saw two women inside the car. A search was quickly started to find the car, but it seemed to have vanished as easily as Ruthie had.

Only a handful of calls came in from people believing they had seen Ruthie this time. When the search for the mysterious black sedan failed, efforts turned to questioning the people who had recently visited her.

A staff psychiatrist named Dean Archer told police that Ruthie had recently boasted to him during a session that "Someone will help me escape." Dr. Conway had recently received a tip that Ruthie was getting outside help to escape but had dismissed it for some reason. Sheriff Cal Boies expressed doubt that Ruthie had actually escaped using the rope - he didn't think the knots were pulled tight enough to support her weight. "She must have gotten out some other way," he suggested.

Dr. Conway agreed. "I think she probably put the rope out the window to mislead any searchers."

And according to Ruthie, they were right. She used that magic key again and tossed the rope out a south window of the building but had exited from a door on the north side. She did have help evading capture for five days, while her friends moved her from place to place. Even during interviews in 1992, she never named the friends who helped her.

Then, on the fourth day, a woman called the sheriff's office to say that Ruthie would turn herself in within 24 hours if she received assurances from the Maricopa County Grand Jury through the newspapers that she would be given a hearing. Another anonymous woman called Dr. Conway and made the same offer. He agreed to the condition.

The following day, Captain Stanley Kimball appeared before the grand jury, and within hours, a subpoena had been issued for Ruthie's appearance immediately upon her return to the state hospital. The grand jury's assurance of a hearing appeared in the two local newspapers, just as the women had asked.

At 11:00 A.M. on Thursday, a secret conference was held at the asylum. It included Dr. Conway, Sheriff's Deputy Herb Barnes, and two unknown men. Whatever this meeting was about, Dr. Conway always insisted it had nothing to do with Ruthie's surrender.

That night, at 10:00 P.M., Ruthie walked up onto the front porch of Dr. Conway's house and rang the bell. When he opened the door, she simply said, "Here I am." They talked for about 45 minutes before Ruthie was returned to the hospital. The only interruption was when a woman telephoned to ensure Ruthie arrived safely. Dr. Conway said it was the same woman who had called earlier in the week.

During their chat, Ruthie told the doctor that she had used the rope to escape despite what the sheriff thought. This was obviously a lie since she didn't want the authorities to know about her passkey. She told him she had moved four or five times to avoid capture and had returned to the institution "half-heartedly." She said that her original plan had been to flee Phoenix by airplane, but ultimately ended up in Guatemala. She didn't want to go to Mexico, where she could be quickly extradited and returned to the United States.

Dr. Conway later quoted her saying, "I've lost faith in anyone doing anything for me."

But he did add that when Ruthie surrendered, she looked like a different person. "It was a moment before I recognized her - she looked so attractive," he said. "She had her eyebrows plucked, her hairline raised off her forehead and seemingly wore some type of makeup which erased wrinkles and other signs of age from her features."

On Friday morning, newspaper reporters were allowed to submit written questions to Ruthie that she would answer in writing. He didn't want to disturb her further with a press conference.

Some of the questions and answers read:

Q: How long have you been planning this escape?

A: I don't plan escapes. It's just that I've been in a sepulcher of living dead for 20 years. As long as I knew I could escape, I pacified myself, but when I read articles of tightening up and putting more nails in the coffin; I got panicky and escaped.

Q. Did you have help making your escape?

A. No.

Q. Did you offer to surrender if the grand jury would permit you to testify before it?

A. I wrote the grand jury two months ago asking them to investigate why my case was in politics. Twenty years ago, the Board of Pardons and Paroles came to see me and told me, "If you will keep everything quiet, as soon as public sentiment dies down, we will do likewise for you." I waited six years - twelve years - three times six years - and then was told by a Rev. Hoffman of the pardon board, "Mrs. Judd, the pardon board is between two political factions in doing anything for you." The whole thing was crooked. My husband said he could raise the money, but he would not trust my life to those dirty double-crossing dogs.

Q: Are you satisfied with the treatment you have had at the state hospital under the present administration?

A: They treat every patient kindly at this hospital.

Q: If you did receive help, was it by local people?

A: No one helped me escape. I cut through a field behind the hospital, through the country up to the Grand Canal. Local people helped me return, not escape, because they knew I was a patient and had hurt myself badly. They cried and cried and said they wanted to see me free legally.

Days passed, and Ruthie was still waiting for her promised appearance before the grand jury. The only thing standing in her way was Dr. Conway, who said he was delaying because he didn't want to see Ruthie more upset and disturbed. He believed there was little, if anything, for her to gain by appearing before the grand jury but admitted that she would make an excellent witness because she had a great memory. If she were compelled as a witness, he would allow her to go - but not until that time.

An editorial appeared in the *Phoenix Gazette* on the Friday after Ruthie returned: "As this editorial is written, Winnie Ruth Judd is back in the Arizona State Hospital. Whether she will still be there by the time this issue reaches the streets is anyone's guess. For the famed murderess apparently can walk in and out of the hospital at will, with cars waiting to take her away and bring her back. She has friends who can take care of her when she is loose, and who can make deals with the hospital authorities before returning to their care. All of which is strange, considering the brutality of her crime. But many old timers who were here at the time of the trial say that all the facts didn't come out."

The mystery surrounding the secret meeting in Dr. Conway's office was solved on Friday when reporters discovered the identities of the two unnamed men - Rev. A.R. Hudson and Ralph J. Tucker, a private detective.

Dr. Conway had lied about the purpose of the meeting because it had been about Ruthie, although it wasn't about her surrender.

Rev. Hudson stated that he was merely "an old friend of Mrs. Judd's family" and had been working to gain her freedom since she'd been judged insane in 1933. He said he had affidavits from jurors which, when presented in court, would prove "Mrs. Judd was railroaded to protect other persons." He wanted to submit them to the ground jury, adding, "I must have dynamite in my possession because several persons would like to get their hands on the evidence I now have. Some unknown persons have broken into my home and stolen pictures and other papers which have a direct bearing on the case I'm trying to prove."

Tucker said that he had been working on the case for more than two months, retained by private interests who didn't want to be named at that time. But, thanks to evidence he'd found recently, he expected they'd soon make themselves known.

During his investigation, he'd learned that some of the court records in Ruthie's case had disappeared. "And some of the evidence used has been taken, too," he said. "I've found a receipt that indicates the death gun is now in the hands of an official who played a large part in the case." Bullets from the gun had also been signed for by the same man that took the gun, although since he knew where to find those bullets, he'd make good use of them when the time came for action.

Governor John H. Pyle and O.D. Miller, chairman of the hospital board of control, both conducted investigations into Ruthie's latest escape. They agreed there was no "conspiracy" - it had been accomplished with help from sympathizers outside the hospital. Miller said, "It appears that none of these persons had any ultimate plan in mind other than to simply help her get away from the hospital if that was what she wanted to do."

But Deputy Barnes - who had also been in that secret meeting - had suspicions about not only the escape but also about the "conspiracy." He was convinced that an "underground" existed among hospital employees and patients. "And Winnie is their queen," he claimed. "She seems to have a hypnotic influence over some of the patients."

I'm not sure how Deputy Barnes managed to leave the hospital after his meeting that afternoon. I wouldn't have been surprised to learn that he was kept behind for observation.

16. "I'LL NEVER ESCAPE AGAIN"

ON FEBRUARY 11, RUTHIE GOT THE CHANCE TO TELL HER story again in front of a grand jury. Her story hadn't changed - self-defense, Halloran's maneuvering of everything after the fact, her suspicions about who had cut up Sammy's body - but many other things had.

Ruthie was no longer the beauty she'd been in 1931. She was now a middle-aged, plump woman of 47, which likely made her a little more believable than she'd been back then. It also didn't hurt that women were now allowed to sit on Arizona juries, and the state had seen six governors since Ruthie gave herself up.

And for the second time, a grand jury believed her story. They recommended that her death sentence be commuted to life in prison. The parole board agreed and recommended the commutation to the governor. Governor Howard Pyle also agreed and signed the order on May 11, 1952. Ruthie now had a chance at parole. A sentence of life imprisonment usually amounted to 10 years or so in those days. Ruthie had already been locked up for 21 years. If her years in the hospital counted as "time served," then her sentence had already been doubly met.

Ruthie's supporters began telling her it was almost over now - she would finally get her freedom.

This turn of events greatly disturbed Lloyd Andrews, the prosecutor who had sent her to the gallows years before. He was now in private practice, but this didn't prevent him from speaking out about the grand jury sessions to the press. He told reporters, "I've been listening to this kind of hogwash ever since the conviction, but I find the present outburst pretty hard to stomach. Mrs. Judd killed a woman in cold blood, confessed to the crime in her own handwriting, and was found guilty - the rest is a baffling hodge-podge based on rumor, falsehood, and innuendo."

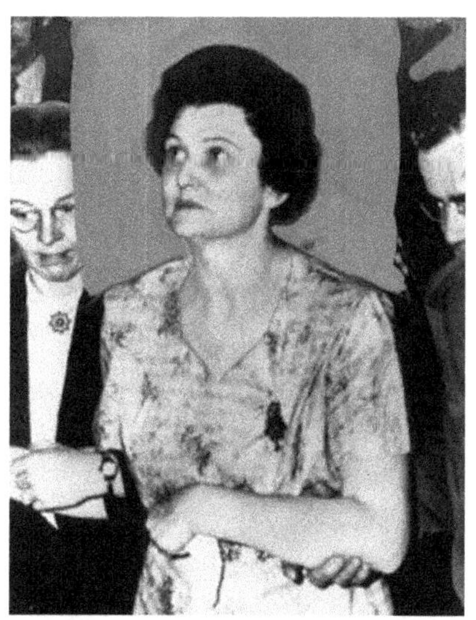

In 1952, Ruthie was allowed to tell her story to another grand jury, who, once again, believed her account of self-defense.

When asked if he thought Ruthie had help dismembering the body, Andrews shot back, "People say now she must have help from a skilled surgeon. More baloney! In trying to sever a leg, the person doing it attempted to cut through a thigh bone. Does that sound like the work of a surgeon or an amateur butcher?"

But no matter how Andrews felt about things, Ruthie was convinced she'd soon be free. Dr. Conway came to see her and gave her the good news. He said Ruthie "registered quite a little joy when I informed her of the governor's action."

She also made a promise to Dr. Conway that day. "I'll never escape again," she told him.

AND SHE DIDN'T - WELL, FOR ANOTHER SIX MONTHS.

Her next "holiday" came on November 27, 1952, which was Thanksgiving night. When it happened, it was difficult to blame her for doing it.

Back in May, Dr. Conway had told Ruthie there was only one formality that had to occur before she could leave the asylum as a free woman -- a sanity hearing. Ruthie was convinced it would happen right away. The guardian of her estate, Elizabeth Harvey, even brought her a new green dress to wear the next day. But there was no sanity hearing that day, the day after, or in the weeks and months to come.

She got tired of waiting. She had been promised her freedom and decided to take it herself when no one gave it to her.

On Thanksgiving afternoon, Ruthie ate a turkey dinner with her mother, whom she was now allowed to visit twice a week. At about 7:00 P.M. that night, Ruthie complained of a headache and a backache and announced that a hot bath would make her feel better. Fully dressed and carrying her bathrobe, she went down the hall to the bathroom on the first floor. Attendants saw her turn on the water and close the door. A half-hour later, they checked the room and found the bathrobe on the floor and a hole cut in the wire screen. Ruthie later confessed she had been cutting little bits of the screen and holding it in place with chewing gum for weeks.

Within 24 hours, three employees who worked in Ruthie's ward had been fired, and a search had started for two former staff members believed to have been involved in her latest escape.

The press was outraged again. The *Phoenix Gazette* published another irritated editorial: "The Winnie Ruth Judd cult probably will applaud Mrs. Judd's escape from the Arizona State Hospital. But the average person will begin to wonder whether Mrs. Judd is bigger than the state of Arizona. One conclusion is inescapable. If and when Mrs. is captured, the authorities should be told to keep her in the hospital "or else." If a dungeon has to be constructed, that should be done. And every effort should be made to find out who is helping the murderess. Ruth Judd and her friends have thumbed their noses at the sovereign state of Arizona long enough."

The public seemed a little less out of sorts by now. A homemade sign appeared on the street outside of the state hospital. It warned, "Drive Slowly - Inmates Escaping!"

But Ruthie remained on the loose for only 46 hours this time. Late on Saturday afternoon, a detective and uniformed officer found her hiding under a pile of clothes in a closet at the home of her guardian, Elizabeth Harvey. When discovered, she complained, "Why don't you leave me alone? I'm so tired of being locked up - it's been long enough."

In December 1952, she wrote a long letter to Governor Pyle, hoping to convince him that she was no longer insane if she had ever been. All she hoped for, she told the governor, just as she had told Dr. Conway, was a sanity hearing.

But no sanity hearing was held.

In February 1953, Elizabeth Harvey and other supporters hired an attorney to file a petition for a writ of habeas corpus, seeking Ruthie's release from the hospital on grounds she was being "unlawfully held and detained." It stated that "Winnie Ruth Judd is not insane within the meaning of Arizona law governing the commitment or detention of persons to and in the State Hospital for the Insane."

Filing the petition was the next step in an effort to gain that sanity hearing, and three months of legal shuffling began, which ended with the petition being dismissed.

No sanity hearing took place.

By then, Dr. Conway had resigned to go into private practice, and Dr. Samuel Wick had become the hospital superintendent. He also promised Ruthie that she would have a hearing, but it didn't happen.

Even with her death sentence commuted, even with the lingering questions about her conviction and her self-defense claim, even with the widespread belief that she had faked her insanity, and even with a growing number of people willing to champion her cause, nothing happened.

Ruthie always claimed she was the victim of the same conspiracy that had haunted her for years. Believe it or not, some people believed her. An attorney named Arthur Johnson had been asked by some of Ruthie's friends if he would help with her case, but he said he was warned away from it from the start.

He said that when he first went to see her at the state hospital, the superintendent offered the opinion that Ruthie had "really gotten screwed." He told Johnson, "The best advice I can give you, son, is forget about it."

Was someone really pulling the strings behind the scenes? Or was this one of Ruthie's delusions? It's easier for some to believe that if she was declared sane and free, someone might listen to her stories and the whole mess would be revived or, worse, reopened as a criminal case than it is for them to believe she stayed locked up because she needed to be.

But what's the truth?

Ruthie could never offer any suggestions about who kept her locked up. She claimed that doctors told her, "Nothing but dirty tricks are being played on you." She said Dr. Conway told her that his call for a sanity hearing had been overruled because "someone had more power than he did, but he would not tell me who, except it was not the governor."

Whether the "conspiracy" was real or not, it didn't matter. Ruthie Judd still wasn't allowed to have a sanity hearing, and she stayed locked behind the walls of the state hospital as years continued to pass.

Security around her increased after her last escape. A maximum-security cell was prepared for her; matrons always accompanied her, and for a time, she was only allowed out of her room twice each day to care for a fishpond and a flower bed. She spent the rest of her time reading and doing needlepoint.

Ruthie settled into life inside the hospital while people outside seemed to forget about her in the 1950s. After World War II, Phoenix began a decade of rebuilding and expansion. Soldiers who had been stationed in the area during the war swore they'd be back when it was over. An entire community of affordable homes appeared on the west side of the city, "starter homes" that General Electric touted across the nation. And why not? They were now mass-producing air conditioners, making life much easier during the Phoenix summers.

New construction followed the arrival of the newcomers to the city. The population reached 440,000 by the end of the 1950s, and Phoenix was no longer a small town.

A group of civic-minded businessmen now controlled local government -- the Charter Government Committee -- who had taken over during the war to rid the city of corruption. When officials at the Army Air Force base west of the city threatened to make Phoenix off-limits to service members, these business leaders finally got serious about cleaning things up. Their version of politics - a handpicked mayor and elections for council members every two years - continued into the mid-1970s.

As things changed around her, whether people talked about her or not, Ruthie's life continued.

In November 1953, she was allowed to attend the funeral services for her mother, Carrie. As time passed, she gradually regained her privileges at the hospital. By late 1956, she was serving as a hospital attendant, had cooking privileges, and was allowed to walk unattended between buildings.

But still, no sanity hearing was held for her. When attorney Arthur Johnson tried again to get Ruthie released in December 1956, he was told by the chairman of the Board of Pardons and Paroles that trying to get her case in front of the board was "a waste of time."

Two years later, her brother, Burton, tried again. He made a personal request to the parole board, but this time, the board sent a letter that said that the board's jurisdiction had ended when his sister was declared insane in 1933. This was the first time this excuse had been used. Burton appealed to the Arizona attorney general, but this also led nowhere.

In May 1959, hospital administrators said they believed Ruthie had given up her fight for freedom, and because of this acceptance, her mental condition was starting to improve. She caused no problems and agreeably complied with hospital regulations. Finally, they said, Mrs. Judd had accepted her situation and no longer planned to escape.

But they were wrong.

Ruthie no longer warranted banner headlines when she escaped for the seventh time on October 8, 1962. A small newspaper story simply announced, "Winnie's Gone Again." There was no frenzy this time, no dogs called out, no rewards offered. The *Arizona Republic* noted, "Nobody seems to be looking very hard for the 56-year-old woman, who is no longer considered dangerous."

Everyone just assumed she'd turn up soon, just like always, but they were wrong once again.

Ruthie didn't show up a few hours or even a few days later. This time, she wouldn't be seen again for seven years.

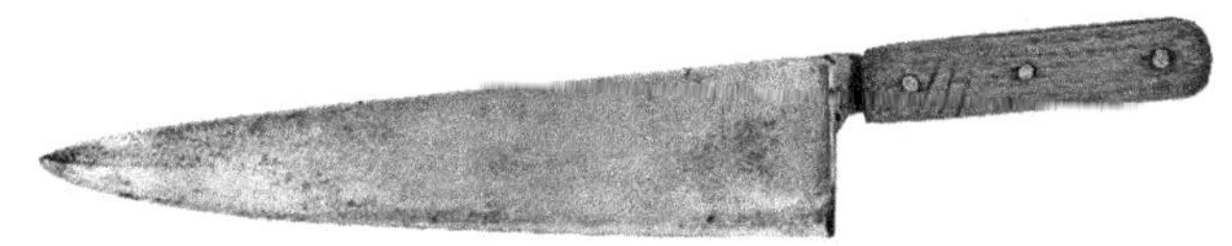

17. MARIAN LANE

WHEN SHE WALKED OUT OF ANOTHER "UNLOCKED" DOOR at the state hospital that day, Winnie Ruth Judd ceased to exist. In her place was a matronly, soft-spoken woman with an ordinary background - a widow who'd spent 20 years caring for her dear departed mother. She was the daughter of a minister, and the only family she had left was her brother, his wife, and their children. She was trained only in housekeeping and caring for the sick and aged.

That woman's name was Marian Ruth Lane. She preferred to use her middle name, and most people who knew and loved her - and there were many - just called her "Ruthie."

When Ruthie slipped out of the hospital, she didn't go far at first. A nephew had been waiting for her with a car outside the hospital that night. He took her to a warehouse near the asylum, ensuring she had warm clothing and food. Ruthie later admitted that church ladies in town prepared hot meals for her nephew to bring to her.

She stayed at the warehouse for five days before the coast seemed clear enough for her to leave town. They headed for Oakland, California, where a niece and a nephew lived. It would be nice to be close to them, but more importantly, it wasn't a place where anyone would look for Ruth Judd. She had no connections to the city. Everyone assumed that she'd flee to Mexico, not northern California.

When she arrived, Ruthie had an apartment her niece had found for her. Burton had sent her the money she needed to set up her new place, but she needed to find a job.

A few days later, Marian Lane walked into an employment agency, and a short time later, she was sent to interview with the Nichols family, who lived in a large home in Piedmont that overlooked San Francisco Bay. She was immediately hired.

Ruthie was hired to call for Ethel Nichols, the matriarch of an old money family. The two women quickly hit it off, and except for her mother, Ruthie admired Ethel more than any other woman she'd ever known.

Ruthie became a loved and trusted member of the household. The family moved her into a lovely apartment behind the Nichols home, a beautiful mansion on a street of opulent houses. Ethel was generous and sweet to her. She paid her $400 a month, plus room and board. She bought all of Ruthie's clothes for her, her uniforms, and her aprons. When Ethel ordered herself some monogrammed handkerchiefs, she would order some for Ruthie, too. One Christmas, Ethel gave her a ruby ring. A simple message was inscribed inside: "E.N. to M.L., Love."

As a maid, caretaker, and companion, Ruthie worked long hours, but she never minded. She got up early to make breakfast and to take Ethel her tray. While she was preparing for the day, a driver would take Ruthie to the market for the day's shopping. During the day, she wore a starched white apron, but in the evening, she served dinner with a formal apron, cuffs, and collar.

Once a week, a laundress came in to do all the washing and ironing. Another woman came in every other week to do the heavy cleaning. There was also a gardener and a full-time driver. Ruthie did the cooking and some light cleaning. The only problem was that she hadn't cooked for 29 years. She took cookbooks to bed with her every night and studied them. It paid off. The Nichols loved to entertain, and Ruthie became the neighborhood's favorite cook for friends and families.

At the age of 60, Ruthie went back to school in her spare time. She enrolled in night school at the Oakland College of Medical Assistants. She did so well that she was offered a job in a doctor's office but decided to stay with the Nichols family.

Ruthie's new identity as "Marian Lane" left her past behind when she created a new life for herself.

The next few years passed peacefully. The two women grew older together, watching the evening news, discussing world events, and sharing stories of their lives - or at least as much as Ruthie dared to share. Mrs. Nichols never knew the real identity of her trusted companion, and Ruthie was thankful for that. She never wanted the new life she'd found to end.

Occasionally, a newspaper somewhere would publish a story, wondering what happened to the notorious Winnie Ruth Judd. Some speculated that she'd taken off to Mexico and was probably helping the sick. The Phoenix police would be quoted in the story saying they had followed up on every tip, but the tips became fewer and fewer as the years passed.

Ruthie joined a church. She continued to do needlepoint and crochet. She made friends with the help of the other houses in the neighborhood, earning a special place among them because her employers treated her so well. She was happy, and she didn't even worry about getting old.

Ethel Nichols had always promised her that she'd always have a home. When she passed away in December 1967, Ruthie discovered that she had been left with all the furniture and $10,000. Mrs. Nichols also provided $85,000 for her daughter to purchase a prefabricated house where Ruthie could live.

But her daughter, also named Ethel, and her husband, John Blemmer, owned a farm north of San Francisco. There was a small guest house on the property, and the younger Ethel suggested it would be a perfect place for Ruthie to live out her retirement. The family adored her, had adopted her as one of their own, and wanted to keep her around.

Ruthie stayed at the big house in Piedmont for the next year and a half, watching over things until the house was sold. By then, she was 64 years old.

She was still unpacking and settling into the house where she planned to live the rest of her life when everything unraveled.

The police finally caught up with her on June 27, 1969.

And how it happened was a series of coincidences caused by a threatened betrayal.

Although Ruthie didn't drive, she bought a car she had loaned to her nephew. She didn't do it out of the goodness of her heart - it was a payoff to keep him quiet. The nephew never hesitated to ask her for money whenever he needed it and he frequently reminded her that if she didn't give it to him, he could have her turned in.

He didn't do it, but what happened was still his fault.

The car was found parked in a San Francisco neighborhood where a woman had been murdered. A routine check of all the vehicles on the street discovered one registered to Marian Lane. As bad luck would have it, the name rang a bell with a veteran police detective who somehow recalled that when Ruth Judd escaped to Yuma, Arizona, in 1939, she had tried to pass herself off as a hitchhiker named "Marian Lane."

It seemed like a long shot, but it paid off.

Ruthie was arrested and fingerprinted, and then the hunch turned into an arrest that made national news. Once again, the name Winnie Ruth Judd was in all the papers.

John and Ethel Blemmer were vacationing in Belgium when Ruthie was caught. They were riding in an elevator, and Ethel had opened the newspaper and nearly fainted. Looking at the picture, she gasped, "Oh God, that's Marian."

Ruthie with her famous attorney, Melvin Belli.

The Blemmers flew home immediately and proved to everyone how much they loved Ruthie. They never questioned anything about her past. They held press conferences and wrote letters stating how much they loved her and would do anything for her.

And that included hiring one of the most famous attorneys in the country for her, Melvin Belli. In 1969, he was so well-known that he was a household name. Always keeping his name in the press, Belli took her on as a client without even meeting her. He'd first heard about Ruth Judd's case when he was in law school, and he followed her exploits as she perfected becoming an escape artist. "She went over the fence more times than Babe Ruth," he joked. This was the perfect case for him.

From the moment he signed on, he made it clear that it was outrageous for anyone to punish this woman further. He unsuccessfully fought her extradition back to Arizona. Then he attacked the length of time she'd already served for her crime, praised her rehabilitation, and did everything he could to paint her in a good light after all the years that had passed.

It was a compelling story, and Belli used his own fame to help arrange for Ruthie's experiences to be turned into an hour-long prime-time television interview. The documentary was hosted by Joe Patrick, the most respected television newsman in Phoenix at the time.

On camera, Mevil Belli used the show to argue for compassion and for how long Ruthie had already served. He was direct and convincing, but when Ruthie followed him onscreen, she was rambling and confusing, much like she had been when she testified against Jack Halloran at the grand jury hearing nearly 40 years earlier.

Joe Patrick wanted to talk about the 1931 murders, but Ruthie had a lifetime of complaints to air - promises made and broken at the state hospital, mistreatment from asylum directors, and her anger at having to plead for her freedom again after proving she had been a solid citizen for the last seven years.

Her story of delf-defense came out in small parts, jumbled with stories about her current life. She talked about how she still put flowers on her husband's grave, about how kind Mrs. Nichols had been to her, and how she wished everyone would leave her alone. She came across as a frightened and complaining older woman, but anyone who listened closely would see it was the same story she'd been telling for years - with the name Jack Halloran left out of it. Every time she used his name, it was edited out. Halloran was still alive then, living in a Phoenix nursing home.

Patrick let Ruthie wander for a bit to show her thinking process, and then he skillfully steered her back to the point with direct questions. He asked her at one point, "Now, do you feel in 1931 you received a fair trial in Phoenix?"

Ruthie snapped, "Do you think it's a fair trial when you can't even take the witness stand and state anything on your behalf?"

Woven in and around Ruthie's story was an interview with a retired Phoenix police officer named Charles Arnold, who was also being quoted in the local newspapers as they scrambled to report on the latest developments in the case.

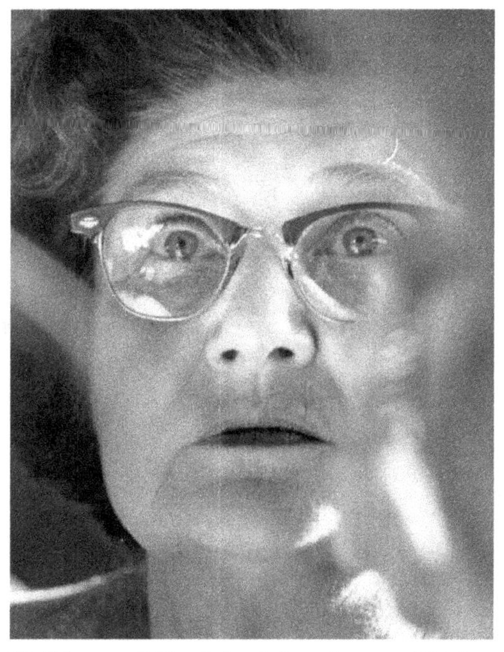

Ruthie used the television show with Joe Patrick to once again plead her case for self-defense and her failure to get a fair trial in 1931.

Arnold claimed that he had overseen the investigation in 1931 and told the camera that he never had any doubts she had committed the murders in cold blood. He added that she had done it alone without help, and she'd done it out of perverted jealousy.

He described interrogating her when she was brought to Arizona from California. "Not, Ruthie, they weren't fighting you. Your story's all wet - you went out to kill them because one rejected your love."

However, Arnold left out or mixed-up undisputed facts about the case several times during his interview. He claimed, for example, that one of the mattresses from the bungalow had bullet holes in it. It didn't. He also claimed a mattress was found with large bloodstains on it. It wasn't. He also said that Sammy's body had been slashed "four or five times" as the person during the dismemberment tried to find a joint. This was also untrue.

But even so, Arnold sounded like he knew what he was talking about. He was presented as a detective with the best information about the case and one with a sharp memory of events from decades before. Anyone who didn't know anything about the case found him convincing and was given the impression that Arizona had once again found a vicious escaped killer.

But there's a slight problem- no one named Charles Arnold was involved with the original case. His name was never mentioned in the thousands of pages of police records. Besides that, even though the Phoenix police were initially called into the case, the county attorney's office conducted the real investigation. If Charles Arnold had been involved in the case at all, then it would not have been in the important role that he had presented to the media in 1969.

The show ended on a dramatic note. Maybe, Joe Patrick said, the whole story of the murders would finally be told. He told his audience: "There are still hundreds of unanswered questions that only Mrs. Judd may answer, for some of her answers are accusations that so far have neither been confirmed or denied. This film report, while only a crack in a 38-year-old closed door, could be the opening of a legal Pandora's box."

Years after the show aired, Joe Patrick retired to Tombstone, Arizona, where he became a freelance writer. In an interview, he confessed that he had been impressed by Ruthie's story. "She was not real bright, but she was sincere," he said. "There's no doubt in my mind that she did the killings, but as far as I could determine, it was not premeditated at all - it just happened. I never believed she cut up the body. It was done with precision, and she didn't have the skill. I think the morals of the time were such that it was demanded they punish her in some fashion."

Ruthie's story wasn't just being told on television. The newspapers were also retelling a story that had become part of Arizona history, but they persisted in misreporting the facts, just as they'd been doing for years. Most claimed that both bodies had been dismembered. None of the stories mentioned the oddities that had raised doubts for so long - the jurors with second thoughts, the ruling that freed Jack Halloran but put Ruthie behind bars, the widespread belief that she had help with the dismemberment, or any of the clues that suggested she had acted in self-defense.

The case was presented as closed, open, and shut, just as it had been 40 years earlier.

But there was good news for Ruthie, too. The Arizona Attorney General, Gary Nelson, declared that the law was clear - Ruthie must get credit for her time at the state hospital. The law read: "When it appeared that a prisoner was sufficiently recovered that he may be returned to the prison without further risk, he shall be returned to serve the unexpired term, and the period he was confined in the state hospital shall be counted as though served in prison."

Subtracting the time away from the asylum during her seven escapes that amounted to 29 years and 154 days. Nelson noted that prisoners sentenced to life terms - as she had been in 1952 - served, on average, only eight to ten years. He recommended that she be released. When asked by a reporter if the board might ignore his opinion, Nelson replied, "They can read the law as well as I can. It obviously applies exactly to Mrs. Judd."

This meant that the highest-ranking law enforcement official in the state agreed with Ruthie's famous attorney that she'd already served the equivalent of three life terms.

When Ruthie got on a plane in San Francisco in the custody of an Arizona sheriff, she had every reason to believe that she wouldn't be in Phoenix for long. Finally, influential people were speaking on her behalf - no more broken promises. All she had to do was endure the heartache for a little while longer, and she would finally be free.

But Arizona was not a place that was willing to forgive and forget.

LARRY DEBUS WAS A YOUNG LAWYER WHO WAS JUST making a name for himself in Phoenix in 1969, so he jumped at the chance to serve as Ruthie's Arizona attorney when Melvin Belli asked him to join the case. He met the plane that brought Ruthie back to Phoenix and then did something that defense attorneys never do - he got her *into* prison.

Arizona still considered Ruthie to be insane, and because of that, she was to be held at the state hospital. But the only way to get her a pardon was to get her out of the hospital and into prison. He handed officials a writ of habeas corpus, claiming she was not insane and would be improperly held at the asylum.

And it worked. Four days later, Ruthie finally got the sanity hearing that she had waited 17 years for, and the panel decided she was sane and sent her to the state prison in Florence.

As soon as she arrived, Debus filed a request with the parole board for a commutation of her sentence, arguing that she had already served so much time that Arizona had no right to hold her any longer. The board planned to meet on October 27, so Ruthie only had to hold on for 66 more days, and it would all be over.

Her time at the state prison was nothing like years before. Back then, there had been only a dozen or so female prisoners, but now, there are hundreds. Some of the inmates threatened her, demanding protection money, pushed her around, and taunted her. Finally, a young woman far more streetwise than Ruthie would ever be stepped in became her friend, and kept others away from her.

It was a long 66 days.

Melvin Belli flew into town a few hours before the parole hearing, and he and Larry Debus drove to Florence together. Belli later said he'd never forget that day. "We went down, and it was a hot day, but they all say in a formal room with stiff collars. They looked like a Grant Wood painting," he remembered. "I knew when I saw them, they were never anyone I'd want on a parole board."

As it always did, the meeting inexplicably began with a prayer. When Belli got up to address the board, he remarked on how touching it was that they would seek divine guidance in their deliberations. And then he brought in a parade of witnesses to plead for Ruth Judd. One after another, they told the board how she was "completely rehabilitated." There were friends, supporters, distant cousins, a professor of psychology, a doctor from the state hospital, and John and Ethel Blemmer, who promised her a lifetime job and to arrange for her care in old age. She would, they promised the board, never be a burden to the state of Arizona.

Four days later, the board announced that Ruthie Judd was not getting a parole.

They had voted against her, two to one. The chairman, one of the negative votes, released a six-page explanation for the decision. It indicated that two of the board members had strong doubts about Ruthie's rehabilitation: "If, as the record shows, she was insane during her time as a fugitive and alleged rehabilitation, then she would not be capable of rehabilitation. On the other hand, if she was actually sane, then she was a fugitive from justice and in violation of the criminal laws of this state and was therefore not subject to rehabilitation."

The report said that Ruthie's explanation of how her car came to be near a murder scene was "vague and unsatisfactory," despite the fact that she had been cleared of any possible connection with the murder by the police in San Francisco.

Sounding like the daily newspapers in Phoenix at the time of her trial, the two board members decided that Ruthie had "cheated the hangman," saying that she "completely escaped the verdict of the jury and the penalty prescribed by it."

The report went on to claim that Ruthie showed a lack of emotion about Anne LeRoi's death. It added, "If, as is claimed by Mrs. Judd, she has suffered enough punishment for this brutal crime, still, she has at least been privileged to live to suffer it, while her innocent victim, whom we must assume had as great a desire to live as her murderer, and certainly as much right, lies cold in death."

The court concluded, "The board is unable, after thorough search of the record, to find any recommendation of mercy from any judge, juror, or prosecutor involved in the trial of this case."

Larry Debus was stunned by the decision. "We hadn't anticipated this. There is a lot more here than meets the eye," he told reporters. He suggested that Ruthie was entitled to some kind of public disclosure of the circumstances that brought the board to its decision.

Belli was less kind. He expressed his outrage to the press, telling them, "I think this board was born too late. They should've been born at the time of the Inquisition... It was the most Victorian thing I've ever seen in my lifetime - utterly unbelievable."

Belli said that legal action might be taken against the board, possibly in a federal district court or the Arizona Supreme Court. "For one thing," he said, "her parole hearing was opened with a prayer. That's unconstitutional, and I'm as a religious man as the next, but I'm going to court on it."

When asked, the board was puzzled by this statement from Belli. When he spoke at the hearing, he complimented them on starting the hearing with a prayer, they said. This just proved the famous attorney's point - the board members were too stuffy and old-fashioned to understand when someone was using sarcasm.

Several days later, on November 5, Belli was still steaming. "Two of those board members must be sick," he said. "There is something sinister in this - either someone or something is being protected." He huffed that he planned to petition the governor to have the board undergo psychiatric evaluations and expressed wonder that Governor Jack Williams would allow them to continue to serve on the board. Finally, Belli added, "I am utterly and completely furious about this. It is one of the blackest marks on your state."

Meanwhile, As Melvin Belli ranted and raved in the newspapers, Larry Debus was stuck with the task of trying to keep Ruthie from falling apart. The board's decision meant she had to spend at least six months behind bars before her case could be considered again. He managed to pull enough strings to get Ruthie a job helping in the prison hospital while he did all he could on the outside to get someone - anyone - to listen.

Every newspaper in the West was trying to get an interview with Ruthie, but he turned them all down. He had a friend, though, Logan McKechnie, who worked for the *Arizona Republic.* Debus promised his pal an exclusive interview for a promise that the *Republic* would print a positive editorial about the case.

The exclusive and the editorial both happened. The *Republic* stated that Arizona had taken its pound of flesh from Winnie Ruth Judd, and "enough was enough." It went on to say, "We believe

Arizona will be serving the joint causes of justice and mercy if it turns Winnie Ruth Judd loose to live the rest of her life as a functioning member of society."

The interview ran, and it got a lot of attention as it presented the first sympathetic portrait of Ruthie that had ever appeared in her hometown newspapers. She told McKechnie: "I had six years of love and happiness. I have been in heaven. I was somebody else and I tried to forget the past. In this atmosphere, with all the love I had, I was happy for the first time in my life. These people loved me. I was not insane Winnie from the insane hospital. I was Marian Lane, and I was loved."

She wanted her freedom, she pleaded to the reporter, saying, "I will prove to everyone who has been kind to me that I can make them proud of me."

The interview fascinated McKechnie, and he started digging into old files about Ruthie's case and even considered writing a book. He never got around to it, though, but he did say something that would've been considered a "spoiler" if the book had been completed: "I was left wondering if she pulled the trigger. She was such a fragile person at that time, she could've been convinced she killed them. I never was."

ON DECEMBER 4, 1969, MELVIN BELLI AND LARRY DEBUS filed suit in the Maricopa County Superior Court, asking that the board be forced to recommend Ruthie's life sentence be commuted. The suit charged that the action of the board "was an arbitrary and capricious abuse of discretion for the reason that no scintilla of evidence was before the board upon which it could base the finding of facts and conclusion."

The issue bounced around Arizona courts for the next seven months. Attorney General Nelson - despite his recommendations - was duty-bound to fight the suit, contending that probation and parole were matters of grace, not right. Thanks to this, the courts didn't have the authority to force the board's decision. "It's their decision," he said, "whether people agree with it or not."

Thousands of letters poured in. And while some of them expressed the belief that the board had been right and that Ruthie belonged behind bars, they were far outnumbered by letters that supported her release. They arrived at the prison warden's office, the office of the parole board, and the office of the governor, who stated that he had no intention of interfering in the case.

Ruthie stayed in prison. Larry Debus didn't seek a second commutation hearing before the board in 1970, even though he could have. Six months had passed. He later explained that he didn't request a hearing then because he wanted the board to see that Ruthie could live inside and outside prison walls as a responsible person.

At least, that's what he claimed to the press. The truth was that a gubernatorial race had heated up between Governor Jack Williams and challenger Raul Castro. Debus wanted to see what happened and whether a new governor would start over with a new parole board. But Williams won the election, so Debus had to push ahead.

There was a different atmosphere when Ruthie got her second parole hearing on February 16, 1971. And Ruthie was a different person. She was now 66, and her hair was completely gray. She looked like what she was - a kindly older woman who just wanted to be free for the final years of her life.

It also didn't hurt that public opinion had now shifted in her favor. Across the country, people demanded that Arizona say just how much more Ruthie should suffer. Why was the state so heartless toward an older woman? Even local newspapers were starting to ask the same questions.

Larry Debus only called two witnesses to be heard by the board - Dr. Herbert Collier and Dr. Otto Bendheim. Both had completed psychiatric evaluations of Ruthie. Bendheim, who had known her since she was in her 30s, concluded: "This person is sound, sane, and absolutely harmless. She presents no danger whatever to society or to herself. There are no suicidal, homicidal, or violent tendencies. She has a potential for constructive and meaningful contributions to society."

Dr. Collier reached the same conclusion. He later recalled, "My initial impression was this woman couldn't have killed anyone. She was a sweet grandmother type. She looked as normal as anyone I'd ever seen."

He told the board during the hearing: "She is entirely within the normal range, except for the area dealing with depression." He attributed this to her imprisonment. "She showed a tremendous need to do good. It seems she is very tuned in to the needs of other people."

Ruthie was teary-eyed throughout most of the 90-minute hearing, losing her composure only once. She said she felt ill and left with a matron for a few minutes before she returned to tell the board, "I want you to know I would never do anything in my life you would be sorry for."

The meeting was adjourned, and a week later, on February 23, their decision was announced. The board again was split two to one - this time in Ruthie's favor. One of the board members who had earlier voted against Ruthie's release had changed his mind.

The report read:

This case is not one you sweep under the rug and forget about. The people of Arizona are very much interested in this case. She has served more than anyone else, possibly in the history of Arizona.

Prior to her first hearing, I was contacted by many people who were not in favor of her being commuted. Apparently, there has been a change in public opinion. Prior to the hearing of February 16, of all the people who contacted me, only one was for denying Mrs. Judd a commutation.

As time passes, more and more people will join the ranks of those who think her sentence should be commuted. What we will see if not a question of modern penology, but the portrayal of out-and-out persecution of an elderly, grandmotherly type, unfortunate woman.

A family in California is very anxious to have her back as their housekeeper, and they have promised her a cottage of her own and employment. Mrs. Judd has a means of livelihood now. It is incumbent upon the board to give her a commutation of sentence now, while she is physically able to work, or forget ever giving her a commutation of sentence."

The report noted that her "excellent adjustment" while living on the run in California showed that she had been rehabilitated. "If circumstances had been different and she had been on parole instead of an escapee, Ruthie would have been classified as an "outstanding parolee," it said.

But the report also stressed that the board strongly believed that "crime doesn't pay" and wanted her parole to include assurances that she would never profit from a book or movie about her life. Hollywood had expressed an interest in Ruthie years before, but the board wanted to make sure that no further embarrassment was going to be faced by anyone in Phoenix.

Debus later recalled that as soon as he reached Ruthie by telephone and gave her the good news, she burst into tears. Now, all they had to do was to wait for Governor Williams to sign the commutation and get Ruthie out of prison for good.

They waited and then waited some more. There was only silence from the governor's office.

SOON AFTER THE BOARD HAD REACHED ITS DECISION, Governor Williams had been approached by reporters about Ruthie's case, but he stated it would be "quite some time" before he decided whether to free her. "There is no deadline," he said. "If I had to rush, I'd keep her in there."

Jack Williams had risen through the political ranks of Arizona during the 40 years that Ruthie had been a part of the state's penal system.

He also had some weird connections to her case. He had been working at a Phoenix radio station at the time of the murder trial in 1932. A reporter covered the trial, and then Williams "rewrote it." Actors took the roles of the real trial participants and would read Williams' script during nightly broadcasts.

Williams had also, at the time of the murders, worked part-time as a baggage handler at the train station in Phoenix. "I could well have handled those trunks," he later said. "Whoever would have thought this would ever come back to haunt me like this?"

Republican Governor Jack Williams had Ruthie's fate in his hands and seemed to relish the power that it gave him. He kept her waiting for months before he finally signed the paperwork that freed her from prison.

Honestly, I could have guessed it. William was a man who evoked some pretty strong emotions from the people in his state. He would freely admit to being an old-fashioned misogynist and an advocate of law and order - the kind of establishment official who was out of favor by the late 1960s and early 1970s. There is a reason that the parole board was made up of the same kind of men - Williams had appointed them.

During his eight years as governor, he made enemies out of every supporter of "liberal causes" in Arizona. He was a right-wing conservative whom college students despised because he didn't believe they had rights. The farm labor movement called him a racist. He seemed to enjoy the most outrageous snubs. When farm labor organizer Cesar Chavez came to see the governor to plead with him not to sign a bill that outlawed unions on Arizona farms, William left him waiting in his outer office until he had already finished signing the bill.

He was so disliked that a recall effort began against Williams in the mid-1970s. The drive collected the required number of signatures, but it was subverted by the Republican attorney general, who found a technicality that disqualified the petition.

This was the politician who held the fate of Ruth Judd in his hands - and he relished the power it gave him. Publicly, he claimed he was still thinking about things. "I don't want her to be rewarded for escaping," he told the press. "I want her to spend a month in prison for every year she'd been on the loose. I don't think we should foster the image that crime pays."

Privately, though, it was about nothing but cruelty. If Ruthie had been sentenced to prison for the murder of Anne LeRoi, she would've been out years before, and Williams knew it.

Months passed, and Williams refused to sign it. Ruthie bided her time behind bars while Larry Debus became more anxious, then angry, then anxious again as more time passed. The anxiety eventually turned into frustration.

Ultimately, Governor Williams finally signed the paperwork on December 22, 1971. He had waited for 245 days.

THE NEXT DAY, RUTHIE GATHERED HER FEW BELONGINGS, said a handful of goodbyes, and walked out of the prison to a car waiting to take her to the Blemmers' home in California.

No reporters were waiting for her as she walked out of the gate, no photographers, no gawking crowds - just an empty street.

She got into the passenger seat of the car and was driven away.

Winnie Ruth Judd never looked back.

IT WAS RAINING ON CHRISTMAS EVE 1971 WHEN Ruthie arrived at the Blemmer house in Danville, California. She really wasn't much concerned with the weather, though. She was just happy to be free.

The Blemmers welcome her home with open arms, and Ruthie returned to her quiet life as Marian Lane. Ethel Blemmer told the *Phoenix Gazette*: "She's a wonderful woman. We saw her at dinner at least twice every week for six years, and she always came at

Christmas loaded with toys she had made for our grandchildren - mostly stuffed animals - and crocheted doilies and placemats for the adults. She does beautiful work. It looks like it's going to be a great Christmas after all."

The next decade passed peacefully with Ruthie in her lovely cottage on the farm. She attended church, did her fine needlework, and helped the family however she could. She also helped the young woman who had protected her in prison. She was paroled herself, found work with the Blemmers for a short time, and then moved to a town nearby. The two women remained friends for the rest of Ruthie's life.

The Blemmer children grew up and became adults with children of their own. Ruthie became a loving "aunt" to the next generation of the family.

She loved Ethel as much as she had loved her mother, Mrs. Nichols, but she never got along with John Bremmer very well. One night, the family celebrated Ruthie's first birthday as a free woman at a fancy restaurant. They were having a good time when John said to one of the waiters, "Do you know who that is? She's Winnie Ruth Judd." After that, the entire staff came by their table, humiliating a woman who was trying to leave the past behind her.

When Ethel passed away in 1982, Ruthie worried about what might happen to her but then reassured herself that both Ethel and her mother had promised her lifetime care.

It broke her heart when she had to sue John Blemmer to make good on their promise. He told her to move out of the cottage given to her because he had another use for it.

At the age of 77, Ruthie was back in court. A lawsuit had been filed that charged she had been kept as an indentured servant without formal wages and a constant fear that her parole would be revoked if she complained. The lawsuit ended in a settlement. Ruthie moved out of the cottage, but in exchange, she received a $50,000 cash payment and a lifetime monthly stipend of $1,250.

Winnie Ruth Judd died in October 1998.
At the time she passed away, Ruthie was finally free.

In 1983, the state of Arizona issued Ruthie an "absolute discharge." That piece of paper meant she was no longer a parolee. Arizona no longer had a claim on her.

Ruthie Judd was finally free.

AFTER MOVING OUT OF THE COTTAGE, RUTHIE WENT to Stockton, California, to be near her niece. She moved into an apartment, joined a church, and even adopted a dog.

Her life had one purpose now - to live as Marian Lane and forget about Winnie Ruth Judd.

But that wasn't the ending to Ruthie's life. She didn't stay in California. Surprisingly, she moved back to Phoenix a few years before her death - and no, I have been unable to find out why - and she died there on October 23, 1998, at the age of 93.

Her death came exactly 67 years after her surrender to the Los Angeles Police Department in 1931.

It was a Friday.

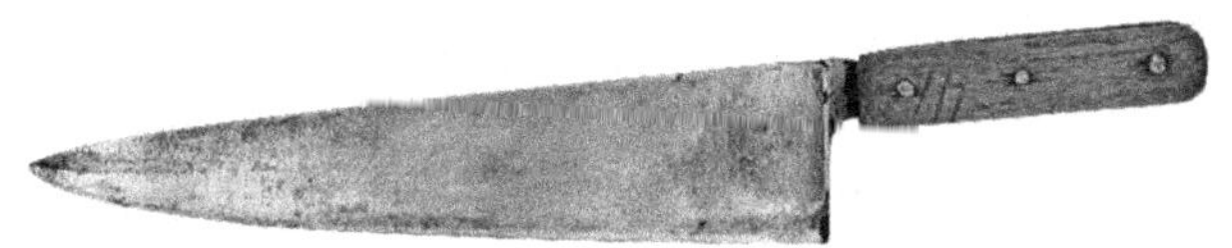

18. ONE NIGHT IN PHOENIX

LET ME START BY SAYING THAT I BELIEVE WINNIE RUTH JUDD was a killer. She murdered her two friends - Anne and Sammy - and she did it for reasons that are completely and utterly human. Those reasons might be wrong, but they're human, nevertheless.

I also believe that someone else was involved in the case and that they deserved to go to prison, just like Ruthie did. However, I don't think that person's involvement was exactly what Ruthie said - and believed - that it was.

So, in my opinion, was Ruthie guilty of murder? Yes, she was. She killed her friends. But was it a cold-blooded, pre-meditated killing that should have sent her to the gallows?

Not really, although I suppose an argument can be made about that - and I will do that later in this chapter.

THERE ARE DOZENS OF THEORIES THAT SURROUND THE story of the "Trunk Murders." Many of them are pretty wild, and others delve pretty deeply into the conspiracies that I've hinted about in earlier chapters. Honestly, I think the whole thing is a lot simpler than has been suggested, but I also think some covering-up was done to keep the names of a prominent person out of the story. And while that failed - Jack Halloran certainly made an appearance - he never suffered from any legal complications because of his connection to Ruthie and the other two girls.

But I do not think Ruthie was innocent as some conspiracies claim.

The most prominent proponent of the "Ruthie was innocent" conspiracy is investigative journalist Jana Bommersbach, who wrote a series of articles about the case, followed by a book in 1992. As part of her investigation, Bommersbach interviewed Ruthie herself and became very friendly with her. In the end, Bommersbach concluded that the police and prosecution were biased against Ruthie, and she uncovered evidence that suggested Ruthie was innocent. Her work is in-depth and very well-written and researched. However, her conclusions and lack of objectivity based on the personal relationship she formed with Ruthie have always had a lot of other researchers questioning her views on the case.

Bommersbach uncovered a lot of evidence that had been long forgotten and even purposely lost. She also did a deep dive into Jack Halloran, which no one had ever done before - mainly because his connections to the case had been covered up for so long. Her evidence revealed that members of the Phoenix police knew Halloran well and were aware of his associates, friends, and girlfriends. She interviewed people who knew Halloran and many who believed that Ruthie hadn't killed anyone -- even in self-defense -- but was only covering up for Halloran and possibly others. And then, of course, there were the sightings of his gray Packard at the crime scene the night of the murders and again the next day, which many believed proved that he had been Ruthie's accomplice.

Bommersbach believed that Ruthie wasn't capable of dismembering Sammy's body - a job that, according to autopsy photos, was performed with surgical skills that Ruthie didn't possess. She also believed Ruthie could not have the strength to move both bodies.

But let's start with her version of the dismemberment. She based the theory that Ruthie didn't do it on a line from Ruthie's story of the crime: "Halloran said that Sammy had been operated on."

Bommersbach theorizes that Sammy's body could *only* have been cut apart by someone with surgical skills. The corpse had been cut into two major pieces at the waist. Then, the legs were severed at the knee. There was also a 10-inch-long, two-inch-deep gash at the hipbone on the right leg, as though someone had intended to sever the torso from the legs but then abandoned the idea.

Ruthie told Bommersbach that she first believed the dismemberment had been completed by Jack Halloran, posing as "Dr. Buckley." But she also knew he had repeatedly tried to reach his old friend Dr. Charles Brown that first night. She never saw Brown at the bungalow, though. And she never asked Halloran to explain who had performed the "operation."

Dr. Brown's name was passed on to Bommersbach through gossip from Stewart Thompson, who had been the jury foreman during Ruthie's murder trial. He said that he'd always believed a doctor was responsible for the dismemberment - and that he knew who the doctor was. He said he reached this conclusion a few months after the trial when he went to see Ruthie in prison. He recalled that the warden told him a strange story while waiting for her to be brought from her cell. Apparently, Dr. Brown had been at the prison a few days before, drunk and yelling that he was the only man alive who knew the truth about the Winnie Ruth Judd case.

Further confirmation of Dr. Brown's involvement came from a nurse named Ann Miller, whom she interviewed for her book. While working at the Arizona State Hospital in 1936, Miller said that Ruthie had confided to her that a Dr. Brown had come to see her while she was in prison and told her he would confess everything. Later, after Miller told a Phoenix attorney of Judd's story, he stated, "I'm sure she told you that. Dr. Brown came up to my office and wanted to tell the whole story. He made an appointment for the next week, but he died the day before the appointment."

Brown died in June 1932 of heart disease at the age of 44. According to Bommersbach, some speculated that he might have been contemplating suicide, writing:

As the New York Mirror *reported the day Halloran's indictment was announced: 'A second man would probably have been indicted, according to widespread rumor, if death had not intervened. Mrs. Judd's story included the declaration that a physician, who has since committed suicide, was summoned to the murder bungalow to aid in the disposal of the bodies.'*

So, Dr. Brown committing suicide is speculation, as is the idea that Ruthie couldn't have dismembered Sammy because she didn't have surgical skills. No hard evidence of any of this exists, but that's what makes it a theory.

It's the cover-up of all this that makes it a conspiracy.

But that's not the end of Bommerbach's theory. She also suggested that a second gun might have been used on the night of the murders, and if that was the case, it was possible, she wrote, that Ruthie hadn't killed anyone at all.

In the original news stories, it was noted that the autopsies of Anne and Sammy showed the women were killed with different guns - Sammy with a .25-caliber like the bullet in Ruthie's hand and Anne with a .32-caliber. That meant that if there were two different bullets, there were two different guns, which made it likely there were two killers, she wrote.

Bommersbach gave little credence to this theory at first. However, when she began reviewing the newspaper stories about the crime - dated between October 20 and October 22, 1931 - she found they were all very specific about there being two guns involved:

Los Angeles Times: "The killer is believed to have used a .25-caliber automatic to murder Miss Samuelson, but a larger caliber weapon was used to kill Mrs. LeRoi.

Los Angeles Examiner: "Police found one of the death-dealing guns" in her hand luggage - a .25-caliber.

Phoenix Gazette: "Another gun is missing, for the autopsy disclosed that each of the women had been shut with a gun of a different caliber."

Arizona Republic: "Two different caliber revolvers were used, autopsy surgeons said."

Phoenix Gazette: "Facts of the killings and butchery which point strongly to the theory that Mrs. Judd, a slight woman, could not have possibly completed the brutal task alone are: 1. The victims were shot with guns of different caliber, according to an autopsy performed in Los Angeles. 2. The weight of Mrs. LeRoi was greater than that of Mrs. Judd, indicating that the task of placing the victim in a trunk would have been too much for one person."

Then, the "two-bullet theory" disappeared, which Bommersbach alleged was part of the conspiracy. She searched the written autopsy reports, the court transcripts, police records - everything she could think of - but there was no more mention of there being two separate guns used in the murders.

She believed that it was because the police were covering up for Jack Halloran, but I think the answer is a lot simpler than that.

It was a mistake.

There's no way to know where the mistake began, whether with the autopsy report - which was later corrected, by the way, since the police found only .25-caliber bullets in the trunk - or in the newspaper stories. I'm going to vote for the newspaper stories. I think it's important that the only mention of two calibers appears in the newspapers printed immediately after the discovery of the bodies. In 1931, reporters were scrambling to get the story into print, and it's no surprise that a mistake was made. But in all those papers? Sure, because as anyone who has done much research into old newspapers knows, stories were often copied word for word in papers across the country. Once a mistake is made, it just keeps repeating until it's fixed - which it was. The "two bullet theory" vanished from the newspapers as soon as the mistake was cleared up.

So, what about the theory that Ruth Judd was completely innocent and never killed anyone at all? That conspiracy came from Bommersbach, too.

In her book, she noted that Ruthie had certainly stabbed Sammy with the bread knife and had shot her during the struggle. She also admitted shooting at Anne, but experts stated that Anne had been shot with a gun pressed to her head, with the bullet traveling backward and downward. Ruthie said that she shot as Anne was bending over to hit her with the ironing board. If true, then the bullet should have struck Anne's head and traveled upward, not downward. And at the distance she was from Anne, on the kitchen floor, the gun would not have left the powder burns found on the body.

Bommersbach used a statement from Ruthie to add weight to her theory: "I shot at Anne. When I woke up, I was lying between two bodies."

Then - using the two different bullets theory, which I think was easily explained - she surmises that someone else was present and that Ruthie came to believe she had killed both women because there was no one else who could have done it.

But what if there was? According to a woman named Virginia Fetterer, whom Bommersbach interviewed for her book, the girls had been killed because they were blackmailing "powerful men in town" over an abortion ring. And, of course, that brings Dr. Brown back into the story again since he was allegedly one of the doctors providing illegal abortions for party girls and "summer wives."

But that wasn't all Virginia Fetterer had to tell Bommersbach. In 1990, Virginia told her that she'd heard Jack Halloran confess to *both* murders.

She claimed she was out celebrating New Year's Eve in the late 1930s with her husband and a group of friends. After dinner, they went to the Adams Grill, the bar at the downtown Adams Hotel. Virginia said that as her group approached the bar, Halloran and some of his friends were coming out.

"Someone asked him a question, like if he could take care of a problem," she recalled. "And he was bragging that, sure, he could fix it. Then he said - I can't recall his exact words, but it was to the effect that if you knew the right people, you could fix anything in this town. He laughed and said that Winnie Ruth Judd was out in the state hospital paying for what he'd done. He was bragging about it."

Then, she said, a drunk Jack Halloran staggered away.

It's not exactly something you could present as evidence in court, but it made an impression on Virginia Fetterer that she recalled more than 50 years later.

Does it prove anything, though? Not really. She could have misheard the comment, or, more likely, Halloran was drunk and playing up the rumors about him for his friends.

Trust me, drunk people say stupid things.

In the end, Bommersbach's book makes for an interesting read. As mentioned, it's well-researched, but I don't think it solves any mysteries - not in the way intended. The "facts" that the book was based on boil down to comments, mistakes, half-forgotten memories, and a lot of speculation.

But there's nothing wrong with speculation if it makes sense, and I'm just about to do the same thing myself.

MY THEORY ABOUT THE "TRUNK MURDERS" IS SIMPLE, as long as you're willing to accept the idea - which I think is well documented - that Winnie Ruth Judd had some pretty serious mental issues. In fact, I think her issues were much more serious than anyone ever realized or imagined.

We should start back in Ruthie's childhood and teenage years when she not only claimed to be kidnapped and raped but also claimed to have been pregnant. I don't believe that Ruthie was lying about these things - she truly believed them to be true. Psychologists refer to this as "Self-Deception," and it's a process where someone actively denies or rationalizes evidence to believe something that isn't true, often to protect their self-image or, in Ruthie's case, to maintain a desired belief.

Joseph Goebbels - the Nazi propaganda chief - said, "If you tell a lie big enough and keep repeating it, people will eventually come to believe it." In this case, Ruthie told herself lies until she was convinced they were the truth.

This wasn't something confined to her childhood when it might have been more forgivable. She continued it after she was married and repeatedly told Dr. Judd that she was pregnant, even when she wasn't, or told others that she'd lost a child, which she hadn't.

But Ruthie wholeheartedly believed those things were true. She wasn't making things up - they were completely real to her.

She would continue her self-deception even after moving to Phoenix and making friends with Anne and Sammy - the two women she later killed.

I think that it's safe to say that Ruthie did have an affair with Jack Halloran. That's one role he had in the whole mess that we can be sure about. Halloran was an admitted "playboy," a prominent businessman with a lot of connections, and someone used to getting his way, especially when it came to women.

When Ruthie first met him - and they began spending time together while she was at her first job in Phoenix - she convinced herself that she was Halloran's "other woman." He was in love with her, and if it weren't for the embarrassment it would cause for his family and the problems it would create for his business, Jack would leave his wife for her.

Of course, this wasn't true. Halloran had a string of women - that probably included Anne and Sammy - and to him, Ruthie was just another notch on his bedpost, so to speak.

But Ruthie was in love.

And she began to believe that Jack was just as in love with her as she was with him. It wasn't a pregnancy or a child this time; it was a man. Ruthie believed it just as much as she believed in those other things in her past.

Ruthie soon became the thing Halloran probably disliked the most - she became clingy and possessive. Based on her conversations with Lucille Moore and others, it's clear that Ruthie was madly in love with

Jack and protective about her relationship with him. She didn't want any other women to interfere in their relationship, including her two best friends.

I think the authorities were correct when they theorized that Ruthie murdered the girls out of jealousy, although I don't think that explains everything. This wasn't just simple jealousy, and it wasn't something that just popped up at the time of the murders. I think her resentment and jealousy had been simmering for quite some time, slowly building until the night when she snapped.

But that's not to imply that the murders were premeditated. I don't think that Ruthie planned them out, which is why it was all such a mess. I don't even think that Ruthie went over to the bungalow that night intending to kill her friends - at least not consciously. But the trouble occurred when her subconscious got the better of her, and she decided that she wanted Anne and Sammy dead.

At some point that night, Ruthie decided she needed to eliminate her competition once and for all. Just as Ruthie had imagined that she and Halloran were engaged in a torrid love affair, she also imagined Anne and Sammy trying to steal Jack away from her. As we've seen from her behavior in the past, when Ruthie imagined something, she was mentally ill enough to make that something become real - even if it was only real to Ruthie.

This is what I think happened that weekend:

Ruthie took the .25-caliber handgun into the bedroom where the girls were sleeping. Did she plan to kill them at that moment? Maybe. Or maybe she just wanted to warn them away from Halloran. Regardless, she entered the room, walked to the bed where Anne was sleeping, placed the gun next to her head, and pulled the trigger.

The bullet penetrated Anne's skull and likely killed her immediately. Since the gun was so close to her head, there was little blood spatter, but there was enough blood that it seeped out onto the pillow and bedsheets, soaked into the corner of the mattress, and dripped onto the floor. This was where the police later discovered the only bloodstains in the room.

The gunshot, of course, woke up Sammy, and that was when the fight between the two women occurred. Ruthie ran into the kitchen, and Sammy followed, trying to get the gun away from Ruthie. During the fight, Ruthie stabbed her friend with the bread knife, but the gun didn't discharge until the two women fell to the floor. One shot went through Ruthie's hand as they fought over the gun. The other gunshot was the one that killed Sammy.

I believe the police had it backward when it came to the order in which the two girls were killed. Anne being killed first in the bedroom explains the evidence that was found there. It also explains why Jack Halloran went into the bedroom and pulled down the window blind, leaving the bloody handprint behind. We'll come back to that in a moment.

At this point, Ruthie had to come to grips with the fact that she had just killed her two best friends. If her mind hadn't snapped yet, it was just about to do so. Somehow, she talked herself into believing that the murders had been committed in self-defense, including Anne attacking her with the ironing board.

There was a reason that juries, doctors, attorneys, politicians, and a lot of other people who heard Ruthie's self-defense story were convinced that it was true. They believed it because Ruthie believed it. Just like her rape and her pregnancies, she convinced herself it happened just the way she imagined it did. She hadn't murdered anyone - she was fighting for her life. She told herself that story starting that night and continued telling herself it was the truth until she absolutely believed it.

Although she was in the midst of convincing herself it had been self-defense, she still panicked and ran. She went home, where she met Jack Halloran, who was coming over, likely because he didn't have another date that night. When she told him what happened - practicing her self-defense story - the pair returned to the bungalow to sort out the mess.

It was at this point that Halloran became an accomplice.

I think what he did next was not to help Ruthie but to hide his role in everything. He knew that if Ruthie was caught and she decided to talk, he would be ruined in Phoenix. He helped Ruthie cover up the murders, but only after he made her promise that she wouldn't talk about his involvement at all. And she didn't - not at first. But, of course, neither of them planned to get caught. They were sure they could erase all traces of the crime, and Anne and Sammy would be written off as a couple of transients who left town one step ahead of a bill collector. They had no real ties to the community, and while they would eventually be missed, there was nothing that could tie Ruthie or Jack Halloran to their disappearance - well, until that steamer trunk started to leak.

In time, Ruthie became resentful after she got caught, went on trial, and was sentenced to death. Halloran had never helped her, and so she revealed his part in the murders. She couldn't understand why he remained silent if he loved her as much as she believed he did. When she finally realized he didn't love her, she went even farther off the deep end.

So, what did Halloran do to help? Not much. He tried to force Ruthie to clean up the blood in the house, but when she balked, he pitched in. He also retrieved Anne's body from the bedroom, which was when he closed the window blind, and he also got rid of the mattresses. Only one of them had bloodstains on it, but if they wanted it to look like the girls left town and no foul play was involved, then *both* mattresses had to disappear. I believe that even though the window blind was closed, Halloran didn't want to alert the neighbors that anything was happening, so he kept the lights turned down low - which is how he missed the blood that had puddled on the floor under Anne's bed.

After that, Halloran placed both Sammy's body and Anne's body into the large trunk that had been in storage. Obviously, the trunk was very heavy, which is why Ruthie had to call a delivery service to move it from the bungalow to her apartment on Brill Street.

The pair then washed up. There's no doubt they had blood on their hands after moving the two bodies and cleaning up the bloodstains on the floor and in the kitchen. This is why Clay George, the plumber who was summoned to the bungalow by the police on October 19, found hair, skin, and blood in the bathroom drain.

Halloran, of course, washed his hands in more ways than one after that. Now, Ruthie was on her own. She didn't offer to move the bodies or do anything else that might link him to the crime. His part was finished, and thanks to his connections, few people in Phoenix believed that he'd have anything to do with the "trunk murders."

The biggest question that most people have about this case is - why would Ruthie have packed up the bodies in her luggage and put them on a train to Los Angeles? Why wouldn't she have driven them out into the hundreds of miles of desert surrounding Phoenix and dumped them someplace where they'd never be seen again? Why would she chance getting caught by putting them on the train?

First, with what car? Ruthie didn't have one, and Halloran certainly wasn't going to drive her. She had no way to move the bodies anywhere, which is why she paid for the trunk to be taken to her apartment and why she begged for help and a ride from her landlord on Sunday.

Second, I think that Ruthie, overwhelmed by fear and helplessness, decided to go to the one place where she knew someone could save her - Los Angeles. Her husband was there, and so was her brother, Burton. She had mentioned to Burton that she wanted him to throw the luggage into the ocean, but if that wasn't feasible, at least her brother or Dr. Judd would know what to do next.

The train was the only way that Ruthie knew how to get there, so she got her tickets, packed the trunks and suitcases, and left town. Should she have predicted that the trunks might leak and give her away? Maybe. She knew the big one had leaked since she'd spotted the stains it left on the front porch when the delivery driver hauled it away, but in her panic and terror, she didn't take any precautions.

And now the question of the trunks - who dismembered Sammy, cutting her into separate pieces so that she'd fit more easily into the luggage. Was it Jack Halloran, or more likely, some doctor who was an acquaintance of his? Was it Dr. Brown who died before he could reveal his secrets?

I don't think so. I think the person who took Sammy's body apart was none other than Ruthie Judd.

But I don't think she did it for some kind of thrill - she did it because she had to. She'd already discovered that the trunk was too heavy for her to move with both bodies in it. Ruthie was too small to move it with only Anne inside, but it was reasonable to ask for help with that kind of weight. She had no other choice but to try and streamline her escape by spreading out the weight of the bodies into separate containers. Turning off her mind to what she was doing, she cut Sammy apart and then packed the luggage just as she later described - by moving one piece of Sammy at a time from the large trunk to the smaller pieces of luggage.

We know what happened next. Ruthie fled Phoenix, her baggage leaked on the train, and the contents of the trunks were revealed. After going on the run, Ruthie eventually turned herself in, was tried, convicted, and sentenced to hang. She was later sent to the state hospital after she was judged to be insane.

From the very beginning of her prosecution, Ruthie had maintained she had acted in self-defense - and truly believed she had. I think she believed everything she told her attorneys, prosecutors, judges, doctors, and everyone else who would listen. She had convinced herself that the things she said were true.

Do I think Ruthie was legally insane? No, I don't. I believe that Ruthie knew right from wrong, and when she had committed the murders, she believed she had a good reason for killing her friends. It wasn't until it was over that she created the deep-seated belief that she'd acted in self-defense.

Do I think that Ruthie had some serious mental health problems? Definitely, I believe her mental illness explains the conspiracy that she created in her mind that important people were out to get her, that the doctors at the hospital were persecuting her, and that there was some grand scheme in the works to get her out of the hospital. None of those things were true - but they were to Ruthie.

I do have sympathy for Ruthie Judd. I don't think she committed cold-blooded murder. She might not have met the *legal* definition of insanity when she murdered her friends, but to put it bluntly, I do believe she was crazy. I don't believe that anyone - based on the earlier mental illness in her life - could have predicted how things were going to end up for Ruthie. Her stories of babies and pregnancy were likely dismissed as her having a "wild imagination" back then. No one could have known that her imagination would eventually drive her to murder.

AM I RIGHT? IS THAT WHAT HAPPENED IN OCTOBER 1931?

I have no way of knowing for sure. It's a theory, just like the ones that so many other people have created about this case. We'll never know for sure what happened that night in Phoenix that left two young women dead. Ruthie did admit that she killed them, but whether it was self-defense or what I believe happened remains a mystery.

How involved was Jack Halloran? Or was her accomplice someone else? I don't believe that Ruthie acted entirely alone, but whether he had a part in the murder or was simply there to clean up the mess she created is also unknown.

And did Ruthie take the bodies to Los Angeles for the reason that I believe she did? Or was it something else? Why else would she have done something so foolish when Phoenix was surrounded by miles of open desert, canyons, and mountains?

Honestly, we'll never know.

The story of Winnie Ruth Judd will always be a mystery that no amount of detective work will ever solve.

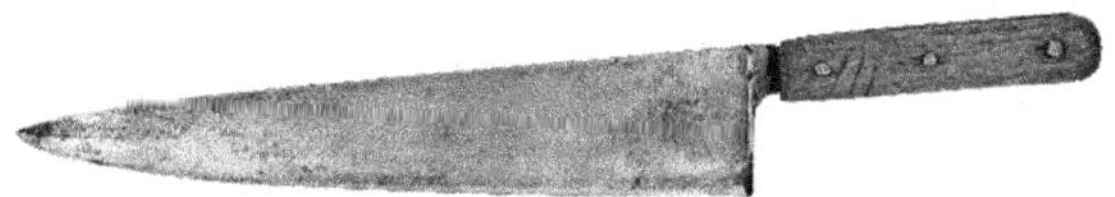

EPILOGUE

BUT THAT'S NOT QUITE THE END OF THE STORY.

In the aftermath of the murders, Anne and Sammy's bungalow became a macabre tourist attraction in Phoenix. The more headlines Ruthie's case garnered, the more people flocked to the house at the corner of North 2nd Street and Catalina. They wanted to see the place where it all happened - where Ruthie had committed murder and stuffed her friends into trunks.

The owner of the house even sold tickets for a time, allowing people a peek behind the locked door and letting them trample what should have still been a crime scene if the police hadn't been so careless.

The duplex began its life in the 1920s as a rental, and it remained a residence for nearly a century, churning through a long list of different owners. In 2016, there were rumors that the house was going to be demolished because it had been surrounded by chain-link fencing. But the property had actually been purchased by a local attorney who remodeled it and turned it into his law office.

And perhaps that's for the best because it had never been a happy place during its time as a family home.

Memories of the past are never far away inside the bungalow. There are original fixtures that survive on both sides of the duplex. Among them are the doorframes, fireplace mantels, and light fixtures that had been there when Anne and Sammy lived in the house.

In the bathroom was the tub Ruthie and Jack Halloran may have washed after cleaning up the crime scene.

The original oak floors - once spattered with Sammy and Anne's blood - also remain, as well as other parts of the original decor.

And those items and the bungalow itself may hold some of the residue from days gone by. The house is not considered to be "haunted"- at least not in the traditional sense- but something has lingered here, becoming an overwhelming presence as the decades have passed.

Locally, the bungalow earned a reputation as "the house where love dies." Couples often bought it together as their dream home, and then things turned sour, ending in arguments, bickering, and divorce.

But was this just a coincidence, the result of America's high rate of divorces, or is there something else to it?

This house seems to have a worse track record than others in the neighborhood - and others in the city of Phoenix. There's just something about the place that no one seems to be able to put their finger on, something weird - something "bad."

Is it a memory of the house's terrible past, making a mark on the present? No one can say, but whatever it is, no amount of distance between the murders that happened there and the present day seems able to make that strangeness go away.

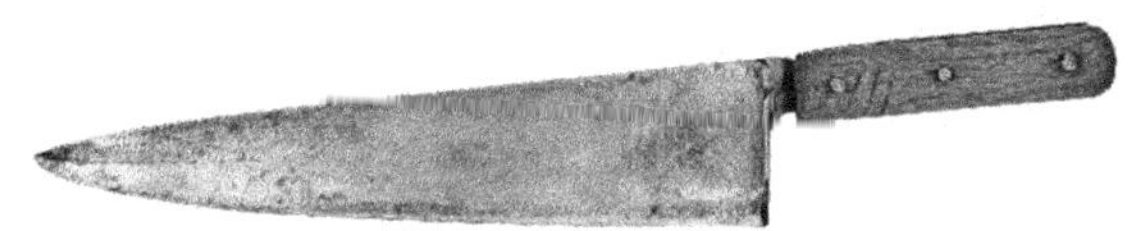

BIBLIOGRAPHY

Arizona Memory Project - Arizona State Library Archives and Public Records

Bommersbach, Jana - *The Trunk Murderess: Winnie Ruth Judd*, New York, NY, Simon & Schuster, 1992

Burns, Stanley and Sara Cleary-Burns - *News Art*, Brooklyn, NY, Powerhouse Books, 2009

-- - *Deadly Intent: Crime and Punishment Photographs from the Burns Archive*, Brooklym NY, Powerhouse Books, 2008

Crimes and Punishment - *Illustrated Crime Encyclopedia*, Westport, CT, H.S. Stuttman, Inc., 1994 edition

Dobkins, J. Dwight and Robert J. Hendricks - *Winnie Ruth Judd: The Trunk Murders*, New York, NY, Grosset & Dunlap, 1973

Dunn, Katherine and Sean Tejaratchi - *Death Scenes: A Homicide Detective's Scrapbook*, Los Angeles, CA, 1996

Heiman, Jim - *Dark City: The Real Los Angeles Noir*, Berlin, Germany, Taschen, 2022

James, Bill - *Popular Crime: Reflections on the Celebration of Violence*, New York, NY, Scribner, 2011

Los Angeles Public Library Tessa Digital Collection

Nash, Jay Robert - *Bloodletters and Badmen*, New York, NY, M Evans & Company, 1995

---------------------- - *Look for the Woman*, New York, NY, M Evans & Company, 1981

---------------------- - *Murder America*, New York, NY, Simon & Schuster, 1980

Odell, Robin - *Mammoth Book of Bizarre Crimes*, Philadelphia, PA, Running Press, 2010

Schechter, Harold - *Murderabilia: A History of Crime in 100 Objects*, New York, NY, Workman Publishing, 2023

Sifakis, Carl - *The Encyclopedia of American Crime*, New York, NY, Facts on File, 1982

Telfer, Tori - *Lady Killers: Deadly Women Throughout History*, New York, NY, Harper Collins, 2017

Wolf, Marvin J. and Katherine Mader - *Fallen Angels: Chronicles of L.A. Crime and Mystery*, New York, NY, Facts on File Publications, 1986

NEWSPAPERS

Arizona Daily-Star
Arizona Republic
Atlanta Journal
Belleville (Illinois) Daily Advocate
Bismarck (North Dakota) Tribune
Brooklyn Eagle

Buffalo (New York) News
Buffalo (New York) Times
Clarksville (Tennessee) Leaf-Chronicle
Columbia (Missouri) Daily Tribune
Corpus Christi Times
Detroit Free Press
Evansville (Indiana) Press
Fort Worth Star-Telegram
Fresno Morning Republican
Great Falls (Montana) Leader
Helena Independent-Record
Indianapolis News
Indianapolis Star
Los Angeles Daily News
Los Angeles Evening Express
Los Angeles Evening Post
Los Angeles Examiner
Los Angeles Times
Memphis Commercial Appeal
Montana Record-Herald
New York American
New York Daily News
Oakland Post-Enquirer
Phoenix Gazette
Poplar Bluff (Missouri) Daily American Republic
Roanoke (Virginia) Times
Rome (New York) Daily Sentinel
Sacramento Bee
San Diego Sun
San Francisco Examiner
San Francisco Examiner
Santa Cruz Evening News
Sedalia (Missouri) Democrat
St. Louis Star and Times
Stockton (California) Evening Record

Tampa Tribune
Ventura (California) Weekly Post and Democrat
Washington Times-Herald
Winston-Salem Sentinel

SPECIAL THANKS TO

April Slaughter: Cover Design
Becky Ray: Editing
Samantha Smith
Athena & the "Aunts" - Sue, Carmen & Rocky
Orrin and Rachel Taylor
Rene Kruse
Rachael Horath
Bethany Horath
Elyse and Thomas Reihner
John Winterbauer
Cody Beck
Trey Schrader
Tom and Michelle Bonadurer
Lydia Rhoades
Cheryl Stamp and Sheryel Williams-Staab
Joelle Leitschuh and Tonya Leitschuh
Scott and Hannah Rob
Victoria & Reese Welch
And the entire crew of American Hauntings

ABOUT THE AUTHOR

Troy Taylor is the author of books on ghosts, hauntings, true crime, the unexplained, and the supernatural in America. He is the founder of American Hauntings Ink, which offers books, ghost tours, events, and the Haunted America Conference, as well as the creator of the American Oddities Museum in Alton, Illinois.

He was born and raised in the Midwest and divides his time between Alton, Illinois and wherever the wind decides to take him. See Troy's other titles at: www.americanhauntingsink.

WINNIE RUTH JUDD —

WANTED

For Double Murder

Murdered and mutilated two young women at Phoenix Ariz. Oct. 16, 1931

Mrs. Judd will no doubt represent herself to be a professional nurse — She has a very pleasing personality, rather slender build, slim legs and thick hair —

Age 25 — Height 5 ft 7 inches — Weight 125 — Eyes Blue grey and large — Hair Light brown —

Arrest and notify Geo. O. Brisboise Chief of Police